ADVANCED
MS-DOS
BATCH FILE
PROGRAMMING

Dan Gookin

 WINDCREST

Published by **Windcrest Books**
FIRST EDITION/FIRST PRINTING

© 1989 **Windcrest Books**. Reproduction or publication of the content in any manner, without express permission of the publisher, is prohibited. No liability is assumed with respect to the use of the information herein. Printed in the United States of America.

Library of Congress Cataloging-in-Publication Data

Gookin, Dan.
 Advanced MS-DOS batch file programming / by Dan Gookin.
  p. cm.
 Bibliography: p.
 Includes index.
 ISBN 0-8306-9197-9 ISBN 0-8306-3197-6 (pbk.)
  1. MS-DOS (Computer operating system) 2. Microcomputers-
-Programming. 3. File organization (Computer science)
 4. Electronic data processing—Batch processing. I. Title.
 QA76.76 063G665 1989
 005.26—dc19
                                                   88-31789
                                                     CIP

TAB BOOKS Inc. offers software for sale. For information and a catalog, please contact TAB Software Department, Blue Ridge Summit, PA 17294-0850.

Questions regarding the content of this book should be addressed to:
Windcrest Books
Division of TAB BOOKS Inc.
Blue Ridge Summit, PA 17294-0850

Ron Powers: Director of Acquisitions
David M. Harter: Manuscript Editor
Katherine Brown: Production

Contents

--PART ONE--

BASICS

PART TWO

BATCH FILE PROGRAMMING

PART THREE
BEYOND BATCH FILES

Appendices

Notices

AST• and **SixPak**•	AST Research, Inc.
AutoCAD•	Autodesk, Inc.
Beyond • *Bat*™	Relay Communications, Inc.
BRIEF™	
and UnderWare™	UnderWare, Inc.
Clipper™	Nantucket Corp.
Compaq•	Compaq Computer Corp.
CompuServe™	H&R Block Co.
CP/M•	Digital Research Inc.
dBase• and **MultiMate**™	Ashton-Tate
Direct Access™	Delta Technology International
Epson•	Seiko Epson Corp.
Hercules Graphics Card•	Hercules Computer Technology.
IBM•, **IBM PC**•, **XT**•, **AT**•, **ProPrinter**•,	IBM Corp.
QuietWriter III•, **PC-DOS**•, **OS/2**• and **PS/2**•	
Intel• and **386**•	Intel Corp.
Kaypro•	Kaypro Corp.
Leading Edge™	Leading Edge Products
Lotus 1-2-3•	Lotus Development Corp.
Lucid™ **3D**	Personal Computer Support Group
Mace Utilities™	Paul Mace Software
Microsoft•, **Xenix**™ and **GW BASIC**™	Microsoft Corp.
Norton™ **Utilities** and **Norton**™ **Editor**	Peter Norton Computing, Inc.
PC Paintbrush™	ZSoft Corp.
PC Write•	QuickSoft, Inc.
R:BASE•	Microrim, Inc.
Solution Systems™	Software Developer's Corp.
SuperCalc•	Computer Associates International, Inc.
TRS-80™ and **TRSDOS**™	Radio Shack, a division of Tandy Corp.
TurboC™, **SideKick**™ and **SuperKey**™	Borland International, Inc.
UNIX™	AT&T Bell Laboratories
VOpt™	Golden Bow Systems
WordPerfect•	WordPerfect Corp.
WordStar™	MicroPro Corp.

What This Book Is About

Batch file programming is more than writing short routines to save keystrokes, run a program, or get you from one place to another. Batch files can offer your computer system more than an AUTOEXEC file to "get you up in the morning." Learning about batch files, and how to program them, teaches you more about DOS. Once you know more about DOS, you know more about your computer; and the more you know about your computer, the more effectively you can use it to make yourself more productive.

Don't let the title fool you. This isn't an advanced, technical book, full of cryptic programmer's talk; nor is this an all-assuming text on the virtues of keeping a clean system, thumping DOS commands into your head, or warning you of the perils of not frequently backing up your hard disk. Instead, this book was written for people who enjoy DOS and want to make it more useful for them. This book offers instruction in the finer aspects of learning to use DOS, and ultimately your computer. This is done through batch file programming.

The funny thing about DOS (if you ever wondered, indeed there are funny things about DOS) is that it's really not that hard to learn. The problem is that DOS is powerful and versatile, and like anything powerful and versatile, it takes time to learn. So rather than sit down and type each command in the DOS manual, which can lead to frustration and immediate greying of the hairs, why not learn about batch file programming?

Batch file programming is a way of communicating with your computer. Fundamentally, "programming" is just a word for human-to-computer com- munications. There are many ways to program a computer, and many programming languages as well. Fortunately, the batch file "language" consists of DOS commands—most of which you already know.

Batch files allow you to type one command—a command you make up yourself—to do many things that would otherwise require a lot of typing. Batch files are really quite simple to do, and, as this book will demonstrate, they can be quite elegant and powerful. Nothing too rough for any DOS dummy to tame.

The underlying theme throughout this book is, "Learn batch file programming and you'll learn DOS; Learn DOS and you'll know more about your computer; know more about your computer and you'll be able to use it more productively." If you're using your computer at work, mastering the batch file is the quickest path to computer "guru-hood"—and we all know how the boss likes to smile on a PC guru.

A "PC guru" is
someone who knows the MODE command.

WHO THIS BOOK IS FOR

For you, of course; or just about anyone who's dabbled with batch files, found them interesting, and then wanted more information but could never find it.

Actually, this book is about more than writing nifty batch files. It's about understanding DOS; learning how DOS controls your programs; hard disk organization; using your computer more efficiently; and so on. It's not that this book deliberately teaches you all of that (and besides, it would be a pain to put all that on the cover), but by learning about batch files, you learn more about DOS and how to control your computer.

This can be compared to learning how to drive. You can take a class and they'll teach you operation of the car, some basic repairs ("remember class, this is a 'lug nut'", and the rules of the road. Yet, that information is just enough to get you started. If you want to be a better driver, or better yet, a race car driver, you'll need to know more. This book teaches you more about DOS by instructing you in the finer aspects of batch file programming.

This book is for anyone who owns an MS–DOS computer, IBM PC/XT/AT, PS/2, IBM-compatible or "clone" computer. You don't need to know anything about batch file programming, though some programming knowledge will help—but don't let that frighten you away from learning more about your computer system.

You should also be familiar with your computer's operating system, or DOS. This means you should have played with your computer for a while, formatted some disks, copied files from hither and thither, renamed files, created new ones, used some software—all the stuff anyone does who owns an MS–DOS computer.

CONVENTIONS, ASSUMPTIONS AND STUFF

IBM, Clone or Compatible?

Hello, IBM and gang! A few years ago, a great deal of emphasis was placed upon computers that were "IBM compatible." That is, computers that could run the same software as the original IBM PC. If those computers carried a national brand name, such as AST, Compaq, Epson, KayPro, Leading Edge, Zenith, and so on, they were called IBM "compatibles." If Larry made the computer in the back of his store and sold it as "Larry's PC"—and it too was IBM compatible—the computer was known as a "clone." There's no official designation for a compatible or clone beyond what's mentioned in this paragraph, though it seems to be an accepted convention. Chances are, if your computer uses MS–DOS (or PC–DOS), you're okay.

In this book, the task of mentioning IBM PC/XT/AT, PS/2, Compatible or Clone is saved by using the abbreviation "PC" or just "computer." Whenever you see PC or read about "your computer," it refers to any popular computer capable of running MS–DOS machines (the old Tandy 2000 and HP 150). If you're a user of one of those systems, the routines demonstrated here may not work with your equipment. Sell it.

HARD DRIVE ANYONE?

This book makes the assumption that you have a hard disk. Everyone should have a hard disk. They're just too inexpensive and there's no reason not to have one. Although all the batch file programs and routines will work on floppy systems, only by using them on a hard drive will you realize their full potential.

In case you do have a floppy-only system, mentally change all references of "drive C" to "drive A" (drive C is the hard drive). You might also want to format a system disk (FORMAT /S) and a blank data disk for use with this book.

ENTER or *RETURN*

Many books and manuals have trouble telling the ENTER and RETURN keys apart. The ENTER or RETURN key is the key you press to complete a line of text—the same key you'd press on an electric typewriter keyboard to move the carriage from one side of the machine to the other. Some keyboards list the carriage return key as ENTER, like the common calculator. Others call the key RETURN, like the common typewriter. Still others, to be novel, seem to have it both ways.

It's been supposed that because IBM couldn't decide if their computer was a calculator or a typewriter that they opted to put a cryptic back arrow symbol on their keyboard (*see* FIG. 1). What is that key?

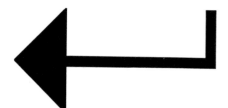

Fig. 1. The funky IBM Return key.

In this book, ENTER is used to represent the carriage return (or RETURN) key. (Presently, IBM is using ENTER in all their documentation.) If your keyboard has a RETURN key or some other symbol, press that key when this book tells you to "press ENTER."

DOS

References to DOS are made throughout this book. The program being referred to is MS-DOS, also known as the Microsoft Disk Operating System, or PC-DOS, IBM's own version of the same. Incidentally, for the last two versions of DOS, 4.0 and 3.3, IBM has been doing the programming. Because of this, the programs presented in this book were tested on an IBM PC computer running IBM's PC-DOS 3.3 and 4.0. However, all the material here applies to all IBM and compatible systems running any version of DOS. Variations, when they occur, are noted.

WHICH VERSION NUMBER?

Generally speaking, you should always have the latest version of DOS. Yeah, it's expensive. Personally, I've spent about $200 every year in DOS upgrades for my computers. (I have DOS 3.1, 3.2, 3.3, and 4.0.) Updating your computer with the latest version of DOS has gotten easier and easier. But it's still time-consuming. Only if you're one of the die-hard and timid—the DOS wary, the compuphobe—should you not upgrade your DOS. Then again, after reading about all the new features offered in the latest version, you'll probably stealthily sneak over to your local authorized dealer and snatch up a copy. You've been warned.

ALL SET?

This book contains material on system management. That implies that you already have a computer and have installed several programs that you use regularly. Granted, DOS all by itself can only be entertaining for a few moments. Without programs to run or things to do, DOS is terribly boring.

Your computer system should be all set up and ready to go. If not, please refer to your DOS manual for setting things up. The setup procedure varies with each version of DOS, so make sure you have the right manual.

If you're being current, a very helpful installation procedure has been introduced with DOS 4.0. This program will install DOS on a new computer system, or update a version of DOS on a current system. I highly recommend it.

YOUR EXPERTISE

As far as prior knowledge about batch files go, you really don't need any. If you consider yourself a more-than-typical DOS user, or you know a programming language, such as BASIC, or you're just enthusiastic, then you have enough knowledge to make the techniques shown in this book work for you.

As was stated earlier, a knowledge of programming could come in handy. You'll probably also want to look into some of the software, including some of the public domain and shareware goodies, discussed in this book. The best stuff has been made available on a companion floppy disk you can order from TAB BOOKS. More information about this disk is provided at the end of this chapter, in Chapter 10, and in Appendix K.

ORGANIZATION OF THIS BOOK

This book is divided into five parts: the basics; batch file programming; beyond batch files; hard disk strategies; and a batch file "cookbook" reference.

PART ONE introduces you to batch files, along with some interesting information about DOS. For some, this may be review material. But, even if you consider yourself an "old hand," you should look it over. There's some information hidden in there that may surprise a few computer gurus.

PART TWO covers batch file programming—how to get things done. Everything is covered from the fundamentals of any programming language: looping, variables, and so forth, on through structure and troubleshooting.

PART THREE goes beyond batch files. DOS merely gives you the basics. "Beyond Batch Files" discusses third-party software that will enhance your batch file programs' performance. Additionally, you'll read about using BASIC and DEBUG to assist your batch files, as well as third-party batch file enhancement programs.

PART FOUR mulls over the basics of hard disk strategy. There are quite a few interesting things batch files can do to make an unruly hard drive behave more efficiently. Also, this section introduces a batch file menu manager and other "shell program" techniques that you can incorporate into your own system.

PART FIVE is the batch file cookbook. This is a virtual encyclopedia of all batch file commands, along with format, description, examples, demonstration programs, and a cross-reference.

Finally, there are over ten appendices full of handy information about DOS to help you go on to write better batch files.

OS/2

OS/2 is in its infancy. In fact, there are far fewer OS/2 applications programs than DOS programs. Because of this, coverage of OS/2 in this book is limited. Most of the OS/2 information in this book is concentrated in Chapter 6. If you have OS/2, it might be a good idea to start reading at that point, and then pick up with Chapter 1. (All the DOS examples in this book work in OS/2's "real mode.")

FOR FURTHER READING

This book does get into two other topics that may catch your interest. Of primary concern would be additional books on DOS. The best book on DOS is your DOS manual. Another handy reference would be *The MS–DOS Encyclopedia*. While it's a hefty and expensive book, it's worth every ounce, and every cent. This book alone replaces half a dozen others on my shelf.

For good information on batch file programming and hard disk management, two books come to mind: *Hard Disk Management with MS–DOS and PC–DOS* written by yours truly and Andy Townsend (from TAB BOOKS). Also, *MS–DOS Batch File Programming* by Ronny Richardson—an excellent introduction and reference manual for any batch file nut (also from TAB).

For BASIC programming, two books I've had the privilege of working on are *Learning IBM PC BASIC* and *The IBM BASIC Handbook*. While geared toward the IBM PC, information in these books generally applies to GW BASIC, a widely available version of PC BASIC.

For assembly language programming, the following three books are recommended: *Assembly Language Primer for the IBM PC & XT*, Ray Duncan's *Advanced MS–DOS*, *The 8086 Book*, and the documentation for Microsoft's Macro Assembler. This information is a little advanced, and only the daring should venture into an area as scary as assembly language programming.

Duncan, Ray, *Advanced MS–DOS*, Washington: Microsoft Press, 1986.

Duncan, Ray et al, *The MS–DOS Encyclopedia*, Washington: Microsoft Press, 1988.

Gookin/Townsend, *Hard Disk Management with MS–DOS and PC–DOS*, Pennsylvania: TAB BOOKS, 1987.

Lafore, Robert, *Assembly Language Primer for the IBM PC & XT*, Virginia: Plume/Waite, 1984.

Lien, David, *Learning IBM BASIC*, California: CompuSoft, Inc., 1984.

Lien, David, *The IBM BASIC Handbook*, California: CompuSoft, Inc., 1986.

Rector/Alexy, *The 8086 Book*, California: Osborne/McGraw-Hill, 1980.

Richardson, Ronny, *MS–DOS Batch File Programming . . . Including OS/2*, Pennsylvania: TAB BOOKS , 1988.

SUPPLEMENTAL DISKETTE OFFER

In conjunction with this book, TAB BOOKS, Inc., offers a companion diskette. On this diskette are: all of the major batch files discussed in this book; several batch file enhancement programs written specifically for this book (that you can't find anywhere else); plus dozens of batch file utilities and other goodies.

To get this diskette, you should complete and mail in the order form at the end of this book. If you get into batch files (and why not?), you'll really enjoy some of the programs on the diskette. For a sneak preview, read Appendix K.

Part One

Basics

WELCOME to advanced batch file programming.

In part one, I'll get you up to speed on batch files and on some aspects of DOS with which you're probably not familiar. The purpose of this section is twofold: first, to acquaint the new DOS gurus with some of the more interesting aspects of DOS; second, to check the knowledge of the older DOS gurus for some real, advanced batch file programming. Whatever your situation, the end result will be the same: you'll know more about your computer and be able to use it more effectively.

1
Batch Files

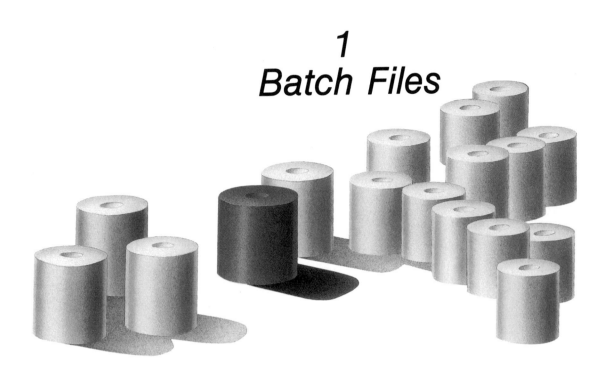

Learning about anything new means that you must build upon what you already know. It's assumed, largely because of this book's title, that you already know a little bit about DOS and batch files. Or, you could be an experienced DOS user and think you don't have the time to mess with an "intro" book. In either case, some background information is in order.

This chapter contains information on batch files, both general and specific. It's assumed that you have some knowledge of batch files, so most of this should be review. Yet, to go beyond that normal knowledge a review is in order.

Most of the information here is also gone over in detail later in the book. In fact, there were so many parenthetical clauses that read "(this is covered in Chapter 900)" that I randomly went through here and deleted a few of them. So, if a few concepts seem fuzzy, keep reading and they'll be detailed later in this book.

Then, to whet your appetite before things get off and running, there are several quick-and-dirty batch file examples at the end of this chapter. While some of them may seem confusing at this stage, type them in and give 'em a try. You're bound to find at least a couple of them useful.

INTRODUCTION

Learning about batch files must be one of the last things people get around to when they learn DOS. It's sad because, by learning about batch files, all the other commands will come naturally. In fact, some of the more bizarre commands actually start to make sense after you take a stab at learning batch file programming.

Normal DOS users, and even a few pros, tend to et stuck in a rut. After a while, they resort to using just a few well-known and trusted favorites: FORMAT, DISKCOPY (sometimes), COPY, REN, DEL (or ERASE), and few others. By knowing those commands you can use your computer—and use it quite effectively. There's nothing wrong with this, except that you're cutting yourself short on the power of your system.

What's missing are batch files. Not just the simple, easy batch files that everyone learns to write. But extremely elegant and powerful batch files. Nothing too complex—just some extraordinary and interesting DOS commands, plus a few hidden secrets that most people (including some professed "power users") ignore.

Remember, what you have sitting in front of you (or near you if you're reading this on the couch) is a computer. Computers can do many things, and many boring and repetitive things over and over gain without complaining. Typing several DOS commands will get the job done. Yet it's possible to cut down on your typing time by taking advantage of batch files.

> *A* batch file program *is simply several DOS commands executing one after the other.*

Batch files give you the capability to issue several DOS commands over and over using DOS's "batch processor." The batch processor was added to DOS on the insistence of IBM. The IBM people wanted to be able to run "scripts" of several commands one after another to test different parts of their new microcomputer. Microsoft, developers of DOS, complied by building a batch file interpreter into DOS.

So, DOS's ability to run IBM's "scripts" blossomed into what we know today as batch files. Over the years, and with each updated version of DOS, the capability of batch files has grown. Now, you can write batch files that can issue multiple DOS commands, make decisions, and extend the power of your system—all by typing the name of a batch file.

Of course, there's more to it than that.

Batch File Programming

Some people jump up and go screaming when they hear "programming language." The odd thing is that most of them program every day without even knowing it. Washing your hair is following a simple program:

1) Lather
2) Rinse
3) Repeat

(Of course, the computer program would need to know exactly what "Repeat" meant and how many times to repeat before it smothered your head with shampoo.)

If those three verbs were DOS commands, "SHAMPOO" would be the basics of a batch file (without the line numbers).

Cooks and chefs—even of the macaroni and cheese variety—follow programs when they make a meal. Even building the office spreadsheet is considered programming. So many people create interesting spreadsheets, yet they'd cry out in pain if you ordered them to "learn programming."

It's all the same thing: telling the computer what you want it to do. Programming puts the power of the computer into your hands. You control what's going on. And to be in control, you only need to know a handful of words, or programming commands.

The BASIC programming language has about 100 commands; the typical spreadsheet user can choose from about 150 commands and functions; the C programming language has only about 25 routines (hard core C nerds will argue over that one); and batch files may use 10 commands, plus the standard DOS commands. Compare this to the 50,000 words the average speaker of English uses. Programming isn't all that hard.

Of course, programming isn't for everyone either. It's assumed that because this book is titled *Advanced MS-DOS Batch File Programming* that you have some inclination toward programming. A little experience helps, but isn't necessary. A strong knowledge of DOS and how your computer works is also recommended. But again, everything you need to know is covered here.

So What Is a Batch File?

In a nutshell: Batch files are simply a list of DOS commands. For example, consider the following two commands. Most people type these two commands to start their word processor:

```
CD \WP
WP
```

CD/WP changes to the WP subdirectory. This is followed by the command to run the word processing program, WP.

Now, suppose both those commands were contained in a batch file. This isn't hard because batch files are simply commands you'd type at DOS. For the sake of reference, call the batch file WP.BAT.

*All batch files
have the filename extension, .BAT*

To execute the above commands, or to "run" the WP.BAT files, you type WP at the command prompt and press ENTER:

```
C> WP ENTER
```

This is the level at which most people are familiar with batch files. Even knowing that you could write such a batch file—just to save a single step over typing the two commands separately—doesn't convince the average person to learn about batch files.

The batch file most people are familiar with is AUTOEXEC.BAT. It's one of the first programs DOS looks for and runs when the computer starts. These same people don't necessarily write their own AUTOEXEC file. No, most people rely on "the store" to set one up for them. Or they use the talents of a DOS-literate friend (that's you) or consultant to build them an AUTOEXEC.BAT file.

This is sad. A lot of important things can take place inside an AUTOEXEC.BAT file. A well-written AUTOEXEC.BAT can save a computer user a lot of time and pain. (Of course, this would put some consultants out of business, so then again . . .)

Recently, many applications have these new "install" programs that automatically alter an AUTOEXEC.BAT file. Personally, I hate them. Running two or three of these INSTALL.EXE programs can mess up a computer system faster than a novice can press *CTRL–ALT–DEL*. Because of this, it's important to know what can be done in a batch file. It's even more important to know what's inside the AUTOEXEC.BAT file.

This book devotes an entire chapter (more or less) to the functions of AUTOEXEC.BAT. Even with all the importance placed on it, AUTOEXEC.BAT is still one of the only batch files many users will ever have. Because of this, I refer to it as a *low-level* batch file.

Mid-Level

Besides simply executing a group of commands, or a script, as IBM wanted it, batch files can do more. While not really a pure programming language, there are certain things a batch file is capable of that can commonly be found in "real" programming languages. (This book will even introduce you to some extraordinary programs that take the concept of the batch file programming language far, far beyond what DOS has to offer.)

Because Microsoft wrote MS–DOS, many of the batch file commands are similar to those found in their popular BASIC interpreter:

FOR
GOTO
IF
REM

Other batch file commands have a unique flavor:

ECHO
PAUSE
SHIFT

These commands could be blended with DOS commands, I/O redirection, and take advantage of system "variables" to make batch file programming quite capable. Batch file programs could create files, evaluate conditions, make decisions, execute specific code, and even execute other batch files. This takes the power of batch file programming beyond the simple WP.BAT programming. But still, there's more.

Take a user who's very familiar with DOS. Because this user has boned up on all the DOS commands, and is familiar with his system, his version of the WP.BAT file may look something like FIG. 1-1.

```
C:
MODE COM1:12,n,8,1,n
MODE LPT#2=COM1
SUBST W: C:\WP
SUBST M: C:\WORK\PROJECTS\MGM\SCNPLAY\ACT01
ECHO Drives substituted:
SUBST
PATH=W:;C:\DOS;C:\UTILITY
M:
W:\WP
SUBST M: /D
SUBST W: /D
PATH=C:\DOS;C:\UTILITY
C:
CD \
```

Fig. 1-1. What WP.BAT file may look like is shown here.

Granted, this program is an extreme example. The difference between this and the previous WP.BAT program is that this one takes advantage of pure DOS power. The user who wrote this knows a lot about DOS. The only real way to do that (without typing yourself to death) is to use batch files.

A few things missing in this batch file are the flow-control and decision making batch file commands: IF and GOTO. Also, the user might have added a few REM, or remark, statements to clue us into what exactly the batch file is accomplishing. (You'd be surprised how many people will gander at their old batch files and not have the slightest idea what some of the commands are trying to accomplish. That is, until the same thing happens to you. And it will.)

This level of sophistication, over simple two liner batch files, is what I call a *mid-level* batch file. This book covers this type of batch file extensively. But more importantly, there's a third, almost secret layer to batch file programming—advanced batch file programming.

Advanced Batch File Programming

Beyond low- and mid-level batch files are (can you guess?) advanced batch files.

What is it that makes an advanced batch file? Several things: DOS tricks; ANSI.SYS; the PROMPT command; the PATH command; Environmental variables; and batch file extensions through DEBUG, BASIC, and third-party software.

DOS tricks are things that DOS can do that no one will ever tell you. Only the intrepid DOS freak will discover them. I've tried to gather most of them from myself and other DOS gurus, and put them here in this book. As a preview: there are ways to get DOS to do things faster than is normally possible with batch files. For example, using TYPE to list a number of text statements instead of multiple ECHO commands; using I/O redirection instead of the pipe (filter) command; and so on. (All this is covered in detail later.)

Another example is the ANSI.SYS screen driver. Most people have a line in their CONFIG.SYS file that goes:

```
DEVICE=C:\ANSI.SYS
```

Yes, no one takes advantage of the things ANSI.SYS has to offer. For example, using ANSI.SYS and the TYPE example mentioned above, you can create a complete menu system, rivaling those of commercial companies—all using DOS. ANSI.SYS can reassign your function keys for speeding up certain activities. And third-party ANSI.SYS replacements can speed up your overall screen output.

The PROMPT command is usually only used once (if at all) in a user's AUTOEXEC.BAT file. But you don't have to keep it that way. Each program can have its own customized PROMPT by using batch files. The same holds true with the PATH command. If you're tired of living with a limited search PATH, then you haven't really read the DOS manual on PATH. (Don't worry, it's covered here.)

Environment variables are another thing most users—and programmers—ignore. It's probably because it's a big, complex word "environment." Or maybe it's because there are too many warnings in the DOS manual about it (or that the examples there are the lamest I've ever seen). A lot can be done with environmental variables to make using your system easier.

Batch files can also be extended beyond what comes with DOS. After all, there are a lot of batch file nuts out there. They scratch their heads and ask themselves questions like "Wouldn't it be neat to have a batch file respond to a yes/no question?" Then they write a utility whose sole purpose is to be included in a batch file. You'll learn how to do this later when the ASK.COM and READKEY.COM programs are introduced.

There are three ways to obtain these batch file extenders. The first two involve creating the program using raw data, assembled via either the DEBUG programming utility or the BASIC programming language—both of which, thank Bill Gates, come with DOS. The third way is to buy a commercial package of batch file helpers, such as EBL, the Extended Batch Language, Beyond.Bat, or the nifty programming utilities that come with Peter Norton's "Norton Utilities." All of these methods allow you to use custom programs that DOS's batch file interpreter doesn't offer.

This book goes into detail about all the goodies you'll need to become an advanced batch file programmer, including what the above commands do and how they can help you.

CREATING BATCH FILES

A Batch file consists of DOS commands, and special batch file directives. The batch file itself is, however, merely a text file on disk. The only thing making a batch file "runable" by DOS is its filename extension: BAT. Whenever you type the name of a file with the .BAT extension at the command prompt, DOS executes that file as a batch file.

Theoretically, if you renamed any text file with a .BAT extension, DOS would interpret it as a batch file. However, if the text file is a letter to mom, you'll see a lot of "Bad Command or Filename" error messages. In order for the batch file to work, it must contain batch file commands.

Text or ASCII?

There are two common types of files under DOS: Text files and program or data files. *Text files* contain characters you can read, usually sentences, figures, quotes, memos—common English text. *Program* or *data files* contain information only digestible by the computer. Even though you can look at and examine the contents of program or data files, only the computer understands the instructions or information.

A batch file must be a text file containing commands—just as you'd type at the command prompt. ASCII is also used to refer to text files because ASCII codes define all the text characters, letters, numbers, and symbols used in a text file. (See Appendix A.)

The object of creating a batch file is to get the batch file commands into a text file and give that file a .BAT extension. There are three methods to do this:

1) Using DOS
2) Using a text editor
3) Using a word processor

All three of these methods get the job done; they're all capable of creating a text file on disk with the .BAT extension. The differences between them are in power and convenience.

The following are brief examples of creating batch files using DOS, a text editor, and a word processor. More detail on these methods, inlcuding some tips and recommendations, are provided in Chapter 7.

From DOS

Creating a batch file from DOS is the quick and dirty method. In fact, most two- or three-line batch files are made this way. Because DOS is device-oriented (which is discussed in detail later), you can directly copy input from your keyboard to a file. The COPY command does the work:

```
COPY CON TEST.BAT
```

This is the famous "copy-con" function. It copies all input from the CON, or CONsole device, to the file TEST.BAT. Incidentally, TEST.BAT is created by the COPY function (just as any other file is created by the COPY function). COPY will not tell you if the file created already exists—the new file will overwrite anything on disk with the same name. (This is a typical oversight on Microsoft's part.)

What the COPY command does is to take the contents of one device and copy them to another. CON, for CONsole, is a fancy term for your keyboard and screen. TEST.BAT is a batch file you hope to create. After typing the above command, each line you type at the keyboard will be copied into the file TEST.BAT:

```
CD \WP
WP
```

Before you press ENTER, you can backspace, use the DOS editing keys, all the normal commands—but nothing fancy. When the line looks good, press ENTER. There's no using the up-arrow to correct a previous line. Once ENTER is pressed, that line is locked into memory.

After typing the last line, you'll need to tell DOS that you're done creating your batch file. Normally, when you're using COPY to copy one file to another, DOS will detect the end of the file by checking the file's size in the directory, or by looking for the CTRL–Z character. Because your CONsole doesn't have a file size, you need to type the CTRL–Z yourself. Hold down the control key and press **Z**:

```
^Z
```

Or, you can press the F6 key, which is the same thing:

```
^Z
```

DOS finishes the action by creating TEST.BAT and putting your commands into it. You'll see:

```
1 File(s) copied.
```

The batch file is created.

This is called the quick-and-dirty method because there's no editing on the file you create. You can't "fix" the file using COPY CON. Instead, you'll have to use a text editor or word processor to make corrections to the batch file.

This quick-and-dirty method is most convenient—especially when you're working on a strange computer, or one that might not have your favorite text editor or word processor handy. In this case, the COPY CON function really comes in handy.

Using a Text Editor

A text editor is a program that lets you edit text (surprisingly enough). It's very similar to a word processor, but it lacks all the printing functions. For example, you can enter text, edit, search and replace, move blocks, delete, cut and paste—but you can't underline, boldface, change typestyle, have footnotes, check your spelling, or print.

Text editors are usually a little more powerful than word processors. They allow a lot of text manipulations that word processor developers probably find too trivial. Because text editors are primarily used by programmers to write code, these tricks come in very handy.

A reason for using a text editor to write batch files is convenience and power. It's convenient because text editors are fast. Several text editors are sold on their loading and saving speeds alone (programmers don't want to waste time). Text editors lack all the printing and "pretty text" commands that word processors do, so there's nothing to slow you down.

Your reasons for using the text editor would be to compose or fix a batch file, then save it back to disk. (Yes, you could print it, but don't expect a Pulitzer for it.)

There are many text editors on the market. The one I personally use costs only $50. Other text editors typically cost less than $100. It may sound like a great expense, but if you're doing a lot of work with batch files (and other programming as well), you'll need it.

Because the various text editors differ in the way they do things, a complete example can't be given here. You just create the text, save it as a .BAT file, then return to DOS to "run" the batch file. Because batch files are interpreted by DOS, you don't need to compile or link them as you would with other programming languages. Also, because the text editor deals strictly with text, there's no special saving techniques or options as you would have with a word processor.

Using a Word Processor

Yes, you can use a word processor to write your batch files. It's a lot like using a 747 to help your child cross the street, but it is possible.

The drawback to using a word processor is that you have a big clunky program doing a small job. The biggest problem is that most word processors save their files in a special document file mode—not a straight text file. Even if you put the .BAT extension on the filename, DOS will not understand the word processor's formatting code. Instead, you must direct the word processor to save your batch file in the text-only, or ASCII, mode. This is an extra step that may not seem worth it—especially when composing small batch files.

Also, unlike a text editor, you'll need to be careful about word wrapping your batch file commands. Batch files can accept a line of commands up to 128 characters long. Most word processors will wrap text at about character position 70. Even if the word processor saves the program in the text mode, it may insert a carriage return in the middle of a long command, breaking the command in two and screwing up your batch file.

If you wind up using a word processor to write batch files, remember to save your work in the text mode. If that seems like too much work, use a text editor. There's one that came free with DOS called EDLIN. Though EDLIN is perhaps the worst text editor you'll ever use, everyone who has DOS also has EDLIN.

No matter which method is chosen, the end result is a text file, with a .BAT extension, consisting of batch file commands. Typing the name of this file (with or without the .BAT extension) executes the commands held within the file.

HOW BATCH FILES WORK

To understand how batch files work, you'll need to know how DOS runs other types of program files. Quite frankly, DOS is very lame when it comes to running programs. This is due primarily to its history; DOS was written to quickly bring the IBM PC into business computing. Back in 1981, all the decent business software was running under the CP/M operating system. Because of this, DOS has its roots in CP/M and uses some of CP/M's conventions to run its programs.

OS/2, the "future" operating system for IBM computers, tried to change the way programs were run, but it still has its roots in the CP/M operating system. Eventually, OS/2 will offer a little more flexibility. But for now, everything relies on the name of the file, not its contents. (Or, as they used to say: never judge a book by its cover, but judge a DOS filename by its extension.)

COM, EXE, and BAT Files

There are three types of files you can "run" using DOS. Unlike other operating systems, the only way DOS knows which files it can run is determined by the file's extension. More sophisticated operating systems use information contained inside the file to determine if it's "runable." But in DOS, everything relies on a filename's extension.

The three "runable" file extensions are:

COM
EXE
BAT

COM is short for COMmand file, and it's the oldest of the file formats. The COM file contains microprocessor instructions and data in the exact format that is loaded into memory. This is considered an older-style format, and behaves exactly like the type of programs that ran under the old CP/M operating system.

Most small programs are written using the COM format because it loads quickly. However, COM files can be no more than 64K in size. This limitation is why most larger files use the more flexible EXE program format.

EXE is short for EXEcutable file. The EXE format saves programs into separate modules, one for the program's code, another for data, and a third for the "stack." A special 512 byte file header contains information about how the three modules are loaded into memory. Because of this independent loading scheme, EXE files are slower to load than COM files, but they can be much larger (terribly huge, in fact).

BAT is short for BATch file. It signals to DOS that the program is actually a batch file, or a series of DOS commands stored in a text file. When you run a batch file, DOS reads in each line from the text file and executes each line as if it had been typed in at the command prompt. Additionally, each line is run through a "batch file interpreter" that performs certain manipulations on certain items in the batch file.

Whenever a file has an extension of COM or EXE, DOS assumes that it's a program file and it will attempt to load and run it. BAT files are interpreted by DOS, and are not loaded in the same manner as COM and EXE files.

DOS assumes a program is runable because, as I've said before, DOS really doesn't know what's in a file and only knows a program by its file extension. So you can rename any file on disk to a COM file. DOS will try to execute that file as a program. But don't expect it to work.

For all three types of runable files, no matter what the file extension, you only need to type the first part of the filename to run the program. For example, to run the program MAILLIST.COM you only need to type **MAILLIST**. To run BACK-UP.BAT, just type **BACKUP**.

Incidentally, if you have three files on disk:

```
HELLO.COM
HELLO.EXE
HELLO.BAT
```

and if you typed **HELLO** at the command prompt, then the file named HELLO.COM would run. Because of the way DOS works, you will never be able to run HELLO.EXE or HELLO.BAT—even if you typed in their full names. If the COM file didn't exist, HELLO.EXE would run. The HELLO.BAT batch file ranks last. The priority scheme with filenames is: COM, EXE, then BAT.

Batch File Execution

Each type of program file (COM, EXE, and BAT) is treated differently by DOS. COM files are loaded into memory ("dumped" actually) directly from disk. EXE files are loaded according to their modules. But how are batch files executed?

The secret lies in COMMAND.COM, the command interpreter. COMMAND.COM interprets a batch file one line at a time. When a BAT file is run, COMMAND.COM reads in one line from the file (all the characters up to the carriage return) and executes that line as if it were typed at the keyboard. Additionally, it expands any environmental variables and keeps track of batch file labels for the GOTO statement. COMMAND.COM also scans the keyboard to see if CTRL–C or CTRL–BREAK was pressed. If so, the user is asked if he wants to stop the batch file and is given a chance to type a Y or an N.

Because batch files are interpreted one line at a time, they tend to be slow. While running some long batch files you may have noticed that DOS is constantly accessing the disk. This is because each line is read from the batch file one at a time. There are ways to avoid this, the first of which is to write better batch files (which, by the way, is what this book is about). The second method is to use a disk caching program. Disk caching isn't directly related to batch file programming. It does speed things up a bit, however.

Batch files are really quite simple then: It's COMMAND.COM that makes them work.

A potential problem when running batch files—especially when you get fancy with them—is that the original file will become "lost." Because DOS fetches one line from the batch file at a time, if you change your system's path or, worse, your batch file erases itself, you'll get an error and the batch file will stop. Normally this shouldn't happen. (But how often do things go normally?)

Another interesting question that usually crops up is "Since a batch file can contain any command you'd normally type at the DOS command prompt, can you have one batch file 'run' another?"

Oh, you mean something like the following (the line numbers have been added for reference):

```
1:  @ECHO OFF
2:  CLS
3:  ECHO About to run another batch file
4:  SECOND.BAT
5:  ECHO How was that?
6:  :END
```

In line 4, SECOND.BAT is the name of another batch file. And to answer the question: yes, the first batch file will run the second. The remaining lines (5 and 6) in the first batch file will not be executed. Once control is passed to another batch file, it takes over. The first batch file stops executing. You can have one batch file execute another, but only by using special tricks covered in the book can you have execution return to the first batch file. Stay tuned.

So, to summarize, batch files are run, or interpreted, one line at a time by COMMAND.COM. A lot of extra translation work is performed by COMMAND.COM, expanding environmental variables, remembering labels, and so on. But ultimately, batch files are the simplest type of program run by DOS.

EXAMPLES

Knowing what you know so far about batch files, you can type in and test the following. These were designed as quick-and-dirty methods for accomplishing things you'd normally have to sort out by hand (or eyeball), or buy an expensive utility program to get the job done.

You can use COPY CON to create these, unless you're intimately familiar with a text editor or word processor. Remember to save these files in the text mode if you're using a word processor.

NOTE: These batch files are written using DOS 3.3. If you have DOS 3.2 or less, do not precede the initial ECHO OFF command with an @ (at) sign.

Directory Sort by Name

All line numbers in the sample batch files are used for reference purposes only; you should not type them in when entering your batch files.

```
Name: DSN.BAT

1: @ECHO OFF
2: REM Sort directory by name
3: DIR | SORT > ZIGNORE.ME
4: MORE < ZIGNORE.ME
5: DEL ZIGNORE.ME
```

(The ZIGNORE.ME file is not displayed in the sorted list of filenames.)

Directory Sort by Size

```
Name: DSS.BAT

1: @ECHO OFF
2: REM Sort directory by file size
3: DIR | SORT/+14 > ZIGNORE.ME
4: MORE < ZIGNORE.ME
5: DEL ZIGNORE.ME
```

Directory Sort by Date Created

```
Name: DSD.BAT

1: @ECHO OFF
2: REM Sort directory by date
3: DIR | SORT/+10 > ZIGNORE.ME
4: MORE < ZIGNORE.ME
5: DEL ZIGNORE.ME
```

Directory Sort by File Extension

```
Name: DSE.BAT

1: @ECHO OFF
2: REM Sort directory by file extension
3: DIR | SORT/+10 > ZIGNORE.ME
4: MORE < ZIGNORE.ME
5: DEL ZIGNORE.ME
```

Directory Sort by Time Created

Name: DST.BAT

```
1: @ECHO OFF
2: REM Sort directory by time
3: DIR | SORT/+35 > ZIGNORE.ME
4: MORE < ZIGNORE.ME
5: DEL ZIGNORE.ME
```

Notes on Directory Sorting

These batch files take advantage of DOS's SORT filter. More information on SORT is provided in the following chapter. If these batch files produce a "Bad Command or Filename" error, it means you may not have the SORT command available. Information on fixing this (by putting SORT on the "path") is provided in Chapter 4. Also, these batch files make use of I/O Redirection and the MORE filter. (That information is also provided in Chapter 2.)

The reason that sorting a directory works is because DOS displays the directory in a consistent format. No matter how long the filename, all filenames start at column 1. The extension always starts at column position 10. The size starts at column 14 (though it may not always display out that far), and so on (*see* FIG. 1-2).

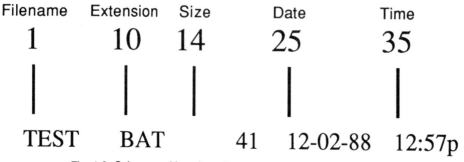

Fig. 1-2. Column positions in a directory listing are illustrated here.

This makes sorting by column an easy way to present a directory. For example, to sort on column 14 (where the file size starts), simply include SORT's column switch, /+, followed by the column number:

```
SORT /+14
```

Note that sometimes you'll see some "garbage files" in with the rest of the files and programs. These are special, temporary files used by DOS and are erased after the SORT is done. Also, when sorting on some columns, you'll see other information interspliced with the rest of the directory listing (*see* FIG. 1-3).

```
DSN       BAT         70    6-08-88   10:25p
DSS       BAT         74    6-08-88   10:24p
DST       BAT         74    6-08-88   10:25p
DSD       BAT         74    6-08-88   10:26p
DSE       BAT         74    6-08-88   10:26p
DISKETTE             129    5-30-88    2:08p
 Directory of  C:\BATCH\DISK
  .              <DIR>      6-08-88   10:24p
  ..             <DIR>      6-08-88   10:24p
       8 File(s)   10389504 bytes free
 Volume in drive C is VERY HARD
 Volume Serial Number is 001C-3246
```

Fig. 1-3. A file directory, sorted by file size, is shown here.

This is a by-product of the SORT command. Because SORT is actually sorting the directory listing as a file, it sorts all the directory information as well as the filenames.

Reversing the Sort

The SORT filter normally sorts in ascending order. That is, from low numbers and letters (1 and "A") to higher numbers and letters (9 and "Z"). SORT can also sort in reverse order by adding an /R switch. Any of the preceding batch file examples can be modified to sort in reverse order by inserting an /R after the SORT command and before the /+ column indicator.

Printing the Sort

To print any of the sorted directory listings, change the line with the MORE command in each batch file to:

```
COPY ZIGNORE.ME PRN
```

This copies the sorted directory file (ZIGNORE.ME) to the printer device, PRN. There will be more sophisticated printing examples presented later in this book.

Gang Copy

You'll find this batch file program extremely useful. It copies a group of files from one place to another. OS/2's COPY command provides this feature. But when you use DOS, you must rely on batch files like the one in FIG. 1-4.

Name: COPY2.BAT

```
 1: @ECHO OFF
 2: REM A 'Gang Copy' batch file example
 3: IF %1NOTHING==NOTHING GOTO HELP
 4: SET DISK=%1
 5: ECHO Copy a group of files to drive %DISK%
 6: :LOOP
 7: SHIFT
 8: IF %1NOTHING==NOTHING GOTO END
 9: COPY %1 %DISK% >NUL
10: ECHO %1 copied to %DISK%
11: GOTO LOOP
12: :HELP
13: ECHO COPY2 Command format:
14: ECHO copy2 [drive:[\path]] [file1] [file2] .... [fileN]
15: :END
16: SET DISK=
```

Fig. 1-4. This batch file copies a group of files from one place to another.

This file takes input such as:

C> COPY2 A: FILE1 FILE2 FILE3.TXT FILE4 FILE5 FILE6

It copies to drive A: all the files listed—any number of files up to 128 characters (the maximum number of characters you can type at the DOS prompt). If you're copying the files to a disk drive, remember to include the letter and colon. Wildcards are allowed, so the input could just as well have been:

C> COPY2 A: C:\SOURCE*.ASM C:\SOURCE*.C

How this relatively "simple" (I wrote it in less than four minutes) batch file works is covered later in this book.

Summary

Batch files are one of three types of program files that DOS can run. The differences between batch files and other program files are that batch files are easy to create—they're text files; batch files are interpreted one line at a time, just like commands typed at the system prompt; and anyone can use batch files to make their system run more efficiently.

Normally, batch files are considered rather humdrum. But as this book will go on to show, batch files can become quite sophisticated, lending even more power to your computer system.

2
DOS

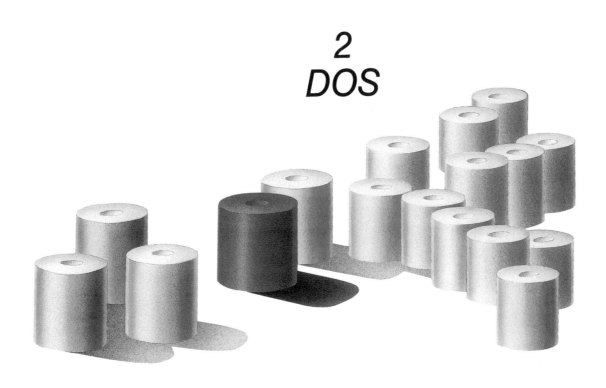

This chapter is about DOS. But it's not your typical "This is the on-off switch" chapter. Instead, this is powerful stuff—information every DOS guru should know. Even if you already think you know all the finer aspects of DOS, the information here may surprise you.

First of all, it's assumed that because this is an advanced book, you already know some of the finer points of using DOS. In fact, all you need to know is how to use the COPY function. But I encourage you to learn more about your system. If you're just starting out, you might want to order a copy of *Hard Disk Management with MS–DOS and PC–DOS*, written by Andy Townsend and myself and available through TAB Books.

SYSTEM OPERATION

You've probably had the opportunity to turn on an MS–DOS or PC–DOS computer and watch it start. Even a novice user has seen this happen maybe one hundred times at the least. When the computer starts, you hear its fan whir, and if there's a hard drive, you hear its gears rev up to 3,600 RPMs. Some clone systems may immediately display a copyright message, or they may show you a visual rendering of their RAM check. IBM computers, for some reason (perhaps because They Were First), just display a blinking cursor on the screen.

Then, suddenly, the floppy disk drive crunches to life. The speaker beeps once. The floppy drive crunches again. Your system tries to load DOS. Eventually, it will get there. If not from the floppy drive, then from that rapidly spinning hard disk.

You may not have a clue as to what's really happening inside your computer at that time (you really don't need to, anyway), but a lot of activity is taking place before you get your second prompt.

That activity, the loading, or *booting*, of a DOS disk, is the subject of this section. Booting the disk is truly trivial information. No one really needs to know this to use a computer, and you only need to have a passing knowledge of it to program batch files.

Why then am I describing it? Because this is a book on Advanced Batch File Programming. This information is important if you expect to know a lot about your system. It's what separates the typical user from an advanced user. The men from the boys, the women from the girls, etcetera. The more you know about your machine, the better you'll understand it. And the information does become useful later on.

Batch files do come into play here, but only toward the end. In the meantime, the following information describes the composition of your system, microprocessor, BIOS and DOS, and how those three items work together to give your computer a personality all its own.

Startup

Three key players compose the personality of your computer system: your microprocessor (or CPU), BIOS, and DOS (*see* FIG. 2-1).

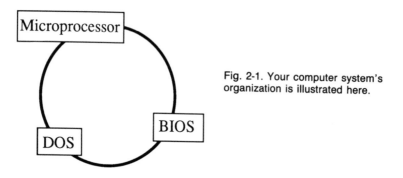

Fig. 2-1. Your computer system's organization is illustrated here.

The microprocessor is your computer's brain. However, the brain really doesn't do any thinking on its own. Instead, the microprocessor must be told what to do. It must be given instructions. The first instructions it gets are from the BIOS, or ROM, inside your computer.

How Does This Work?

According to the documentation for the Intel 8088 microprocessor (Part No. 999-999-845), the chip will innately start executing instructions at memory location FFFF:0000 when it's first turned on. This memory location typically contains "jump" instructions directing the microprocessor to the computer's BIOS (which is another memory location containing microprocessor instructions).

The original IBM PC's BIOS began at memory location F000:0000. The instructions located at the address would systematically warm-up all the various parts of the computer; initialize low-level interrupt vectors; check for port assignment conflicts; determine which type of video display adapter was attached; and perform two memory checks. It also scanned the system for another BIOS, such as an EGA BIOS, and executed it if found. Then, after a time, it attempted to check for a diskette in the first floppy disk drive.

If nothing was found in the first floppy drive, the original PC would load a ROM version of Microsoft BASIC. (The first PC had a cassette port for loading and saving programs, though none ever came out on cassette. This allowed some insane users to use the computer without disk drives. I seriously doubt if anyone ever used their IBM PC as a cassette tape-only computer.)

If a disk was found in the first drive, the BIOS would read in the first 512 bytes of that diskette. Then, once that information was in memory, BIOS would check to see if it was program code, or just garbage (meaning an unreadable disk.)

If the first 512 bytes of the disk contained program code, plus special identification bytes, the BIOS would "jump" right into the code and keep on going. If the disk contained DOS, an initialization procedure would begin whereby the first 512 bytes would load information from another part of the disk, and eventually, somewhere down the line, code would be executed to look for and load DOS from disk.

Since the addition of hard drives, the BIOS was modified to check to see if a hard disk is installed. If a diskette isn't found in the first floppy drive, the BIOS will attempt to load information from the hard disk. If DOS is on the hard drive, it will be loaded and executed similar to a floppy disk—only must faster.

This is all a simplified explanation of a very complex process. A lot of work is involved in getting DOS up in the morning. By the way, this entire process is called *bootstrapping*, and is illustrated in FIG. 2-2.

If all goes well, DOS takes over and begins loading itself into memory. Of course, it's really not as easy as that (as you'll discover in the next section). If DOS can't be loaded, an error message is displayed and, typically, your heart goes pitter-patter.

Since Then

The previous instructions were written based on the operations of an original IBM PC modified with hard disk ROMs. They also apply to your typical PC/XT. Since then, many more IBM computers, as well as a whole slew of clones and compatibles, have come to market. They generally follow the same scheme as above, though a few of the more eccentric computers may deviate here and there. The premise is basically the same as detailed in FIG. 2-2.

Along with the new computer systems came upgrades to the BIOS and to the microprocessor itself. No matter what configuration is being used, the procedures are still the same (*see* TABLE 2-1).

Power on, jump to memory location FFFF:0000, which passes control to the BIOS

Does power-on self-text (POST) routines, checks memory, then attempts to load information from disk.

Information is loaded from disk into memory by the BIOS. The information loaded is then executed. If the disk is a DOS disk, the code will attempt to load DOS.

If a floppy disk isn't in Drive A, the BIOS will check for a hard disk.

As with the floppy disk, information from the hard disk is loaded into memory by the BIOS. If the disk is a DOS disk, DOS will be loaded.

Fig. 2-2. The boot strapping sequence is illustrated here.

Table 2-1.

Computer	Microprocessor	Speed
IBM PC	8088	Average
IBM PC/XT	8088	Average
IBM PC-AT	80286	Faster
IBM PS/2	80386	Much Faster

Loading DOS

DOS is a general term that refers to the entire MS–DOS, or PC–DOS, operating system. Actually, there are many programs and files that make up DOS. Currently, DOS comes on two 360K 5 ¼-inch floppy disks, or one 720K 3 ½-inch disk. There are a total of 52 files (programs, filters, "sys" files, and overlays) that come with DOS version 3.3.

At the core of DOS are three programs. Their names differ depending on whether you have PC-DOS or MS-DOS (*see* TABLE 2-2).

Table 2-2.

PC–DOS	MS–DOS	Function
IBMBIO.COM	IO.SYS	DOS BIOS
IBMDOS.COM	MSDOS.SYS	DOS "kernel"
COMMAND.COM	COMMAND.COM	User interface, or "shell"

These files are your DOS—your Disk Operating System. Their responsibilities vary from integrating DOS with a computer's individual components to interfacing with a human being.

All three of these files will make the minimum DOS system disk. IBMBIO.COM and IBMDOS.COM are the first two files on disk. (It's done that way so that the bootstrap loader can easily find the files.) Both files are hidden, meaning they aren't listed by the DIR command. With DOS versions prior to 3.3, IBMBIO.COM and IBMDOS.COM had to be the first two files on a system disk, and both files had to be contiguous or the bootstrap loader wouldn't consider the disk a DOS disk (even if they were elsewhere on disk).

COMMAND.COM is the third required file to create a minimum system disk. Unlike IBMBIO.COM and IBMDOS.COM, COMMAND.COM is a visible file and doesn't need to be one of the first files on disk. Individually, the functions of these files are as follows:

IBMBIO.COM   is the first system file loaded into memory by the bootstrapping routines. This program serves two functions: It contains all the low-level DOS-to-hardware code, and it performs other DOS functions that come under the term SYSINIT.

The DOS-to-hardware code is referred to as the MS–DOS BIOS. It's customized by each computer manufacturer (or OEM for Original Equipment Manufacturer) to personalize DOS with the computer's hardware. These BIOS routines and low-level device drivers interface DOS directly to a computer's hardware. Once in place, the SYSINIT routines take over and continue loading DOS.

IBMDOS.COM   is loaded by the SYSINIT routines of IBMBIO.COM. This file is considered to be the MS–DOS kernel, containing all the meat of the operating system: file management, memory management, device and character input/output, time and date support, the system environment and configuration. Additionally, the routines in IBMDOS.COM set up the low-level interrupt services that are used by other programs to access DOS functions.

The next thing SYSINIT does (after loading IBMDOS.COM) is to check for a CONFIG.SYS file. If the file exists, SYSINIT reads it and sets any environmental variables listed as well as loads any user device drivers, such as a screen driver (ANSI.SYS) or a mouse driver if the computer has a mouse. (CONFIG.SYS is covered in detail in Chapter 5.)

The final act of loading DOS is to run the COMMAND.COM program. COMMAND.COM is the user *shell*, or a program that allows a human being access to DOS and all the DOS routines. (The shell insulates the user from the kernal. What a nutty idea.)

Because MS–DOS can have other shells besides COMMAND.COM, SYSINIT checks for a SHELL command in the CONFIG.SYS file. If another shell is listed, SYSINIT loads it instead of COMMAND.DOM. Otherwise, SYSINIT looks for the good old COMMAND.COM that came with DOS (*see* FIG. 2-3).

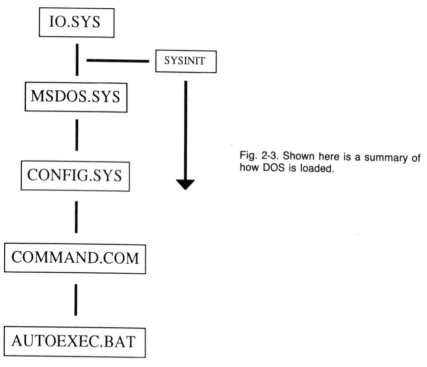

Fig. 2-3. Shown here is a summary of how DOS is loaded.

Anyone can write their own COMMAND.COM program to be used as a user shell. The only stipulation is that it be named COMMAND.COM, or specified in the CONFIG.SYS file using the SHELL command. As far as the scope of this books is concerned, the COMMAND.COM Microsoft supplies must be used because it contains the batch file interpreter.

COMMAND.COM has three parts, or modules: Initialization, Transient, and Resident. The first duty of COMMAND.COM is to fire up the initialization module.

This module copies the transient part of COMMAND.COM to higher memory. The transient module is part of COMMAND.COM that displays the command prompt and accepts commands. The resident module stays in memory all the time. It's the resident module that accepts control from a program after the program runs. It then checks to see if the transient portion of DOS is still up there in high memory. If everything's intact, the command prompt again appears. Otherwise, if the transient portion of COMMAND.COM is not present or was overwritten by a program, the resident portion reloads COMMAND.COM from disk. (This is when, on some floppy disk systems, you'll see the message "Insert disk with COMMAND.COM in Drive A and strike any key when ready.")

Why split the command processor into Transient and Resident parts? Primarily to give you more memory to run your programs. In the early days of computing, memory size was restricted. The original PC came with only 64K of RAM, so any memory that could be released to a running program was important. Even with today's memory-hog programs, every byte of RAM is important.

Batch Files

Batch files are part of the user shell, COMMAND.COM—the one supplied by Microsoft. COMMAND.COM is called a CLI, or Command Line Interface. It accepts commands typed in from the keyboard (as opposed to a pull-down menu interface or graphic environment interface). These commands are then translated by a command interpreter and the instructions passed to the DOS kernel.

At the time DOS was developed, this was the way most computers operated. Since then, and because computing power has increased and memory prices have dropped, other types of interfaces have been developed. For using batch files, however, the command line interface is the only way to get the job done. (Later, in Part III, you'll see how to use a PC Mouse to get around the command line interface.)

Batch files were originally a scripting language. The first implementation of batch files under DOS version 1.0 was quite limited. In fact, the first version of DOS had only these two batch file commands:

PAUSE
REM

Other batch file commands were simply DOS commands or program names. (There wasn't even an ECHO command to suppress the listing of a batch file as it was executing.) This all stems from the original script-like nature of batch files per IBM's request.

When DOS version 2.x came out, several commands were added to the batch file repertoire:

ECHO
FOR
GOTO
IF
SHIFT

And with DOS version 3.3, a final and very useful batch file command was added:

CALL

Additionally, all the DOS commands can be used in batch files, as well as interesting third-party software, some of which is custom designed to integrate with batch files.

ANATOMY OF AN OPERATING SYSTEM

Most of you probably claim to know DOS quite well. Personally, I'll never make a mistake and admit to something like that. Because, just as soon as I think I have DOS mastered, along comes a friend or associate who shows me some simple trick I would have never guessed. "It's in the manual," they usually say. This is a good argument for reading the manual. Again.

The material covered here is not introductory, nor is there any hand holding or DOS tutorial. Instead, this is mid-level to advanced material dealing with the finer aspects of DOS. The purpose of this section is twofold: first, it will reacquaint you with some things about DOS you may already know—or already think you may know. Second, it will introduce you to some things about DOS you may not know.

The items covered in this section include some trivia about the history of DOS (facts with which to amaze your friends), details about DOS's organization, the way it handles files and devices (more facts), and information on some of the less-practiced aspects of DOS, filters, pipes, I/O redirection, and shelling (even more facts).

History

This first version of PC–DOS came on one 160K, single-sided floppy diskette. Three programs came with DOS (EDLIN, FORMAT, and DEBUG) and it needed only 8K of RAM to run. The latest version of DOS comes on five 320K diskettes, consists of 83 files, and needs a minimum of 256K to run. (Even then, there is little room left over for running any of today's software.)

PC–DOS was written by Microsoft for IBM's first personal computer. At the time, the CP/M was the most popular microcomputer operating system. CP/M ran on the 8-bit 8080, or Z80, microprocessor. It had the lure of the largest base of business software, which meant that most businessmen interested in personal computers were buying CP/M machines. IBM wanted a piece of that action.

Under encouragement from Bill Gates, president of Microsoft, IBM planned their new machine around the 8086 microprocessor. The 8086 was a 16-bit chip and far more powerful and capable than the 8080. (For cost reasons, the 8088, a similar chip, was used instead on the first PC.)

Because the 8086 had no operating system and could not run CP/M programs, Microsoft promised IBM it would write on—and make that operating system similar to CP/M. This would make it easy for software developers to rewrite, or *port*, their software over to the IBM machine.

The initial release of DOS, version 1.0, looked a lot like CP/M. Even the filenames and structure were similar. Microsoft wanted to pave the way for CP/M business applications to move up to DOS, so everything was done accordingly. There were even translation programs built that would take Z80 and 8080 CP/M code and re-output it as 8086 MS–DOS code.

Programs started to appear for the IBM PC and PC–DOS almost overnight. This made the PC a magnificent success. Because Microsoft owned the rights to DOS (they merely licensed it to IBM), they soon released their own version called MS–DOS. This version could be sold to clone and compatible manufacturers and customized for each machine. It also ensured the popularity of what is now generically called "DOS" in the microcomputer world.

With the release of DOS 2.0, DOS began to move away from CP/M. Bill Gates was quoted as saying the second release of DOS was the version they wanted to do in the first place. Many new features were added to DOS 2.0, which coincided with the release of IBM's PC/XT.

The most attractive addition of DOS 2.0 was the hierarchical file structure, similar to the one used by Microsoft Xenix, a clone of AT&T's UNIX operating system. This file system made storing and organizing files and programs on a large volume disk, such as the 10 megabyte hard drive on the PC/XT, much easier.

DOS 2.0 also offered support for different types of floppy drives. Besides the single-sided 160K and 180K diskette formats, DOS 2.0 could support double-sided drives. This brought floppy disk storage (which was still the most popular form of storage) up to 320K. Incidentally, since version 2.0, almost every new release of DOS has centered around some new, funky disk drive format.

DOS 3.0 was designed to deal with the needs of the IBM PC/AT. The AT had a new format of floppy disk drive (see?) and a new processor: the 80286. Still, you didn't need to have a funky 1.2 megabyte drive to use DOS 3.0. It was compatible with all machines and any serious user should always upgrade to the latest version of DOS. (Make a note of that.)

One of the best additions to DOS with version 3.0 is the ability to run programs from any subdirectory. For example, suppose dBASE is in your /DB3 subdirectory. You happen to be in the /WP directory. To run dBASE under DOS 2.x, you'd have to type two commands:

```
CD  \DB3
DBASE
```

(Astute users will know that dBASE III wasn't around when DOS 2 was the rage.)
Under DOS 3.x, you can type:

```
\DB3\DBASE
```

This would normally result in a Bad Command or filename error message. But DOS is smart enough to recognize a full pathname and execute the file. (There's more on subdirectories later in this chapter.)

DOS 3.1 quickly followed DOS 3.0, primarily to fix bugs in version 3.0 and to add some networking capabilities. DOS 3.2 was introduced with the IBM laptop computer, and yet another diskette drive format: the 3 ½-inch disk. (This gets worse and worse.)

DOS 3.2 was a dog in the opinions of most consultants. It was little improvement over DOS 3.1 and offered few new features. Most people waited for DOS 3.3 and then immediately upgraded.

DOS 3.3 was a vast improvement over previous versions of DOS, with one remarkable feature: It's almost entirely re-written by IBM.

As far as batch files are concerned, DOS 3.3 added a nice new command: @. This command (usable only in batch files) suppresses the echoing of batch file commands to the screen. This eliminated the almost mandatory ECHO OFF command at the head of each batch file. They also added a new CALL command that made running second batch files easier (more on that later).

DOS 3.3 additionally provided (probably thanks to IBM) a better and smarter BACKUP command, an improved method of upgrading DOS versions, and support for yet another funky type of disk drive: the 3 ½-inch 1.44 megabyte drive on the PS/2 series of computers. (Time to throw in the towel on different disk size formats. In fact, the optional switches for the FORMAT program are so complex only the truly insane bother to memorize them.)

DOS 4.0 is the latest version of DOS as this book goes to press. Strangely enough, it wasn't coupled with the announcement of a new disk drive format. Also strange is that this version is, once again, written entirely by IBM and not Microsoft.

Version 4.0 of DOS offered three things that DOS users have wanted for a long time: The first support for very large capacity hard drives. DOS 4.0 can handle really large hard drives, way beyond the imposed 32 megabyte limit of earlier versions of DOS.

The second was that DOS 4.0 incorporated support for enhanced memory, that is, memory beyond the 640K "boundary." Certain DOS commands could now take advantage of that extra memory, leaving more room in main memory to run your applications.

Finally, DOS 4.0 comes with a mouse-driven shell program. This program is really nice, similar to those offered by other software developers—but free with DOS. The shell can be customized somewhat, making DOS painless for the first-time user.

Because of the dominance of OS/2 (discussed in Chapter 6), many people have made predictions that DOS 4.0 will be the last version of DOS ever written for PCs. This may be wishful thinking on the part of OS/2 pundits, but only time will tell. With over 13,000,000 computers that can run only DOS, rumors of its death may be "greatly exaggerated."

The purpose of this section was purely review—and trivia. About the most important thing to be gained from all this is to make sure that your system always runs on the most current version of DOS. To see if this is true, you can use the trivial VER command, which displays the version of DOS your computer is using:

```
C> VER

IBM DOS Version 4.00
```

DOS Operation

Because this is an advanced book, it's assumed that you know how to operate DOS. This includes being able to:

- copy a file from one place to another
- rename a file
- delete a file
- format disks
- copy a group of files from one place to another
- run a program and quit properly

As long as you can do these simple operations, continue reading. (Really, that's all it takes to be an intermediate DOS user. If you're rusty on any of those items, take a moment to read over your DOS manual, or read the self-promotional plug in the next paragraph.)

Again, the best book for boning up on DOS is the one I wrote with Andy Townsend, *Hard Disk Management with MS–DOS and PC–DOS*. It's available from TAB Books. Even though it says "Hard Disk" on the cover, the first several chapters offer an excellent DOS tutorial. (I promise this will be the last self-promotion in this book. Maybe.)

Device-Oriented

DOS is *device oriented*. This means that everything in the system is considered a *device*. The disk drives are devices, your keyboard is a device, the screen is a device, everything's a device. So what is a device?

A *device* is something DOS can deal with. It's typically a source for input or output. A device can receive information or produce information (or both). DOS controls your computer by processing information through various devices.

The simplest device is the disk drive. It's an I/O device, capable of input and output. DOS can both write information to disk and read it back. With some operating systems, disk drives are the extent of the devices they can handle. With DOS, however, the disk drive isn't the only device.

Another example of a device is the printer. DOS treats the printer as a device just like the disk drive. Other operating systems may only deal with the printer at a low level, or not at all.

The advantage of having the printer as a device means that DOS is able to deal with it just as it would a disk drive. So, for example, instead of putting information into a file on disk, DOS could just as easily send the information to the printer. (Both are devices.)

Because, according to DOS everything is a device, DOS can easily deal with various parts of your computer. Later in this chapter, you'll see how input and output can be redirected from one device to another. A non-device-oriented DOS wouldn't be capable of this. But MS–DOS/PC–DOS is capable, and much more versatile because of it.

Table 2-3.

Device	Device Name	Input	Output
First floppy drive	A	X	X
First serial port	AUX	X	X
Second floppy drive	B	X	X
Hard drive	C	X	X
System Clock	CLOCK$	X	X
First serial port	COM1	X	X
Second serial port	COM2	X	X
Third serial port	COM3	X	X
Fourth serial port	COM4	X	X
Console	CON	X	X
First printer	LPT1		X
Second printer	LPT2		X
Third printer	LPT3		X
Null device	NUL	X	X
First printer	PRN		X

A list of the devices that DOS recognizes is shown in TABLE 2-3.

DOS knows each of these devices by their Device Name. For example, the first serial port is AUX, or COM1. The first floppy drive is "A" (though floppy drives are not normally included in a device list; still, they are devices).

Listed in the chart is whether a device is capable of Input, Output, or both. Only the printers are output-only devices. Other devices can accept input or produce output. A variation on this is the CON, or console, device. CON is actually a combination of the keyboard and screen. When CON is selected for input, the device monitored is the keyboard. When CON is selected for output, the information is displayed on the screen.

Device Tricks

Because DOS treats everything in the system as a device, you can take advantage of some file manipulation commands for use with devices. The best trick is to use the printer device, LPT1 or PRN, as a file. For example say you want a hard copy of your favorite batch file. Try:

```
C> COPY FAVORITE.BAT PRN
```

This copies the file FAVORITE.BAT (a test file) to the printer device, PRN. The net effect is that your batch file is now printed.

A better example of this type of trick is to get hard copy from within a text editor. Remember, text editors lack any decent printing capability. Some text editors even lack a printing function. However, the text editor will let you save a file to disk. So . . . to get a hard copy from within your text editor, choose the "Save" command and for the filename type **PRN**. Voilá, you have instant hard copy.

Another device trick involves listing files on the screen. Normally, to see the contents of a text file, you'd use the TYPE command. If you wanted to look at your FAVORITE.BAT file, you'd type:

```
C> TYPE FAVORITE.BAT
```

Your batch file would be displayed on the screen in all its glory. Because the screen is also a device, the following command does the same thing:

```
C> COPY FAVORITE.BAT CON
```

You get the same result. The file is just "copied" to the screen, just as it was earlier copied to the printer.

Using COPY instead of TYPE has one distinct advantage. During your travels, you might come across some files that won't display to the screen with the TYPE command. This is because TYPE (and COPY, for that matter) looks for the end of file marker, CTRL–Z, to determine where a file ends. Some clever (?) programmers will stick a CTRL–Z at the start of their programs to prevent you from TYPEing them on the screen. There's a way to get around this using the COPY command.

Normally, COPY will look for the CTRL–Z, character, just like the TYPE command does. So, if a file starts with a CTRL–Z, COPY will have the same effect as TYPE: you won't see the file. However, COPY has a special switch /B which allows the file to be copied in the *binary* mode. This mode relies upon the file's size to determine the end-of-file position, not the CTRL–Z.

```
C> COPY FILENAME/B   CON
```

This command will "TYPE" any file on disk to your screen. But beware: many of these files contain programming code that you won't be able to read. Worse, if the files contain the CTRL–G character, your computer will beep at you each time a CTRL–G is "displayed." To stop the COPY display, press CTRL–BREAK.

Something Different

An odd little device is the null device. NUL comes from the UNIX "null" device. It's an input/output device that's basically treated the same as other devices, except that NUL is non-existent. When output is sent to NUL, the output goes nowhere and is not saved. However, because NUL is a device, DOS treats writing to the NUL device just as writing to any other device. In fact, when copying a file to NUL, DOS responds accordingly:

```
C> copy TEST.BAT NUL

1 File(s) Copied
```

Because NUL is a device, DOS really did do something. But don't expect to find an extra copy of TEST.BAT anywhere.

NUL is also an input device, but don't count on it for too much input. When the NUL device is read by DOS, and immediate end-of-file character is produced. So, copying from the NUL device to a file produces a very short file:

```
C> copy NUL TEMP

0 File(s) Copied
```

Actually, no file was created. But you can still use NUL for input. Later in this chapter, when I/O redirection is covered, you'll see how the NUL device can be used to create an empty file. Those are the scary directory entries with a byte size of zero (that usually indicate something is dreadfully wrong with your system—but not in this case).

As is shown by the above examples, devices can be used like filenames when manipulating information. This is the key to understanding devices and what they can do. The ability to manipulate these devices through the DOS commands covered in this book is a cornerstone to writing good batch files.

DOS Commands

DOS is famous for its cryptic commands. Using these puzzling commands is how you communicate with your computer. Once you learn them, they don't seem as cryptic anymore. Still, they seem to baffle the neophyte.

DOS's commands deal with files—their storage and organization. Because files are stored on devices, DOS commands also deal with devices, and they allow the devices to interact with each other.

There are other maintenance and utility commands, as well as setup commands and, of course, batch file commands. But DOS is there primarily to help you manipulate files and devices—and to keep the computer novices from messing with your system.

Table 2-4.

Command	I/E	Filter	Abbreviation	Network
APPEND	I/E			
ASSIGN	E			
ATTRIB	E			
BACKUP	E			
BREAK	I			
CHCP	I			
CHDIR	I		CD	
CHKDSK	E			
CLS	I			
COMMAND	E			
COMP	E			No
COPY	I			
CTTY	I			

Command	I/E	Filter	Abbreviation	Network
DATE	I			
DEL	I			
DIR	I			
DISKCOMP	E			No
DISKCOPY	E			No
DOSSHELL	E			
ERASE	I			
FASTOPEN	E			
FDISK	E			
FIND	E	X		
FORMAT	E			No
GRAFTABL	E			
GRAPHICS	E			
INSTALL	E			
JOIN	E			No
KEYB	E			
LABEL	E			
MEM	E			
MKDIR	I		MD	
MODE	E			
MORE	E	X		
NLSFUNC	E			
PATH	I			
PRINT	E			
PROMPT	I			
RECOVER	E			No
RENAME	I		REN	
REPLACE	E			
RESTORE	E			
RMDIR	I		RD	
SELECT	E			
SET	I			
SHARE	E			
SORT	E	X		
SUBST	E			No
SYS	E			No
TIME	I			
TREE	E			
TYPE	I			
VER	I			
VERIFY	I			
VOL	I			
XCOPY	E			

DOS commands come in two flavors: Internal and External. The internal commands are in that transient portion of COMMAND.COM you read about earlier. The external commands are actually stand-alone support files that came on the disk with DOS.

TABLE 2-4 shows all the DOS commands, internal and external, that came with DOS version 4.0. Also shown is if the command is a filter (covered later), if that command has an abbreviation, and if the command is considered network compatible.

NOTE: TABLE 2-3 is limited to DOS commands and doesn't contain other programs that come with DOS, including BASIC, the BASIC demonstration programs (PC–DOS), DEBUT, EDLIN, or any system drivers.

In the above chart, I and E are used to designate a command internal or external. Internal commands are part of COMMAND.COM. In some cases, you don't even need to have a disk in the drive to use these commands. External commands are typically .COM or .EXE files on disk.

APPEND is an internal/external command. It's actually what is known as a memory resident program (covered at the end of this chapter). APPEND starts out on the disk as APPEND.EXE. Once you type APPEND, it loads itself into memory and there it stays until you reset or turn off your computer. It is, therefore, an internal/external command.

A *filter* is a special type of program. Three come with DOS: FIND, MORE, and SORT. These filters can be used to control or manipulate the flow of input and output between various devices. They're covered later in this chapter.

Four DOS commands have shorthand versions: CHDIR, MKDIR, RENAME, and RMDIR can be abbreviated CD, MS, REN and RD respectively. Most people use the shorthand versions rather than the longer versions. Don't ask me why two versions exist (possible compatibility with Xenix/UNIX). Some intrepid DOS programmers have even taken to "patching" out the longer versions of the command names and replacing them with programs of their own.

Finally, the "Network?" category indicates those commands that are not network compatible. They can, however, be used on a single-user system, normally to allow disk and file control that would really foul up a network.

Beyond those simple categories of DOS commands, I've divided them up further in TABLE 2-5. For better descriptions, refer to your DOS manual.

Hierarchical File System

With Version 2.x, DOS incorporated a hierarchical file system. This was DOS's first step away from CP/M and a giant leap toward Xenix, Microsoft's version of the popular UNIX operating system.

A hierarchical file system employs subdirectories, or directories within directories, to store files. A disk is no longer one large set of files. Instead, you can create a number of subdirectories and organize your files into them. Furthermore, you can create subdirectories within subdirectories for more organization. This is also commonly referred to as a *tree structured* directory (although the tree in this case is upside down). The main, or top, directory is called the *root*. Branching off from it are the subdirectories much like the (upside-down) branches of a tree (*see* FIG. 2-4).

Table 2-5.

Device and File Commands

COMP	*Compares two files*
COPY	*Copies between devices*
DEL	*Deletes files*
DIR	*Displays files*
ERASE	*Deletes files*
RENAME	*Renames files*
TYPE	*Displays contents of a file*
XCOPY	*A faster version of COPY*

System Maintenance Commands

ATTRIB	*Sets or resets file attributes*
BACKUP	*Archives files*
CHDIR	*Changes the current directory*
CHKDSK	*Checks files and disks*
FORMAT	*Formats/erases disks*
INSTALL	*Installs DOS onto a new system or updates an older system*
LABEL	*Adds or changes a disk's label*
MEM	*Displays information about memory usage*
MKDIR	*Creates a new subdirectory*
REPLACE	*Updates old files, adds new ones*
RESTORE	*Restores BACKUP archives*
RMDIR	*Removes subdirectories*
SYS	*Installs/updates DOS onto a properly formatted disk*

Utility Commands

APPEND	*Modifies the search path*
ASSIGN	*Reroutes I/O from one drive to another*
CHCP	*Changes the Code Page*
CTTY	*Changes the console device*
DATE	*Changes the system date*
DISKCOMP	*Compares two diskettes*
DISKCOPY	*Copies two diskettes*
FASTOPEN	*Buffers the last few disk reads (makes opening files faster)*
FDISK	*Partitions a hard drive*
FIND	*Locate string filter*
GRAFTABL	*Loads extended ASCII character set for graphics*
GRAPHICS	*Allows graphics characters to be printed*
JOIN	*Deceives DOS into thinking a disk drive is a subdirectory*
KEYB	*Loads keyboard information for non-U.S. users*
MODE	*Controls the serial ports, screen and printers*
MORE	*A display paging filter*

Table 2-5. Continued.

NLSFUNC	*Used with CHCP for foreign users*
PATH	*Set the search path*
PROMPT	*Sets the system prompt*
RECOVER	*Attempts to restore damaged files*
SELECT	*Installs DOS for other countries*
SET	*Establishes system variables*
SHARE	*Used with file sharing*
SORT	*A filter used to sort information*
SUBST	*Deceives DOS into thinking subdirectories are disk drives*
TIME	*Changes the system time*
TREE	*Graphically displays the hierarchical file system*

Miscellaneous Commands

BREAK	*Monitors Control-Break for halting programs*
CLS	*Clears the screen*
DOSSHELL	*Starts up a user-friendly DOS interface program*
PRINT	*Starts a background print spooler*
VER	*Display the DOS version number*
VERIFY	*Set the diskette verify-write function on*
VOL	*Display the disk's volume name (set with LABEL)*

The reason for the hierarchical file system is to allow DOS to make the best use of a large volume drive, or hard disk. Face it, a 10-megabyte drive with one thousand files all in one directory would be a total mess. And besides, the programmers at Microsoft originally wanted DOS to have the hierarchical file structure, but time constraints forced them to make it a later addition.

With the introduction of the hierarchical file system came three new DOS commands, which have similar counterparts in UNIX, as shown in TABLE 2-6. (CHDIR has two counterparts in UNIX.)

Table 2-6.

Command	Abbreviation	UNIX	Function
MKDIR	MD	mkdir	Create (make) a directory
CHDIR	CD	cd	Change (sub)Directory, go "home"
CHDIR	CD	pwd	Print working directory
RMDIR	RD	rmdir	Remove a directory

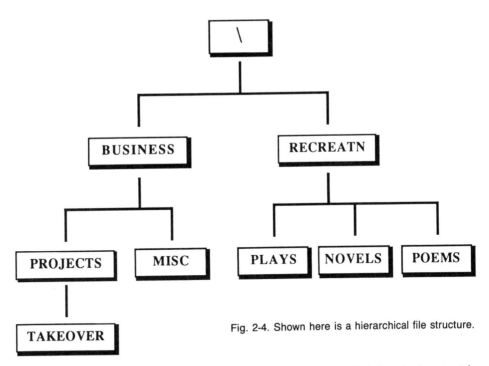

Fig. 2-4. Shown here is a hierarchical file structure.

MKDIR, or MD, is used to make a new subdirectory. All disks start out with one directory, the root. This is signified under DOS by a single backslash character. To create a subdirectory, you type MKDIR followed by the name of the subdirectory. Subdirectories are named just like files, though they usually don't have a file extension. (Filenames are covered in the next section.)

```
C> MKDIR DB3
```

This command creates the subdirectory DB3. If you're in the root directory, you've just created /DB3. If you're in another directory, you've just created a subdirectory of that directory. So, if you're in the DATABASE subdirectory, you've just created:

```
\DATABASE\DB3
```

CHDIR, or better, CD, is the most common of the directory commands. Under DOS, CD changes to the directory specified. For example:

```
C> CD \SYSTEM\UTIL\MACE
```

This command changes from the current directory to the /SYSTEM/UTIL/MACE subdirectory. /SYSTEM/UTIL/MACE is now the current directory. The same command would work under UNIX—except UNIX wouldn't understand the long-hand version 9(CHDIR), and UNIX uses forward slashes and lower case directory names, usually.

The reason why DOS doesn't use forward slashes is primarily to annoy UNIX people. Actually, in DOS 1.x, the forward slash was used as a "switch" to specify options for certain commands. To be consistent, Microsoft decided to use the back slash, \, to separate directory names. A painful, regrettable decision, but one we have to live with. (There are third party programs that will patch DOS to accept both the forward and reverse slashes to separate directory names. However, because most computers don't use these patches, this book remains consistent with DOS as is.)

Another difference between DOS and UNIX is that typing CD by itself under DOS displays the current working directory. If after the above command you typed CD, you would see:

```
C> CD
C:\SYSTEM\UTIL\MACE
```

Also, typing CD followed by a drive letter displays the current working directory for that drive:

```
C> CD A:
A:\
```

Under UNIX, the pwd command is used to print the "working" (currently logged) directory. Typing CD by itself in UNIX changes you back to your "home" directory.

RMDIR, or RD, is one of the least-used directory commands. Very rarely does anyone remove an entire subdirectory. The only limitation to RD is that the directory must be empty before you can remove it. All files must be deleted first, or you'll get an Invalid path, not directory, or directory not empty error message. This can be annoying at times because some DOS programs deposit these hideous invisible files that DEL *.*, or ERASE *.*, do not remove.

To summarize, the hierarchical system gives your hard disk better organization than could be possible otherwise. (You can still use subdirectories on floppy diskettes, though it's not necessary.) There is no limit to the number of ways you can organize your system using subdirectories, though a common philosophy seems to be "keep the root directory clean." This means, keep as few files in the root directory as possible (otherwise it gets junked up).

For trivial purposes (again, TABLE 2-7 shows a few of the files that must be in the root directory.

Table 2-7.

File	Comments
IBMBIO.COM	Hidden
IBMDOS.COM	Hidden
CONFIG.SYS	Must be in the root directory
COMMAND.COM	Could be elsewhere (see previous section)
AUTOEXEC.BAT	Must be in the root directory

Some other programs may require files in the root directory, but it's not common. Other than the above files (two of which are invisible), most root directories have only subdirectory names. The number of subdirectories you have off your root directory is up to you. Several suggestions for keeping the number small are offered in PART THREE of this book.

Why keep the number small? First, because a crowded root directory is usually the sign of an inexperienced DOS user. Second, because the root directory can only hold so many files. Once that number of files has been allocated, DOS will tell you the disk is full—even if you have several megabytes of free space on the drive (*see* TABLE 2-8).

Table 2-8.

Disk Format	Maximum files in the root directory
160K	64
180K	64
360K	112
720K	112
1.2MB	224
1.44MB	224
Hard Disk	512

A directory utility that comes with DOS is the TREE command:

FORMAT   TREE *drive* /F /A

TREE is used to display a graphic rendition of your hierarchical file system. Optionally, it will also display all the files on your hard drive and where they're located.

drive is the name of the disk drive that you want to examine. If *drive* is omitted, the current drive is used.

/F is an optional switch that displays all the files in the subdirectories encountered.

/A is an optional switch that uses ASCII character graphics to display the tree, as opposed to the Extended ASCII characters (which won't copy correctly to some non-IBM printers).

What TREE does is to start with the current directory and work its way alphabetically down the hierarchical directory structure, displaying each directory as it's encountered. If you specify another drive or directory, TREE will display a graphic picture of that drive's hierarchical file structure.

DOS 4.0 offers the most elegant version of TREE—one that displays your directory structure using character graphics rather than simply listing directory names. (For older versions of DOS, try TREE by Charles Petzold.)

FIGURE 2-5 is an example of the TREE program's output when the /A switch is specified.

```
Directory PATH listing for Volume 20 MEGGER
Volume Serial Number is 001C-3246
C:\
+---AEPRO
|   \---DATA
+---ASM
|   +---BATCH
|   +---CFONT
|   +---COM
|   +---EDITOR
|   +---MAKETAB
|   \---TELECOM
+---BASIC
+---BOOKS
|   +---BATCH
|   |   +---RYAN
|   |   +---DISK
|   |   \---OTHER
|   +---GROWING
|   +---SK
|   \---PAN
+---PLAN
+---SYSTEM
|   +---BORLAND
|   |   \---DATA
|   +---DOS
|   +---HERCULES
|   +---NORTON
|   +---TOOLS
|   +---UTIL
|   \---MOUSE
|       \---PAINT
+---TEMP
+---TURBOC
|   +---BGI
|   +---INCLUDE
|   |   \---SYS
|   +---LEARN
|   \---LIB
\---WORDP
    +---BB
    |   +---CFNSC
    |   +---COLUMN
    |   \---MAJOR
    +---DATA
    \---MJ
```

Fig. 2-5. Shown here is an example of the TREE program's output.

File Organization and Manipulation

Most of the DOS commands deal with files.

> *A file is a collection of stuff on disk.*

Generally speaking, files contain either data or instructions. Data files can be documents for a word processor, text files, spreadsheet data—anything that doesn't "run" as a program. Instruction files contain programming instruction, which include binary overlays, system drivers, utilities, and applications programs. Blandly speaking, this is all there is to a file system: storing files on disk, using some files as data, and using other files as programs (instructions for the microprocessor).

No matter what's in the file, all files share a similar name format. The format of a filename is as follows:

drive path filename.ext

drive is optional. It specifies the disk drive where the file is located. If the file in question is not on the current disk drive, **drive** must be specified. **drive** is followed by a colon:

A:**filename**

path is the full pathname (all the subdirectories) indicating where the file is on the drive. If the file is in the subdirectory GAMES, then the path is:

\GAMES

A second backslash must follow games to indicate the complete path:

\GAMES**filename**

For files in the root directory, only a single backslash is specified:

filename

or:

C:**filename**

If the file is in the current directory, the **path** can be omitted. **filename** is the important part of a filename. It's a one- to eight-character string (no spaces) identifying the file. Any ASCII or Extended ASCII character can be used to identify a file, save for the following riffraff:

. " / \ [ ] : * ! < > + = ; , ?

Also, the space character and control characters (ASCII 0 through 31) are not allowed in the filename. A period can be used, but only once, and then only to define the start of the filename extension.

ext is an optional one- to three-character extension. The power of this extension is one of the most overlooked aspects of DOS file management. Even so-called "experienced" users fail to see the convenience of naming files in a similar category with the same extension. I will now rant on this considerably.

DOS uses only three file extensions to define a program file:

COM   "Old style" program file
EXE   Executable program file
BAT   Batch file

Additionally, these extensions are used by DOS:

BAK   EDLIN (and other program's) backup file
BAS   BASIC program file
CPI   Code page information file
MOS   Mouse driver
SYS   Device driver

Aside from these, there can be over 9,129,329 possible filename extensions. (That's 256 ASCII characters, minus 32 control characters, space, and 14 reserved characters, cubed.) Granted, not everyone uses the 128 extended ASCII characters in a filename, but it is possible. In fact, using those 128 extended ASCII characters is a clever way to provide system security. (Without the extended ASCII characters, you still have 531,441 variations. Golly.)

TABLE 2-9 is one of the lists you've probably come across at one time or another in your PC travels. Due to space considerations, of course, TABLE 2-9 is only a small sample of the over eight dozen "common" extensions I found:

Table 2-9.

Extension	(Usually) Defines
ARC	Archive file (multiple files, data compression)
ASM	Assembler source code (text file)
BIN	Binary image file
C	C language source code (text)
CAL	*SuperCALC* spreadsheet data file
CBL	COBOL source code (also COB)
CFG	Configuration file
DAT	Data file
DBF	dBASE database file
DEF	Definition file
DIF	Data Interchange Format spreadsheet file
DOC	Text file containing documentation, or *Microsoft Word* document
FOR	FORTRAN source code (text)
FNT	Font file
H	C language include file
INC	PASCAL include file
LIB	Library file
MNU	*Microsoft Mouse* menu file
NDX	An index file in dBASE format
OBJ	Linker or compiler object code

Extension	(Usually) Defines
OVR	Overlay file
PAS	PASCAL source code (text)
PIC	*Lotus 1-2-3* graphic file
PIF	Program Information File for Windows
PRG	dBASE program file
RBS	R:BASE database file
SLK	SYLK formatted spreadsheet file (also SYL)
TXT	Text file
TMP	Temporary file
WKS	*Lotus 1-2-3* spreadsheet (also WK1)
XLC	*Excel* spreadsheet (also XLM, XLS, XLW)

What's the point?

The point to all this is that file organization is easier when you have similar file extensions. In some cases, organizing by file extensions is easier than splitting small items off into subdirectories. For example, at the magazine I work for there are three types of files in my editorial directory. Each of them is marked by a special file extension to make dealing with them easier:

WP	WordPerfect document
DOC	Microsoft Word document
TXT	Text document
U	Unknown format (probably text)
@	Document has been edited (now in WordPerfect format).
@^	Edited document has typesetting codes inserted
DON	Edited document in pure text format (no codes)

These extensions hold meaning for only the people in the editorial department. Yet they make transferring and copying files much easier. When the finished editorial needs to go to production, it's a simple DOS command:

```
COPY *.@^ A:
```

This copies all the finished editorial to the diskette in drive A without someone manually searching through a directory for the proper files—or scanning several subdirectories for lost files.

Anyone can do this with any files. For example, if a number of people use the same program on one computer, it's a good habit to have each of them use their initials as a file extension. If you have a subdirectory into which you place miscellaneous word processing documents, use the filename extension to provide a little organization. Use LTR for letters, MM for mail merge documents, LST for lists, and so on. (This is all provided that your software allows you to supply your own filename extension. That's not always the case.)

Using Wildcards

Don't be confused about the use of wildcard characters. There are only two of them: * and ?.

? is the single character wildcard. ? matches only one character in the filename. For example:

`D?N`

This matches any filename with D as the first letter and N as the third. You can use more than one character ? to match for more than one character. However, the character ? still matches only a single character:

`FILE?.D??`

This matches all five-letter filenames, the first four letters of which are FILE. The machine files must also have an extension starting with character D but followed by any other two characters.

A special note: Even though the character ? can replace one character, it also replaces none. If a file named "FILE.D" were on disk, it will also match the above wild card.

The character * matches a group of characters. The character * isn't as smart, however, as most people assume:

`C> DIR *.*`

displays a directory of all files in the current directory.

`C> DIR T*.*`

displays a directory of all files in the current directory that start with the letter T and have any file extension.

`C> DIR T*`

does the same thing as DIR T*.*

`C> DIR T*.`

displays all the files in the current directory starting with the letter T that have no file extension.

`C> DIR T*ING.*`

displays all files in the current directory that start with the letter T. The ING is ignored because the character * wildcard is not as logical as you may assume. In fact, internally, DOS replaces the character * with a series of question mark wildcards. So the following:

`T*.*`

becomes:

`T???????.???`

The following two commands both display all filenames in the current directory starting with the letter T:

`C> DIR T*.*`

`C> DIR T???????.???`

The most common wildcard is *.*, for the "whole shebang," or every file in the currently logged directory. It's not common knowledge that this wildcard has an abbreviation. It's "." The period is used in the hierarchical file structure to indicate the current directory. (Two periods mean the "parent" directory.) So:

`C> DIR *.*`

and

`C> DIR .`

both display a directory of the current directory. Additionally:

`C> DEL .`

attempts to delete every file in the current directory. Be careful with that one.

XCOPY

Besides the DIR command, a popular command for using wildcards is the COPY command. COPY is slow, however. It reads and copies one file at a time—even when you specify a group of files using wildcards.

The way the COPY command works internally is to take the file to be copied, read it from disk into memory, then copy it to the destination. If you use a wildcard, DOS translates it (see above), then searches for each match one at a time. As each match is found, that file is read into memory, then copied to the destination. This is tedious to say the least.

Rather than fix the COPY command, Microsoft introduced the XCOPY command with DOS 3.2. XCOPY does everything the COPY command does and more. The best improvement is that XCOPY reads all the files to be copied into memory all at once—then it copies them to the destination.

Orientation

DOS keeps track of every drive in your system, as well as which directory is currently logged for that drive. All DOS computers have an A drive, the first floppy disk drive. Some computers have a second internal floppy drive, B, and nearly all computers now have hard drives, C.

If your computer only has one internal floppy drive, it's A. However, a second "logical drive," B also exists. To prove it, type B: on your single drive system:

Insert diskette for drive B: and strike any key when ready

The physical drive A has just become the logical drive B. Microsoft did this to make copying disks (and using a single drive system—which is crazy) possible. DOS keeps track of whether the physical drive A is presently logical drive B or logical drive A, and it will instruct you to change disks if needed.

Besides all these logical assumptions, DOS keeps track of the currently logged directory for each (logical) drive in the system. To see how this works, you can use the CD command to display the currently logged directory of a specific drive. Just type the drive letter and colon after **CD** (see FIG. 2-6).

```
C> CD A:
A:\
```

```
C> CD B:
B:\EBL
```

Fig. 2-6. You can use the CD command to display the currently logged directory of a specific drive.

```
C> CD C:
C:\WP\BOOKS\BATCH
```

It's important to know that DOS remembers the currently logged directory when dealing with multiple file systems. In fact, quite a few gurus will make a so-called bozo mistake by typing in the following:

```
C> COPY *.* A:
```

Most would assume that this means to copy all the files in the current directory to the root directory on drive A. In fact, many people assume that if you're not logged to a particular disk drive, then all references to that drive are to the root directory. Wrong. Wrong. Wrong. If, for the above example, drive A is logged to /BACKUPS, then all the files will be copied to the subdirectory BACKUPS. This could possibly cause some devastating effects, including mental anguish.

Because of this mistake, it's important to know about DOS's orientation, or "where everything is." Never assume anything to be where you "think" it is. This gets very important later when you'll use the JOIN and SUBST commands to create a multitude of pseudo disk drives and subdirectories on your system.

DOS *orientation* refers to its ability to keep track of where everything is. Orientation allows you to type COPY A:*.* and have DOS know that you want all the files from drive A to be copied to your current directory. DOS knows the orientation, so this is possible.

As an example of orientation, consider the following. A group of files are in the /GAMES/KIDS directory on drive C. You want to copy them to the subdirectory /DAVID on drive A. The absolute safest way to do this is:

```
C> COPY C:\GAMES\KIDS\*.* A:\DAVID
```

This makes no assumptions. Yet, it's a lot of typing for one command. Three other (separate) commands could do the same thing, as follows.

```
C> A:
```

```
A> CD \DAVID
```

```
A> COPY C:\GAMES\KIDS\*.*
```

In the last command, DOS assumes the target directory (where all the files are to be copied to) is the currently logged directory on Drive A. The full pathname for all the files could have been omitted if the following command were used first:

```
C> CD \GAMES\KIDS
```

This initially logs drive C to the KIDS subdirectory. Now the final command could be:

```
A> COPY C:*.*
```

It's very easy to mess up a complex system by making assumptions. It's even easier when you use batch files (and it's harder, in that case, to detect and trap the errors). So be aware of DOS's orientation when writing batch file copying routines.

Filters, Pipes, and I/O Redirection

Besides being able to bandy about the various devices using DOS's file copying function, you can also take advantage of devices using filters, pipes and I/O redirection. This is one of the best aspects of DOS and one of the least understood.

You know DOS deals with the input and output of each of the various devices. There are ways of using DOS, however, that allow you to intercept the input or output of a device, modify it, change it, or send it to someplace else. For example, you can send output that normally goes to the screen to the printer, or to a file, or to any other device. Or, you can modify the input or output of a device by use of a filter program. All this is possible because DOS is device oriented.

Before getting into this, you should know that only programs using the standard input and output DOS calls can take advantage of filters, pipes and I/O redirection. These include all of the DOS functions, plus a few utilities. Rarely will sophisticated applications programs, such as spreadsheets, data bases, and word processors, use DOS's input and output functions.

I/O Redirection

Normally, unless told otherwise, DOS uses so-called standard devices for input and output. The standard input device is the keyboard. The standard output device is the screen. An example of using standard output is the DIR command. Normally, DIR sends its output to the CONsole device. Standard input is done by the keyboard, also the CONsole device. When a DOS program, such as EDLIN or DEBUG, asks for input, the input is provided by the keyboard. However, DOS allows you to perform input/output redirection, meaning that the standard input and output devices don't necessarily have to be the CONsole (keyboard and screen).

To redirect standard input or output, the less-than and greater-than symbols are used. (This is why they are reserved characters and cannot be part of a filename.)

<   Redirect standard input

>   Redirect standard output

Both symbols are followed by the name of a device that will either provide input or output, replacing the standard devices. When DOS evaluates a command you've typed at the system prompt, it looks for either character < or >. If either one or both is encountered, DOS makes the appropriate adjustments and redirects input or output to the indicated device(s).

For example, the output of the DIR command normally goes to the standard output device, the CONsole. You can redirect the output to the printer device, PRN, to get a hard copy of your directory listing:

```
C> DIR > PRN
```

or, just as easily, you could direct the output of the DIR command to a file. This would allow you to look at and edit the directory listing using a word processor or text editor:

```
C> DIR > DIRFILE.TXT
```

An interesting use of redirected output is a small DOS command I use to eject a page from the printer. I use the ECHO command, which is normally a batch file command to "echo" a string of text to the CONsole. Using I/O redirection, however, I can echo my string to the printer:

```
C> ECHO ^L > PRN
```

This sends the character Control–L to the printer, forcing a new page. If you use batch files to print lists of information, you might want to include this at the end of the file to eject a page for the user.

You can also use redirected output to make a copy of a text file. Suppose you have a text file DOCS. To make a copy of it, try:

```
C> TYPE DOCS > DOCSCOPY
```

Normally, TYPE sends its output to the standard output device. However, the character > redirects the output to the file DOCSCOPY. Remember the NUL device? I mentioned that using I/O redirection and the NUL device, you can create blank files. Here's how:

```
C> TYPE NUL > TEMP
```

The output of the NUL device is sent to a file TEMP. Because NUL contains nothing, the file TEMP will as well (*see* FIG. 2-7.)

One drawback to redirecting output to a file is that, like so many other DOS commands, if the file already exists, it will be overwritten. With the example in FIG. 2-7, if TEMP is already on disk, the redirected output from the NUL device will overwrite the old TEMP file, effectively erasing it. DOS will give you no warning when this happens. But there is a half-way solution.

```
C> DIR TEMP

    Volume in drive D is DIRTY
    Volume Serial Number is 00CC-1701
    Directory of  D:\EXAMPLES

TEMP                      0    6-14-88   10:55p
              1 File(s)      165920 bytes free
```

Fig. 2-7. The NUL file TEMP's contents are displayed here.

A variation on output redirection is the double greater-than, > >. This works just like output direction with a single greater-than sign, except when the output is directed to a file, it's *appended* to that file. (This is yet another trick borrowed from UNIX/Xenix.) For example:

```
C> DIR > DIRFILE
```

The output of the DIR command is sent to the file DIRFILE. If DIRFILE already exists, it's overwritten, otherwise DIRFILE is created. If you type a second command:

```
C> DIR >> DIRFILE
```

the output of the DIR command is now appended to whatever is already inside DIRFILE. Again, if DIRFILE doesn't exist, it's created. (Later you'll see how >> can be used to create an ongoing log of who uses the computer at what time.

Redirected input using the less-than sign < is a little trickier than redirected output. Because all input is provided from a device other than the keyboard, that device (usually a file) must have all the proper keystrokes stored in it. (This isn't as difficult as it seems, just tricky.)

The following commands are used with EDLIN to create a brief text file:

```
I
This is a brief text file.
^C
E
```

Each line is followed by a carriage return, just as you'd press *ENTER* when typing those commands in EDLIN. Note that ^C represents CTRL–C.

Normally, all those keystrokes would be used to create a very short text file in EDLIN. However, consider that the keystrokes are saved in a text file called INPUT. INPUT can be used with the character < to provide the input for EDLIN. When typed at the system prompt, you'll see what is displayed in FIG. 2-8.

```
C> EDLIN BRIEF.TXT < INPUT
New file
*I
            1:*This is a brief text file.
            2:*^C

*
*E

C>
```

Fig. 2-8. The file INPUT can be used to provide the input for EDLIN.

This all happens quickly—you never touch the keyboard. DOS reads the input from the file INPUT to create BRIEF.TXT. Later in this book, you'll see how complex programs are created using redirected input and the DEBUG program.

First, a word of warning: When providing input to a file using the character <, *all* of the program's input must be in the file. If for some reason the file supplies the wrong input, your computer may freeze. Your keyboard control may be lost with some programs because, after all, you've told DOS to get input from a file or other device. In this case, the only recourse is to whack the reset button.

As long as you're careful about your keystrokes and know the program you're redirecting the input to very well, you should normally have no problems.

Filters and Pipes

Filters and pipes also deal with I/O redirection, but in a different way. The filter intercepts the input, or more commonly the output, of a program and modifies it. The pipe is a device that allows the output of one program to be used as the input for another. Pipes and filters are not two separate items. Instead, they work together to modify the input or output of DOS and other programs that use standard input and output.

DOS comes with three filter programs:

FIND	Locates a string in a text file
MORE	Pauses the display after a screen full of text
SORT	Sorts text files

Note that even though "text files" are mentioned, the filter programs actually rely upon standard input. In fact, I've found that quite a few neophyte DOS users will often type the following at their command prompt to test the SORT filter:

```
C> SORT
```

They press ENTER and DOS just sits there. No, nothing is wrong. It's just that SORT is waiting for something to sort, in this case, standard input from the keyboard. If you type:

```
APPLES
ORANGES
GRAPES
```

And then press CTRL–Z, SORT displays:

```
APPLES
GRAPES
ORANGES
```

SORT has just sorted standard input and displayed the results as standard output. Normally, SORT doesn't use standard input and output in this way. Instead, as with the other two filters (and any additional filters other programmers may write), SORT relies on a text file or other DOS command to replace standard input.

For example, to sort a text file containing a list of items, I/O redirection is used:

```
C> SORT < FRUIT
```

Suppose FRUIT is a file containing an alphabetical list of fruits. The SORT filter will read input from that file (provided by DOS's I/O redirection) and display the sorted list to the CONsole. If you want the sorted list in another file, use I/O redirection to create the file:

```
C> SORT < FRUIT > FRUITSRT
```

The MORE filter is used to pause long displays of text. MORE displays the message "Press any key to continue" after every 23 lines of text have scrolled up the screen. This avoids the necessity of pressing CTRL–S every so often to pause a long display.

To use MORE as a filter for displaying a long text file, use I/O redirection as follows:

```
C> MORE < LONGTEXT
```

There will be more examples of these and other filters later in the book. Just remember that they rely upon standard input and, most often, that input is provided from a file (or DOS command) using I.O redirection.

Using these filters on DOS commands is different than using them on plain text files. After all, if you type:

```
C> DIR > MORE
```

you create a text file called MORE that contains the current directory. And you can't type:

```
C> MORE < DIR
```

unless you have a text file on disk named DIR.

The way around this is to use the pipe. The pipe uses the output of one command as the input for another. Because DIR uses standard output, you can use the pipe to make that output the standard input of a filter.

The pipe character is the vertical bar ¦ . Some displays show that character with a space in the middle, so it looks like a tall lower case I. To use the pipe, position it between the command providing the output and the command requiring the input:

```
C> DIR | SORT
```

This reads: take the output of the DIR command and use it as the input for the SORT command. What you'll see on the screen is a sorted directory listing. (This example was used at the end of Chapter 1 for a sorted directory batch file.)

If you want the sorted directory saved to a file, you can add I/O redirection:

```
C> DIR | SORT > ZIGNORE
```

To summarize, use I/O redirection to channel output or input of a program from the standard output or input device to another device. Use a filter to modify the output or input of a device. And use the pipe to cause the output of one command to be used as the input of another.

One final note:

*You cannot use piping or I/O redirection
on the same command line with a batch file*

The symbols ¦ < and > are not allowed after the name of a batch file on the command line. Don't expect them to work.

Multiple Programs at Once

A final interesting thing about DOS is it's ability to run more than one program at once. This isn't the classic sense of multitasking, where more than one thing is going on at a time. Instead, DOS has the ability to load and execute more than one program. It's like stacking several books inside a box: you can have a number of books in the box, but you're only allowed to read from or use one of them at a time.

There are two ways DOS runs more than one program at at time. The first is by making the program *memory-resident*. The second method is where DOS leaves one program to run a second program. Both of these methods involves different programming, and they lead to different results.

Memory-Resident

Memory-resident programs in every respect except for the way they quit. When a program quits, it calls one of the many DOS quit functions (there are five of them). These quit functions, shown in TABLE 2-10, are low-level machine-language vectors to internal DOS routines.

To quit and return to the DOS command prompt, a programmer will choose one of the functions in TABLE 2-10. The normal way programs quit is through Interrupt 20h and Interrupt 21h: functions 0h and 4Ch. These three functions simply return control to COMMAND.COM and release the memory taken by the program, freeing it up for other functions. Interrupt 21h function 4Ch is considered the most preferable method because it allows the program to generate a "return code." This return code can be evaluated by batch files, as you'll discover late in this book. The other two functions will also quit to DOS, but without a return code.

Table 2-10.

Interrupt	Function	Description
20h	none	Return to COMMAND.COM
21h	0	Terminate program (same as above)
21h	31h	Terminate and stay resident (TSR)
21h	4Ch	Terminate with return code (best)
27h	none	Terminate and stay resident (semi-dangerous)

Memory resident programs use Interrupt 21h function 31h, or Interrupt 27h to quit. These are known as the "Terminate but Stay Resident" routines, which is why some call memory-resident programs "TSRs."

Unlike a normal program, a TSR exit quits the program but does not release the memory used by the program. DOS keeps the program in memory and then loads a new copy of COMMAND.COM "on top" of the memory-resident program.

The user can go on using DOS without knowing the program he just ran is still lurking in memory.

The tricky part about memory-resident programs is that they hook into low-level routines inside the computer. For example, they may steal the keyboard routines to check for certain keystrokes. Most likely, they steal a low-level interrupt used by the PC's timer chip. This chip "ticks" 18.5 times a second. A programmer will modify the interrupt used by the timer chip so that his code will be executed every time the chip ticks. When this happens, the dormant code in memory becomes active and the program runs, suspending whatever else is going on. Needless to say, writing these programs is tricky and only a few can peacefully exist in many computers.

The reason memory-resident programs were written so they'd always be available, or to allow them to modify some part of your system. A simple type of memory-resident program is a clock that may display the current time in the upper right corner of your screen. The memory-resident clock program may monitor the system's time and display it on the screen—even though you may be using some other program.

The most popular type of memory-resident program is the "pop-up" application. These are usually (though not limited to) mini-programs that serve some handy function, such as an appointment calendar or calculator. These programs monitor keyboard input for certain key combinations. For example, a calculator program may wait for you to press ALT–C. Once pressed, the memory-resident program suspends all other computer operations and, zip!, you have a calculator on your screen.

Some users love these programs. They just can't live without their memory-resident software. Personally, I must profess that I find these programs annoying. They take up too much memory and often are incompatible with other software.

Another drawback to memory-resident software is that, once it's in memory, it's usually there to stay. Only a few memory-resident programs allow themselves to be removed. Even then, they must be removed in the exact order in which they were placed in memory. Otherwise, your system will go down in a blaze of glory.

Shelling

The second method of running more than one program at a time is technically referred to as the MS–DOS EXEC function. Commonly, it's known as *shelling* out of a program. The primary difference between leaving a program memory-resident, and shelling, is that shelling provides a quick way to get back to the original program.

Shelling operates similarly to the terminate-but-stay-resident situation. The difference is that the program you leave in memory just waits there, unlike a memory-resident program that could "pop-up" at any given time. What shelling allows you to do is leave one program in memory, return to DOS and run another program. You can also, optionally, avoid DOS and just run the second program directly.

A good example of shelling is in the writing of this book. If I need to write a quick demonstration batch file, I can "shell out" of this word processor and return to DOS. My word processor, complete with my text, is still in memory—sitting there, waiting. While in DOS, I can write batch files, even run other programs (though there's not much memory left over). Then, once I'm done, I return to the word processor by using the EXIT command. Shelling lets me do this and save a few steps.

Why shell?

The reasons for shelling will differ depending on who uses it. Most people don't understand what's going on, so they never bother. What it boils down to is that shelling is handy. When a program allows you to shell, it gives you the freedom to immediately return to DOS to perform some other activity. The original program, the *parent*, is still in memory, intact. To return to it, type EXIT and you're back where you started. This avoids having to save your information, quit the program, then return to DOS, do what you want done, re-load the program, and start over. It's handy.

An Example

When you shell you have two choices. The MS–DOS EXEC function allows a program name to be specified as a *child*. So, you can shell to a second child program, or you can shell to DOS by specifying COMMAND.COM as the child program. (Most applications do this automatically.)

In fact, you can shell to a new copy of COMMAND.COM at any time by typing \COMMAND at your system prompt. This runs the COMMAND.COM program in your root directory. You'll see something like:

```
C> \COMMAND

IBM DOS Version 4.0
        (C) Copyright International Business Machines Corp
        (C) Copyright Microsoft Corp 1981, 1986
```

You are now in a shell program. In this case, you're running a second copy of COMMAND.COM. The original copy is still there in memory, just as an applications program would be had you shelled from it.

To prove that you're running COMMAND.COM, you could check your system's memory size and notice a decrease of several thousand bytes. Or, better yet, change your command prompt. Type:

```
C> PROMPT I'm in a shell$g
```

This changes your command prompt to:

```
I'm in a shell>
```

When the second copy of COMMAND.COM was loaded, it copied what is known as the system environment over from the old, original copy of COMMAND.COM. One of the items contained in the environment is your system prompt. In the new copy of COMMAND.COM, you've just changed that prompt. When EXIT is typed, the new COMMAND.COM will be removed from memory, and you'll be returned to the original COMMAND.COM with your original system prompt. Type EXIT to get out of the shell:

```
I'm in a shell> EXIT

C>
```

You're now back at the original command prompt. The second copy of COMMAND.COM, with its modified environment and prompt is gone. If you had shelled from a word processor or other application, you'd now be back in that program. (The PROMPT command and the environment are covered in Chapter 4.)

Shelling is another way that DOS can run more than one program at a time. Running a second copy of COMMAND.COM may seem a little redundant now, but later you'll learn that sometimes it's necessary to create a larger environment, or when you want to modify your system without messing with the original COMMAND.COM.

SUMMARY

There is more to DOS than many users think. The fact that this is the fattest chapter in this book is proof. Yet, this chapter has only begun to scratch the surface. The important points covered were:

- DOS is based on older operating systems, and this explains why some things are done some ways (such as filenames and the way programs are loaded).

- DOS is device-oriented. This means that DOS isn't limited to manipulation of files on disk. Different devices can interact via DOS, which makes it a more flexible operating system, and allows such things as I/O redirection and the use of filters and pipes.

- DOS uses a hierarchical file system, similar to UNIX and Xenix. This allows files to be organized into subdirectories. DOS's method of naming files can also be used for further file organization.

- DOS remembers the currently logged directory for each drive in your system. This should be taken into consideration when copying files.

- Using I/O redirection, filters and pipes, the input and output of DOS commands can be manipulated.

- DOS allows more than one program to be in memory at a time. Memory-resident programs are loaded and then stay in memory. Shelling also allows a program to stay in memory, but provides a way to return to the original program.

3
Extra Control with ANSI.SYS

One of the most misunderstood, yet most often used, goodies that comes with DOS is the ANSI.SYS driver. ANSI.SYS not only provides codes that enhance the way information is displayed on the screen, but it can also redefine your keyboard, give you the ability to create more interesting system prompts, and really spice up some boring batch files.

Very few users bother to tread on the grounds of ANSI.SYS: ANSI commands aren't well documented, and there aren't enough interesting or useful examples to build upon. This chapter provides both of those: All the ANSI.SYS commands documented, as well as interesting examples for everything.

As an added bonus, two ANSI.SYS replacements are covered: FANSI-CONSOLE and NANSI.SYS. These two alternative screen-drivers offer more ANSI compatibility than the ANSI.SYS driver provided with DOS, and that means you can do more tricks with them.

All of these ANSI tricks can be incorporated into your batch files later, giving you more control over your computer system.

ANSI.SYS TRICKS

ANSI.SYS is a device that controls your screen and keyboard—the CONsole device. A device driver is a low-level routine loaded when DOS is booted (specified in the CONFIG.SYS file). The purpose of a device driver is to modify the input and output of a device. Because DOS is device oriented, it's easy to control the way devices behave by using a device driver.

Table 3-1.

Driver Name	Device	Controls
ANSI.SYS	Console	Character display and can be used to modify keyboard input.
DISPLAY.SYS	Screen	Used with the Enhanced Graphics Adapter (EGA), laptops, and foreign computers to allow "code page switching."
DRIVER.SYS	Disk	Sets the capacity of external drives; indirectly allows PCs and XTs to support a 720K 3½-inch floppy drive.
PRINTER.SYS	Printer	Used with IBM's Proprinter and QuietWriter III printers to allow code page switching, similar to the DISPLAY.SYS driver.
VDISK.SYS	none	Simulates a disk drive using Random Access Memory (RAM).
XMAEM.SYS	none	Emulates IBM's PS/2 80286 Expanded Memory Adapter in 80386 computers. This driver must be installed before using XMA2EMS.SYS.
XMA2EMS.SYS	none	An expanded memory driver, allowing your system and several DOS commands to use expanded memory.

DOS comes with several device drivers, seven of them with version 4.0 (see TABLE 3-1).

Two other SYS commands also come with DOS. These are not device drivers, and should never be used in a CONFIG.SYS file:

COUNTRY.SYS Contains time, date, capitilization and other information for using DOS in various countries besides the USA.

KEYBOARD.SYS Used by the KEYB command to allow non-American keyboards to be used with DOS.

There are also third-party device drivers, for examples, MOUSE.SYS, which controls the Microsoft mouse. Two public domain/shareware ANSI.SYS replacements, NANSI.SYS and FANSI-CONSOLE (actually called FCONSOLE.DEV), are covered at the end of this section.

ANSI.SYS Installation

Device drivers are installed into your system's CONFIG.SYS file and loaded when you boot your machine. (If you change CONFIG.SYS, you must reboot for the change to take effect.) They are used by the CONFIG.SYS directive DEVICE, followed by an equal sign (=), followed by the full filename of the device driver (including a path if the driver isn't in the root directory).

For example, my PC's CONFIG.SYS file is:

```
BUFFERS = 32
FILES = 20
DEVICE = C:\SYSTEM\DOS\DRIVER.SYS /D:1 /T:80 /S:9 /H:2 /F:2
DEVICE = C:\SYSTEM\DOS\ANSI.SYS
DEVICE = C:\SYSTEM\MOUSE\MOUSE.SYS
```

(More information about CONFIG.SYS is provided in Chapter 5.)

For years I was putting the ANSI.SYS device driver into my CONFIG.SYS file and never knew what it did. Oh, I knew that it controlled the screen display. In fact, on one clone I had to have the ANSI.SYS driver installed or my screen wouldn't clear when I typed CLS at the command prompt. But ANSI.SYS goes beyond controlling the screen.

To install the ANSI.SYS driver in your system, simply add the line:

```
DEVICE = ANSI.SYS
```

to your CONFIG.SYS file. If ANSI.SYS is not in your root directory, include its full pathname. Once the above line (or something similar) is in CONFIG.SYS, reboot your machine and you'll be able to access the ANSI device driver. Now the fun begins.

DOS version 4.0 has added three optional switches to ANSI.SYS: /X and /L and /K. These switches give the ANSI.SYS drive more control over your system.

/X   is used for re-assigning extended keyboard keys. (Normally these keys cannot be detected by the ANSI.SYS driver.)

/L   is used by ANSI.SYS to retain the number of rows on the screen. Using ANSI.SYS, the MODE command, and a high resolution graphics adapter, you can change the number of rows displayed on your monitor. Some applications programs may change that value back to the default of 25. When the /L switch is specified, ANSI.SYS will attempt to keep the number or rows you want, regardless of whether or not an applications program changes it.

/K   suppresses the detection of extended keyboard functions. This switch can be used with older programs that might not understand, or detect, extended keyboard functions.

ANSI

ANSI stands for the American National Standards Institute. The institute defines a number of standards for use with computers. For example, there's the ANSI standard BASIC programming language. The funny thing about that language is that no one uses it; Microsoft GW BASIC is by far more popular than the ANSI standard. (Which makes you wonder who pays ANSI people.)

ANSI has also defined a method for screen and keyboard control, and this is the standard that's employed by DOS's ANSI.SYS driver. These screen controlling commands use "escape sequences" to control output to the screen, as well as to redefine the keyboard. An escape sequence is a series of codes sent to the screen, with the first code being the ESCape character, ASCII 27.

The ANSI.SYS driver included with DOS actually uses a subset, or only a few, of the commands defined by ANSI. Other screen drivers, NANSI.SYS and FANSI-CONSOLE, use most or all of the ANSI-defined escape sequences. (The drawback is that not all DOS machines use those two alternative drivers.)

There are good and bad things about the ANSI.SYS driver. The good thing is that, assuming all DOS machines have it installed, programs that take advantage of the ANSI escape sequences to control the screen are compatible with all DOS machines.

The bad thing about the ANSI.SYS driver is that it's slow. Because of this, most programs write to the computer's screen hardware directly, circumventing DOS and the ANSI.SYS driver. But from DOS, and in the case of batch files, ANSI.SYS is a blessing.

ANSI Escape Sequences

All ANSI commands start with the Escape character (ASCII 27). This is immediately followed by a left bracket [(ASCII 91). Following those two characters are the codes that tell ANSI how to control your console; these codes are similar to DEC's VT100 terminal control codes, though far more limited.

The problem with the ANSI control sequences starting the Escape is that you can't readily enter the Escape character from your keyboard. From DOS, pressing ESC cancels the current line. In most word processors, ESC changes mode or performs some other command. Even using the ALT–keypad trick (see Appendix A) won't work properly. One common way around this, however, is EDLIN.

Though everyone who uses DOS hates EDLIN, it's one of the few text editors around that lets you enter the Escape character safely and sanely from the keyboard. No, you can't press ESC in EDLIN—that cancels the current line just as with DOS (both EDLIN and DOS use the same keyboard input routines). Instead, you type CTRL-V and then follow that with the upper case ASCII character corresponding to any control key.

> EDLIN Trick: *Press* CTRL–V *and follow it with an upper case letter to insert a control character.*

TABLE 3-2 shows which control characters are associated with other ASCII characters (also refer to Appendix A).

Table 3-2.

Control	Char.	Decimal	Hex	ASCII Char.
^@	NUL	0	00h	@
^A	SOH	1	01h	A
^B	STX	2	02h	B
^C	ETX	3	03h	C
^D	EOT	4	04h	D
^E	ENQ	5	05h	E
^F	ACK	6	06h	F
^G	BEL	7	07h	G
^H	BS	8	08h	H
^I	HT	9	09h	I
^J	LF	10	0Ah	J
^K	VT	11	0Bh	K
^L	FF	12	0Ch	L
^M	CR	13	0Dh	M
^N	SO	14	0Eh	N
^O	SI	15	0Fh	O
^P	DLE	16	10h	P
^Q	DC1	17	11h	Q
^R	DC2	18	12h	R
^S	DC3	19	13h	S
^T	DC4	20	14h	T
^U	NAK	21	15h	U
^V	SYN	22	16h	V
^W	ETB	23	17h	W
^X	CAN	24	18h	X
^Y	EM	25	19h	Y
^Z	SUB	26	1Ah	Z
^[	ESC	27	1Bh	[
^\	FS	28	1Ch	\
^]	GS	29	1Dh	]
^^	RS	30	1Eh	^
^_	US	31	1Fh	—

To include an Escape in an EDLIN file, first type CTRL–V, then a left bracket. EDLIN displays this as ^V[. When you edit the file a second time, however, you'll see ^[listed for the Escape character. Note that you must type the exact corresponding ASCII character because it is case sensitive. Typing CTRL–V followed by lower case **a** does not insert a ^A into your text. It must be an upper case **A**, just as in the above chart.

Of course, if you have a word processor that allows embedded control characters, then you can use them. The purpose here is to get the Escape character into a file to control the ANSI.SYS driver. Once this is done, you can write batch files that take advantage of the ANSI commands. (Escape is the only ASCII control character used by the ANSI driver; all other code values are entered using the ASCII characters "0" through "9")

Once you get Escape into a file, you'll want to output it to the screen via DOS. ANSI codes only work when they're interpreted by DOS. Spitting the same codes out to the BIOS or directly to the screen (two common and faster display methods than using piddly old DOS) won't be interpreted by the ANSI driver. So, to use ANSI, you can either TYPE the file or redirect its output to the screen—or use any command that sends its output directly to the CONsole device.

ANSI Commands

There are two categories of ANSI commands: screen formatting control and keyboard control. Screen formatting commands are further divided into cursor movement commands and character display commands (*see* TABLE 3-3).

Table 3-3.

ANSI Commands	Cursor Movement
Locate Cursor	Move cursor to row/column coordinate
Position Cursor	Same as above
Move Cursor Up	Move cursor up one row
Move Cursor Down	Move cursor down one row
Move Cursor Right	Move cursor right one column
Move Cursor Left	Move cursor left one column
Save Cursor Position	Stores cursor's current position
Restore Cursor Position	Restores position saved with above command
Character display	
Erase Display	Clears the screen (same as CLS)
Erase Line	Erases from the cursor's position to the end of the line
Set Graphics Rendition	Changes color/attributes of displayed text
Set/Reset Mode	Changes screen mode
Character Wrap On/Off	Turns character wrap on/off
Keyboard Control	
Key Reassignment	Replaces one character with another
String Reassignment	Replaces one character with a string

Each of the commands in TABLE 3-3 is associated with an ANSI escape sequence. The escape sequence for each ANSI commands is prefixed by two characters: Escape and the left bracket [. Any other characters appearing in the command string are case sensitive. All capitals must remain capitals and lower case letters must be used in lower case for the ANSI commands to work.

Various examples of the commands are placed through the rest of this chapter. A complete list of ANSI commands is provided in Appendix B.

Screen Manipulating Examples

TABLE 3-4 is a list of ANSI commands that will do strange things to your display. "ESC" is used to represent the ESCape character. Because ESC is always followed by a [(left bracket) in the ANSI scheme of things, don't let ESC[confuse you.

Table 3-4.

ANSI Command	ESC Sequence	What it does
Erase Display	ESC[2J	Clear screen, home cursor
Set Graphics Rendition	ESC[34m	Change text color to blue
Position Cursor	ESC[12;1H	Move to row 12, column 1

Erase Display clears your screen the same as typing CLS. In fact, to prove that, try the following:

```
C> CLS > TEMPFILE
```

This redirects the output of CLS (which is redirectable, by the way) to the file TEMPFILE. If you have a file-peeker program, you can examine the contents of TEMPFILE to see that it contains the ANSI escape sequence for Erase Display (in hex: 1B 5B 32 4A). Also, if you have the ANSI.SYS driver installed (and you should), you can type TYPE TEMPFILE at your command prompt and it will clear your screen. Nifty.

Set Graphics Rendition is one of the more popular ANSI commands—on a color display. It changes the text color, foreground and background, as well as other display attributes. (If you try changing color on a monochrome monitor, it usually changes display attributes to underline, flashing, bold, or a combination of each—including the dreaded invisible text.)

If you've studied the way color text graphics are programmed on the PC, you'll notice that there's little logic to the way ANSI programs its screen colors (see below). Normally, the PC uses bit positions to determine text foreground and background color, so a logical pattern is created among the various text color commands. But ANSI's text color commands are different. (It's probably because ANSI is a standard across many computers, not just the PC.)

The ANSI command to Set Graphics Rendition, or change the color, is:

ESC[*n;nm*

n is replaced by an ASCII number sequence (rather than a numericvalue) to change the color of the text display. There can be any number of *n*'s listed in this command, but usually only two are listed, separated by a semicolon.

The code values to change the color are in TABLE 3-5.

Table 3-5.

ANSI Code	Text Color	Monochrome
0	Normal	Normal (white on black)
1	High-intensity	High-intensity
2	Normal-intensity	Normal-intensity
4	Blue	Underline
5	Blinking	Blinking
7	Inverse video	Inverse video
8	Invisible text	Invisible text
30	Black foreground	
31	Red foreground	
32	Green foreground	
33	Yellow foreground	
34	Blue foreground	Underline
35	Magenta foreground	
36	Cyan foreground	
37	White foreground	
40	Black background	
41	Red background	
42	Green background	
43	Yellow background	
44	Blue background	
45	Magenta background	
46	Cyan background	
47	White background	

Finally, the *Position Cursor* sequence in TABLE 3-4 does what it says: move the cursor to any row or column on the screen. If you've programmed a PC compatible before, and used the BIOS cursor positioning routines, note that ANSI starts numbering rows and columns with one, not zero.

The format for *Position Cursor* is:

ESC[*row;column*H

A second, though unpopular, version of the same command is:

ESC[*row;column*f

The values for **row** are from 1 (the top row) through 25 (the bottom row). For **column**, the values range from 1 (left side) through 80 (right side). If either **row** or **column** is omitted, 1 is used. (If you leave out **row**, remember the semicolon.)

An ANSI Example

The following batch file uses the commands in TABLE 3-4 to clear the screen, display text in blue (or underline), and then move the cursor to line 12. It uses the ECHO command to send the ANSI sequences to the screen.

Just to show you how EDLIN can be used, the following describes a step-by-step outline for entering the batch file. First, type the name of the batch file, EXAMPLE.BAT, after EDLIN at the command prompt:

```
C>EDLIN EXAMPLE.BAT
New file
*
```

EDLIN displays it's * prompt character. To insert the lines of this batch file, press I, then type:

```
1:*@ECHO OFF
2:*ECHO ^V[[2J
3:*ECHO ^V[[34m
4:*ECHO Feeling Blue?
5:*ECHO ^V[[0m
6:*ECHO ^V[[12;1H
7:*^C
```

CTRL–C is typed to stop input. Remember to press CTRL–V to get ^V to display. Typing a caret followed by a V does not activate the control character entering ability of EDLIN. (You need to get those ESC characters in there.) Also, if you're using a DOS version prior to Version 3.3, don't precede the ECHO command in line one with the @, "at" sign.

After CTRL–C is pressed, you're returned to the * prompt. Type **1P** to "print" from the first line to the last, displaying your input:

```
*1P
        1:  @ECHO OFF
        2:  ECHO  ^[[2J
        3:  ECHO  ^[[34m
        4:  ECHO Feeling Blue?
        5:  ECHO  ^[[0m
        6:*ECHO  ^[[12;1H
```

Finally, type E to save the file EXAMPLE.BAT to disk.

When you run EXAMPLE.BAT, it will clear your screen, display "Feeling Blue?" in the color blue (or underline on monochrome screens), then move the cursor to line 12.

Before moving on, I should point out what's wrong with this batch file. First, there are no REM statements commenting the code. This is bad because it makes modifying the code difficult. For example, what does line 5 do? (It returns the text back to normal, otherwise everything displayed after this batch file is run will be blue.)

Second, this whole batch file could be written in one line. If you can do it, go ahead and use EDLIN to create the new batch file. Otherwise, take a peek at this example:

```
@ECHO ^[[2J^[[34mFeeling Blue?^[[0m^[[12;1H
```

The only reason that the first example wasn't all one line was to make it easier to read. You may elect to move all your ANSI commands on one line when doing your own batch files. It has the advantage of being much faster than the above example (because DOS doesn't have to keep reading the batch file from disk for each new screen formatting command).

Also, you should intersplice them with some comments to make future reference easier (see FIG. 3-1).

```
 1: @ECHO OFF
 2: REM ANSI display example
 3: REM First, clear the screen
 4: ECHO ^[[2J
 5: REM Turn on Blue foreground color, underline monochrome
 6: ECHO ^[[34m
 7: REM Display our message
 8: ECHO Feeling Blue?
 9: REM Reset color back to normal
10: ECHO ^[[0m
11: REM Move cursor to row 12, column 1
12: ECHO ^[[12;1H
```

Fig. 3-1. Intersplice batch files to make future reference easier.

More Examples

The following batch file examples demonstrate some ANSI.SYS tricks you can incorporate into your batch files. Use EDLIN to create them if you feel up to it.

Change of Colors   The ANSI batch file in FIG. 3-2 draws an American Flag (more or less) on a color display.

Name: FLAG.BAT

```
 1: @ECHO OFF
 2: REM American Flag ANSI display program
 3: CLS
 4: ECHO ^[[37;44m * * * * * * ^[[41m(25 blank spaces)=
 5: ECHO ^[[37;44m  * * * * *  ^[[47m(25 blank spaces)=
 6: ECHO ^[[37;44m * * * * * * ^[[41m(25 blank spaces)=
 7: ECHO ^[[37;44m  * * * * *  ^[[47m(25 blank spaces)=
 8: ECHO ^[[37;44m * * * * * * ^[[41m(25 blank spaces)=
 9: ECHO ^[[47m(38 blank spaces)=
10: ECHO ^[[41m(38 blank spaces)=
11: ECHO ^[[47m(38 blank spaces)=
12: ECHO ^[[41m(38 blank spaces)=
13: ECHO ^[[0m
```

Fig. 3-2. This ANSI batch file draws an American flag on a color display.

NOTE: There are 25 spaces used in the first group of ECHO statements, and 38 spaces used in the second group. The equal signs are used as a positioning guide for entering the spaces—they do not need to be part of the final batch file.

Only the *Set Graphics Rendition* command is used in this example (I could have used ESC[2J to clear the screen, but CLS is easier to type). The only thing odd about this use of color is the display of the red and white stripes on the flag—they're actually space characters with the background color set to either white or red. Don't forget the final ANSI command to set the screen mode back to normal.

Want More Color?　　There is a public domain shareware program available called *ANSIDRAW*. What it does is allow you to create "graphics" on a text screen using the IBM graphics characters (the extended ASCII line drawing characters). You can change colors, draw patterns, cut and paste, and move graphics around one screen. Then, the program allows you to save the graphics screen as an ANSI text file on disk.

For example, you could create the American Flag (above) using *ANSIDRAW*, then save it to disk as FLAG.DAT. To see the final result, simply type at the command prompt:

C> TYPE FLAG.DAT

ANSIDRAW is available from public domain houses like PC–SIG, or from many bulletin board services.

Graphics/Screen Mode　　The ANSI batch file example in FIG. 3-3 displays a menu in the 40 column mode. Note how screen positioning is used. Unfortunately, this batch file only displays the menu. After the display, you're returned to the command prompt where, sadly, you can't enter options three or four. However, in Part IV of this book, you'll learn how to coordinate your PROMPT command with a menu like the one in FIG. 3-3.

Name: MENUEX.BAT

```
 1: @ECHO OFF
 2: REM ANSI batch file to create a 40-column menu
 3: CLS
 4: REM Set 40 column screen mode (color):
 5: ECHO ^[[=1h
 6: ECHO ^[[5;15HM A I N   M E N U
 7: ECHO ^[[8;10H1. Break into company computer
 8: ECHO ^[[10;10H2. Look at payroll files
 9: ECHO ^[[12;10H3. Give me raise
10: ECHO ^[[14;10H4. Give Jamison demotion
11: ECHO ^[[16;10H5. Stealthily log off
12: ECHO ^[[20;15HEnter choice:
```

Fig. 3-3. This ANSI batch file displays a menu in the 40-column mode.

The LOCATE Batch File   The ANSI batch file example in FIG. 3-4 will come in really handy. Basically, it uses the ANSI screen positioning commands to move the cursor to a specific spot on the screen.

Name: LOCATE.BAT

```
 1: @ECHO OFF
 2: REM LOCATE batch file, positions cursor on the screen
 3: REM input is %1=row, %2=column, %3 through %9=message
 4: REM if insufficient input, cursor is unchanged
 5: REM First, save the cursor position:
 6: ECHO ^[[s
 7: IF !%1==! GOTO OOPS
 8: IF !%2==! GOTO OOPS
 9: ECHO ^[[%1;%2H%3 %4 %5 %6 %7 %8 %9
10: GOTO END
11: :OOPS
12: REM Error condition, restore cursor position
13: ECHO ^[[u
14: :END
```

Fig. 3-4. This ANSI batch file moves the cursor to a specific spot on the screen.

LOCATE.BAT accepts three input parameters: The row, the column, and a string to display. Because of the way batch files accept information from the command line, all parameters, %3 through %9, must be specified for the string to be displayed. For example:

C> LOCATE 12 40 Hello

displays "Hello" near the center of the screen.

```
C> LOCATE 12 40 Hello there
```

displays "Hello there" near the center of the screen. "Hello" and "there" are actually two command line parameters. This is why LOCATE specifies parameters %3 through %9—just in case a long string needs to be displayed.

Because LOCATE.BAT needs both a row and column coordinate, testing for those two parameters must be done. If either one is missing, locate does nothing. (Actually, because the initial cursor position was saved, the error condition, OOPS in FIG. 3-4, restores the cursor's position.)

More information is provided later in this book about replaceable parameters, as well as information on testing for missing parameters.

Character Wrap Demo   Character wrap is a rather strange addition to the ANSI.SYS driver. Character wrap controls how characters are displayed after the 80th column on the screen. Normally, with character wrap on, any character displayed after column 80 is displayed in column one on the next row down. With character wrap turned off, however, all characters after column 80 in the current row are displayed in column 80.

Turning character wrap off seems kind of dumb, yet I assume there's a reason for it. To see how character wrap works you can write two batch files:

```
Name: WRAP-ON.BAT

1: @ECHO OFF
2: ECHO ^[[=7h
3: ECHO Character wrap is on

Name: WRAP-OFF.BAT

1: @ECHO OFF
2: ECHO ^[[=7l
3: ECHO Character wrap is off
```

NOTE: the command to turn character wrap off ends in a lower case L, not a one character.

To demo character-wrap-off, run the WRAP-OFF batch file, then type on the command line until you reach column 80. Once the cursor is at column 80, it will stay there. Each character you type will be echoed in that one spot until you press ENTER or hit the ESCape key. (You can type 128 characters at the command prompt.)

To turn the wrap back on (face it, it's annoying to have it off), just run the WRAP-ON batch file.

Keyboard Key Reassignment

ANSI has the ability to replace any key you press on the keyboard with another key. Actually, what goes on is that you press one key and a character not necessarily associated with that key will be displayed. For example, you could assign the "N" key to display a "G".

On the surface, keyboard key reassignment sounds fun. I once had a boss who thought it would be neat if the "5" key on the numeric keypad could double as the down-arrow key. This would give him a keen "inverted-T" cursor pattern, like he was used to on an older computer. Unfortunately, ANSI keyboard key reassignment wouldn't work with the "5" key on the keypad. (It's considered a "dead key" by DOS.) Also, the program he was using ignored the DOS keyboard input routines and read the keyboard directly. *C'est la glabre glace*[sic].

The ANSI format for keyboard key reassignment is:

ESC[*n1;n2*P

n1 and *n2* are usually ASCII values. *n1* is the value of the key you're replacing, and *n2* is the character to replace it with. The only time this command gets complex is when you're replacing various CTRL and ALT key combinations. In those instances, you're not using ASCII character codes, but rather keyboard scan codes—an entirely different thing. But for most substitutions, ASCII characters are all you'll ever use. (A list of keyboard scan codes is in Appendix C.)

Their are two exceptions to the above format. The first is when zero prefixes the first code, *n1*. Typically, these are with ALT–*key* values. For example:

ESC[0;104;65p

This command reassigns the ALT–F1 key combination (0;104) with a capital A (ASCII 65).

Also, though it's not written down in any manuals (until now), you can place two ASCII values next to each other in quotes. For example, to reassign "A" to "G" you can use either of the following commands:

ESC[65;71p

or

ESC["AG"p

Examples   So what can you do with keyboard key reassignment? An interesting application comes from the "glabre glace[sic]" sentence in a previous paragraph: Foreign text characters.

Say you write a lot of Spanish, yet you don't want to reconfigure your computer under DOS to a Spanish configuration (covered in Chapter 5). About the only character you need to type is ñ, an n with a tilde over the top. This character is crucial to the pronunciation and meaning of dozens of Spanish words.

The following batch file can be written to use ANSI to assign the key combination ALT–N and CTRL–N to the ñ and Ñ characters respectively.

The ALT–N character code is 0;49. The character ñ has an extended ASCII code value of 164. CTRL–N has a character code of 14. The character Ñ has an extended ASCII code value of 165.

Name: EN-AY.BAT

```
1: @ECHO OFF
2: REM change Alt-N to ñ
3: ECHO ^[[0;49;164p
4: REM change Control-N to Ñ
5: ECHO ^[[14;165p
```

Some users may find it easier to assign an unpopular key to a foreign language character, rather than messing with ALT–this and CTRL–that. The following batch file program reassigns the tilde key to produce an é and an É when shifted:

The character ' has a character code of 96. The character é has an extended ASCII code value of 130. ~ has a character code of 126. The character É has an extended ASCII code value of 144.

Name: ACCENT-E.BAT

```
1: @ECHO OFF
2: REM change ` to é
3: ECHO ^[[96;130p
4: REM change ~ to É
5: ECHO ^[[126;144p
```

Keep in mind when you do this that the key reassignment only works from DOS, and programs that use the DOS keyboard scanning routines. This rules out most common applications, such as word processors and databases (where this kind of stuff would really come in handy).

Dvorak Keyboard Layout   Another example of switching keys around would be a batch file program to make your keyboard respond as a Dvorak-style keyboard. The Dvorak keyboard layout was designed with the most-often-used keys logically placed on the "home row," making typing faster and easier than the old QWERTY keyboard English-speaking people are used to.

To cause DOS to interpret your keystrokes as if you're typing on a Dvorak keyboard, you could write an ANSI batch file to change all the necessary QWERTY keys to Dvorak keys. Some keys, "A" and "M" for example, don't change. Others change according to FIG. 3-5.

Standard Keyboard Layout

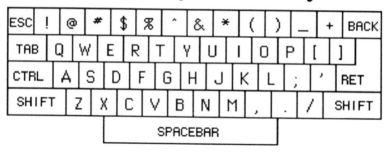

Dvorak Keyboard Layout

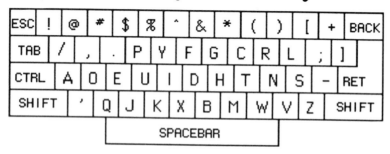

Fig. 3-5. Dvorak and QWERTY keyboard layouts are shown here.

The translation simply involves replacing the differing upper case, lower case, and control characters on the standard keyboard with those found on a Dvorak keyboard. Some things won't work properly: for example, translating CTRL–H (backspace) on a standard keyboard to a CTRL–D on a Dvorak keyboard means that your backspace key (interpreted by DOS as CTRL–H) is translated as CTRL–D. Also, there's no way to read CTRL–;,CTRL–', or CTRL–\ from the PC keyboard to translate them into CTRL–S, CTRL–_ and CTRL–Z for a Dvorak keyboard.

Therefore, an exercise in writing an ANSI batch file to create a Dvorak keyboard wouldn't really have any practical applications. If you're curious, though, it would look like FIG. 3-6.

```
@ECHO OFF
REM Dvorak keyboard Layout:
ECHO Installing Dvorak Keyboard Layout
ECHO Press Control-Break to stop, or
PAUSE
REM - to [, _ to {
ECHO ^[[31;27p
```

Fig. 3-6. This is a Dvorak keyboard layout batch file.

```
ECHO ^[[45;91p
ECHO ^[[95;123p
REM q to /, Q to ?
ECHO ^[[113;47p
ECHO ^[[81;63p
REM w to ,, W to less-than
ECHO ^[[119;44p
ECHO ^[[87;60p
REM e to ., E to greater-than
ECHO ^[[101;46p
ECHO ^[[69;62p
REM R to P
ECHO ^[[18;16p
ECHO ^[[114;112p
ECHO ^[[82;80p
REM T to Y
ECHO ^[[20;25p
ECHO ^[[116;121p
ECHO ^[[84;89p
REM Y to F
ECHO ^[[25;6p
ECHO ^[[121;102p
ECHO ^[[89;70p
REM U to G
ECHO ^[[21;7p
ECHO ^[[117;103p
ECHO ^[[85;71p
REM I to C
ECHO ^[[9;3p
ECHO ^[[105;99p
ECHO ^[[73;67p
REM O to R
ECHO ^[[15;18p
ECHO ^[[111;114p
ECHO ^[[79;82p
REM P to L
ECHO ^[[16;12p
ECHO ^[[112;108p
ECHO ^[[80;76p
REM [ to ;, { to :
ECHO ^[[91;59p
ECHO ^[[123;58p
REM S to O
ECHO ^[[19;15p
ECHO ^[[115;111p
ECHO ^[[83;79p
```

Fig. 3-6. Continued.

```
REM  D to E
ECHO  ^[[4;5p
ECHO  ^[[100;101p
ECHO  ^[[68;69p
REM  F to U
ECHO  ^[[6;21p
ECHO  ^[[102;117p
ECHO  ^[[70;85p
REM  G to I
ECHO  ^[[7;9p
ECHO  ^[[103;105p
ECHO  ^[[71;73p
REM  H to D
ECHO  ^[[8;4p
ECHO  ^[[104;100p
ECHO  ^[[72;68p
REM  J to H
ECHO  ^[[10;8p
ECHO  ^[[106;104p
ECHO  ^[[74;72p
REM  K to T
ECHO  ^[[11;20p
ECHO  ^[[107;116p
ECHO  ^[[75;84p
REM  L to N
ECHO  ^[[12;14p
ECHO  ^[[108;110p
ECHO  ^[[76;78p
REM  ; to S
ECHO  ^[[59;115p
ECHO  ^[[58;83p
REM  ' to -
ECHO  ^[[39;45p
ECHO  ^[[34;95p
REM  Z to '
ECHO  ^[[122;39p
ECHO  ^[[90;34p
REM  X to Q
ECHO  ^[[24;17p
ECHO  ^[[120;113p
ECHO  ^[[88;81p
REM  C to J
ECHO  ^[[3;10p
ECHO  ^[[99;106p
ECHO  ^[[67;74p
```

Fig. 3-6. Continued.

```
REM  V to K
ECHO  ^[[22;11p
ECHO  ^[[118;107p
ECHO  ^[[86;75p
REM  B to X
ECHO  ^[[2;24p
ECHO  ^[[98;120p
ECHO  ^[[66;88p
REM  N to B
ECHO  ^[[14;2p
ECHO  ^[[110;98p
ECHO  ^[[78;66p
REM  , to W
ECHO  ^[[44;119p
ECHO  ^[[60;87p
REM  . to V
ECHO  ^[[46;118p
ECHO  ^[[62;86p
REM  / to Z
ECHO  ^[[47;122p
ECHO  ^[[63;90p
```

Fig. 3-6. Continued.

Keyboard String Reassignment   The second form of keyboard reassignment replaces a single key with a string of characters. So, instead of getting "A" when you press the A key, you could get "Alameda."

The format for this ANSI command is the same as the single-key reassignment program, except that the *n2* value is a string enclosed in quotes:

ESC[*n;"string"*p

n is the ASCII code of the key to reassign. For example, to reassign "A" as "Alameda" you would use:

```
ESC[65;"Alameda"p
```

The number 65 is the ASCII character code for capital A. Every time you press A in DOS, or when running an application that uses the DOS keyboard functions, you'll see "Alameda" displayed. Nifty.

Extended keyboard codes, such as ALT-*key* combinations and the various function keys, all start with zero. So their format includes the leading zero, followed by a semicolon. For example, the following code changes ALT-F1 to the string "Alt-F1":

```
ESC[0;104;"Alt-F1"p
```

Now, pressing ALT-F1 in DOS displays "Alt-F1" (golly, won't that come in handy some day?).

Example   Here is a keyboard reassignment trick. This batch file assigns strings to your function keys. The unshifted function keys are needed for editing DOS commands and for EDLIN. ALT–*function* keys, however, are rarely used. The batch file in FIG. 3-7 assigns strings to the function keys ALT–F1 through ALT–F10 with various, useful DOS commands.

You could replace the strings in FIG. 3-7 with whichever DOS commands or application names you use most frequently. Notice how some of the strings are followed by "13"? That's the carriage return character. By tacking on a "13" before the "p" and after the string, the keyboard string reassignment function automatically adds a carriage return to the end of the command—just as if you'd pressed ENTER at the keyboard.

```
Name: NIFTY.BAT

 1: @ECHO off
 2: ECHO ^[[0;104;"DIR";13p
 3: ECHO ^[[0;105;"COPY "p
 4: ECHO ^[[0;106;"DEL "p
 5: ECHO ^[[0;107;"CD ";13p
 6: ECHO ^[[0;108;"CD ..";13p
 7: ECHO ^[[0;109;"CD \";13p
 8: ECHO ^[[0;110;"WP";13p
 9: ECHO ^[[0;111;"123";13p
10: ECHO ^[[0;112;"DBASE";13p
11: ECHO ^[[0;113;"PARK";13p
```

Fig. 3-7. This is the batch file NIFTY.BAT.

NANSI.SYS and FANSI.SYS

Two public domain/shareware ANSI.SYS replacements are NANSI.SYS and FANSI.SYS, or FCONSOLE-DEV as it's called. These are two ANSI.SYS replacements that implement more of the ANSI standard features, as well as added speed that ANSI.SYS doesn't provide.

FANSI.SYS   FANSI.SYS is a public domain ANSI.SYS replacement that's also known as FANSI-CONSOLE. FANSI-CONSOLE has many advantages over ANSI.SYS. For one, it's faster—you have the option of writing directly to the screen hardware using FANSI-CONSOLE, and bypassing all the relatively slow DOS routines.

FANSI-CONSOLE offers more ANSI compatibility, including more VT100 commands. Also, extended control for EGA monitors is available. The actual system driver file for FANSI-CONSOLE is called FCONSOLE.DEV. It's placed in your CONFIG.SYS file, just like ANSI.SYS:

```
DEVICE=FCONSOLE.DEV
```

There are optional switches that follow FCONSOLE.DEV, but, alas, I'm unable to locate any further documentation to tell you what they are, and what they do.

There are two drawbacks to FANSI-CONSOLE. The first is that, like other ANSI.SYS replacements, there's no guarantee that every system you come across will have it. Also, FANSI-CONSOLE is a bear to find. The version I have was written in 1985/86, and there's no information included with the file for obtaining updates. Even public domain software libraries have trouble nailing down FANSI-CONSOLE. So if you find it, check it out. Otherwise you might have better luck with NANSI.SYS.

NANSI.SYS   Of the two ANSI.SYS replacements mentioned in this book, NANSI.SYS seems to be the better option. Like FANSI-CONSOLE, it's a fast and more complete ANSI console device driver than plain old ANSI.SYS.

There are four NANSI device drivers you can use:

```
NANS88.SYS
NANS88B.SYS
NANS286.SYS
NANS286B.SYS
```

The NANS88 files are for older, PC and PC/XT compatible computers (using the 8088 microprocessor). The NANS286 files take advantage of the extended instruction set offered with the 80186 and 80286 and NEC V series chips. In other words, they're fast.

The "B" version of each NANSI driver allows the ANSI codes to be interpreted by the BIOS write-character function in addition to the DOS write-character functions. This means some applications programs that wouldn't accept the ANSI.SYS commands will accept NANSI's commands.

Also, better than FANSI-CONSOLE, NANSI.SYS comes with complete documentation, and it's easy to find. It's listed in the PC–SIG catalog and is included with a game (*NetHack*) that proves how useful NANSI.SYS can be. (Ask for Disk #1000 if you'd like *NetHack* and NANSI.SYS. *See* Appendix M for ordering information.) The copy of NANSI.SYS that comes with *NetHack* also includes documentation. So, if you order *NetHack*, you also get NANSI.SYS and it's documentation for use in your own programs. I recommend it above FANSI-CONSOLE. If you enjoyed playing with the ANSI.SYS batch files in this chapter, you'll go nuts with NANSI.SYS.

Summary

ANSI.SYS is a console device driver that can modify your keyboard and the way items are displayed on the screen. Although the power of the ANSI.SYS driver included with DOS is quite limited, it can be used to give your batch files more power, as well as make them more visually interesting.

If you're looking for more screen formatting power, you might try to locate FANSI-CONSOLE or NANSI.SYS, two ANSI.SYS replacements that offer greater functionality than the version that comes with DOS.

For a complete list of the ANSI.SYS command, refer to Appendix B.

4
The Environment

DOS has many layers to it. The more you learn about DOS, the more there is to know. In fact, there are some very thick books on DOS (such as the MS-DOS Encyclopedia at 1570-odd pages) that still don't tell everything there is to know about the operating system. One of those important items, not mentioned in most books, is the *environment*.

The environment is DOS's variable storage area—a scratch pad, if you will. The nice thing about this storage area is the DOS lets you modify it, and you can take advantage of the information stored there in batch files. In fact, there are some interesting and incredible things you can do, and all you need to know about is the environment.

This chapter covers the environment, the place were DOS keeps important information that your batch files can use. Remember, just because other books and manuals may overlook the environment doesn't mean that it's not important.

ABOUT THE ENVIRONMENT

The Environment is where DOS keeps important information, similar to a variable pool that would be used by a programming language such as BASIC. Because this information can be changed or modified by DOS, applications programs, or us users, the environment is kept in RAM (as opposed to disk).

There are two ways you can view the environment. The first is via the SET command. The second is by peeking into your computer's RAM using the DEBUG utility that comes with DOS. Most DOS aficionados would prefer that you use the first method. But because this is an advanced book and I happen to be in an exceptionally good mood today, I'm going to show you both methods.

SET

The SET command is one of those strange DOS commands that is "bi-modal." That means it does two nearly different things, depending on how you use it. Normally, SET is used to set, or create, an environment variable. However, when typed by itself, SET displays a copy of the current DOS environment on the screen:

```
C> SET
COMSPEC=C:\COMMAND.COM
PROMPT=
PATH=C:\SYSTEM\DOS;C:\SYSTEM\BATCH;U:;..
MASM=/V /Z
```

If you type SET, doubtless what you see will be different. Each computer system will probably have a different environment set up, depending on how much the user knows (or doesn't know) about DOS.

Most of the above items are set by commands in an AUTOEXEC.BAT file. If a user doesn't have an AUTOEXEC.BAT, or they don't bother to set a PATH or PROMPT or any environment variables, the environment looks like this:

```
C> SET
COMSPEC=C:\COMMAND.COM
PATH=
```

Boring. These items are the only two that DOS automatically assigns unless you change them. Actually, nothing has been assigned for the PATH. The COMSPEC is set by DOS when the system boots. It indicates the location of the COMMAND.COM program. COMMAND.COM will typically be in the root of the boot disk, or a floppy disk if you boot from it.

The second way of viewing the environment is via DEBUG. This is the dangerous way that most power users will tell you to avoid. By using DEBUG you can look directly at the environment as DOS stores it in memory. Scary.

DEBUG is a tool provided with DOS that can do many interesting things. With DEBUG, you can examine raw information on disk, "peek" at memory locations, disassemble program files (and change them), or create new programs. DEBUG is quite versatile, yet it's cryptic and backwards (or just "simple" if you don't want to be mean about things), so many people avoid using it.

In order to examine the environment using DEBUG, we have to know where the DOS keeps a copy of its environment. This information is obtained by examining what's known as the *Program Segment Prefix*, or PSP.

Each time DOS runs a program, it creates a PSP. The PSP is a 256 byte block of memory into which DOS places all kinds of interesting stuff. For example, there are important memory locations and vectors; there is information about any filenames typed on the command line, the command line itself (a copy of the command line you typed to run the program—which is how some programs know that information); there are various reserved buffers and storage places. As far as the environment is concerned, one of those storage places holds the address of your system's environment.

Because the environment location differs with each computer, observe the following directions carefully. The numbers you type will be different from the ones in the example.

First, enter DEBUG:

```
C> DEBUG
-
```

DEBUG's cryptic command prompt is the hyphen. To display the PSP (actually, this is a special PSP created by DEBUG—but it looks like the normal PSP), type D0 L100. This displays memory locations starting at address zero through address 100. The numbers are in hexadecimal, so 100 is really 256:

```
-D0 L100
```

You will see about 16 lines of information scroll up the screen, similar to what is shown in FIG. 4-1. DEBUG breaks down this display as shown in FIG. 4-2.

```
159C:0000   CD 20 00 A0 00 9A EE FE-1D F0 F4 02 ED 11 2F 03    . . . . . . . . . . . . ./.
159C:0010   ED 11 BC 02 ED 11 6F 0F-03 04 01 00 02 FF FF FF    . . . . . . .o. . . . . . . .
159C:0020   FF FF FF FF FF FF FF FF-FF FF FF FF AD 11 4E 01    . . . . . . . . . . . . . .N.
159C:0030   27 15 14 00 18 00 9C 15-FF FF FF FF 00 00 00 00    '. . . . . . . . . . . . . .
159C:0040   00 00 00 00 00 00 00 00-00 00 00 00 00 00 00 00    . . . . . . . . . . . . . . .
159C:0050   CD 21 CB 00 00 00 00 00-00 00 00 00 00 20 20 20    .!. . . . . . . . . . .
159C:0060   20 20 20 20 20 20 20 20-00 00 00 00 00 20 20 20    . . . . .
159C:0070   20 20 20 20 20 20 20 20-00 00 00 00 6E 67 65 73    . . . .nges
159C:0080   00 0D 20 0D 6E 20 6B 69-6C 6C 0D 61 74 63 68 00    .. .n kill.atch.
159C:0090   0D 3A 5C 53 59 53 54 45-4D 5C 42 41 54 43 48 3B    .:\SYSTEM\BATCH;
159C:00A0   55 3A 3B 2E 2E 0D 70 6C-65 3A 0A 0A 43 3E 20 43    U:;...ple:..C> C
159C:00B0   44 20 5C 53 59 53 54 45-4D 5C 55 54 49 4C 5C 4D    D \SYSTEM\UTIL\M
159C:00C0   41 43 45 0A 0A 54 68 69-73 20 63 6F 6D 6D 61 6E    ACE..This comman
159C:00D0   64 20 63 68 61 6E 67 65-73 20 66 72 6F 6D 20 74    d changes from t
159C:00E0   68 65 20 63 75 72 72 65-6E 74 20 64 69 72 65 63    he current direc
159C:00F0   74 6F 72 79 20 74 68 65-20 74 6F 20 5C 53 59 53    tory the to \SYS
```

Fig. 4-1. DEBUG displays your PSP.

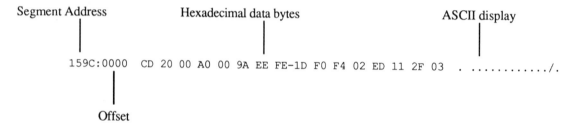

Fig. 4-2. The display is broken down in this way.

Each line starts with a segment address, followed by a memory offset. The segment address value varies the most from machine to machine. The more memory resident programs you load in when you start your system, the higher this number will be. The offset value is the byte offset within the segment. For everyone, this will start with 0.

The hexadecimal data bytes display shows the value of each byte at each memory location. The ASCII display shows the bytes as ASCII characters. Non-ASCII characters are displayed with a dot. You may see some readable characters around line 80. These are the remnants of any previous commands you've typed at the keyboard. The other information displayed is of trivial importance right now—except for the two bytes at offset 2C. To specifically see these two bytes, type:

```
-D2C  L2
```

This displays the two bytes at offset 2C. What you'll see is something like what is shown in FIG. 4-3.

```
-d2c l2

159C:0020        AD 11
```

Fig. 4-3. This shows the segment of your environment table.

Again, the numbers you see will probably be different. On my system I got the above: AD 11. This is the segment address value of my computer's environment. Note that it's a segment address and not an offset. The offset is really 0 (so it's not listed). To see your environment, simply display the block of information at that address.

The numbers displayed are in reverse order (because that's the way the 8088 stores them in memory, and it's a long story). So, to display the information at that segment address, use DEBUG's "D" command followed by the segment address (in reverse order):

```
-D11AD:0
```

This command is different from the others because the segment address is included. The segment address should be followed by a colon and a zero. After pressing ENTER, your system's environment is displayed, as shown in FIG. 4-4. Items are in the exact order in which they are displayed by the SET command. A few things to note:

• Each item in the environment is separated by a "null" character, zero.

• The last item in the environment is followed by two nulls.

There's really nothing else that can be done at this point. After all, you've seen the environment in memory—what an honor! Seriously, if you mess with anything

```
-d11ad:0

11AD:0000   43 4F 4D 53 50 45 43 3D-43 3A 5C 43 4F 4D 4D 41   COMSPEC=C:\COMMA
11AD:0010   4E 44 2E 43 4F 4D 00 50-52 4F 4D 50 54 3D 2E 20   ND.COM.PROMPT=.
11AD:0020   00 4D 41 53 4D 3D 2F 56-20 2F 5A 00 50 41 54 48   .MASM=/V /Z.PATH
11AD:0030   3D 43 3A 5C 53 59 53 54-45 4D 5C 44 4F 53 3B 43   =C:\SYSTEM\DOS;C
11AD:0040   3A 5C 53 59 53 54 45 4D-5C 42 41 54 43 48 3B 55   :\SYSTEM\BATCH;U
11AD:0050   3A 3B 2E 2E 00 00 01 00-43 3A 5C 53 59 53 54 45   :;......C:\SYSTE
11AD:0060   4D 5C 44 4F 53 5C 44 45-42 55 47 2E 43 4F 4D 00   M\DOS\DEBUG.COM.
11AD:0070   5A B5 11 4B 8E 00 00 00-00 00 00 00 00 00 00 00   Z..K............
-q
```

Fig. 4-4. Your RAM environment is shown here.

at this point, you could damage your system. Nothing severe: you just may need to reboot to right things again.

To exit DEBUG, type a Q:

-Q

C>

Now you're back at DOS.

Important Environment Notes

Don't pollute. Don't feed the animals. Etc.

On a more electronic note, you should keep the following items in mind when dealing with the environment. Items are placed in the environment at boot time, or by the SET command. Beware of programs (besides SET) that change the environment. You will notice how items in the environment will move around as you use SET to assign and un-assign items. The order is not important, so don't let it bother you.

Because more programs can be loaded on top of the environment, its size is limited. One of the most common errors you may see with your batch files is "Out of environment space." This means the environment is full and you can't stick anything else into it. (Later, in this chapter and the next, you'll read about expanding the environment.)

When you "shell" a program, or leave a memory-resident program in memory, DOS makes a new copy of the environment. A simple way to keep a safety copy of your environment is to use COMMAND to start a second command processor shell. You can then modify the environment and, when you're done, type EXIT to return to your original command processor and your original environment.

COMSPEC

Your system's environment will contain only two variables unless you tell it otherwise: COMSPEC and PATH. COMSPEC tells DOS where to find COMMAND.COM should the transient portion need to be re-loaded. Also, programs that take advantage of DOS's "shelling" capabilities (see Chapter 2) will examine the environment to look for COMSPEC = in order to run a second copy of the command processor.

Normally, if you have a hard drive, COMSPEC will look like this:

```
COMSPEC=C:\COMMAND.COM
```

or, if you boot from a floppy drive:

```
COMSPEC=A:\COMMAND.COM
```

Apparently, DOS (possibly the SYSINIT function) simply figures out which drive you booted from, then assigns COMSPEC to COMMAND.COM in that drive—whether it's actually there or not. For example, if you boot from drive A, then remove your boot disk, COMSPEC is still set to A:\COMMAND.COM. This is why some programs request that you "Insert DOS diskette in Drive A, and strike any key."

You can change the location of COMSPEC using the SET command. (SET is covered in detail below.) SET simply assigns a new valve to an environment variable, or creates a new variable if one doesn't already exist.

```
C> SET COMSPEC=Z:\COMMAND.COM
```

This command resets COMSPEC in your system's environment to the COMMAND.COM file in the root directory of drive Z. You can type SET alone on the command line to verify this:

```
C> SET
PATH=
COMSPEC=Z:\COMMAND.COM
```

The only drawback to this is that if you need to reload the transient portion of COMMAND.COM, DOS will look for it on drive Z. It better be there.

So why change the COMSPEC?

Because COMMAND.COM doesn't need to be in your root directory. In fact, you can tuck COMMAND.COM away somewhere in your deepest, darkest subdirectory where no one will ever find it. You do so with the SHELL command.

SHELL is a command used in your CONFIG.SYS file. If you recall from Chapter 2, CONFIG.SYS is run before COMMAND.COM is loaded. If DOS is informed via the SHELL command that COMMAND.COM is in another directory, it will look for it there. This has one clear advantage: it keeps your root directory clean.

To move COMMAND.COM out of your root directory, add the SHELL command to your CONFIG.SYS file:

```
SHELL=C:\DOS\COMMAND.COM
```

This instructs DOS to look for and run the file "COMMAND.COM" in the \DOS subdirectory. (SHELL also allows you to run other command processors besides

COMMAND.COM, simply by specifying their name.) If you add this command to CONFIG.SYS, you can go ahead and move COMMAND.COM to your /DOS subdirectory and delete the old COMMAND.COM from your root directory.

A drawback to using the SHELL statement this way is that your AUTOEXEC.BAT file won't run. To run AUTOEXEC.BAT, you need to specify the /P option:

```
SHELL=C:\DOS\COMMAND.COM /P
```

This instructs COMMAND.COM to look for AUTOEXEC.BAT in the root directory (you can't move AUTOEXEC.BAT—it must stay in the root) and execute it.

A second option, /E, is used to adjust the environment space. This option is covered later in this chapter.

If you boot your machine now, DOS will look for and run COMMAND.COM from your\DOS directory. Also, if /P is specified, AUTOEXEC.BAT will run from the root directory. One thing that doesn't change, however, is your COMSPEC. It will still read that COMMAND.COM is found in the root directory of whatever drive you booted from. (It appears that, whatever command creates the initial COMSPEC entry in your environment, it isn't that smart.)

To fix this anomaly, you'll need to add the following line to your AUTOEXEC.BAT file:

```
SET COMSPEC=C:\DOS\COMMAND.COM
```

This patches up any possible future "Insert DOS diskette in drive C, and strike any key" messages. (You can't reinsert your hard disk—you must reboot if this happens.)

So, if you move COMMAND.COM to a different subdirectory remember the following:

- Specify the full pathname of COMMAND.COM using SHELL in CONFIG.SYS
- Specify /P if you want AUTOEXEC.BAT (in the root) to run
- Add a SET COMSPEC= line in AUTOEXEC.BAT to tell DOS where to look for COMMAND.COM

Otherwise, you can avoid this by keeping COMMAND.COM in your root directory. This will keep the COMSPEC variable "normal" the entire time you use your computer.

THE PATH

The second environment variable DOS automatically gives you is PATH. Unlike COMSPEC, which DOS apparently makes a wild guess with, PATH starts out set to nothing. A blank path, if you will.

The reason that the path is blank is simple. DOS doesn't really know your directory structure, where your files or located, or how you use them: and that's the key to the PATH command's power. Because DOS doesn't know, how can it assign a PATH that works best for you?

Down the Beaten Path

Aside from being one of the "must haves" in your AUTOEXEC.BAT file (along with PROMPT and the command to set the system clock—more on this in the next chapter), little is ever done with the PATH command. It's sad, because a bad PATH can cause a lot of grief.

The PATH command was implemented along with subdirectories in DOS version 2.0. Before then, all your files were kept in one big directory: the disk you were using. But because of the way DOS handles subdirectories, there needed to be a way for you to access commands, utilities, and applications that are not necessarily in the same subdirectory you're in.

Unless told otherwise, DOS only looks for program files in the current directory. If you type HELLO, and HELLO.COM (or HELLO.EXE or HELLO.BAT) is not in the current directory, then nothing will happen. (Well, you'll get an error message, but the program won't run.)

The answer is the *search path*—yet another trick borrowed from the UNIX operating system. The search path gives DOS a list of other subdirectories to search through to look for files. So, you no longer need to be in the same subdirectory as a program to run that program. If that program's subdirectory is on the path, it doesn't matter where you are when you type the program's name.

Setting the Path

To set the path you simply type PATH, followed by the names of the subdirectories you want DOS to look through. Subdirectory's pathnames are separated by semicolons, and it's a good idea to include a drive letter in case you happen to be on another drive when you type a command. Also, unlike other environment variables, there's no need to type SET to set the path. PATH alone does the job.

To see your current system path, type PATH at the command prompt:

```
C> PATH
PATH=C:\SYSTEM\DOS;C:\SYSTEM\BATCH
```

Two directories are specified: C:/SYSTEM/DOS and C:/SYSTEM/BATCH. Theoretically, you could have as many directories as would fit on the command line (up to 128 characters). The drawback to long search paths is that it takes time for DOS to hunt through those directories for your commands—especially when you mistype something. (For example, if you accidentally typed BLECH, DOS would look for BLECH.COM, BLECH.EXE, or BLECH.BAT in each of the subdirectories listed on your path—a potentially time consuming process.)

When your system starts, the PATH is set to zero, or only the current directory. To reset your PATH to zero at any time, simply follow the PATH command with a single semicolon:

```
C> PATH ;
```

This resets the path to nothing.

To change the path, simply specify the new directories to search through:

```
C> PATH C:\SYSTEM\DOS;C:\WP
```

Rarely does the path need changing. In PART FOUR of this book, however, you'll see various examples that do change the path.

Nifty Trick

Without going too deeply into hard disk organization, there's a nifty trick you can play on the PATH command that alleviates typing complex subdirectory names, or maintaining a complicated PATH.

Most hard disks are organized into subdirectories that contain program files. For example, if you use *dBASE, Microsoft Word,* and *SuperCalc* as your primary applications, you may have four subdirectories on your system's hard disk (*see* FIG. 4-5). Underneath these subdirectories, you'll typically have the data files that work with the applications in the appropriate subdirectories (*see* FIG. 4-6).

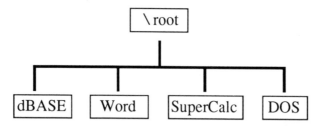

Fig. 4-5. Typical subdirectories are shown here.

Fig. 4-6. Typical data directories are shown here.

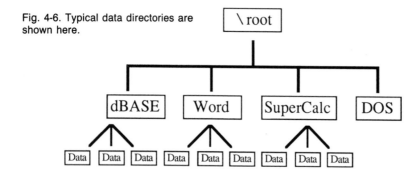

In this instance, you would probably want a path that looks something like the following:

```
C> PATH C:\DOS;C:\DBASE;C:\WORD;C:\SUPRCALC
```

This would ensure that wherever you were on your hard disk, you could access the appropriate applications file without necessarily having to be in that subdirectory. Right? Yes, but there's a better way.

The answer is ". ."—that's *double-dot*, and it's the way DOS abbreviates the parent directory. Every directory except for the root has a parent. You may have wondered what those two "dot" entries where in your directory listing, as shown in FIG. 4-7.

```
Volume in drive C is LONELY
Volume Serial Number is 0000-0001
Directory of  C:\STUFF

.            <DIR>       2-17-88    8:56p
..           <DIR>       2-17-88    8:56p
        2 File(s)    9758720 bytes free
```

Fig. 4-7. The double-dot abbreviates the parent directory.

. indicates the current directory.

Typing the following, displays the current directory:

```
C> DIR .
```

Typing the following will attempt to delete all the files in the current directory:

```
C> DEL .
All files in directory will be deleted!
Are you sure (Y/N)?
```

Two periods indicate the parent directory. This command displays the directory of the parent directory:

```
C> DIR ..
```

If you wish to change directories to the parent directory, type:

```
C> CD ..
```

It's much easier than typing the full name. As far as the PATH command is concerned, the following path:

```
C:\DOS;C:\DBASE;C:\WORD;C:\SUPRCALC
```

can be changed to:

`C:\DOS;..`

This means that DOS will first look for applications programs in the current directory (the default), then in the DOS subdirectory, then in the parent directory. If you're in one of the data subdirectories listed in FIG. 4-6, this would guarantee that you'd always have access to your applications program.

Of course, ". ." isn't the solution to everything. If you were on drive A and needed to access SuperCalc, ". ." wouldn't pass muster. So, for some important programs, especially those that you'll use often, it's best to keep their subdirectory on the path.

SUBST

The SUBST command was introduced with DOS version 3.1. Because DOS version 3.x is often cited for its "network support," many people assumed that SUBST was a network-only command. It's not. (In fact, it can't be used with a network drive at all.) Instead, SUBST can be used in a number of ways, one of which greatly boosts the performance of your search path.

Basically, SUBST lets you assign, or "alias," a disk drive letter to a pathname. For example:

`C> SUBST D: C:\DOS`

This command SUBSTitutes the pathname C:\DOS with the drive letter D. If you typed D: to move to "drive D," DOS would pretend that you are on a drive D:

`C>D:`

`D>`

While it looks as though you've just logged to drive D, in actuality you're in the \DOS subdirectory on drive C. If you did a DIR command now, it would appear as though you were in the "root" directory of drive D. Any subdirectories under \DOS (which is really where you are) would appear as subdirectories on drive D.

Note that while you can SUBST drive letters for subdirectories, the subdirectories have not been removed from your system. In the above example, you can still go to the subdirectory \DOS on drive C. It's the same thing as going to drive D.

There are some limits to the SUBST command. The first of which is that DOS only lets you have five "logical" drives—no matter how many physical drives are in your system. If you have only one hard drive "C", then DOS allows you to use D: and E: with the SUBST command. Otherwise, you have to reset the number of available logical drives with the CONFIG.SYS command LASTDRIVE. (This is covered in Chapter 5.)

The next limit is that quite a few commands will not work on a substituted drive: ASSIGN, BACKUP, DISKCOMP, DISKCOPY, FDISK, FORMAT, JOIN, LABEL, and RESTORE. Also, take care if you plan on using CHDIR, MKDIR, or RMDIR on a substituted drive. You're actually creating subdirectories from a subdirectory—not a disk drive.

To see which drives you've substituted, use the SUBST command alone:

```
C> SUBST
D: => C:\DOS
L: => C:\1-2-3
T: => C:\SYSTEM\TEMP
U: => C:\SYSTEM\UTILITY
W: => C:\WP
```

Finally, to remove a substitution, specify the /D (disable) switch after the substituted drive letter:

```
SUBST D: /D
```

This un-does the earlier example where drive D was substituted for C:\DOS. In the future, you may come across some utility programs that won't recognize the substituted drives. When this is the case, simply use the full pathnames instead of the substituted drive letters.

Why SUBST?

There are more reasons to use SUBST than any other command introduced with DOS Version 3. The first thing many users found out is that SUBST allows quick, abbreviated access to long subdirectory names. Typing U: was easier than typing CD \SYSTEM\UTILITY. Also, a number of popular, well-frequented directories could be abbreviated using SUBST. This made writing and updating a PATH command much easier:

```
PATH=D:\;E:\;U:\;W:\;..
```

Some users only use SUBST with directories they want to put on their path. This way, SUBST allows them to place a number of directories on the path by using drive letters instead of full pathnames. (Remember, though this will let you put more directories on your search path, it still means DOS will slow down as it looks through the entire path to find a program.)

A second blessing SUBST offered was a way around certain older, CP/M-ish programs that didn't understand subdirectories. Yes, even in 1985, with millions of DOS users, *WordStar* didn't understand what a subdirectory was. SUBST allowed *WordStar* users to specify a drive letter instead of the subdirectory name that the program didn't understand. When word got out about this, thousands of users upgraded to DOS version 3.1.

JOIN

The JOIN command is usually mentioned in conjunction with SUBST. JOIN is nearly the opposite of SUBST. Instead of assigning a drive letter to a subdirectory, JOIN lets you access another disk drive (particularly a floppy drive) as a subdirectory:

```
JOIN A: C:\DEV\DRIVEA
```

This command allows you to reference all the files and directories in drive A as the subdirectory \DEV\DRIVEA on drive C. So:

```
C> A:
```

is the same as typing:

```
C> CD \DEV\DRIVEA
```

You'll end up in the same place.

This command also makes dealing with partitioned hard drives easier. In earlier versions of DOS, a hard disk could only be 32 megabytes in size. When your system had a 40 megabyte (or larger) hard drive, you had to partition it into divisions smaller than 32 megabytes. So the 40 megabyte drive would become two logical drives: a 32 megabyte drive C and a 10 megabyte drive D. When this happened, you could use JOIN to make drive D a subdirectory of drive C (and keep yourself sane in the process).

```
C> JOIN D: C:\DRIVED
```

Now drive D is just a subdirectory of C, easily referenced without having to train yourself to type D: each time you want to access files there.

As with SUBST, to remove a JOIN substitution you specify the /D switch:

```
C> JOIN D: /D
```

This removes the assignment. Also, to display a list of joined drives, type JOIN on a line by itself:

```
C> JOIN
D: => C:\DRIVED
```

Also, the following commands will not work properly on a JOINed drive: ASSIGN, BACKUP, RESTORE, DISKCOMP, DISKCOPY, and FORMAT. And, for Pete's sake, don't mess around with JOINing and SUBSTituting the same drives and subdirectories over and over—unless you have a recent backup of your system.

APPEND: A Swell Addition

DOS 3.3 added a new PATH-like command to the search path repertoire: APPEND. It works a lot like path. In fact, many people confuse the two. What APPEND does is to create a search path for non-program files; any files on disk without a .COM .EXE or .BAT file extension.

APPEND works almost exactly like PATH. The exceptions are that APPEND doesn't normally store its information in the environment. Instead, APPEND is actually a memory resident program. Once you type APPEND, it stays in memory and keeps track of its own search path. To start APPEND, type APPEND on the command line:

```
C> APPEND /X/E
```

The /X switch is used to accommodate the DOS function's "search first," "find first," and "exec." These functions are used by DOS commands, such as COMP, BACKUP and RESTORE, to locate files.

The /E switch is used to place APPEND's search path into the environment. This way, you can modify that search path using either APPEND or the SET command (discussed below). The manual recommends that you not use the environment, however, and instead let APPEND keep track of its own search path.

After typing APPEND, you can set a search path for non-program files, just like the PATH command. For example:

```
C> APPEND C:\1-2-3\JUNE\DATA;C:\DOS\MISCINFO
```

This command places two subdirectories, \1-2-3\DATA and \DOS\MISCINFO, on APPEND's search path. If the data file PHONE# was in the \DOS\MISCINFO subdirectory, and you were currently logged to the \DOS subdirectory, then the following command:

```
C> TYPE PHONE#
```

would display the PHONE# file. Normally, you'd get a "File Not Found" error message. But because APPEND is loaded and you've specified \DOS\MISCINFO on the search path, the PHONE# file was found and displayed, like magic.

Just like PATH, typing APPEND on the command line alone displays the current search path:

```
C> APPEND
APPEND=C:\1-2-3\JUNE\DATA;C:\DOS\MISCINFO
```

Also, if the /E option was specified at startup, you'll see a copy of APPEND in the environment:

```
C> SET
COMSPEC=C:\COMMAND.COM
PROMPT=
PATH=C:\SYSTEM\DOS;C:\SYSTEM\BATCH;U:;..
APPEND=C:\1-2-3\JUNE\DATA;C:\DOS\MISCINFO
```

To reset the APPEND search path to nothing, type APPEND followed by a semicolon:

```
C> APPEND ;
```

To verify that nothing is there, type APPEND again:

```
C> APPEND
No Append
C> SET
COMSPEC=C:\COMMAND.COM
PROMPT=
PATH=C:\SYSTEM\DOS;C:\SYSTEM\BATCH;U:;..
APPEND=
```

APPEND is a useful and sometimes necessary command. Some problems may occur with other applications, however, especially when the /X option is specified. Also, because APPEND is memory-resident, once it's in there there's no way to get it out again.

THE SYSTEM *PROMPT*

The system prompt provides a place for input from the user. It's the first thing you become familiar with when you use DOS. Yet, it doesn't necessarily need to be so intimidating.

Normally, the system prompt is set to the current drive letter, followed by a greater-than sign:

```
C>
```

The prompt can be changed, however, to just about anything you'd like, using the PROMPT command. With the PROMPT command, you can use special prompt commands to customize your prompt, and even incorporate ANSI commands. The only limitation is the 128 input length at the command prompt—no prompt command can be more than 128 characters long.

The format of the PROMPT command is:

PROMPT = *commands*

The equal sign is optional. If you don't include any **commands**, the prompt is reset to the default drive letter plus greater-than sign. More likely than not, however, you'll use some of the nifty PROMPT commands to create your own custom prompt.

Prompt Commands

There are 13 prompt commands. Each of them is prefixed by a dollar sign. Any other character included in the PROMPT command becomes part of the prompt. Note that the characters > ¦ and < can be included in your system prompt only via the commands in TABLE 4-1. If you attempt to use them straight (as if you wanted to perform I/O redirection with them), you'll get an "Unable to create file" message.

Table 4-1.

Command	Displays
$$	$, dollar sign character
$b	¦ character
$d	the date (according to the system clock)
$e	the ESCape character
$g	> character
$h	backspace (erase previous character)
$l	< character
$n	the logged disk drive letter
$p	the logged disk drive and subdirectory
$q	= character
$t	the current time (according to the system clock)
$v	DOS version
$_	Carriage return/linefeed (new line)

Note that in TABLE 4-1, the alphabetic commands (P, G, B and so on) can be in either upper or lower case.

In addition to the commands in TABLE 4-1, ANSI cursor and screen control can be introduced into the system prompt. The $e command provides the ESCape character, so you simply supply the other information. The only drawback to this is that some prompts (see below) will look awfully confusing.

Popular System Prompts

The most popular system prompt is:

```
PROMPT=$p$g
```

Some users will follow the $g with a space (which you can't see above). This makes the prompt read:

```
C:\SYSTEM\MOUSE>  _
```

The cursor is one space after the > character. Some potentially claustrophobic users prefer this to the straight pg prompt, which puts the cursor right-butt-against the final > character:

```
C:\SYSTEM\MOUSE>_
```

There are so many things you can do with your prompt. But first, a confession: My personal system prompt, the one I use all the time, is merely a dot. That's right, a single dot—just like dBASE gives you. This is perhaps the most cryptic and unusual prompt I've ever seen, and it also keeps the neophytes from messing with my system. (I even wrote an assembly language program called QUIT that displays "This isn't dBASE!" This is in case the unsuspecting power user saunters along and tries to use my system without knowing what my personal dot prompt is!)

Most UNIX lovers change their system prompts to "$" or "#", depending on which flavor of UNIX they love the most. But before you choose your own favorite cryptic system prompt, make sure you've memorized your directory structure. The good ol' pg prompt is the best one for navigating a directory-laden hard drive. (Which makes you wonder why Microsoft didn't make it the default system prompt starting with DOS version 2.0.)

Date and Time

This system prompt is quite popular around the office. It displays the current date, time, and directory:

```
PROMPT=$d$_$t$_$p$g
```

The next effect of this prompt is something like:

```
13:19:57.26
Sun 11-30-88
C:\SYSTEM\TEMP>
```

Quite a few people like this prompt because it gives them the current date and time by simply pressing ENTER at the DOS prompt. Others don't like the prompt because it takes up three lines on the display, sometimes scrolling important information "off the top."

Memory Daze Prompt

My first computer was a Radio Shack TRS-80. It's system prompt can be emulated under MS-DOS:

```
PROMPT=TRSDOS Ready$_$e[s.... (64 dots) ...$e[u
```

(There are 64 dots between the ESC[s and ESC[u commands.)

UNIX-Lovers Prompts

UNIX is boring and cryptic—if you've ever thought the two could go together. Here are some popular UNIX-type prompts:

```
PROMPT=#
```

This is the "root" user's prompt, a number sign followed by a space.

Rarely will the UNIX nut use the lower-level user's prompt: the dollar sign. If they did, the PROMPT command to do so is:

```
PROMPT=$$
```

Because the dollar sign is the prefix character with the prompt command, two of them are issued to create a dollar sign system prompt. An interesting variation on this would be a system prompt you could write for your greedy, money-mad boss at the office. Try:

```
PROMPT=Think$$
```

Prompts That Use Backspace

The backspace prompt command, $h, can be used for a number of special prompt effects. Most often, however, it's used to erase the seconds and decimal portions of the time (and sometimes the date) display. For example:

```
PROMPT=$t$h$h$h$h$h$h$g
```

This prompt displays something like:

```
13:19>
```

The $t displays the time. But the time is displayed with seconds and hundredths of seconds as follows (in the U.S.—for other countries, see the following chapter):

```
13:19:57.26
```

To erase the six extra characters (:57.26), six backspace characters are added to the prompt command, hhhhhh. This is followed by the $g, and optionally followed by a space.

The backspace command, $h, is most often used with date and time strings to erase extra information. The only drawback is that the prompt appears to be displayed twice—the first time the entire time string is displayed, then you can see the backspacing, then the ">" character is displayed. Some users may find this annoying. (Remember, it's also possible to use the ANSI backspace command, ESC[D or $e[D, to backspace without erasing.)

The following system prompt is one of my favorites.

Screen Update

The screen update prompt displays the current directory, date and time at the top of the screen. The system prompt is then just a > character somewhere else on the screen. This system prompt makes heavy use of ANSI commands to move the cursor around the screen, save it's position, change color, and whatnot.

```
PROMPT=$e[s$e[1;1H$e[7m$e[K$p$e[1;45H$d @ $t$e[0m$e[u$g
```

I'm going to break this down into its several elements to make reading easier:

$e[s	Save the current cursor position
$e[1;1H	"Home" the cursor
$e[7m	Set inverse video on
$e[K	Erase that line
$p	Print the current directory and path
$e[1;45H	Move the cursor to just past the middle of the screen, still the top row
$d	Display the date
@	Display a space, then the "at" character
$t	Display a space, then the current time
$e[0m	Change the color back to normal video
$e[u	Restore the cursor position
$g	Display a > character, followed by an optional space

All this makes sense—move the cursor around, displaying the date and time (the character @ may confuse, but it separates the date and time strings well), and the rest. But the Erase Line command ESC[K may seem odd. Why erase the top line? Two reasons:

First, the screen may have scrolled over the old directory/date/time display. If so, the new directory/date/time display would look awkward printed over the old.

Second, if the line is not erased, only the directory, date and time will be displayed in inverse video. That would look rather tacky. Instead it's a better effect to have the entire line in inverse video. That's what erasing that line does (with the inverse video mode set on).

Making complex system prompts like this can be really fun. There's an example in Chapter 14 that works with a batch file menu program. A major drawback to overworking the ANSI commands, however, is that some users will do some unpredictable and stupid things that can ruin the effectiveness of your prompt.

Limited Input Prompt

The limited input prompt is designed for the user who will only be typing in a few single-letter commands:

```
PROMPT=Commands are:$_1 - Help$_2 - WP$_3 - 123$_4 -
       dBASE$_Choice [ ]$e[D$e[D
```

This PROMPT displays as follows:

```
Commands are:
1 - Help
2 - WP
3 - 123
4 - dBASE
Choice [ ]
```

The cursor is positioned between the brackets by the two ESC[D commands. This way, the system prompt appears as a menu, and to the unsuspecting user it would look as though only one command is allowed. (Supposedly batch files would be named 1.BAT, 2.BAT and so on to carry out the commands.)

This is just a fancy display for the normal system prompt, however, and a user could type DIR or COPY, or any DOS command in the choice box, and that information will ruin the menu effect. There's no way to limit input at the system prompt, so the reasoning behind such prompts should be carefully taken into consideration.

ENVIRONMENT VARIABLES

Environment variables come into play in two areas: those few applications programs that take advantage of them, and with (are you ready?) batch files. In fact, because so few applications programs bother to take advantage of environment (or system) variables, only those who have bothered to learn batch file programming know about variables.

Environment variables can be created at any time, though it's best to create them early, such as in your AUTOEXEC.BAT file. The reason is that they take up space. Without knowing otherwise, the environment is limited to a size of 127 bytes (it varies with the version of DOS). This fills up rather quickly when you assign a lot of variables.

Normally your environment space won't overflow. When it does, or if you plan on using a lot of environment variables, you'll need to increase the size of your system's environment. This is covered below, as well as in the next chapter under the CONFIG.SYS file's SHELL command.

The SET Command

Of all the environment commands, COMSPEC, PROMPT, and PATH, the most important one as far as batch files are concerned is SET.

Earlier in this chapter, you saw how SET is used to display the current contents of the environment. Also, at other points in this book (especially a few of the batch file examples), you may have seen SET used to create a variable. This is the primary function of the SET command: it places an environment variable into your system's environment.

> SET *is used to assign a value*
> *to an environment variable*

Set is really simple to use. In fact, knowing Microsoft, it's a wonder they didn't call it "LET". After all, the BASIC language command to assign a variable is LET.

In BASIC:

```
LET A$ = "DATA
```

In DOS:

```
SET ASTRING=DATA
```

In both examples, the variable name comes first, followed by an equal sign, and finally the data the variable is assigned to. You must use the equal sign with SET to create the assignment or you'll get a "Syntax error." And, unlike some traditional programming language, all the variables SET deals with are strings—not values. So, assigning the number 123 to a variable simply assigns the string "123" to that variable—not the value one hundred and twenty-three.

```
SET myname=dan
```

This assigns the string "dan" to the environment variable MYNAME. To make sure of it, type SET to see your environment:

```
C>SET
COMSPEC=C:\COMMAND.COM
PROMPT=
MYNAME=dan
```

Internally, DOS capitalizes the variable names—but it leaves your string data exactly as entered. The variable name, as well as the data you assign to it, can be as long as a DOS command line. (Well, 128 characters minus 3 for "SET" and 2 for the space after set and the equal sign, plus the length of your variable name, etc.)

```
SET long=this is a long string assigned to the variable long
```

This command places "this is a long string assigned to the variable long" into the environment.

```
SET unusualvariablename=hi
```

This command assigns "hi" to the variable name USUALVARIABLENAME.

There may be a temptation to enclose strings in quotes. Don't do it unless you want the quotes to become part of the variable data. For example:

```
SET greetings="Hello"
```

This command assigns the seven characters "Hello," including the quotes, to the variable GREETINGS.

Also, SET pays attention to spaces:

```
SET TEST = HELLO
```

This sets the variable "TEST" (note the space) to "HELLO" (note the space). There's nothing wrong with those extra spaces, but they do take up room in the environment table and they could lead to confusion later on.

To remove a variable, simply assign it an empty string:

```
SET temp=
```

By pressing ENTER after the equal sign, the variable TEMP, as well as whatever string was assigned to it, is removed from the environment. This is good to remember: environment space can get tight, and it's wise to remove unneeded variables after you've used them. Otherwise, they'll sit in the environment table taking up space that can be used by other variables.

Using Variables

Obviously, it's nice that DOS allows you to create variables. They can be used in two circumstances:

1) With programs that recognize the environment

2) With batch files

Quite a few applications programs are taking advantage of the environment, and use it for setting certain values. Where normally you would type something like the following:

```
C> LM /A/P/T=C:\TEMP
```

programs are letting you SET an environment variable to pass along the same information:

```
SET LM=/A/P/T=C:\TEMP
```

Programs (that are smart enough) will examine the environment and use any data there to assist running the program. Typically, these SET statements will be issued in an AUTOEXEC.BAT file, though they could better be issued in a batch file to run the program—and then reassigned to nothing after the program is run. An example of this is in FIG. 4-8.

```
1: @ECHO OFF
2: REM Batch file to run "LM" program
3: C:
4: CD \LM
5: SET LM=/A/P/T=C:\TEMP
6: LM
7: SET LM=
8: :END
```

Fig. 4-8. This is an example of a smart program.

This batch file will first move to the /LM subdirectory, set the environment, then run the LM program. After LM is through, the environment variable LM is cleared and the batch file is done.

The second example of using environment variables is to use the variable names in batch files. This is similar to using replaceable command line parameters, but don't confuse the two. (Replaceable command line parameters are covered in Chapter 7.)

DOS's batch file interpreter uses the character %, percent sign, to translate environment variables. When surrounded by percent signs, the batch file interpreter expands the environment variable to its string assignment. This happens only in batch files—not on the command line.

For example, suppose the variable NAME is assigned to ''Fred Flintstone'' by an AUTOEXEC.BAT file:

```
SET NAME=Fred Flintstone
```

The following batch file is used to extract that variable:

```
1: @ECHO OFF
2: ECHO Glad to meet you, %NAME%.
```

When you run the GREET.BAT file, you'll see the following:

```
C>GREET
Glad to meet you, Fred Flintstone
```

Because NAME is an environment variable, and it's surrounded by percent signs, the batch file interpreter expands it to whatever string is assigned in the environment table. If you change NAME to something else with the SET command, that new data will appear when you run GREET.BAT.

The secret is the expansion of the variable names by the batch file interpreter. This explains why the following happens when you try to use an environment variable on the command line:

```
C> ECHO %NAME%
%NAME%
```

The information on the command line does not pass through the batch file interpreter. DOS does exactly what you tell it to: "Echo '%NAME%' to the console."

To see how the expansion works, simply remove the @ECHO OFF command from the GREET.BAT file and watch your screen as the batch file works:

```
C>GREET
ECHO Glad to meet you, Fred Flintstone
Glad to meet you, Fred Flintstone

C>
```

The batch file interpreter is converting the names even as the lines are displayed. This just doesn't happen in the command line.

Out of Space

The only error you can get with the SET command, besides the above mentioned "Syntax error," is "Out of environment space." As you may discover, environment variables can use a lot of memory.

Normally, unless told otherwise, DOS only gives you 127 bytes for the environment. (Some versions of DOS may go up to 160 bytes.) That's only 127 bytes for everything: variable names, their assignments, the equal sign, and the final null, or zero, character. That 127 bytes can go rather quickly when each character you type is one byte.

If you plan on using more than 127 bytes for storing environment variables, you'll need to increase your environment size. Sure, you can reassign some variables to nothing. That will clear some space, but that's not really the answer.

Creating an environment larger than 127 bytes is done with the SHELL command in CONFIG.SYS (discussed in the following chapter). SHELL is used to specify a command interpreter other than COMMAND.COM, or to specify a different location on disk for COMMAND.COM (see above), or to change the environment size. It's the /E: switch that does the trick:

SHELL = COMMAND.COM /E:*n*

The *n* is a number ranging from 160 through 32,768. It specifies the number of bytes DOS allocates to the environment. If the number is less than 160 or greater than 32,768, then those two values are used (respectively). Incidentally, DOS will round the number you specify up to the nearest multiple of 16.

If you suppose that you'll be using 1K (1,024 bytes) of environment space, you can boost it up to that by adding the following line to your CONFIG.SYS file:

```
SHELL=C:\COMMAND.COM /E:1024
```

This CONFIG.SYS command still uses COMMAND.COM in the root directory (just like normal), but sets aside 1K, or 1,024 bytes, of storage for the environment. Also, if you still want COMMAND.COM to run your AUTOEXEC.BAT file, remember to specify the /P switch:

```
SHELL=C:\COMMAND.COM /P/E:1024
```

SHELL is a nifty way to increase the size of your environment. Unfortunately, it's only available with DOS versions 3.2 or later. So what can you do if you're "stuck" with an older version of DOS and want a bigger environment size?

The answer always lies in those busy geniuses who write utility programs. One utility (not in the public domain) is called *SETENV*. It comes with the *Microsoft Macro Assembler* package and was specifically written to alter the environment size for users of DOS 2.0 through 3.1.

The drawback to *SETENV* is that you must pay $150 retail (often $99 discounted) for it, and you get the Macro Assembler package that you may never, ever use. The happy part is that there may be some public domain programs that do the same thing. Offhand, I don't know of any—but if they do pop up, a public domain/shareware software warehouse like PC–SIG would know about it. See Appendix L for information on contacting PC–SIG.

THE ENVIRONMENT AND BATCH FILES

You can use any or all of the environment commands: SET, PATH, and PROMPT, in any of your batch files. In fact, you probably already use PATH and PROMPT in your AUTOEXEC batch file. But the use of those commands, and of environment variables, need not be limited to AUTOEXEC.BAT.

Saving the Old

One important use of batch files is to run other programs. This will be demonstrated in detail in PART FOUR of this book. But for now, consider some batch files that run other programs, like the LM.BAT program mentioned earlier in this chapter.

For each batch file that runs a program, you can modify the PATH and SET environment variables. For example, say you have a batch file that you use when writing programs in the C language. Because you only use the C compiler and all the other C goodies when you're programming, you don't need to have those subdirectories on your patch all the time. So, you write a batch file called DO-C that sets up your computer's environment for writing C programs (*see* FIG. 4-9).

```
Name: DO-C.BAT

 1: @ECHO OFF
 2: REM Set up environment for C compiler
 3: C:
 4: CD \TURBOC
 5: PATH C:\DOS;C:\TURBOC;C:\UTILITY;..
 6: REM Set APPEND to look for include files and such
 7: APPEND C:\TURBOC\INCLUDE;C:\TURBOC\LIB
 8: REM Set TURBOC environment variable 87=N (no 8087)
 9: SET 87=N
10: ECHO Welcome to Turbo C, Phillipe thanks you.
```

Fig. 4-9. The DO-C batch file creates a C environment.

A new path is set for the C program in line 5. In line 7, APPEND is used to set a search path for the include and library file directories. Line 9 sets the environment variable 87 to "N", meaning that this system lacks an 8087 numeric co-processor.

The disadvantage to this type of batch file is that you will need to manually reset all the above items once you're done working in the C programming language environment. A second batch file, UNDO-C, can be written to do just that (see FIG. 4-10).

```
Name: UNDO-C.BAT

 1: @ECHO OFF
 2: REM Reset computer back to normal
 3: PATH C:\DOS;C:\UTILITY;..;C:\WORD
 4: APPEND ;
 5: SET 87=
 6: ECHO System back to normal.
```

Fig. 4-10. The UNDO-C batch file undoes the C environment.

In FIG. 4-10, the PATH is reset to its previous value (supposedly), APPEND is disabled, and the environment variable 87 is cleared. (You should always clear environment variables once you're done with them.)

Though these two batch files will help you set your environment for programming in Turbo C (or any other program—simply change the directories and other variables), they lack a wee bit of elegance. For example, you can use an environment variable to temporarily store your old path rather than having to re-enter it in UNDO-C.BAT. Try:

```
SET OLDPATH=%PATH%
```

The batch file interpreter will expand the variable %PATH% into your system's current path, making the variable OLDPATH equal to the path. Now, you can mess with your systems path and restore it back to what it was simply by using:

```
PATH %OLDPATH%
```

In fact, quite a few intrepid users may already have an OLDPATH variable set in their AUTOEXEC.BAT file. Because OLDPATH always contains a copy of the original path, resetting it is as easy as typing the above command.

Status Variables

Another interesting use of variables is to check the status of your batch file. On the *Supplemental Programs Diskette* is an interesting batch file called HELP.BAT. HELP.BAT actually runs a "main menu" program, which in turn runs more batch file programs. When the secondary batch file programs are done, they re-run HELP.BAT. But before they do, they set a special environment variable called IN.

IN is used to determine which program is running the batch file HELP.BAT. If a secondary batch file is running HELP.BAT, then the value of IN is equal to YES. Otherwise, IN isn't equal to anything (in fact, it doesn't exist). This way, if IN is equal to YES, HELP.BAT will not display its initial screen and move right to the main menu. It uses the IF statement to determine if IN is equal to YES:

```
IF "%IN%"=="YES" GOTO MAIN
```

If IN has already been set to YES, then the IF statement passes the test and batch file execution branches to the MAIN label. Otherwise, the startup screen is displayed. At the end of the batch file, IN is reset to zero to conserve environment space.

This is about the best use of environment variables in batch files. Sadly, batch files are not interactive. You can't assign the variables values as the batch file runs, at least not based upon a user's input. In a later chapter you'll see how a special batch file variable, ERRORLEVEL, can be used to get input from the user. But for now, environment variables are best used for saving useful information, or keeping track of a specific status.

Summary

The environment is DOS's scratch pad, where it holds important information, and where you can place environment variables for use by your batch files.

The SET command is crucial to the environment. It's used to assign variables, reset variables, and display the contents of the environment.

Other than the environment variables you create, the ones DOS offers are: COMSPEC, to give the location of COMMAND.COM; PATH, to set a system search path; and PROMPT, for a system prompt.

Because the environment table is rather small, the SHELL command can be used to increase its size. This avoids those nasty "Out of environment space" error messages, but takes up more of your system's valuable RAM.

5
CONFIG.SYS, AUTOEXEC.BAT, and SHUTDOWN.BAT

This chapter deals with the most important files on your computer system, which also happen to be the only two system files you have direct control over: CONFIG.SYS and AUTOEXEC.BAT.

Because it's loaded first, CONFIG.SYS is covered first. CONFIG.SYS sets up your system by loading and running specific programs and device drivers. While it's not a batch file, some of the items you place into CONFIG.SYS will greatly enhance the performance of your batch files.

AUTOEXEC.BAT is the first program you write that your computer runs (or vice versa). It's the primary batch file that controls how you want your computer to behave for the rest of the day. Sad to say, often AUTOEXEC.BAT is the only batch file anyone ever uses. But since this is an advanced book and you, of course, are a power user, you'll want to gather as much useful information on this batch file as possible. And there is a lot of ground to cover.

Finally, just to be goofy, I've thrown in a third program called SHUTDOWN.BAT. I don't know why Microsoft never saw fit to include this batch file, or something like it, in DOS. After reading about how useful a SHUTDOWN.BAT file can be, you may wonder yourself.

CONFIG.SYS

CONFIG.SYS is your system configuration file. It's used to customize your system. It's also the first one of your personal efforts that DOS pays heed to.

Because DOS lets you create your own CONFIG.SYS file, you can put into it whatever you want. Generally, it's a good idea to fill it up with just about anything you may think you'll need—even though you may not use it at the present.

DOS does let you modify CONFIG.SYS to remove or add commands at any time. The only stipulation is that you need to reset your computer to have the new configuration loaded into memory. (This isn't as bad as it sounds; you may only do it a few times—not the 200 or so I had to while researching this chapter.)

A well-written CONFIG.SYS file can make your system perform at top efficiency. Yet, there are only twelve commands that CONFIG.SYS uses:

BREAK	FCBS	REM
BUFFERS	FILES	SHELL
COUNTRY	INSTALL	STACKS
DEVICE	LASTDRIVE	SWITCHES

These commands can be divided into two categories: Those that set your system's conditions, establish parameters, set limits, allocate buffers, etc., and those that load system device drivers (*see* TABLE 5-1).

Table 5-1.

Condition Commands	Device Drivers
BREAK	COUNTRY
BUFFERS	DEVICE
FCBS	SHELL
FILES	
INSTALL	
LASTDRIVE	
REM	
STACKS	
SWITCHES	

The condition commands lay down the rules as far as DOS is concerned. Each one of the commands tells DOS how far to go, or how to handle a certain situation. Briefly, what the condition commands cover is shown in TABLE 5-2.

Table 5-2.

Command	Does what?
BREAK	Monitors the pressing of CTRL–BREAK to cancel commands
BUFFERS	Allocates buffer space for file I/O
FCBS	Used with file sharing to control number of open files
FILES	Scts the maximum number of open files at a time
INSTALL	Runs a memory-resident program during system setup
LASTDRIVE	Sets the maximum number of drive letters available
REM	Allows comments to be included in CONFIG.SYS
STACKS	Allows you to increase stack storage space
SWITCHES	Provides compatibility for programs that don't understand the extended keyboard functions.

The device driver commands load a special type of memory-resident program that monitors, alters, or filters the I/O of a device. The most versatile, all-purpose command here is the DEVICE command (logically). The other two commands are more specific (*see* TABLE 5-3).

Table 5-3.

Command	Does what?
COUNTRY	Set formatting instructions for date, time, etc.
DEVICE	Loads a device driver into low memory
SHELL	Specifies an alternate COMMAND.COM

The only drawback to stuffing your CONFIG.SYS file with every conceivable command configuration, is that several of the commands take up valuable memory. On a computer system with 640K (the "max"), this doesn't present a problem. But if you have 512K or 256K, and your programs require a lot of memory (most of them do), saving a few bytes here and there will help.

For reference, TABLE 5-4 describes approximately how much memory is taken by each of the CONFIG.SYS commands. This isn't an absolute, "final authority" type of table—just my own calculations based on a 640K PC with the latest version of DOS.

Table 5-4.

Command	Sucks up this much memory
BREAK	Nothing
BUFFERS	528 bytes per buffer
COUNTRY	Nothing
DEVICE	Approximate size of driver (.SYS) file, except for VDISK
FCBS	Nothing
FILES	48 bytes for each value greater than 8
INSTALL	Approximate size of the memory resident program
LASTDRIVE	80 bytes for each drive letter after "E"
REM	Nothing
SHELL	Depends on environment size
STACKS	From 32 to 512 bytes, depending on the number of frames
SWITCHES	Nothing

The DEVICE or INSTALL directives will take up the most memory, depending on the size of the driver or memory-resident program installed. For example, my *Microsoft Mouse* driver, MOUSE.SYS is about 7K in size, yet only uses about 4K of memory after it's loaded. VDISK is an exception. Because VDISK creates an electronic, or "virtual," disk from your system's memory, it will use that much memory plus the size of the VDISK device driver.

Figuring out the amount of memory LASTDRIVE uses is tricky. The amount of memory used per each drive letter after "E" varies. Yet, for calculation purposes, factor the drive letter (above "E") by 80 bytes and you'll get an approximate size.

Again, the point to all this may be to save a few bytes here and there on systems that are memory-sparse. There's no use in being petty over bytes—especially for those huge database programs that require you to set FILES and BUFFERS to something ridiculous like 32 or 40. In that case, the one or two K you lose in system memory is made up for by the extra speed of the database. Trust me.

CONFIG.SYS Commands

There's no need to dwell on CONFIG.SYS in a batch file book. So the following are brief descriptions of the CONFIG.SYS commands, followed by some examples I've gotten from computers around the office and from various friends and not-friends. As far as batch files are concerned, and what's mentioned later on in this book, pay special attention to the DEVICE, LASTDRIVE, and SHELL commands.

BREAK

BREAK is set either on or off.

BREAK=ON

or

BREAK=OFF

BREAK's use is confusing to most readers. Normally, you can press CTRL–BREAK to stop any action in DOS, or to return to DOS from any program that uses the standard DOS keyboard and write-to-screen functions. If a program doesn't use those functions, however, setting BREAK-ON in CONFIG.SYS allows some applications to be halted by pressing CTRL–BREAK.

For example, if BREAK were set ON in CONFIG.SYS, and a program was adding a long list of numbers, or sorting, but not writing to the screen, then DOS would still monitor CTRL–BREAK. If pressed, the program would immediately stop. Otherwise, with BREAK-OFF, DOS would wait until the program wrote to the screen, or made some other I/O call.

BUFFERS

BUFFERS sets the number of file buffers DOS uses:

BUFFERS = n,s /X

n can be any number, from 1 through 99, indicating how many disk buffers your system will use. Remember, each buffer uses 528 bytes of RAM.

s was introduced with DOS 4.0, and it specifies the number of sectors DOS will read in advance—a sort of "buffering ahead" to speed up disk access.

If *s* is omitted, DOS won't bother with buffering ahead. Otherwise, you can specify a value from 1 through 8 for *s*.

The /X switch is used to put the buffers into expanded memory on systems that have expanded memory (of course).

The DOS manual babbles on and on about BUFFERS. Basically, the more buffers you have, the better your system will be able to handle programs that read and write to disk a lot.

Unless told otherwise, the *n* value for BUFFERS is set internally as shown in TABLE 5-5.

Table 5-5.

If Your System Has	BUFFERS =
Nothing specific	2
A 720K, 1.2M or 1.44M disk drive	3
More than 128K of RAM	5
More than 256K of RAM	10
More than 512K of RAM	15

By not setting BUFFERS in your CONFIG.SYS file, DOS "gives" you the amount shown in TABLE 5-5. Note that by setting BUFFERS to something less than what DOS would give you, you can save memory. But, never mind! Setting a large buffer size makes your system run faster. As a suggestion, set your BUFFERS to a value of 32 or greater:

BUFFERS=32

This is generally what some of the more disk-intensive database programs will request. So set BUFFERS to that value now, so you won't have to do it later.

COUNTRY

COUNTRY is used to load country-specific information formatting routines.

COUNTRY = *phone code, code page, country file*

phone code is a three-digit number that specifies a specific country. The code is based on the international telephone access code you use to dial foreign countries.

The code must have been developed in the USA because that code is 001 (the one DOS automatically assumes if you don't specify COUNTRY in your CONFIG.SYS file).

code page is an optional three-digit number used to specify a character set to be used for different countries. Basically, the ASCII characters stay the same, but the characters for codes 128 through 255 (the Extended ASCII set) can be altered. These alternative code pages will use some foreign characters that aren't available in the standard, ''USA'' code page. If **code page** is omitted, you must specify the second comma.

country file is the name of a country information file, usually COUNTRY.SYS that was supplied with DOS. If COUNTRY.SYS is not in your boot disk's root directory, you should specify a full pathname to it.

COUNTRY basically deals with the way DOS formats certain information, such as the date and time. For example, normally, or in the United States, the date has a specific format:

month, day, year

Some European countries, however, use other formats. In England (the United Kingdom), the following format is used for the date:

day, month, year

By using the COUNTRY command in CONFIG.SYS, you can tell DOS to format its date and time information, as well as the currency sign and decimal separator (which, in some countries, is a comma, not a period) for a specific country. *See* TABLES 5-6 and 5-7 for a listing of **phone code** and **code page** values.

Table 5-6.

Country/Region	Phone Code
Arabic	785
Australia	061
Belgium	032
Canada	001
Canada (French)	002
Denmark	045
Finland	358
France	033
Germany	049
Israel (Hebrew)	972
Italy	039
Japan	081
Korea	082
Latin America	003
Netherlands	031
Norway	047
Portugal	351

Table 5-7. Continued.

Simplified Chinese	086
Spain	034
Sweden	046
Switzerland	041
United Kingdom	044
United States	001

Table 5-7.

Country/Region	Code Page
Arabic	864, 850
Australia	437, 850
Belgium	850, 437
Canada	437, 850
Canada (French)	863, 850
Denmark	850, 865
Finland	850, 437
France	437, 850
Germany	437, 850
Israel (Hebrew)	862, 850
Italy	437, 850
Japan	932, 437
Korea	934, 437
Latin America	437, 850
Netherlands	437, 850
Norway	850, 865
Portugal	850, 860
Simplified Chinese	936, 437
Spain	437, 850
Sweden	437, 850
Switzerland	850, 437
United Kingdom	437, 850
United States	437, 850

The following COUNTRY command sets up your system's formatting information for a computer in the United Kingdom:

The number 044 is the international phone code for the United Kingdom. The 437 is the code page value (a good, general-purpose code page). COUNTRY.SYS specifies the full pathname.

Changing Keyboard Definition

If you want to further define your system for a foreign country, you can use the KEYB command. KEYB reassigns the keyboard layout to match common typewriters for foreign countries. This allows users in non-English speaking countries to have access to their own, unique alphabetic characters.

To complete the transformation to a U.K. computer, you could add the following line to your AUTOEXEC.BAT file:

This loads the standard keyboard layout that an English typist would be used to. Various keys are replaced and re-assigned on that keyboard, including the # key replacing the # sign.

You can type KEYBUK, or any one of the other KEYB*.COM programs after starting DOS to change your keyboard layout. To switch to the standard keyboard, press CTRL–ALT–F1. To switch back to the foreign keyboard, press CTRL–ALT–F2.

DEVICE

DEVICE is used to load a device driver.

DEVICE = *pathname*

pathname is the full pathname of the device. It's important to specify a full path because no PATH command has been set yet (it's done in AUTOEXEC) and no drive aliases have been assigned (using SUBST). The full pathname should include the drive letter and directories indicating the driver's location. In my own system, I put all the system drivers in my DOS directory and simply list the full path for each DEVICE I load (see below for an example).

There are seven device drivers included with DOS 4.0:

ANSI.SYS
DISPLAY.SYS
DRIVER.SYS
PRINTER.SYS
VDISK.SYS
XMAEM.SYS
XMA2EMS.SYS

Two other .SYS files should never be used with the DEVICE command:

COUNTRY.SYS
KEYBOARD.SYS

Also, other device drivers may be available, including alternative ANSI.SYS drivers and mouse device drivers, such as MOUSE.SYS, the *Microsoft Mouse* device driver.

FCBS

FCBS is used with file sharing to set the maximum number of files (actually File Control BlockS) that DOS can have open at one time.

FCBS = *max,close*

max is the maximum number of FCBS that can be opened at one time. It can be any value from 1 through 255.

close is a number from 0 through 255. It specifies the number of FCBS that will not be closed by DOS, should the total number of FCBS opened by DOS exceed *max*. *close* is used to protect a given number of FCBS from being automatically closed by DOS when an application tries to open more than *max* files. *close* should always be less than *max*.

If you don't set FCBS in your CONFIG.SYS file, DOS automatically assigns values of 4 and 0 to *max* and *close* respectively.

FILES

FILES specifies the maximum number of files that DOS can have open at a time.

FILES = *n*

n sets the maximum number of files that can be open. Its value ranges from 8 through 255. If you don't set FILES in your CONFIG.SYS file, DOS uses 8.

FILES is similar to BUFFERS. It's generally a good idea to set FILES to a high number, generally equal to the value of BUFFERS. (After all, if DOS won't let you open that many files, why have the BUFFERS?)

A question that usually comes up concerning FILES is "Why set them at all?" The answer is that DOS controls access to all files on disk. If a program asks to create or access a file and there are already the maximum number of files open (according to FILES), your program gets an error. These errors are rather uncommon because DOS automatically gives you eight files whether FILES is set by CONFIG.SYS or not. But just to be on the safe side, FILES should be set to a high number, with values greater than 20 being the most common. For example:

FILES = 32

This command would make a perfect companion to a BUFFERS = 32 command (as any good maitre d' would let you know).

INSTALL

INSTALL allows you to load memory-resident applications in CONFIG.SYS, rather than during execution of your AUTOEXEC.BAT file.

INSTALL *filename*

filename is the full path and name of your memory-resident program. INSTALL will load and execute that program, leaving it in memory for later use. Using INSTALL, as opposed to including the memory-resident program's installation in AUTOEXEC.BAT, make more efficient use of memory.

At present, four DOS 4.0 programs can be used with CONFIG.SYS's INSTALL command:

FASTOPEN
KEYB
NLSFUNC
SHARE

Other, third-party memory-resident applications should also work with INSTALL.

LASTDRIVE

LASTDRIVE is used to set the maximum number of disk drives your system can have.

LASTDRIVE = *n*

n is the highest drive letter your system can have. It can be any letter from A to Z (which implies that your system can only handle a maximum of 26 drives). The default minimum value is the number of drives you have in your system. If you have a hard disk, then it's drive C. If LASTDRIVE isn't specified, DOS gives you up to drive E.

LASTDRIVE comes in handy when you're assigning "fake" drives using the SUBST command (see Chapter 4). If you want to SUBST a number of drive letters for directories, simply specify LASTDRIVE equal to the maximum number of drives you want substituted. As long as your system isn't short on memory, make it drive Z:

```
LASTDRIVE=Z
```

This command lets DOS know that your system can handle up to Z drives. You don't need to use all those drives—it's just the letters you want.

REM

REM allows you to include comments in your CONFIG.SYS file.

REM *comment*

comment can be anything—any string of characters. This allows you to **comment** the operation of your CONFIG.SYS file, to include important notes, or to "comment out" certain CONFIG.SYS commands that no longer apply to your system (without deleting them entirely). CONFIG.SYS will not execute any commands after a REM.

Aside from REM, you may also include blank lines in your CONFIG.SYS file to "clean it up" a bit.

SHELL

SHELL allows you to specify another command file instead of COMMAND.COM, or to specify a different location for COMMAND.COM. Additionally, by using COMMAND.COM with SHELL, you can adjust the size of your computer's environment.

SHELL = *pathname*

pathname is the full filename, including drive letter, colon, and path, for an alternate COMMAND.COM file, or an alternate location for COMMAND.COM. When you specify COMMAND.COM as your shell, two optional switches can be used: /P and /E.

The /P switch instructs DOS to load and execute a batch file named AUTOEXEC.BAT in the root directory of your boot disk after COMMAND.COM is executed. Otherwise, without the /P switch specified, COMMAND.COM will simply display a copyright message and then the default command prompt. (It won't even ask for the date and time.)

The /E switch is used to change the size of COMMAND.COM's environment. An optional value **n** sets the size of the environment and it ranges from 160 to 32,768 bytes. For example:

```
SHELL=C:\COMMAND.COM /P/E:2048
```

This command directs DOS to use the COMMAND.COM file found in the root directory of your hard drive, load and run AUTOEXEC.BAT after it's done, and allocate 2K, or 2,048 bytes of space, for the environment. This example is a must for your CONFIG.SYS file if you want more environment space.

Also, as was mentioned in the previous chapter, SHELL doesn't change the COMSPEC= value in your default environment. That needs to be done in AUTOEXEC.BAT with the SET command.

STACKS

STACKS allows you to increase internal stack storage space.

STACKS = *frames,size*

frames is a value ranging from 8 through 64. It indicates the number of stack frames DOS is to allocate. The default value for a PC/XT computer is zero, for AT and faster computers, DOS sets **frames** to 9 unless otherwise specified.

size indicates the size (in bytes) of each stack frame. It can be a value from 32 through 512, with the default value for PC/XTs equal to zero and AT computers equal to 128.

Normally, DOS uses an internal stack to keep track of return addresses from interrupt calls. So what does that mean to you? Not much, unless you see a very rare error message: "Out of stack space, System Halted." This can be devastating. (I almost fainted when I first saw it.)

On AT machines that can run multiple processes (or so they claim), it may be a good idea to allocate a few internal stacks. Otherwise, unless your software application mentions using the STACKS command in CONFIG.SYS, never mind.

SWITCHES

Suppresses the use of extended keyboard functions.

SWITCHES = /K

/K is used to suppress the extended keyboard functions, preventing them from being used.

Some older software packages may not properly interpret the extended keyboard's functions. When SWITCHES /K is specified in your CONFIG.SYS file, the computer is forced to use the older, conventional keyboard functions. This will make your system more compatible with older applications.

CONFIG.SYS Examples

One of the best ways to become familiar with advanced CONFIG.SYS files is to take a look at some. The following are CONFIG.SYS files that I use on my computers, and that various friends employ. Each of them is followed by an explanation of what they do and why:

Standard CONFIG.SYS

```
BUFFERS = 32
FILES = 20
DEVICE = C:\DOS\ANSI.SYS
```

Two of the most common commands you'll see in CONFIG.SYS are BUFFERS and FILES. Most databases want you to have at least 20 of each. The CONFIG.SYS file above is configured for a "worst case scenario." Just about any program, no matter how disk intensive it is, will probably not want more than 32 buffers and 20 files.

Even if you're sour to the entire idea of a CONFIG.SYS file, you should always include the FILES and BUFFERS statements. Have extra files and buffers available not only makes certain programs run smoothly, it also speeds up DOS in certain instances. For example, DOS takes a long time to display the last few files of a long, fragmented directory (one with, say more than 200 files in it). Increasing the BUFFERS and FILES values will alleviate this problem.

ANSI.SYS is also thrown into this CONFIG.SYS file to give the system the extra control that ANSI.SYS offers. Note that the full pathname, including drive letter, was given for ANSI.SYS. Again, this avoids having to keep the file in your root directory.

My Own CONFIG.SYS   FIGURE 5-1 is the CONFIG.SYS I use on my IBM PC. Two REM statements in FIG. 5-1 start my CONFIG.SYS, telling me which computer the CONFIG.SYS file is on (I call my PC "Denise"), and the date the file was last updated.

```
REM CONFIG.SYS File for Denise
REM September 9, 1988

BUFFERS = 32,8
FILES = 20
DEVICE = C:\SYSTEM\DOS\DRIVER.SYS /D:1 /T:80 /S:9 /H:2 /F:2
DEVICE = C:\SYSTEM\DOS\ANSI.SYS
DEVICE = C:\SYSTEM\MOUSE\MOUSE.SYS
```

Fig. 5-1. This is the CONFIG.SYS that I use.

FILES, BUFFERS, and ANSI.SYS are specified, as are the device drivers DRIV-ER.SYS and MOUSE.SYS.

DRIVER.SYS is used to establish my second internal floppy drive as a 720K 3½-inch drive. Originally, I had two 5¼-inch drives, but replaced drive B with a 3½-inch drive for compatibility with the new PS/2 machines, as well as laptops. Also, the disk holds more information and makes backing up less tedious.

The DRIVER device driver configures my drive B as an "external" logical drive D that can hold 720K. When I access the drive as D, it's a 720K drive. But the same drive, logically accessed as B, is only a 320K drive. This is because DOS (and IBM and the gang) assumes that you cannot have a 720K drive in a PC/XT. Therefore, anything that's 720K must be an "external" drive, hence it's drive D. Confusing? Yes. But the DRIVER.SYS command in CONFIG.SYS allows me the 720K drive (as D).

Incidentally, an undocumented MS–DOS CONFIG.SYS command, DRIVPARM, works exactly like the DRIVER.SYS file—except it allows you to use drive B as the 720K drive—no messing with drive D. DRIVPARM is, at present, an undocumented command, but the parameters are the same as for DRIVER.SYS above. Simply put something in your CONFIG.SYS file like:

```
DRIVPARM D:/1
```

and your drive B will be a 720K drive (providing, of course, that you have the hardware).

MOUSE.SYS is the Microsoft Mouse driver. You need to load the mouse driver into memory in order to use your mouse hardware. (Because the mouse isn't a part of the normal system, you must load its BIOS routines.) There are two ways you can load the mouse driver: MOUSE.COM and MOUSE.SYS.

MOUSE.COM is a memory-resident program that installs the mouse BIOS. You type MOUSE.COM, or just "MOUSE," at the DOS prompt right before you run a mouse-operated program. Once it's in memory, it stays there, so you don't need to type MOUSE a second time. (If you do, you get an "already installed" message.)

MOUSE.SYS is the same mouse driver that's packaged in MOUSE.COM. The difference is, it's a device driver and can be loaded when CONFIG.SYS runs. By using MOUSE.SYS in CONFIG.SYS, you never have to worry about typing MOUSE before you run a mouse-driven program, and then having that program not work. The mouse driver is always in memory when you use MOUSE.SYS, so it's an easier way to do things.

Multi-Drive CONFIG.SYS

```
BUFFERS = 32
FILES = 20
LASTDRIVE = Z
DEVICE = C:\DOS\ANSI.SYS
SHELL = C:\DOS\COMMAND.COM /P
```

Aside from BUFFERS, FILES, and ANSI.SYS, this user's CONFIG.SYS file adds the LASTDRIVE and SHELL configuration commands.

LASTDRIVE allows up to Z drive letters to be assigned. Normally, DOS will give you 5, A through E. But by setting LASTDRIVE to Z, this user can take advantage of the SUBST command and have up to 23 subdirectories substituted as disk drives (the other three are drives A, B, and C).

SHELL is used here to specify a new location for COMMAND.COM. Normally, SHELL is used to specify a new command processor. Here, the command simply directs SYSINIT to look for COMMAND.COM in the \DOS subdirectory. Also, the /P switch was added, allowing the user's AUTOEXEC.BAT file to run. There is one drawback to this command, the user must place the following line into their AUTOEXEC.BAT file:

```
SET COMSPEC=C:\COMMAND.COM
```

That will patch up the minor bug of DOS not recognizing from whence it loaded COMMAND.COM.

RAM Disk Example

```
BUFFERS = 32
FILES = 32
DEVICE = C:\DOS\ANSI.SYS
DEVICE = C:\DOS\VDISK 360 512 64
```

The only new addition to this CONFIG.SYS file is the new device, VDISK. VDISK is DOS's idea of a RAM disk. (A RAM disk is a superfast, electronic disk drive that uses memory instead of a physical diskette.) There are much better RAM disk drivers out on the market than VDISK, most of which come with memory upgrade boards. (But VDISK is free with DOS, so what the heck?)

This VDISK driver has the options "360 512 64" tagged on. This directs VDISK to create a 360K disk from memory with 512 byte sectors. The disk will allow up to 64 entries in the root directory.

If your system has extended memory, you can specify the /E switch to place the RAM disk there. The following CONFIG.SYS command would place a one megabyte RAM drive into extended memory:

```
DEVICE = C:\DOS\VDISK 1000 512 64 /E
```

DOS 4.0's Suggestion

When you run the DOS 4.0 INSTALL program, it builds a suggested CONFIG.SYS file for you, and places it on your hard drive. The file is named CONFIG.400, so that it won't overwrite your existing CONFIG.SYS file (thank goodness—and thank you IBM).

The CONFIG.400 file DOS suggested for my system is shown in FIG. 5-2. DOS 4.0 knew a lot about my system, including the location of some device drivers. I took some of its "suggestions" to heart and put them into my CONFIG.SYS file. Otherwise, I thanked the INSTALL program for the suggestions, and then filed CONFIG.400 away for later perusal. (The INSTALL program also came up with an

```
BREAK=ON
BUFFERS=25,8
FCBS=20,8
FILES=8
LASTDRIVE=E
SHELL=C:\SYSTEM\DOS\COMMAND.COM /P /E:256
DEVICE=C:\SYSTEM\DOS\ANSI.SYS /X
INSTALL=C:\SYSTEM\DOS\FASTOPEN.EXE C:=(150,150)
```

Fig. 5-2. This is the CONFIG.400 file DOS suggested for my system.

AUTOEXEC.400 batch file suggestion. My personal copy is listed in the next section.)

All Told

CONFIG.SYS is an important part of your system and you should know what to put into it. Above all, be very careful of programs that do self-modification to your CONFIG.SYS file. As long as you stick by some of my recommendations above, you should be doing okay.

AUTOEXEC.BAT

AUTOEXEC.BAT is your system's startup file. It's also the most common batch file, and the most important. Its primary function is to set up your system and customize your operations. Because of this, you must be careful about what you place into AUTOEXEC.BAT. Also, there may be a few things your AUTOEXEC.BAT may be missing. The only way to find out is to keep reading.

Behind the Scenes

Reviewing how DOS is loaded, first comes IBMBIO, the DOS BIOS, followed by IBMDOS, the "kernel." This is followed by CONFIG.SYS (if present), and finally COMMAND.COM. The COMMAND.COM that comes with DOS will look for and execute a batch file named AUTOEXEC in the root directory of your boot disk. (If you use the SHELL command to place COMMAND.COM in a subdirectory, the /P switch must be specified in order for AUTOEXEC.BAT to be executed.)

If AUTOEXEC.BAT isn't found, COMMAND.COM asks for the date and time to be entered, displays a copyright notice, and displays the default system command prompt, as shown in FIG. 5-3.

If AUTOEXEC.BAT is found, COMMAND.COM warms up its batch file interpreter and starts executing the commands found inside that batch file.

```
Current date is Tue   1-01-1980
Enter new date (mm-dd-yy): 7-17-89
Current time is 0:01:06:07
Enter new time: 15:54


IBM DOS Version 4.00
        (C)Copyright International Business Machines Corp
        (C)Copyright Microsoft Corp 1981-1986

C>
```

Fig. 5-3. When AUTOEXEC.BAT isn't found . . .

Things to Do: Setting the Clock, Path, Prompt and MODE

What you put in AUTOEXEC.BAT is up to you. Some people write complex AUTOEXEC files that spiff-up their entire system (and take about fifteen minutes to run). Other people only include the name of a program they want to run immediately after booting their computer. Both examples are fine because both express how you can personalize your system using AUTOEXEC.

But for the majority of people, AUTOEXEC does some "standard" operations, more or less. Consider that AUTOEXEC is the first program that does anything on your computer. (CONFIG.SYS just loads drivers and sets system settings.) Because it gives you control over your system each time you start your computer, there are some things you can do in your AUTOEXEC that should be done first.

Most people develop an AUTOEXEC strategy. There are always a certain number of things that should be done by the AUTOEXEC.BAT file. These include:

- Setting the system clock
- Setting a search path via the PATH command
- Setting a system prompt with the PROMPT command
- Setting the screen mode, or setting up the printer with the MODE command
- Changing the screen color
- SUBSTituting or JOINing drives and subdirectories
- Setting environment variables via the SET command
- Executing startup programs
- Executing applications programs or user "shells"

These are only a few of the many things that could be done in an AUTOEXEC file. Additionally, you can use any of the regular DOS commands (after all, they were why batch files were originally invented). For example, you can use CLS to clear the screen, TYPE to list a text document (rather than use repeated ECHO statements), CD to change directories—any of the DOS commands are legal in AUTOEXEC, and in some cases, necessary.

The following descriptions go into more detail on the above categories:

Setting the System Clock   Because DOS asks you to if you don't have an AUTOEXEC file, the first thing most people put in their AUTOEXEC file is a command to set the system clock. DOS offers two commands, TIME and DATE, that get it up to speed.

These two commands in AUTOEXEC.BAT will prompt the user to enter the date and time—just as DOS normally would, had AUTOEXEC.BAT not been present.

Most PC/XTs, however, can have internal clocks added to them, either on a special clock card or a multi-function card that has a "real-time" clock and battery backup.

If your PC has such an internal clock, you'll need to issue the command to read the time from the clock in your AUTOEXEC file. For example, with the AST Six-pac multi-function card, the command is ASTCLOCK. Other real-time clocks may use programs such as GETCLOCK or TIMER. These programs simply read the time from the real-time clock hardware and set DOS's internal clock.

So, depending on your hardware, you would add a command in AUTOEXEC.BAT that looked something like the following:

```
ASTCLOCK
```

or

```
GETCLOCK
```

or

```
TIMER/S
```

AT computers don't need a time setting command in their AUTOEXEC file. The reason is that the AT BIOS automatically reads the time from the AT's battery backed-up RAM. So for an AT computer, a set-the-time command in the AUTOEXEC file is unnecessary.

Setting a Search Path   Typically, the next command to be issued by AUTOEXEC.BAT is the PATH command. This sets up the search path for any files that may be included later:

```
PATH=C:\DOS;C:\UTILITY;C:\1-2-3
```

Of course, this isn't a "must have" command early on in a batch file. As long as full pathnames are specified for any programs AUTOEXEC.BAT may run, there's no need to set a path until later.

Setting a System Prompt   After the PATH is set, the next command most users include is the PROMPT command. This sets the system prompt, though the system prompt may not be visible until AUTOEXEC.BAT finishes running:

```
PROMPT $p$g
```

Alternately, you can choose from a variety of interesting prompts, all covered in Chapter 4.

Setting the MODE   MODE is one of those totally useful and confusing commands. It started out rather innocently. But in the fine tradition of all-purpose commands, MODE has mushroomed into an ugly, multipurpose mess.

The MODE command has several functions, ten with DOS 4.0. Ten! With MODE you can do the following:

- Control the printer
- Control the display
- Control the serial port
- Redirect printer output to the serial port
- Prepare a code page
- Select a code page
- Display current code page
- Refresh the code page
- Requesting a status
- Setting the keyboard's "type-a-matic" rates

Most of these are things you may need to do in AUTOEXEC.BAT. Two of the most common are setting the screen mode (only needed for color monitors) and creating a serial printer port:

```
MODE CO80
```

This enables your color monitor to display color on an 80-column screen. If you are vision impaired, you could try:

```
MODE CO40
```

This sets up a color monitor in the 40-column mode.

Though not related to the MODE command, users with Hercules Monochrome Adapter cards may want to issue a command to set up their monochrome monitors. HGC is the command to enable a Hercules graphics card. It could easily replace, or serve the same function as, the MODE command would for a color monitor:

```
HGC FULL
```

This command enables the Hercules Graphics Card (HGC) to its full graphics potential.

A few users need the MODE command to set up a serial printer. This involves two steps:

1) Setting up the serial port
2) Redirecting printer output from the printer port to the serial port

This takes two steps with the MODE command as well:

```
MODE COM1:1200,N,8,1
MODE LPT1=COM1
```

The first command sets the first serial port (COM1) to 1200 bps (bits per second), No parity, an 8-bit word length, and 1 stop bit. (See the DOS manual for other settings.)

The second command reassigns output from LPT1, the first printer port, to COM1, the first serial port. These two MODE commands enable the user to use COM1 and a serial printer as any other user would use LPT1 (or the PRN device).

Before moving on, it should be noted that MODE (and HGC) is a program on disk. If used in AUTOEXEC.BAT, a full pathname should be specified—or the PATH should be set to include the subdirectories where those files are located.

Changing Colors

There are many ways to change the color of the screen. The first, and cheapest, is with the ANSI.SYS driver the nice people who sold you DOS have given you. (You do have ANSI.SYS in your CONFIG.SYS file, don't you?)

If you create or edit your AUTOEXEC.BAT file with EDLIN, it's possible to ECHO an ANSI display string in AUTOEXEC.BAT, allowing you to start up with a colorful display:

```
ECHO ^[[37;44m;
```

This command would give you that prestigious white-on-blue screen that so many users clamor for. The problem with this is that some programs will change the color back to boring white-on-black. To get around this, there are several screen color programs available. The most popular of which comes with the highly touted *Norton Utilities*. SA, for Screen Attributes, is a small utility program that comes with the *Norton Utilities*. It allows you to change screen color to any foreground or background color that your monitor is capable of. For example:

```
SA white on blue
```

This sets the foreground (character) color to white, and the background color to blue. (It sure beats the heck out of remembering what the ANSI numbers stand for.)

SUBST or JOIN Commands

Those users who make use of SUBST and JOIN will want to make their substitutions early on. AUTOEXEC is the perfect place to make drive substitutions and to JOIN disk drives as subdirectories. In some instances, these commands should be issued before the PATH statement is set:

```
SUBST U:  C:\UTILITY
SUBST W:  C:\WP\WORDSTAR
SUBST T:  C:\RELAY

JOIN A:  C:\DEV\DRIVEA
```

These substitutions help prepare your system. It might even be helpful to ECHO a substitution message to the console (especially if you've turned ECHO OFF). So the above commands may be followed by:

```
ECHO Drives substituted:
SUBST
ECHO Drives joined:
JOIN
```

The SUBST and JOIN commands by themselves simply list out the substituted and joined drives.

Setting Environment Variables

Quite a few programs rely on environment variables: Borland's *Turbo C*, the design package *AUTOCAD*, the *Clipper* database, and on and on. This is the ideal place to set them:

```
SET 87=N
```

The environment variable "87" is used by Borland's *Turbo C* compiler to determine if your system has a math co-processor present. If 87 equals "N" you don't; if it equals "Y" you do.

You can and should set a whole slew of environment variables in your AUTOEXEC.BAT file. (Refer to Chapter 4 for additional information.)

Executing Startup Programs

This is perhaps the most diverse area of AUTOEXEC.BAT: the ability to run other programs that help to set up your system. These programs are usually of two types, *utility* and *memory-resident*.

The *utility* programs are run to do various things with your system. For example, the *VOpt* program from Golden Bow Systems will quickly unfragment your hard drive. Unfragmenting the hard drive means your system will run faster and more efficiently. It's something that should be done regularly, so why not do it each time you start your computer?

Another utility comes as part of the *Mace* hard disk utilities. The *RXBAK* program will make a duplicate of your hard disk's boot sector, as well as your system's root directory—a safety copy if you will. This safety copy is used by another one of the *Mace Utility* programs to successfully recover from the hard disk being accidentally reformatted.

The second type of program is a *memory-resident* program. These programs include RAM disks and print spoolers, as well as the popular memory-resident utilities. There's no problem with setting up your system with these "goodies"—as long as you've got the memory for it.

Another point is that certain memory-resident utilities insist upon being loaded last. The greatest offender is Borland's *SideKick* (or "suicide-kick" as it's been dubbed). *SideKick* must always be the last program to be loaded in your AUTOEXEC.BAT file—according to Borland. Also, the manual specifies that you must be in your *SideKick* directory when you load the program:

```
CD \MEMRES\SIDEKICK
SK
CD \
```

These commands move you to the *SideKick* directory, load the program, then return you to the root directory.

Executing Applications Programs

Applications programs can be of two types. The first is a program that you normally use when you start your computer. The second type is a DOS shell program.

Quite a few users will stick to the basics when writing an AUTOEXEC.BAT file. However, they never pay attention to what they type after they run AUTOEXEC. For some, the next thing they type is:

```
CD \WORDSTAR
WS
```

If they're so consistent, why not include those two commands as the last two in AUTOEXEC?

Sure, by not adding an applications program at the end of AUTOEXEC, you're affording yourself a tiny bit more freedom. But if you can save the keystrokes, why not?

The second type of program that can be run immediately by AUTOEXEC is a DOS shell. These are the infamous "User-Friendly" programs that supposedly make using DOS a snap. They offer menus for choosing programs, or pretty graphic interfaces that are supposed to take the pain away from using DOS.

Bah!

If you bought a DOS computer, learn DOS.

This doesn't mean you can't buy the shell and install it at the end of someone else's AUTOEXEC.BAT file. Just in case, there are a few shell programs that do rank quite high in their usefulness, and you may consider one if another user or yourself would rather use the computer that way.

One of the most impressive efforts of IBM was to include a shell program with DOS 4.0. *DOSSHELL* is actually a batch file that runs the DOS 4.0 menu-driven shell program. With that program, you can use an optional mouse to control your computer. My overall impression of the program is that it's quite capable. I prefer, however, to use the command prompt rather than *DOSSHELL*.

AUTOEXEC Strategies

Your AUTOEXEC.BAT file can get a lot done. Yet, you don't really need to toss the kitchen sink into the works just to get your system up and running. There is a certain strategy to composing your own, personal AUTOEXEC file. Not all of the previous section's examples need to be used. Instead, this section concentrates on some strategies you may want to take to make your AUTOEXEC.BAT file more personal.

The following are some tips on creating effective AUTOEXEC.BAT files:

First Things First   The first command in most people's AUTOEXEC.BAT file is ECHO OFF, or @ECHO OFF. This shuts off the echoing of the various commands, which may confuse some users. Also, it pleases the advanced user who enjoys a "clean" display when his computer starts.

Some systems forego the initial ECHO OFF. In fact, one of the computers I use has ECHO OFF omitted intentionally. Because this system has a long, detailed AUTOEXEC.BAT file, I want to be certain that everything is executing properly. (Batch files don't stop if a program errors unless you direct them to—more on that later.)

More importantly, the echoing of some commands may be necessary during some intense disk operations, or long pauses, just to let you know things are proceeding. An alternative to turning ECHO off, of course, is to use ECHO to display what's going on. Such as:

```
ECHO Optimizing Hard Drives...
ECHO (this takes a few seconds)
VOPT C: /N
VOPT D: /N
```

No ECHO   Sometimes you may want to suppress the output of all commands. For example, using some commands in any batch file may display only brief and sometimes confusing messages:

```
11 file(s) copied

Memory-resident portion installed

CF (C)Copyright 1988 Nice 'n' Soft, Inc.
```

To suppress these types of messages from being displayed you can use an old, old DOS 2.1 trick. This involves I/O redirection to send the file's output to the NUL device:

```
COPY C:\WORD\SPELL.DAT E:\ > NUL
```

This command copies a word processor's spelling checker data to drive E:\ (possibly a RAM disk). The > NUL portion of the command redirects the normal DOS message "1 file(s) copied" to the NUL device, effectively concealing it from view.

> NUL can be used with a variety of commands, and in just about any batch file, to suppress the superfluous display of trivial information.

REMming Out   Another popular AUTOEXEC trick is using the REM statement to "comment out" some commands that may not always be necessary. (This trick applies to all batch files, but is used most often in AUTOEXEC.)

Normally, you'd use REM to comment exactly what your AUTOEXEC.BAT file is doing. Believe me, I've looked at dozens of them to research this chapter. I've given several people phone calls asking them "what does CL/I mean?" It would have helped a lot if they would have put a REM command in there telling everyone what the CL program is and what the /I switch does.

```
REM HGC FULL
MODE CO80
SA white ON blue
```

or

```
HGC FULL
REM MODE CO80
REM SA white ON blue
```

These are two snippets from an AUTOEXEC file. The first is for a system with a color monitor. The REM statement blocks out the HGC FULL command, normally used for a monochrome Hercules-compatible system. Then the MODE command is used to set the 80-column color mode, and the *Norton Utilities* SA command is used to change screen color.

The second example is from the same AUTOEXEC file. In this case, a monochrome monitor is used. Notice how the color statements are now REMmed out and the Hercules command is included? This shows an effective use of the REM command to temporarily block out commands without having to totally rewrite your AUTOEXEC.BAT file.

Positioning Crucial Commands   Another interesting strategy is to place the set-time, path, and prompt commands at the top of your AUTOEXEC.BAT file. This allows you to "break out" of the AUTOEXEC.BAT file if you'd like and still have a useful system.

Some people crowd their AUTOEXEC.BAT file with a lot of trivial displays, backflips, twists and turns. If you've ever had to reset your system a few times during a programming session, you know how annoying it can be waiting for your AUTOEXEC.BAT file to dazzle you with screen displays. With all the important commands at the top of your AUTOEXEC.BAT file, however, you could press CTRL–BREAK to stop the file and still have a working system (complete with TIME, PATH and PROMPT) without having to wait through a bunch of meaningless display material.

An Occasional Pause   In several of the above examples, messages were displayed, indicating exactly what was going on. There may be a time when you would actually want AUTOEXEC.BAT to stop after displaying some information. For example, the following snippet from an AUTOEXEC.BAT file runs a program called SCHEDULE that creates a TO-DO file:

```
SCHEDULE < SINPUT
TYPE TO-DO
ECHO ^G
PAUSE
```

This snippet of code shows the SCHEDULE file running using standard input from the SINPUT file. SINPUT probably contains the keystrokes used to create the TO-DO file, a list of things that need to be done that day.

The next step is to display TO-DO: the list of things the user needs to do. This is followed by a BEEP (the ECHO ^G command sends the ^G character, the bell, to the console), and the PAUSE command. This allows the user to see what needs to be done, acknowledge it, and then move on.

Time Savers   The first time you type DIR on a hard drive, it takes a long time to return to the command prompt. The reason is that the DIR command must calculate how much space is left on the hard drive as the last part of its display (*see* FIG. 5-4). This happens when you first start your system, or after you use any disk utility that also calculates how much space is on the hard disk (such as CHKDSK).

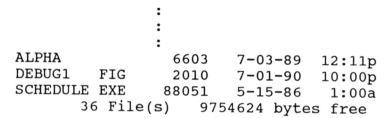

```
        :
        :
        :
ALPHA              6603    7-03-89   12:11p
DEBUG1    FIG      2010    7-01-90   10:00p
SCHEDULE  EXE     88051    5-15-86    1:00a
        36 File(s)     9754624 bytes free
```

Fig. 5-4. This is the display when you first DIR a hard drive.

You can avoid the wait easily by including the following command in AUTOEXEC.BAT:

```
DIR > NUL
```

or, you can eliminate the > NUL if you're interested in seeing your directory displayed. By "pulling a directory" in your AUTOEXEC file, you're making the next directory you display move a lot quicker (because the initial, slow display was already done).

Memory Saving Tips Generally speaking, it's a good idea to save any modifications to the environment for the last part of your AUTOEXEC file.

The reason for saving environment modifications for last—especially after you run memory-resident programs—is that each memory-resident program makes a copy of the environment. If the environment is already full of variables (besides COMSPEC, PATH, and PROMPT), each one of those variables is copied to a new environment when the memory-resident program exits.

In a worst-case scenario, suppose you have boosted the size of your environment to 2K or 3K to allow for a ton of environment variables. After you load your first memory-resident program, a copy is made of that 3K environment. Theoretically, what used to take 3K now occupies 6K in your system (the original 3K environment is still there). Add two more memory-resident programs and you've used 12K, 9K of which is useless to you.

So, if you're going to use SET to create a lot of environment variables, save it for last—after the memory-resident programs are loaded.

Directory Strategies In several instances, your AUTOEXEC batch file will be running other programs. In the case of DOS commands and common utilities, those should already be on your path. But some commands may be of the run-only-once type and you wouldn't want to include their directories on your path. In those instances you have two choices: Use the file's full pathname (only under DOS 3), or use CD to move to the file's directory and run the file there.

Full pathnames are the preferred way to run these programs. After all, DOS 3 allows you to specify a program by its full pathname—so why not do it?

```
C:\UTILITY\GOLDNBOW\VOPT C: /N
```

This causes the VOPT program in \UTILITY\GOLDNBOW to run. The alternative method, using CD, would be a little more involved:

```
CD \UTILITY\GOLDNBOW
VOPT C: /N
```

It's important to note that some programs may insist that you be in their directory when you run them. A good example is *SideKick* which insists, among other things, that you be in your *SideKick* directory when you first start the program. In that case, you must CD to that directory to run the program in your AUTOEXEC batch file:

```
CD \MEMRES\SIDEKICK
SK
```

Before moving on, there are some cautions when dealing with the CD command in a batch file. First, make certain that you're on the drive the directory is on. In some cases, this involves using the drive letter before the CD command. For example, if you've substituted the drive letter U for your\UTILITY subdirectory, you may need to do the following:

```
U:
CD GOLDNBOW
VOPT C: /N
```

Also, after using CD in a batch file, remember to return yourself to whichever directory from which you would like to start. For most cases, that's the root directory on drive C. So the final command in the batch file may be:

```
C:
CD \
```

AUTOEXEC Examples

The following are AUTOEXEC.BAT files I've collected. The most amazing thing about this assignment was the reaction I got from most people when I told them I wanted a printout of their AUTOEXEC file. Most people thought their's was boring. In fact, no two of them were alike (except in an office situation, and then only two from the same dealer were alike).

The line numbers used in FIG. 5-5 are for reference, and are not a part of the batch file. Scott's AUTOEXEC is pretty simple. He starts with the traditional ECHO OFF (1) and then sets his path (2). The three directories on his path are DOS, DB# (*dBASE*) and PCW (*PC Write*). These are the only three programs he uses so it makes sense for him to have them on the path.

```
1:  ECHO OFF
2:  PATH=C:\DOS;C:\DB3;C:\PCW
3:  PROMPT $t$_$d$_$p$g
4:  AUTOTIME
5:  CD\UTILITY\SIDEKICK
6:  SK
7:  CD\
8:  CLS
```

Fig. 5-5. This is Scott M's AUTOEXEC.BAT.

Scott's prompt setup is typical of others found in the same office: display the time, a new line, the date, a new line, and the standard directory and greater-than prompt (3):

```
12:36:24.97
Thu   7-21-1988
C:\DB3\JUNE>
```

AUTOTIME (4) is the real-time clock setting program for Scott's computer. Again, this varies from system to system, depending on who made the clock.

To run the memory-resident program *SideKick*, first you need to log to the *SideKick* directory (5) and then load the program (6). This is part of the loading procedure described in the *SideKick* manual. After loading *SideKick*, CD changes directories back to the root (7) and the screen is cleared (8).

Kent has a pretty complex AUTOEXEC.BAT file (he's read this book), as shown in FIG. 5-6. After the initial ECHO OFF (1), Kent has REMmed out his time-setting command (2). I asked him why, and he said because the battery on his real-time clock was dead and he hasn't gotten around to changing it. After he replaces the battery, he can edit out the REM statement.

```
 1: ECHO OFF
 2: REM \SYSTEM\UTIL\TIMER/S
 3: PROMPT . $A
 4: PATH = C:\SYSTEM\DOS;C:\SYSTEM\UTIL;C:\SYSTEM\BATCH
 5: SUBST E: C:\ETC
 6: SUBST F: C:\ISSUES\FUTURE
 7: SUBST G: C:\GAMES
 8: SUBST I: C:\ISSUES
 9: SUBST M: C:\WORDP\BB\MAIN
10: SUBST T: C:\TALK
11: \SYSTEM\MACE\RXBAK
12: DIR
13: CLS
14: GREET Kent!
15: VER
16: BANNER HELLO THERE, KENT
17: DATE
18: TIME
```

Fig. 5-6. This is Kent's AUTOEXEC.BAT.

Kent's prompt is a cryptic dot prompt, ala *dBASE* (3). The "$A" is used as a place holder for the space character after the cryptic dot. Kent's path is set to three directories, a DOS directory, a UTILity directory, and a special BATCH file directory. (This technique is covered in Part III.)

Lines 5 through 10 contain SUBSTitution commands to set up Kent's directory the way he wants. Note that, unlike line 2, here he can just use the SUBST command without a path prefix because the PATH command has already set the path.

Line 11 runs the RXBAK program, part of the Mace Utilities. RXBAK is kept in the \SYSTEM\MACE subdirectory and a full pathname is specified.

Line 12 pulls a directory, speeding up any further DIR commands Kent may issue. From here on, the AUTOEXEC file gets "pretty." All the work is done, and now it's time for Kent to amuse himself, starting with a clear screen (13).

The GREET program (14) is included on the supplemental disk you can order with this book. Basically, it reads the real-time clock and displays "Good Morning,"

"Good Afternoon," or "Good Evening," followed by whatever is on the command line. In Kent's case, he'll see:

Good Morning, Kent!

(He'll always see "Good Morning" because, remember, his real-time clock is broken.)

Next, DOS displays its version number (15) and this is followed by huge letters scrolling up the screen displaying, "HELLO THERE, KENT" (16). (BANNER is a program with many variations, one of which displays huge messages on the screen.)

Finally, because the real-time clock is broken, Kent must enter the date and time manually (17, 18) to finish out his AUTOEXEC.BAT file. Tina's AUTOEXEC file, shown in FIG. 5-7, is rather uncomplicated, doing only the necessary commands and then running a shell program (6). This computer's real-time clock setting command is RCLK (3) and, before Tina runs her shell, she runs a special program in her \LIBRARY subdirectory, CL. This program displays a list of "things to do today."

```
1:  PROMPT $P$G
2:  PATH C:\DOS;D:\;D:\LIBRARY;C:\UTIL
3:  RCLK
4:  CD \LIBRARY
5:  CL/I
6:  SHELL
```

Fig. 5-7. This is Tina's AUTOEXEC.BAT.

Sean's AUTOEXEC batch file, shown in FIG. 5-8, is unique in that it doesn't have an ECHO OFF command. Instead, Sean relies entirely on DOS 3.3's @ command to suppress the listing of his batch file to the screen.

```
 1:  @SET COMSPEC=c:\command.com
 2:  @SET PATH=E:\; C:\; C:\BIN; C:\DOS; C:\POINT; C:\NORTON;
     C:\WORD; C:\TURBOC; C:\FONTS; C:\MENUS; C:\LUCID; C:\GAMES
 3:  @chkdsk c:/f
 4:  @chkdsk d:/f
 5:  @SET PROMPT=$P$G
 6:  @sfreak 0400
 7:  @timer/s
 8:  @SUPERSPL LPT1:/M=256/EXTM=2560
 9:  @SET term=ibmpc-ega
10:  @SET PCPLUS=C:\PROCOMM
11:  @SET LUCID=C:\LUCID
12:  @CED -fc:\bin\ced.cnf
13:  @kcsetpal
14:  @egafont c:\fonts\thin.ega
```

Fig. 5-8. This is Sean's AUTOEXEC.BAT.

SET COMSPEC (1) really isn't necessary here because DOS does it automatically (unless there is a SHELL command in Sean's CONFIG.SYS). Sean sets a pretty long path (2), but again, as in line 5, doesn't need to use the SET command for either PATH or PROMPT.

Two CHecK DiSKs are run (3, 4) to look for bad files on both of Sean's hard drives. SFREAK slows down the computer's RAM refresh rate (6). TIMER is used to set the system clock (7), and a print spooler is activated in line 8.

Lines 9 through 11 set environment variables for game software, ProComm (a telecommunications package), and Ludic (spreadsheet). CED (12) is a program that Sean claims "makes DOS a little less inconvenient" (I think it allows you to replace some DOS commands with two-letter equivalents). KCSETPAL (13) sets the computer's EGA monitor to the standard color palette and EGAFONT (14) loads a "readable" font into the EGA display.

```
 1: echo off
 2: mouse
 3: cpanel
 4: \bin\util\setdos
 5: \bin\util\respro
 6: \bin\util\1 48
 7: prompt $e[1;1H$e[7m Date $d $e[1;30H Directory $p $e[0m
    $e[25;1HCommand
 8: copy c:\command.com d:\ >nul
 9: set comspec=d:\command.com
10: set procomm=c:\usr\telecom\prcm\
11: path d:\;c:\;\bin;\bin\sys;\bin\util;\etc\filefix;\usr\ws
12: search d:\; c:\usr\ws; \usr\telecom\aems;
    \usr\telecom\prcm; \tn
13: cd\bin\util
14: ced
15: pf k 5
16: mark >nul
17: \usr\ws\wf
18: echo Moving job files into RAM drive D:
19: copy c:\etc\dev\*.bat d:\ >nul
20: copy c:\etc\dev\*.exe d:\ >nul
21: copy c:\etc\dev\*.com d:\ >nul
22: cls
23: echo  E n v i r o n m e n t  i s:
24: echo -----------------------------
25: chkdsk /f
26: echo Standby while defragging hard disk
27: vopt
28: cls
29: cd\
```

Fig. 5-9. This is Mike's AUTOEXEC.BAT.

Sean's AUTOEXEC.BAT file is a perfect example of customization. He knows exactly what he wants, and uses AUTOEXEC to set his computer up that way.

When I asked my friends to send me their AUTOEXEC.BAT files, I received a whole slew of them. Some I really don't have the room for (there is one that's over 2K in length—a monster!). FIGURES 5-9 to 5-12 are several more AUTOEXEC.BAT files, without the liberal comments I gave on the previous examples.

Look at FIG. 5-10. PK and SCRNSAVE are both screen saver programs. BACKSCRL is a back-scrolling utility, allowing you to review data that has already scrolled off your screen. Note that the ECHO ON (12) is never necessary at the end of a batch file.

```
 1: echo off
 2: prompt .
 3: path
 4: c:\; c:\bin; c:\dos; c:\batch; d:\turbo; d:\utils;
    d:\norton; d:\games; d:\dfedit; d:\vi;
 5: timepark 5
 6: backscrl 5
 7: scrnsave
 8: set PROCOMM=\TERM\PRO-COMM
 9: set TC=D:\TURBO
10: set DFEDIT=D:\DFEDIT
11: cls
12: echo on
```

Fig. 5-10. This is Jim's AUTOEXEC.BAT.

Notice the nice use of REMs in FIG. 5-11. With all the REMs in there, it makes commenting Scott O's AUTOEXEC.BAT file a little redundant. (See how nice remarks can be?)

```
 1: echo off
 2: cls
 3: REM echo Switching to monochrome monitor...
 4: \dos\mode mono
 5: echo Setting system defaults, please wait...
 6: set user=SAO
 7: REM
 8: REM ---- Set path information for DOS & UTILITY commands
 9: REM
10: path c:\;c:\batch;c:\dos;c:\util;c:\db3
11: REM
12: REM ---- Run Vopt to optimize hard disk.
13: REM
14: vopt
```

Fig. 5-11. This is Scott O's AUTOEXEC.BAT.

```
15: if not errorlevel 4 goto ok
16:     echo There are hard disk errors!   Check HARD DISK!
17:     pause
18: :ok
19: REM
20: REM ---- Set prompt for "\dir >"
21: REM
22: prompt $p$g
23: REM
24: REM ---- Install PRINT with a 20 file queue
25: REM
26: rem print /b:1024 /q:20 /d:prn > nul
27: REM
28: REM ---- Install Video-7 CGA Emulation & Screen Saver
29: REM
30: rem vega save:8 > nul
31: REM
32: REM ---- Set hard disk park for 5 minutes
33: REM
34: timepark 5 > nul
35: REM
36: REM ---- Install Mouse driver
37: REM
38: rem mousesys > nul
39: REM
40: REM ---- Set keyboard repeat rate
41: REM
42: REM quickeys
43: REM
44: REM ---- Set-up DOS EDIT feature
45: dos-edit > nul
46: REM
47: REM ---- Turn keyclick OFF
48: REM
49: mode: cli=0
50: REM
51: REM ---- Install PC-193A Okidata TSR setup
52: REM
53: REM PC-193A > nul
54: REM
55: REM ---- All done, return to user
56: type \dos\logo.ans
57: C:\quicken2\billmind /c=C:\QUICKEN2
```

Fig. 5-11. Continued.

See, in FIG. 5-12, how Donald needed to go to his *SideKick* subdirectory in order to run *SideKick*. Did you notice the batch file subdirectory in line 3? This nifty idea crops up again in PART FOUR.

```
 1: @echo off
 2: ver
 3: path=c:\mouse;c:\batch;c:\msdos;c:\util;c:\util\norton;
    c:\util\sideways
 4: set clipper=c:\clipper
 5: fast
 6: mode co80
 7: sa bright yellow on black
 8: prompt $v$_Current Directory $p$_$n$g
 9: getclock
10: menu
11: click
12: cd\
13: fastopen c:=100
14: cd\util\sidekick
15: sk
16: cd\
17: cls
18: C:\QUICKEN2\BILLMINDER /C=\QUICKEN2 /P
```

Fig. 5-12. This is Donald's AUTOEXEC.BAT.

DOS 4.0 Suggests . . .

Earlier, you read about how DOS 4.0's INSTALL program created a suggested file for my system's CONFIG.SYS file. It did the same thing with AUTOEXEC.BAT. INSTALL created a file called AUTOEXEC.400 that contained what it thought would be a good AUTOEXEC.BAT for my system (*see* FIG. 5-13).

The first thing the suggested file does is to turn off the ECHO (1). In line 2, it sets my COMSPEC to where its CONFIG.SYS file specified using the SHELL command (pretty smart, eh?). Other things done in this batch file seem rather ordinary (after all, INSTALL doesn't know everything about my system). For example, I don't personally like the APPEND command (5, 6) because quite a few of my directories contain the same filenames. Also, my system doesn't have an IBM printer, so the GRAPHICS command (8) is useless to me. Also, I dislike the PRINT spooler program (10) and I prefer to use the command prompt rather than the shell program (11).

I know—picky, picky. But at least DOS 4.0 gives you the option of using this batch file or not. In fact, for a beginner, this wouldn't be a bad way to start.

```
 1: @ECHO OFF
 2: SET COMSPEC=C:\SYSTEM\DOS\COMMAND.COM
 3: VERIFY OFF
 4: PATH C:\SYSTEM\DOS
 5: APPEND /E
 6: APPEND C:\SYSTEM\DOS
 7: PROMPT $P$G
 8: C:\SYSTEM\DOS\GRAPHICS
 9: VER
10: PRINT /D:LPT1
11: DOSSHELL
```

Fig. 5-13. INSTALL created this file called AUTOEXEC.400.

Non-Booting Disk Example

Some older computers, and some computers with special types of fixed disks (such as the older Bernoulli drives), could only boot from the first floppy drive. This can be annoying—requiring you to keep a system disk in the first floppy drive even when you use a hard disk. But there's a way around it with only a simple change to your AUTOEXEC.BAT file.

The object is to fake a "boot" from the hard drive. This is done by loading a second copy of the command processor from the floppy boot disk.

Essentially, your system would have two COMMAND.COMs, and two AUTOEXEC.BATs. The first set would be on a bootable floppy disk. The AUTOEXEC.BAT file would look something like this:

```
@ECHO OFF
C:
COMMAND C:\ /P
```

This directs your system to log to drive C, then reload COMMAND.COM (a secondary shell). The C:\ option tells COMMAND.COM to reload itself from the root directory on drive C. The /P switch directs COMMAND.COM to execute the AUTOEXEC.BAT file, this time on the root directory of drive C. Now you can safely remove the boot disk from drive A and use the system as a hard disk system should be used (and much faster, as well).

This strategy also applies to flaky, and marginally operational, hard disks. In fact, it would be a good idea to keep a boot disk around with an AUTOEXEC.BAT file just like the above example. This way, if ever the boot sector on your hard drive went south, you'd still be able to boot your system, then back up all your files before rushing out to buy a new hard disk. (Of course, it's always best to have a recent backup handy "just in case.")

SHUTDOWN.BAT STRATEGIES

An interesting concept in system batch files is a SHUTDOWN.BAT file. Just like AUTOEXEC.BAT is the first batch file your system runs, SHUTDOWN.BAT should be the last file your system runs. The designers of the original PC (and of DOS) didn't see fit to include such a program. So you must write it yourself.

Before continuing, it should be noted that a few computers do come with SHUTDOWN routines. For example, the Epson PC runs a special BIOS routine when the "off" button is pressed. Rather than turning itself off immediately, an Epson first parks the hard drives and then shuts itself off. This is a nice safety feature, but frustrating because there should be some way to access and modify those routines so you could perform other functions at shutdown time.

Because there is no official SHUTDOWN.BAT file, let's make one up. The following tasks should be done by a SHUTDOWN batch file:

- Erase any un-needed files/clear out "junk" directories
- Print any files in a "spool" directory
- Back up most recently worked on, or important, files
- Optimize the hard drive
- Park the hard drive

Generally speaking, SHUTDOWN.BAT should take care of all the things that you normally do at the end of the day, just before shutting down the computer (or just turning the monitor off, which is what I usually do).

The SHUTDOWN.BAT file in FIG. 5-14 tries to accomplish most of the above strategies. This SHUTDOWN file accomplishes most of the things that I typically do at the end of my computing session. I've spiced it up a bit, adding some variety and showing some examples that apply to just about everyone's situation.

```
 1: @ECHO OFF
 2: REM Display shut down message
 3: ECHO ^G
 4: ECHO System Shutdown
 5: ECHO Cleaning directories...
 6: REM Remove temporary files...
 7: C:
 8: CD \TEMP
 9: DEL *.* < C:\SYSTEM\BATCH\YES >NUL
10: REM Use SWEEP utility to remove temporary files
11: CD \
12: SWEEP DEL *.BAK > NUL
13: SWEEP DEL KILL*.* > NUL
14: SWEEP DEL TEMP*.* > NUL
15: ECHO Printing spooled files...
16: IF NOT EXIST E:\SPOOL\*.* GOTO SKIP1
17: E:
18: CD \SPOOL
19: COPY *.* PRN > NUL
20: DEL *.* < C:\SYSTEM\BATCH\YES >NUL
```

Fig. 5-14. The SHUTDOWN.BAT file.

```
21: :SKIP1
22: REM Backup most recently worked on stuff/important files
23: ECHO Backing up spreadsheet data
24: HOLD Put spreadsheet backup disk in Drive A and
25: CD \LOTUS
26: BACKUP C:\LOTUS\*.* A: /S/M
27: HOLD Put word processing backup disk in Drive A and
28: CD \WORDP
29: BACKUP C:\WORDP\*.* A: /S/M
30: REM Optimize the hard drive
31: ASK Optimize the hard drive now? (y/n)
32: REM ERRORLEVEL 1 IS "NO"
33: IF ERRORLEVEL 1 GOTO SKIP2
34: VOPT /N
35: :SKIP2
36: REM all done, park the hard drive
37: CLS
38: ECHO Shutdown completed, parking hard disk
39: GREET Dan
40: PARK
```

Fig. 5-14. Continued.

First comes the traditional ECHO OFF (1), followed by messages informing the user what's going on (3, 4). If the SHUTDOWN file takes a while to perform its duties, you may want to add a message here telling the user how long the operating will take, or give them the option to cancel the shutdown procedure.

The batch file removes temporary files (6) from the \TEMP directory on drive C (7, 8). (Some users name this directory \JUNK.) Line 9 removes all the files and uses I/O redirection to first provide the input for the "Are you sure?" question that DEL *.* always asks, and second to redirect the output to the NUL device, reducing possible confusing by the user.

Next, the SWEEP utility is used to clean through all directories and remove all *.BAK (12), KILL*.* (13), and TEMP*.* (14) files. If SWEEP is used starting at the root directory (11), it looks through all subdirectories. Otherwise, you could use it to sweep only selected subdirectories.

Line 16 checks drive E (possibly a RAM disk) for any files that need to be spooled to the printer. If there are any files (16), they are copied one by one to the printer (19) and then deleted (20).

About the most important thing a SHUTDOWN.BAT file can do is ensure that crucial files are backed up. As opposed to backing up your entire system, which should be done once a month or so, backing up recently worked-on files should be done every day. Lines 23 through 26 and lines 27 through 29 back up all the spreadsheet and word processing files on this system that have been modified since the last backup.

The HOLD command (24 and 27) is part of the program disk available with this book. It's a "smart" version of the DOS pause command, which doesn't always display a message before the "press any key to continue" prompt.

Lines 30 through 35 are for optimizing the hard drive. As you saw with the AUTOEXEC.BAT examples, many users opt to do this before they run their computer. There's nothing wrong, however, with putting an optimizing utility in a SHUTDOWN.BAT file. In this instance, the ASK command (31) is used to determine if the user wants to optimize now or not. If so, the hard drive is optimized (34), otherwise execution skips to the SKIP2 label (35).

Finally, the screen is cleared (37), the user is informed that SHUTDOWN.BAT is done running (38), and the user is presented with a friendly greeting (39). Line 40 parks the hard drive. Depending on the parking program, the system may "lock up" and the user may be forced to shut off the system. Other parking programs may simply return to DOS, in which case the user can shut off the system at that time.

You'll notice in this batch file how "> NUL" was used in several places to re-press the display of some messages. Also, the ASK command could have been used more liberally to control what SHUTDOWN.BAT does and doesn't do.

The BACKUP commands are really rather simple. A more realistic example might have the user enter specific directories to back up as part of the batch file's replaceable parameters (covered in Part II). Over all, this file would take a long time to run, even on a fast computer. Still, with all its drawbacks, this example provides an excellent base upon which you could build your own SHUTDOWN.BAT file.

Summary

CONFIG.SYS and AUTOEXEC.BAT are the two most important files you control on your system.

CONFIG.SYS sets up your system, allowing you to customize and configure it to your tastes. Only three CONFIG.SYS commands are important to batch file programming. They are: DEVICE, LASTDRIVE, and SHELL.

AUTOEXEC.BAT is the first program your computer system runs—and you get to write it. There are many things you can do in AUTOEXEC, some of which are important and others can simply be your own strategy on how you want your system to start. The important thing to remember is that a well-written AUTOEXEC.BAT file will do wonders for your system.

SHUTDOWN.BAT is not an official DOS batch file, but it can come in handy. The SHUTDOWN batch file can take care of all sorts of miscellaneous duties that you normally perform before turning your system off. Just remember to type SHUTDOWN.BAT, as unlike CONFIG.SYS and AUTOEXEC.BAT, DOS will not run it automatically.

6
OS/2

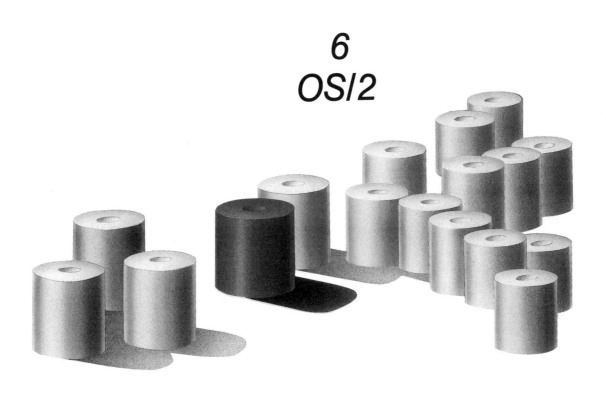

Just when you thought you knew everything about DOS, along comes OS/2.

Actually, OS/2 is nothing to be afraid of. In fact, it's quite an impressive piece of work. Regardless of what all the doomsayers have to say (most of whom have a vested interest in keeping DOS alive), OS/2 will eventually be "the" future operating system for PCs.

OS/2 has many powerful features and, just to put all your fears aside, it's very, very similar to DOS. In fact, they should have called DOS 3.0, 3.1, 3.2, 3.3 and 4.0, versions 2.2, 2.3, 2.4, and 2.5. OS/2 is really DOS 3.0. It's an improvement. It's better. You'll like it.

The problem with OS/2 is that there's really no reason to buy it right now. Sure, I spent $325 for it to write this book. (Actually, it was more like $1000 when you add in the cost of my memory upgrade.) But I have no OS/2 software other than OS/2 itself. And the current trend shows that people won't be rushing out to buy OS/2 for at least a few years.

This chapter scratches the surface of OS/2. It's not designed as a comprehensive tutorial, nor is there space to explain all the details of OS/2. Instead, this should help get those few of you who use OS/2 off to a better start writing OS/2 batch files. If you don't own OS/2, the information here is optional reading.

HISTORY OF OS/2

The history of OS/2 starts with IBM's decision to put Intel's 80286 microprocessor in their PC/AT. The 80286 was a giant technological leap up from the old 8088 in the original PC and the PC/XT. It was also a leap up from the 8086 chips (a true, 16-bit version of the 8088) used in some of the faster PC clones, such as Compaq.

The 80286 could address much more memory than the 8088. Also, it offered a special "protected" mode. In this mode the processor can restrict access to certain areas of memory. Hence, when run in the protected mode, an 80286 program couldn't just go out and grab memory like an 8088 program could. Instead, the 80286 program must ask for the memory. (Under normal circumstances, the 80286 behaves just like a fast 8088—so this memory control stuff is trivial if you're just running DOS programs on your AT clone.)

The protected mode meant the 80286 chip could offer programs a lot more flexibility when running. It also meant that a crude form of multi-tasking would be possible. That is, in the protected mode, the 80286 could conceivably run two or more programs at the same time. While it sounds a bit much for a microcomputer (which, after all, is based on the one computer-one human concept of getting work done), multitasking opens up a whole new area of capable computer programs.

The problem with the 80286, and really all computer hardware advances, is that it takes the software a long, long time to catch up. Developing hardware and getting the bugs out is an involved process. But once it's done, it's done. Software, on the other hand, takes a lot longer. Because of this, software specifically for the 80286 chip lagged. Also, software developers weren't anxious to write 80286-only programs with the abundance of 8088 computers. Software for the 8088 can run on the 80286 (and run quickly). But 80286-specific software cannot run on the 8088.

Because of the power of the 80286, Microsoft set out to write what was internally called "DOS 3." It would be a multi-tasking version of DOS that took advantage of the 80286's protected mode. In the course of events, DOS 3 (the MS-DOS version) was released instead. Then the older DOS 3 project became DOS 4, and then DOS 5. Finally, coupled with IBM's introduction of their new PS/2 computers, Microsoft decided to start the whole numbering shebang over with OS/2, for Operating System Two.

It took the team at Microsoft, working closely with IBM, quite some time to develop OS/2. But the results are worth it. It takes advantage of the power of the 80286 chip. And because the newer 80386 chip can run 80286 programs, users with those computers can run OS/2 as well. (The 80386-specific version of OS/2 is planned, but not available at this writing.)

Additionally, OS/2 allows compatibility with DOS via the *DOS 3x box*. This is a special operating mode of OS/2 that allows it to "fake" MS–DOS version 3.3, albeit slowly. The DOS 3x box is also referred to as the OS/2 "real" mode.

Concerns

As I said in the introduction, there are no OS/2 software packages available yet. In fact, there probably won't be anything specific to OS/2 that everyone must have for at least a few years. (OS/2 is now in its infancy, just as DOS was in the early '80s.) Because of this, OS/2 needed to be very compatible with existing computer systems. The DOS 3x box plays a leading role in this. But there are other items of importance as well. They are:

Hardware compatibility

File structure compatibility

Memory compatibility

Program compatibility

Hardware

Hardware compatibility determines the success of the operating system. DOS was successful for three reasons (two hardware and one software): it ran on a lot of computers; you could read diskettes formatted on another DOS computer, regardless of who made that computer; DOS programs could run on any "compatible" computer. All this has to do with hardware compatibility. For OS/2 to follow successfully in DOS's footsteps, it needs to incorporate those three items.

Hardware compatibility also refers to which systems can run OS/2. As you might know, just about everyone and anyone can make a DOS compatible computer. What about OS/2?

It turns out that most 80286 computers that are DOS compatible are also OS/2 compatible. (Older 8088 and 8086 computers cannot run OS/2.) In fact, most major IBM-compatible manufactures now offer a version of OS/2 for their 80286 and 80386 computers. I have tested OS/2 on an 80286 "clone" computer and it ran fine. You cannot "buy" OS/2 like you can MS–DOS, so if you're looking for a copy to run on your clone computer, you'll need to locate a version distributed by a national manufacturer, or visit your local IBM authorized dealer to buy a copy.

You also need at least 1.5 megabytes of RAM to run OS/2. The more RAM you have, the more OS/2 can do for you. Presently, about 4 megabytes seems to be a "comfortable" amount. By the way, most AT computers come with 512K of RAM. That's the ".5" part of 1.5 megabytes. To run OS/2, you'll need to add that extra megabyte of memory. You'll also need to specify that extra megabyte as "extended memory" rather than enhanced memory.

Also, OS/2 requires a hard drive, and will use approximately three megabytes of storage on that drive. Presently, OS/2 comes on either 1.2 megabyte 5¼-inch or 1.44 megabyte 3½-inch diskettes, so you need those sized disk drives to read the OS/2 diskettes and install it on your system.

Fortunately, all of these items are presently available on quite a few DOS machines. (This is, of course, assuming that you need OS/2 in the first place.)

File Structure

OS/2 uses the same file structure as DOS. Presently, that means OS/2 uses eight-character filenames with an optional three-character extension, pathnames with the backslash separator, drive letters with colons—the whole nine yards. You can install OS/2 on a hard disk that already has DOS on it—no changes are necessary.

Future versions of OS/2 will incorporate a filename "module" that will allow different types of filenames (maybe longer names, or names including spaces). But, for now, and to keep compatible, OS/2 uses the same file structure as DOS. In fact, some versions of the OS/2 installation program will let you keep DOS on your hard drive. You'll have the option of running either one or the other operating system when you reset your computer.

Memory

OS/2 requires 1.5 megabytes of RAM to run. The first megabyte is configured roughly the same as a DOS computer (*see* FIG. 6-1). Memory above the 1 megabyte mark is used exclusively by OS/2 programs. Remember, OS/2 will need 1 megabyte of extended memory to run. That's memory in the address space between 1 and 2 megabytes in FIG. 6-2.

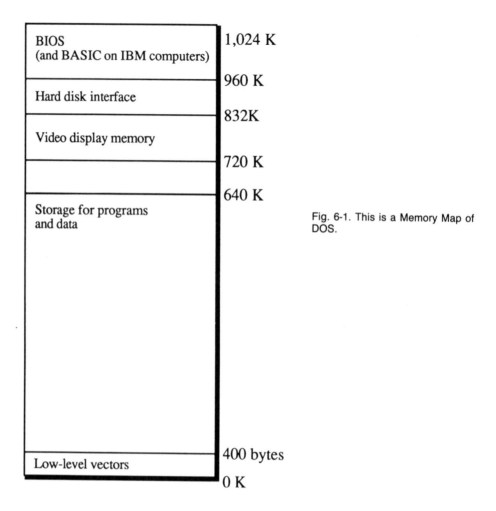

Fig. 6-1. This is a Memory Map of DOS.

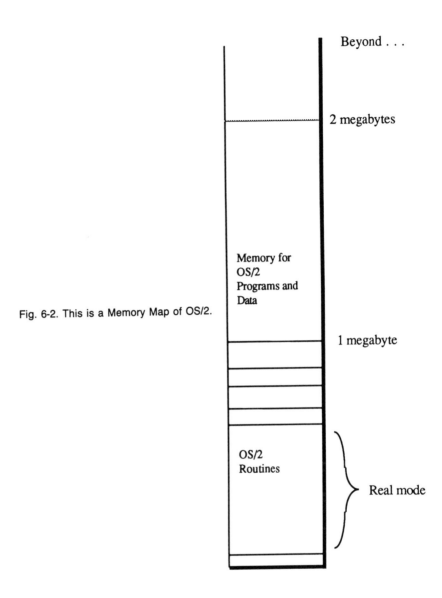

Beyond . . .

2 megabytes

Memory for
OS/2
Programs and
Data

Fig. 6-2. This is a Memory Map of OS/2.

1 megabyte

OS/2
Routines

Real mode

REAL AND PROTECTED MODES

OS/2 comes in two flavors, the real and protected modes. Eventually, the protected will be the only OS/2 mode. The *real* mode was added to maintain compatibility with DOS and the many applications programs that can only run under DOS. The *protected* mode is where the real power of OS/2 lies.

The Real Mode

The real mode is configured to work just like DOS. In fact, it was created because Microsoft knew there wouldn't be any OS/2 specific (which means "protected mode") software for quite some time. So the real mode allows you to run DOS programs.

But don't be confused. The real mode is not DOS. It's simply an optional mode of OS/2. In fact, when you start the real mode under OS/2, you see the following displayed:

```
Microsoft Operating System/2 Command Interpreter
Version 1.00 - DOS Mode

C:\>
```

The command prompt looks the same as the DOS command prompt. You have all the same DOS commands—even a copy of GW BASIC (depending on who sold you OS/2). Everything works the same as DOS, but you're really using a special OS/2 mode.

The real mode is also referred to as the *DOS 3x box*, or the *compatibility box*. Though you can run DOS programs there, some people claim that they will work slower than if you just use DOS. My advice is to install the dual-boot option with OS/2, so you can run your machine as a DOS-only computer and leave OS/2 out of the picture when you don't want it.

The real mode also lacks some commands that were available under the latest version of DOS 3.3 (DOS 4.0 is a step-and-a-half in a different direction). Among the commands missing are:

CTTY

FASTOPEN

KEYB (though there is a protected mode version of this command)

NLSFUNC

SELECT

(There's a complete commands reference listed later in this chapter.)

If you choose to run your computer in dual modes (that is, you have the option of booting OS/2 or running your system only for DOS when you turn the computer on or reset), then some of the OS/2 filenames may change. Specifically, if you run a dual-mode system, the names for AUTOEXEC.BAT and CONFIG.SYS will be different in the OS/2 mode.

Because you have a dual system, the DOS mode will want to boot using the files AUTOEXEC.BAT and CONFIG.SYS. These two files, however, are also needed on the OS/2 side. AUTOEXEC is used by the OS/2 real mode when the real mode session is first started. CONFIG.SYS is used by both modes when OS/2 first boots.

If you run your system in the dual mode, OS/2 changes the names of AUTOEXEC.BAT and CONFIG.SYS. For the real mode, AUTOEXEC.BAT becomes AUTOEXEC.OS2. For both modes, CONFIG.SYS becomes CONFIG.OS2.

The reason for the renaming is compatibility. Because some versions of OS/2 can boot either as an OS/2 or DOS system, there had to be some way to separate the AUTOEXEC file for OS/2's real mode and the AUTOEXEC file for the DOS mode.

The solution was to rename the AUTOEXEC file for the real mode as AUTOEXEC.OS2.

CONFIG.OS2 is the system configuration file for both the real and protected modes. (There's more on OS/2's CONFIG file later in this chapter.) If you run your system as an OS/2 computer, however, your system configuration file will be named CONFIG.SYS.

The Protected Mode

I don't find the title "protected mode" as silly as the real mode's title. The protected mode is a nice title, in fact. It means that your software is protected by the processor from other programs. The memory used by one program can never be interfered with by another program. Everything is protected.

The protected mode is what OS/2 is all about. It's where you can run multiple programs and perform multitasking. The protected mode offers a new face, and looks quite different from DOS. For example, the default prompt is the current drive and path enclosed in brackets:

```
[C:\OS2]
```

(Though, as with DOS, you can change the prompt using the OS/2 PROMPT command.)

Also, some of the commands are souped up. You can now type:

```
DIR *.COM *.EXE
```

to display a directory of all your COM and EXE files.

You cannot run DOS programs in the protected mode, however. Only programs specific to OS/2 will run. If you try to run a DOS program, you'll get an error message like:

```
SYS0193: C:\DOS\EDLIN.COM cannot be run in Microsoft
Operating System/2 mode.
```

Eventually, there will be some OS/2 protected mode software. Until then, about the only programs you can run are (can you guess?) batch files.

Sessions

Using OS/2, you can have multiple "sessions" running at a time. A session is an independent process. For example, you could be formatting a disk in one OS/2 session, and then use another session to run a text editor. Both operations work at the same time and are independent of each other.

An example of running multiple sessions would be to have a word processor working in one session while a database is sorting a long list in a second session, and you're connected with a mainframe computer downloading a program in a third session. All processes are running independently of each other. From the operator's point of view, everything is happening at once—and with no loss of speed. (This is the primary purpose behind the new operating system.)

The real mode is also considered an OS/2 session, though you can only run one copy of the real mode at a time. (In the protected mode, you can run as many sessions as you like, or until whenever your system's memory fills up.) You can switch back and forth between the real mode session and the protected mode sessions, but once you leave the real mode, its actions are suspended. (Protected mode sessions continue to run after you leave them.)

One nice thing about these independent sessions is that, if a program crashes in one session, it doesn't bring down the whole system. You simply return to OS/2's Program Switcher and start up a new session. The old, crashed session still stays in memory, but it doesn't stop you from using your computer.

To start a new session, you press ALT–ESC. That activates the OS/2 Program Selector where a list of programs and running sessions are displayed. You choose a new program to run, or a new session to switch to, using the arrow keys and the Enter key.

To finish a session, type EXIT at the protected mode command prompt. (You cannot end the real mode session.) To switch between two running sessions, press CTRL–ESC.

Batch Files

Both the real and protected modes of OS/2 use batch files. The real mode runs the same batch files that run under DOS. All the same commands are used and the batch files end with the .BAT file extension.

In the protected mode, batch files behave the same as they do in protected mode. The only difference is that the CMD extension is used rather than BAT:

.BAT   Real
.CMD   Protected

Also, there are additional batch file commands that work only in the protected mode. If you don't use the new protected mode commands, however, you can run any real mode batch file in the protected mode, and vice versa, simply by renaming the batch file. (The new commands are covered below.)

SIMILARITIES BETWEEN *OS/2* and *DOS*

OS/2 and DOS are really close. As I said earlier, OS/2 should really be called DOS 5.0 (or something). Anyone who's comfortable with DOS will learn OS/2 in no time. In fact, only a few subtle clues will tip you off that you're not running DOS.

Error Messages

One annoying thing I've found with OS/2 is its cryptic error message handling. Rather than getting a simple "File not found" message, OS/2 confronts you with the following:

`SYS0002:` `The system cannot find the file specified.`

Is this supposed to be friendly?

 If you type HELP followed by the number (after SYS above), you'll get a more detailed explanation of what went wrong:

`EXPLANATION: The file name in the command`
`does not exist in the current directory or search path`
`specified.  Or, the filename was entered incorrectly.`
`ACTION: Retry the command using the correct filename.`

 Of course, this is a definite improvement over some earlier operating systems that merely displayed a single question mark, leaving you totally in the dark as to what you did wrong.

 Fatal error handling has been "improved" as well. Instead of the now "classic" Abort, Retry and Fail message, OS/2 displays a fancy box with a help screen and detailed instructions.

 Supposedly, OS/2 will be taking on a new face, and these subtle differences will grow more remote. The OS/2 *Presentation Manager* will eventually offer OS/2 users a graphic interface, like Apple's Macintosh computer. The *Presentation Manager* will doubtless improve the usability and appearance of OS/2.

OS/2 Commands

 TABLES 6-1 and 6-2 list a comparison of DOS 3.x and OS/2 commands. (DOS 3.x was chosen over DOS 4.0 because OS/2 claims compatibility with DOS 3.3—not DOS 4.0.) The OS/2 commands have been grouped into real and protected modes in TABLE 6-1.

Table 6-1.

DOS 3.x Command	Real Mode OS/2 Command	Protected Mode OS/2 Command
—	—	ANSI
APPEND	APPEND	DPATH
ASSIGN	ASSIGN	—
ATTRIB	ATTRIB	ATTRIB
BACKUP	BACKUP	BACKUP
BREAK	BREAK	—
CHCP	CHCP	CHCP
CHDIR (CD)	CHDIR	CHDIR
CHKDSK	CHKDSK	CHKDSK
CLS	CLS	CLS
COMMAND	COMMAND	CMD
COMP	COMP	COMP
COPY	COPY	COPY
CTTY	—	—
DATE	DATE	DATE
DEL	DEL	DEL

DOS 3.x Command	Real Mode OS/2 Command	Protected Mode OS/2 Command
—	—	DETACH
DIR	DIR	DIR
DISKCOMP	DISKCOMP	DISKCOMP
DISKCOPY	DISKCOPY	DISKCOPY
—	—	DPATH (see APPEND above)
ERASE	ERASE	ERASE
FASTOPEN	—	—
FIND	FIND	FIND
FORMAT	FORMAT	FORMAT
GRAFTABL	GRAFTABL	—
GRAPHICS	—	—
—	HELPMSG	HELPMSG
JOIN	JOIN	—
KEYB	—	KEYB
LABEL	LABEL	LABEL
MKDIR (MD)	MKDIR	MKDIR
MODE	MODE	MODE
MORE	MORE	MORE
NLSFUNC	—	—
—	PATCH	PATCH
PATH	PATH	PATH
PRINT	PRINT	PRINT
PROMPT	PROMPT	PROMPT
RECOVER	RECOVER	RECOVER
RENAME (REN)	RENAME	RENAME
REPLACE	REPLACE	REPLACE
RESTORE	RESTORE	RESTORE
RMDIR (RD)	RMDIR	RMDIR
SELECT	—	—
SET	SET	SET
—	SETCOM40	—
SHARE	—	—
SORT	SORT	SORT
—	—	SPOOL
—	—	START
SUBST	SUBST	—
SYS	SYS	SYS
TIME	TIME	TIME
TREE	TREE	TREE
TYPE	TYPE	TYPE
VER	VER	VER
VERIFY	VERIFY	VERIFY
VOL	VOL	VOL
XCOPY	XCOPY	XCOPY

Table 6-1. Continued.

Table 6-2

Renamed Commands:

APPEND is called **DPATH** in the protected mode
OS/2's COMMAND.COM is called **CMD.EXE**

New Commands:

Command	What it does
ANSI	Turns the extended screen and keyboard control on or off.
DETACH	Sends a process off into the background. You can "detach" a command that will function while you're doing something else.
HELPMSG	A program that displays helpful information about OS/2's cryptic error messages. You type the error message number after HELPMSG. (This program works with a batch file named HELP.CMD or HELP.BAT depending on which mode of OS/2 you're using.)
PATCH	Used to alter or update the code of a program. You can apply a "patch" to the program by specifying a file containing the patching code.
SETCOM40	Controls access to the serial ports for the real mode. Because some real mode programs will just "take control" of a serial port, SETCOM40 is used to avoid conflicts with protected mode programs and to make the port available to the real mode program.
SPOOL	Starts a background printer spooler.
START	Starts a new protected mode process. You can use START to begin a new protected mode session.

Special Directories

Unlike DOS, OS/2 must be installed. Depending on the version of OS/2, there will be several installation strategies. My advice (for everyone) is to use the automatic installation the first time. Later, as you get to know OS/2, you can move the files around. But when you start, it's frustrating not knowing which files do what, and where you can put them.

OS/2's installation program will also tell you if your system has what it takes to run OS/2. For example, you need that 1 megabyte of extended memory to run OS/2. If you don't have it, the installation program will simply sit there and be stubborn.

OS/2 creates for itself a number of directories into which it places its files (*see* FIG. 6-3). In the root directory are CONFIG.SYS, AUTOEXEC.BAT (for the real mode), STARTUP.CMD (for the protected mode), and OS2INIT.CMD (for each subsequent session under the protected mode). Additionally, OS/2 will place a bunch of .SYS and a few .COM and .EXE files into your root directory, disobeying the law of "keeping the root clean."

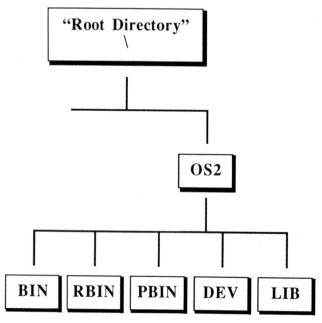

Fig. 6-3. This is the OS/2 directory structure.

If you're running a dual mode computer, CONFIG.SYS for OS/2 will be named CONFIG.OS2, and AUTOEXEC.BAT for the real mode will be named AUTOEXEC.OS2. These files will exist in addition to CONFIG.SYS and AUTOEXEC.BAT for the DOS mode. (You'll have one heck of a crowded root directory.)

\OS2   The OS2 subdirectory holds all the OS/2 commands, program and data files. It can have five directories under it: BIN, RBIN, PBIN, DEV, and LIB.

\OS2\BIN   The BIN subdirectory holds all the executable files that run under both the real and protected modes.

\OS2\RBIN   The RBIN subdirectory holds only those files and programs used by the OS/2 real mode.

\OS2\PBIN   The PBIN subdirectory holds only those files and programs used by the OS/2 protected mode.

\OS2\DEV   The DEV subdirectory is used to hold device drivers.

\OS2\LIB   The LIB subdirectory contains OS/2's dynalink (.DLL) library files.

Anyone who's familiar with DOS will realize that this makes for quite a mess. Yet, it's organized (more or less).

CMD.EXE

CMD.EXE is the COMMAND.COM of OS/2. It serves virtually the identical function of COMMAND.COM, and also contains the OS/2 batch file interpreter.

CMD has two optional switches, /C and /K.

/C works exactly like the /C switch for COMMAND.COM. You follow /C with the name of a program to run, such as a batch file. CMD.EXE executes that command, then returns. (So you could use CMD /C with a batch file to "call" the batch file. However, the CALL batch file command works in the protected mode, so this would be unnecessary.)

/K works like /C except that, after the optional program runs, OS/2 stays in the new shell created by CMD.EXE. To return to the previous shell, simply type EXIT (just as you would exit from a COMMAND.COM shell).

CONFIG.SYS

The OS/2 system configuration file for both the real and protected modes is called CONFIG.SYS. (If you're running a dual mode system, then the OS/2 configuration file will be named CONFIG.OS2. The DOS mode will use a second file named CONFIG.SYS.)

TABLE 6-3 is a brief list of OS/2's CONFIG.SYS commands. If a "Yes" appears in the second column, it means that command applies only to the real mode. Otherwise, most of the commands are specific to the protected mode or a combination of both modes.

Table 6-3.

Command	Real Mode	Description
BREAK	Yes	If set equal to YES the system will check for CTRL–C (break) to halt programs.
BUFFERS		Specifies the number of buffers to be used by OS/2 for file reading and writing.
CODEPAGE		Selects the code page to be used by your system (for foreign language computers).
COUNTRY		Selects time, date and currency display formats for different countries.
DEVICE		Loads a device driver into memory.
DEVINFO		Prepares a specified device for use with code pages.
DISKCACHE		Allocates space for a disk cache.
FCBS	Yes	Specifies the number of file control blocks that can be open at a time.

Command	Real Mode	Description
IOPL		Controls access to hardware, such as screen memory.
LIBPATH		Specifies the path of OS/2's dynamic-link library modules.
MAXWAIT		Specifies the maximum number of seconds a process will be ignored before OS/2 gives it some time.
MEMMAN		Sets memory management options.
PAUSEONERROR		If set equal to YES, the system will pause if there is an error in the CONFIG.SYS file.
PRIORITY		Specifies how priority will be allocated to different processes.
PROTECTONLY		If set equal to YES, then only OS/2 protected mode programs will be allowed to run.
PROTSHELL		Specifies a program shell and a command processor for the protected mode.
REM		Used to include comments in the CONFIG.SYS file.
RMSIZE		Sets the real mode's memory size.
RUN		Specifies a program or background process to run during system initialization.
SHELL	Yes	Specifies a real mode command processor.
SWAPPATH		Specifies the location for a "swap" file, used when swapping memory to disk or vice-versa.
THREADS		Specifies the maximum number of threads (individual processes) allowed.
TIMESLICE		Selects the minimum and maximum number of milliseconds allowed per timeslice (time allocated to each thread).

Table 6-3. Continued.

The following device drivers are available under OS/2. As with DOS, they are installed using the DEVICE = command in the CONFIG.SYS file:

ANSI.SYS   Loads the ANSI.SYS console driver into memory for use in the real mode only.

COM01.SYS   A device driver that controls the serial port.

EGA.SYS	Used to support a mouse in the various EGA (Enhanced Graphics Display) screen modes and resolutions.
EXTDSKDD.SYS	A device driver that allows the addition of external floppy drives.
MOUSEA??.SYS	Loads device drivers for support of the various mouse pointing devices made by Microsoft.
POINTDD.SYS	Creates a pointer image (from the mouse pointing device) on the screen.
VDISK.SYS	A device driver used to configure parts of memory as a RAM disk.

OS/2 BATCH FILES

Like everything else with OS/2, its batch files are remarkably similar to the old DOS batch files. The only visible difference is that the protected mode batch files have the extension .CMD rather than .BAT.

OS/2 can only run three different types of programs, all based on the program's filename extensions. As with DOS, these are .COM, .EXE and .CMD. In real mode, they are .COM, .EXE, and .BAT.

Besides the new .CMD filename extension, OS/2 adds the following batch file commands to protected mode batch files:

ANSI	Turns extended keyboard and screen control on or off.
ENDLOCAL	Restores the drive, directory and environment to what they were when the SETLOCAL command was issued.
EXTPROC	Defines an external batch file processor.
SETLOCAL	Saves the current drive, directory and environment. These can then be altered by the batch file and subsequently restored to their original states via the ENDLOCAL command.

A final difference with OS/2 is how it reacts to a user pressing CTRL–BREAK to halt a batch file. In the real mode, this works just like it does under DOS: you see the famous "Terminate batch file (Y/N)?" prompt and are allowed to press Y to continue the batch file or N to stop it. Under OS/2's protected mode, however, pressing CTRL–BREAK immediately stops the batch file and returns you to the OS/2 command prompt.

OS/2 uses two types of AUTOEXEC.BAT file. The first is STARTUP.CMD. The second is OS2INIT.CMD. Both serve the same functions as AUTOEXEC.BAT, yet they are customized to work in the OS/2 environment. (AUTOEXEC.BAT, or AUTOEXEC.OS2, is used when the real mode first starts.)

STARTUP.CMD

STARTUP.CMD is the batch file run when you first boot your OS/2 system. Like DOS, OS/2 reads in various system files, including CONFIG.SYS, and then it looks for and executes the commands in STARTUP.CMD. This batch file is run only once, when you first boot OS/2.

OS2INIT.CMD

OS2INIT.CMD is run each time a new session is started in the protected mode. So, if you want to start another OS/2 "Command Prompt" session, the OS2INIT.CMD batch file will be run again—once for each new session you start. Typically, OS2INIT.CMD is the final command in STARTUP.CMD.

This may sound confusing at first, but as you work with OS/2 you'll find some interesting applications for both of these startup batch files. For example, my STARTUP.CMD file looks like this:

```
1:  @ECHO OFF
2:  ECHO This is OS/2
3:  VER
4:
5:  OS2INIT.CMD
```

Very simply, this displays the message "This is OS/2" followed by the OS/2 copyright notice (VER—the same as the DOS VER command):

```
This is OS/2

The Microsoft Operating System/2 Version is 1.00
```

The final thing my STARTUP.CMD file does is to run OS2INIT.CMD. Realistically, this should be an automatic operation. Unfortunately, you must specify OS2INIT if you want it to run for your initial protected mode session.

My OS2INIT.CMD file looks like this:

```
1:  @ECHO OFF
2:  PATH=C:\;C:\OS2\BIN;C:\OS2\PBIN
3:  PROMPT = [$p]
4:  ANSI ON > NUL
5:  ECHO Welcome to OS/2
6:  ECHO Now whatcha gonna do?
```

This sets my path to all the important protected mode directories (and the root directory, of all places). Then I set my prompt to the standard OS/2 prompt: the current drive and path between brackets. The ANSI ON command turns on the ANSI.SYS driver for this OS/2 session; > NUL redirects the output to the NUL device, which suppresses the "ANSI is on" message. Finally, I display a funny little rhyme:

```
Welcome to OS/2
Now whatcha gonna do?

[C:\]
```

This is in reference, of course, to the fact that I own no OS/2 software, and having nothing to do with OS/2 other than write silly little batch files.

For each new protected mode session I start OS2INIT.CMD runs, setting my path and prompt and displaying that silly, yet accurate, rhyme.

Summary

OS/2 is the next generation of operating system for IBM compatible computers. It runs only on 80286 and 80386 computers. Older, 8088 and 8086 systems will be unable to run OS/2. Also, your 80286 or 80386 system will need at least 1.5 megabytes of RAM to accommodate OS/2.

There are two operating modes in OS/2. The *real* mode, also called the DOS 3x box, operates similar to DOS version 3.3. Older DOS programs can run in the real mode, though they cannot take advantage of OS/2's true power.

The *protected* mode is the true OS/2 mode. In this mode, several programs can be run simultaneously. Each program is called a session and you can run as many sessions as your system allows.

As far as batch files are concerned, OS/2 real mode batch files are identical to DOS batch files. In the protected mode, batch files end with the .CMD extension. Also, there are four new batch file commands you can use in the protected mode: ANSI, ENDLOCAL, EXTPROC, and SETLOCAL.

OS/2's AUTOEXEC is divided into two batch files. STARTUP.CMD is run the first time OS/2 boots (only once). A second type of AUTOEXEC file, OS2INIT.CMD, is run each time a new OS/2 protected mode session is started.

Part Two

Batch File Programming

NOW that you are all boned up on DOS, you're ready to apply that knowledge to your batch files. That's what PART TWO is all about: programming batch files. Because batch files use DOS (or is that what makes DOS easier to use?), after wading through all the information in PART ONE, you should come up with some interesting concoctions. The information in this part of the book will help.

7
Programming Tools

All programming languages, even batch files, have many parts. In all cases, the end result is a program you've written that instructs your computer to do something. How you get from the basic idea in your head—the "Hey, I need a program (or batch file) that does blah blah," —to the actual program that does blah blah—is what this chapter is all about.

Of primary concern here are programming tools: those things you need to write, edit and run batch files. The tools include a text editor or some other method of writing the batch file; the batch file commands themselves; the DOS commands that are used with batch files; and the variables that batch files employ. Put them all together and you have advanced batch file programming.

STANDARD PROCEDURES

Perhaps the best thing about computers is that you can tell them exactly what to do—and they'll do it (even when it's wrong). For most people, this means telling the computer that they want to use a word processor to write a letter. But for others, it means that you can program the computer, instructing it to do exactly what you want it to do.

There are varying degrees of programming language complexity, depending on how "friendly" you want them, or how close you want to get to programming the computer hardware directory. Just about the friendliest programming language around is the batch file programming language. Another friendly language is BASIC. Pascal is a bit more rigid in its structure than BASIC, but still friendly (and popular). C is getting toward the obscure-yet-powerful end of the spectrum. And assembly language is as close as you can get to telling the computer's microprocessor exactly what it is you want it to do (almost like grunt and point).

All the above languages and more can be grouped into two types: interpreted and compiled. Only BASIC and the batch file programming languages are interpreted. This means, simply, that the computer examines each instruction one at a time, then carries out that task.

Compiled languages involve a few more steps. First, a compiled language has source code, written with a text editor. The source code contains all the programming instructions and information for a compiler. The compiler translates the source code, which is basically English text, into an "object" format, or sometimes directly into machine-readable code. The object format is then run through a "linker" that creates the final program (see TABLE 7-1).

Table 7-1.

Compiler Steps	Interpreted Steps	Tools Used
Edit/Create	Edit/Create	Editor
Compile	(not needed)	Compiler/Assembler
Link	(not needed)	Linker program
Run	Run	DOS

The extra steps, compile and link, make a compiled program run much faster than an interpreted one. But compiled programs take longer to write, test and debug. Interpreted programs, on the other hand, are easy to write and run. For example, you simply write the text for a batch file, then type the batch file's name at the command prompt and it runs. Because it's interpreted, however, batch files can be really slow—especially because they fetch each line of text from the disk one at a time.

Compiled programs may offer speed of execution and interpreted programs offer quick development. For batch file programming, all you need are tools to create the programs. These are: editing tools to write the batch file; the batch file programming language, which consists of DOS commands, batch file directives, and third party utilities; DOS itself to translate, or interpret, each line of the batch file. Fortunately, you get most of these items free with DOS.

EDITORS

Batch files must be text files, composed solely of ASCII characters.

The ASCII limitation isn't really a hard and fast rule. After all, as seen in Chapter 3, it's possible to embed control characters in batch files. It's also possible to have the extended ASCII character set used, for example, to display line graphics. If a non-ASCII character is used in a batch file, for example a word processing code, chances are that the batch file won't work properly.

So, the first step to writing a batch file is to find the proper tool to do the job. As was discussed in Chapter 1, there are three popular methods of creating a batch file:

- A Word Processor
- DOS
- A Text Editor

These are listed in order from top to bottom as "worst" to "best" based on my recommendations. The end result always must be the same: a text file on disk with the .BAT filename extension. How you get there is up to you.

Word Processors—Not the Best Way

If you're going to be doing any serious batch file programming, or any programming, you're going to need to get a text editor. Word Processors are nice for writing, composing letters, writing stories, books and plays—creative verbal stuff. But programming requires only text. You don't need all the pretty margins, headers, footnotes, spell checkers, underline printing and whatnot. Just plain text.

For example, most word processors "wrap" a line of text, rather than insisting that you press ENTER at the end of each line (like a typewriter). The batch file interpreter needs that *ENTER* character to signal an end of line. Actually, it really needs the combination carriage return and line feed characters. Some word processors simply put a carriage return character at the end of a line. If you ever encounter a "Bad Command or Filename" error message, or notice that not all your batch file's commands are executing, it's probably because you're missing a line feed character somewhere.

Some word processors save their files in a unique format, keeping their formatting codes, font changes, and other pretty things intact. You don't want that in a batch file. So, in order to save a batch file program in a word processor, you'll need to specifically save the file as a non-document, text, or ASCII formatted file. Furthermore, some word processors have different formats for ASCII files. If so, you'll want the "DOS" text format, with a carriage return and linefeed character at the end of every line: a major bother.

If you like using a word processor, by all means stick with it. Just make sure that you save your batch files in the text mode. Also, be prepared to wait, seeing that most word processors take longer to load and save text files than any of the text editors discussed later in this section.

Quick and Dirty: Using DOS

I would estimate that 100 percent of the batch files that are less than four lines in length were created using DOS. It's the quickest and easiest way to create any text file, and you don't even need a program.

On the other hand, using DOS to create a batch file means no editing. Once a line of text is entered and sealed with the ENTER key, it's done! I don't need to tell you how many times I've used DOS to create a batch file, then absentmindedly pressed the up-arrow key to fix a previous line. No matter how hard I try, it just doesn't work.

This quick and easy way, of course, is using the famous COPY CON "function" of DOS. Actually, this is simply using DOS to copy a file from the CONsole device to a batch file name. Because DOS is device driven, this is possible:

```
C> COPY CON TEST.BAT
```

DOS is now ready for you to type your text. The characters you enter will be copied to a DOS file named TEST.BAT. If TEST.BAT doesn't exist, it will be created. If it does exist, DOS will overwrite it with the new information.

If you've never done this before, or even if you have, here are the rules for creating a text file using COPY CON:

- You are allowed to edit each line up until the time ENTER is pressed. The DOS editing keys (see below) are available for working on the current line only. Once ENTER is pressed, the line is locked into memory.
- Pressing CTRL–Z ends input and creates the file. You must follow CTRL–Z with ENTER. CTRL–Z can be at the end of a line or on a line by itself.
- Pressing CTRL–C cancels the COPY CON operation and returns you to DOS.

The following is an example of a short batch file created with COPY CON:

```
C> COPY CON SHORT.BAT
@ECHO OFF
VOL
VER
^Z
        1 File(s) copied
```

On the last line, CTRL–Z was pressed to end input. The final file was "copied" from the console to disk and named SHORT.BAT. Presto! You have created a batch file.

Using COPY CON isn't as limited as it may appear. For one, you have access to the DOS editing keys. These are the often ignored function key commands for manipulating information in DOS's input buffer. (They're also available at the command prompt.)

By using the editing keys in TABLE 7-2, you can have limited control over the line you're currently working on. Also, because DOS retains the previous line in the input buffer's "template," you can edit or re-use it as well. Further explanations of the function keys in TABLE 7-1 are provided in Appendix F.

Most people would use COPY CON more often if they were aware of these function keys and what they could do. For creating fast batch files, nothing beats it. But, when you need more sophistication, one step above COPY CON (actually, a giant leap toward batch file writing nirvana) is the text editor.

Table 7-2.

DOS Editing Function Keys

F1	Right Arrow	Move cursor right, display next character in the template (if any)
F2		(Followed by a character) Search for character, display template up to that character
F3		Display the rest of the template
F4		(Followed by a character) Delete up to the character
F5		Reset the template, replacing it with the Characters entered so far
	CTRL–Z	End input, write file after pressing *Enter*
Enter	CTRL–M	Accept current line, begin new line
ESC	CTRL–[	Cancel current line, start over
Backspace	Left Arrow	Move back one character
DEL		Remove character from template
INS		Insert characters into the template (can be toggled on and off)

Text Editors

Text editors differ from word processors because they only edit text. There are rarely any text formatting abilities, and only a handful of the popular text editors have any printing facilities. You can forget underline, bold, superscript and italics. Instead, text editors were designed to create and edit text files. This is ideal for programming and any other type of work where text files are required.

Like all microcomputer software, there are dozens of text editors on the market. Some are free, some shareware, and some cost more than most word processors do. The power and capability of the text editor determines its price. Believe it or not, just because a text editor isn't a word processor doesn't mean its short on features. For programming work, there are a lot more goodies you'll require than when you're writing prose.

Recommendations

If you don't already have a text editor, there are two that I recommend in addition to EDLIN that came with DOS. They are *PC Write*, which is really a full featured word processor but serves well as a text editor, and the other is my personal favorite, *See* (pronounced S–E–E). There are other text editors on the market and they are discussed later in this section.

PC WRITE

PC Write isn't just a text editor. It's a full fledged word processor, but still a favorite for writing dBASE, assembly langauge, C, and batch file programs. Also,

PC Write is an interesting computer software success story. Offered since the early days of the PC as "shareware," QuickSoft eventually became a full fledged and thriving company that now sells its product commercially.

Even though it's a word processor, *PC Write* saves its text in ASCII format. As long as you turn word wrap off (SHIFT–F7), *PC Write* is quite a handy editor to have. In fact, you may want to incorporate it as the default editor for programs such as *ProComm* and *dBASE* that allow a secondary editor program.

The only limitation to *PC Write* is that it's files can be only 60K in size. This is more of a limitation on the word processor size of the program because it's doubtful that you'll write any batch file that's 60K in length. (Most text editors have a limited file size.)

Presently, version 3.0 of *PC Write* is under production by Quicksoft. Supposedly, this new version of the program will make it even more powerful. In the meantime, *PC Write* can be obtained from a number of sources and, in most cases, for free. As part of the shareware agreement, you can use the program for a while to test it. Then, if you keep on using it, you're asked to pay a nominal fee for registration. Full registration for *PC Write* is $89, which includes the manual and full support.

PC Write
Quicksoft, Inc.
219 1st Ave N #224-B
Seattle, WA 98109-9911
206-282-0452

See

See is the editor I personally use. I downloaded it from a BBS a long time ago, thinking it was shareware or public domain. It's not. The author is Michael Ouye (oh-way), who now writes Macintosh software. The asking price is $50 for the program, or for $100 you can get the source code.

See's best advantage is that it's quick-loading and -saving. This comes in handy for quickly editing things like batch files. You simply load the text, edit it, then save it back out to disk. No waiting.

See is a modal text editor. The ESCape key toggles you between text entering and editing modes. Once you get used to this, editing can get quite fast. *See* is able to handle any size file up to about 64K—which is more than enough room for batch files.

Some users may find *See* annoying because it's more along the lines of a program editor rather than a word processor. Yet, once you know the commands, editing with *See* is fast and easy.

See Editor
C Ware Corporation
PO Box 428
Passo Robles, CA 93447
805-239-4620

And, of Course, EDLIN

No one ever has anything nice to say about EDLIN. Well, how about this: it's free. Everyone has it, and, as pointed out earlier in this book, it's one of the few word processors that will let you enter the ESCape character into the text (and other control characters as well).

There are two problems with EDLIN that make everyone hate it. The first is its confusing command structure. Sure, it's easy to remember that I is insert and D delete, but do the line numbers come before or after the command? Here's a hint:

> *In* EDLIN, *the line number comes*
> before *the command.*

1D means to delete line 1. D1 means delete the current line, then edit line one. Confusing? Yes.

Also, the second problem with EDLIN is that it's line-oriented. You can only edit one line of text at a time—and you're limited to DOS's function key editing, meaning you can't really see what you're working on.

On the bright side, EDLIN automatically makes a backup copy of your work, so you'll never lose any originals. Of course, some people don't like their disks littered with .BAK files.

The DOS manual has a complete reference and a brief tutorial on EDLIN. Also, Appendix G of this book has a command summary and reference.

Other Text Editors

Besides the above, other popular text editors are *Brief*, the *Norton Editor*, *SideKick*, and *WordStar*.

Brief   *Brief* is the most sophisticated programming editor you can buy—and the most expensive. It's abilities go beyond what I could describe here. Because of Brief's advanced features, and the fact that it's really designed for a C, assembly language, or dBASE compiling efforts, a few would accuse it of being too powerful for writing batch files. Though this may be the case, you should seriously look into purchasing *Brief* if you plan to be doing any extensive programming.

Brief
Solution Systems
541 Main Street Suite 410
South Weymouth MA 02910

The Norton Editor   Contrary to popular belief, master programmer Peter Norton did not write the *Norton Editor*. Someone else did. Still, now that you're crushed, the *Norton Editor* is a handy text editor, written for only one purpose: writing programs. (What else would you expect from Peter Norton Computing?)

The Norton Editor
Peter Norton Computing, Inc.
2210 Wilshire Boulevard, # 186
Santa Monica, CA 90403

SideKick   *SideKick* is the venerable "good buddy" program. Not only does it have an editor that you can pop-up and use at any time, but it has other memory-resident utilities as well, including a handy calculator.

SideKick is nice because, once loaded, it's always there. The only drawback to the *SideKick* editor is that it has a clumsy way of saving and loading files. Also, it sucks up a great deal of memory and may conflict with some of your other programs.

SideKick
Borland International
4585 Scotts Valley Drive
Scotts Valley, CA 95066

WordStar   *WordStar* is an official, deluxe word processor. The current version even supports spell checking and offers a thesaurus—things you rarely need when batch file programming. By the way, I'm talking about the old *WordStar*, the unfriendly, cursor-diamond pattern, control-key WordStar of the CP/M days of computing. This isn't the behemoth slug WordStar 2000 (or whatever they're calling it nowadays).

Believe it or not, *WordStar* was every famous programmer's first text editor. Even *SideKick* and *dBASE* use its famous key commands. Back in the good old days, *WordStar* was all a programmer had to write long expanses of code. Today, with *WordStar*'s added features, it would make an excellent choice as both a text editor and word processor.

WordStar
MicroPro International
PO Box 7079
San Rafael, CA 94901
1-800-227-5609

There are other editors as well, including a whole slew of editors that mimic the UNIX-style editors "vi" and *EMACS* (or *JOVE*). Because I can't stand UNIX, I didn't bother with any of these. If you must, however, several of these public domain/shareware editors are available from the PC–SIG library. (Their number is in Appendix L.)

BATCH FILE COMMANDS

Besides an editor to create batch files, another tool you'll need is the batch file programming language itself. Batch file commands are a mixture of DOS's command and the special batch file directives included with DOS. This section covers an introduction to the batch file commands. This section covers some interesting DOS commands that augment the batch file commands. Of course, any DOS command names and programs can be part of a batch file.

Batch file commands are those DOS commands and functions that were written to specifically aid in the writing of batch files. Some of these commands can be used at the command prompt. Others only have meaning in batch files.

TABLE 7-3 briefly describes the various batch file commands and what they do. PART FIVE of this book contains a complete "cookbook" of all the batch file commands, along with descriptions and examples. (Yes, there are only eight official batch file commands.)

Table 7-3.

Batch File Directives	Description
CALL	"Runs" a second batch file, like a BASIC subroutine
ECHO	Turns ECHO on/off, sends strings to the console
FOR	Repeats a command for a given group of files
GOTO	Transfers execution to a label
IF	Executes a command on a given condition
PAUSE	Displays a pause message and waits for any key
REM	Allows REMarks in batch files
SHIFT	Rotates, or shifts, replaceable parameter variables

There are other elements of batch files, certain functions and variables such as EXIST, ERRORLEVEL, DO, NOT and " = = ", which are also incorporated into the batch file language. The following descriptions elaborate on those batch files commands and the use of them. Again, refer to the cookbook section for more details.

FOR

The FOR command is used by both batch files and on the DOS command line. Like the BASIC programming language's FOR–NEXT loop, the batch file statement FOR allows you to do a number of commands at a time. The format is:

FOR %*variable* in (*file selection*) DO *command*

variable is a one character variable. In DOS, *variable* is preceded by a single percent sign; in batch files, there must be two percent signs.

file selection is a list of files, including wild cards, full pathnames, or just a list of individual filenames.

command is a DOS command. Usually *command* incorporates *variable* to perform some action on the list of files in *file selection*.

In a nutshell, FOR repeats the DOS command listed after DO for as many times as there are files in *file selection*. The *variable* is used to represent each individual file.

```
FOR %A IN (MENU*.* SUB*.* CTRL*.*) DO COPY %A B:\STOW
```

This FOR command operates on three groups of files, MENU*.*, SUB*.* and CTRL*.*. For each of those files, FOR will DO the command:

```
COPY %A B:\STOW
```

Each time FOR executes the DO command, %A is replaced by one of the three filenames. So the single FOR command does the same thing as the following three commands:

```
COPY MENU*.* B:\STOW
COPY SUB*.* B:\STOW
COPY CTROL*.* B:\STOW
```

Fundamentally, that's the extent of the FOR command. It performs a single DOS command on a variety of files as specified between the parentheses. But keep in mind that, when used in a batch file, two percent signs are used instead of one.

IF

IF is used in batch files to evaluate a condition—just like the BASIC IF programming statement. The only difference is that there is no THEN or ELSE statement to follow IF:

IF [NOT]*condition command*

condition is an evaluation or compare. If **condition** is true, then **command** is executed. Otherwise, batch file execution continues with the next line.

NOT is a logical switch that can be placed before condition. When NOT is specified and **condition** is true, then **command** is executed—the opposite of IF's normal operation.

command is another batch file command. Typically it's a GOTO, though it could be any command—even another IF statement.

condition is evaluated using two batch file commands, the EXIST test and the ERRORLEVEL variable. Also, a double equal-sign operator is used for string comparisons.

EXIST tests the existence of files:

IF EXIST *.* . . .   If any files exist (*.*), then **condition** is true and **command** is executed.

IF EXIST JUNE.DAT . . .   If the file JUNE.DAT exists in the current directory, **condition** is true and **command** is executed.

NOT can be used to see if a file doesn't exist:

IF NOT EXIST JUNE.DAT . . .   **condition** is evaluated as true here only if the file JUNE.DAT does not exist. If it exists, then **command** isn't executed and the batch file continues with the next line.

ERRORLEVEL is used to test the return code from certain programs.

When programs return to DOS, they can do so in four manners (*see* Chapter 1). If they return properly (according to Microsoft), they'll return a code value from 0 to 255. The ERRORLEVEL variable is used to hold the program's return code.

ERRORLEVEL is followed immediately by a comparison code value. If ERRORLEVEL is greater than, or equal to, that value, the **condition** is true and **command** is executed:

IF ERRORLEVEL 1 . . .   If an ERRORLEVEL value of 1 or greater is returned by the previous program, **command** is executed. (Appendix I contains a list of DOS programs and their return codes.)

= = (double equal signs) are used to compare string values. These can include environment variables or replaceable parameters, as well as string constants. Incidentally, both strings must be exact, upper case for upper case and lower case for lower case. If both strings are identical, **condition** is true, and **command** is executed.

IF %LOGIN% = =STEVE . . .   This command tests to see if the value of the environment variable LOGIN is equal to the string "STEVE". If so, **command** is executed. To see if the strings are not equal, use NOT:

IF NOT %LOGIN% = =STEVE . . .   Keep this rule in mind:

> *When comparing strings with* IF,
> *two equal signs are used*

This is to avoid confusion with BASIC, where only one equal sign is used when comparing variables.

command is executed in this case only if the contents of the environment variable LOGIN are not equal to "STEVE".

The batch file example in FIG. 7-1 shows how the IF statement is used to test for the existence of a file. The batch file simply scans two directories on disk,\ TEMP (5) and \ASM\BATCH (7), and deletes any *.BAK files found. IF EXIST is used to first test if any *.BAK files exist. If so, the **command** DEL *.BAK is used to remove those offending files.

Name: KILLBAK.BAT

```
 1: @ECHO OFF
 2: REM Remove .BAK files from where they may be lurking
 3: ECHO Removing ugly .BAK files...
 4: C:
 5: CD \TEMP
 6: IF EXIST *.BAK DEL *.BAK
 7: CD \ASM\BATCH
 8: IF EXIST *.BAK DEL *.BAK
 9: ECHO Done
10: :END
```

Fig. 7-1. An IF statement tests for the existence of a file.

DOS COMMANDS

The following is a list of several DOS commands that work quite well with batch files. In fact, some of them have become "hall of fame" tricks used with most advanced batch file programming.

This is not a list of all DOS commands that can be used with batch files (because, well, all DOS commands can be used with batch files). Instead, the following are some DOS commands that you can use to enhance your batch files.

A TYPE of Shortcut

One of the worst examples of batch file programming is the overuse of the ECHO command. I cringe each time I see an entire screen full of text scroll up one line at a time, meaning someone used 24 ECHO statements to get his point across.

Rather than use multiple ECHOes to get the job done, use the DOS TYPE command. TYPE will quickly and nicely display an entire screen of text—a lot faster than ECHO (which needs to go to the disk each time it executes).

The only drawback to using TYPE is that you must know the exact name and location of the file you'll be typing. As long as you specify a full pathname (and are certain that the file exists), however, TYPE really makes displaying text a lot smoother than over-using ECHO.

Speed Trick

When displaying a long file, for example, with TYPE, information may scroll off the screen before the user has a chance to read it. You can solve this problem by putting at the top of the file:

"Press Control-S to pause the display, Control-Q to continue"

but most users won't see that message until it's too late. Instead, you can use the MORE filter that came with DOS. There are two ways to use MORE:

```
TYPE MESSAGE.TXT | MORE
```

```
MORE < MESSAGE.TXT
```

Both of these methods will display the contents of the text file MESSAGE.TXT. Each method correctly uses the MORE filter to pause the display of text after each screen. The second method is faster than the first, however.

The first method uses the TYPE command to send the contents of MESSAGE.TXT to the MORE filter. This takes time because both TYPE and MORE are being used at once. Because the second method uses I/O redirection to send the contents of MESSAGE.TXT directly into the MORE filter, it's faster.

IF EXIST

So many users write batch files that run quite smoothly—except for those occasional "File not found" error messages. There's a simple way around this: Use

IF EXIST. In fact, adding the IF statement to any command that deals with a file is easy. For example

```
DEL *.BAK
```

This command can be used in a batch file to delete all those terrible .BAK files that accumulate all over your hard disk. But what if they're all gone? Then your batch file will display a string of those "File not found" messages. Instead, you can modify the above line as follows:

```
IF EXIST *.BAK DEL *.BAK
```

Painless—and no more phantom error messages.

>NUL

This is a popular trick you might have seen at various locations in this book. The NUL device is the "door to nowhere." Though it's a real device, and can be used with I/O redirection like any other device, it really doesn't put anything anywhere. So, it's a safe bet that when you redirect output to the NUL device it will be invisible.

>NUL is most often used in "silent" batch files. When you don't want the user to see something, or when the results of a command need not be displayed, simply redirect them to the NUL device. For example:

```
COPY *.* E:\SPOOL
```

This command copies a whole gang of files to the directory \SPOOL on drive E (assume it's an electronic disk). If this line were in a batch file, and ECHO were turned off, either one of the following may be displayed on the screen:

```
3 File(s) copied
```

or

```
File not found - ????????.???
        0 File(s) copied
```

(The number of files copied varies depending on how many files *.* represents.)

Needless to say, those messages, especially the latter, will be confusing. So, rather than risk confusion, simply use >NUL to redirect any output to the NUL device. Whatever the results of the COPY command, the screen will remain clean.

By the way, you can avoid the above situation by using the IF EXIST command, as shown in FIG. 7-2.

```
1: @ECHO OFF
2: CD \WS\PRINT
3: IF EXIST *.* GOTO COPYTHEM
4: ECHO No files found to copy
5: GOTO END
6: :COPYTHEM
7: COPY *.* C:\TEMP >NUL
8: ECHO Files copied to spool directory
9: :END
```

Fig. 7-2. To keep the screen clean, use the IF EXIST command.

IF EXIST tests for the existence of any files in the directory \WS\PRINT (3). If any file (*.*) is found, the EXIST test proves true and execution branches to the COPYTHEM label (6). Otherwise, the "No files found to copy" message is echoed (4) and the program stops (5, 9).

>NUL is used in line 7 to suppress the listing of the files as they are copied, as well as the final DOS message telling you how many files were copied. Line 8 ECHOes a message to the screen telling the user what has happened. This is always a wise idea after any potentially long disk activity.

YES, NO, ENTER, ENTERN

Another I/O redirection trick is the use of small files that contain the answers to some familiar questions:

```
Are you sure (y/n)?
```

```
Press ENTER to continue
```

When running a batch file, you may want to perform some actions that make it necessary for the user to press Y or press ENTER to confirm some choice. This is risky. First, who really knows what a user will press? Second, why risk them messing up your batch file by insisting that they press Y when they don't even know why (or wouldn't understand the reason even if you told them)?

The trick is to use I/O redirection to provide the answer for them. They'll never know the difference.

Somewhere on your system you should have several small files. The first file should contain a "Y" followed by a carriage return/linefeed, the second should contain an "N" followed by a carriage return/linefeed, and the third should contain only the carriage return/linefeed. These files should be named YES, NO, and ENTER respectively. You can use DOS to create them (see FIG. 7-3).

```
                              C> COPY CON YES
                              Y
                              ^Z

                              C> COPY CON NO
                              N
Fig. 7-3. To create files YES, NO and ENTER . . .   ^Z

                              C> COPY CON ENTER

                              ^Z

                              C>
```

A fourth file can be named ENTERN. It's to be used with I/O redirection to replace pressing ENTER and then the N key:

```
C> COPY CON ENTERN

N
^Z

C>
```

Remember to press ENTER after Y and N. The character ^Z is obtained by pressing CTRL-Z, or F6. These files are now ready to be used to answer common questions that pop up during batch file execution.

As an example, I use the batch file in FIG. 7-4 on an update disk at the end of my work day. I don't want to use the BACKUP program because it saves the

```
 1: @ECHO OFF
 2: REM Program files update
 3: REM can be run from any subdirectory on drive
 4: C:
 5: ECHO Updating program files subdirectory
 6: ECHO Insert diskette "ONE" in drive A and
 7: PAUSE
 8: ECHO Formatting . . .
 9: REM "ENTERN" must be cr/lf + "N" + cr/lf or
    keyboard locks
10: FORMAT A: <C:\SYSTEM\UTIL\ENTERN >NUL
11: ECHO Done!  Copying files . . .
12: COPY \BATCH\DISK\*.* A: >NUL
13: ECHO Done!
```

Fig. 7-4. This batch file I use to back up my files.

files in a funky format that I can't use. A disk created with BACKUP can only be undone by the RESTORE command (and from the same version of DOS). So I just want a disk full of files. As long as my files don't occupy more space than is on the disk, that's fine.

Also, I want to make sure no other files are on the disk before I copy my files to it. There are two ways I could ensure this. The first is to reformat the disk each time, before I copy the files to it. And the second is to delete all files already on the disk. The first is safer—the second is quicker. The batch files in FIG. 7-4 demo both versions.

This is a "silent" batch file (1, 10, 12). Because of that, there are quite a few ECHO statements to let the user know what's going on. The first two ECHO statements (5, 6) direct the user to put the diskette ONE into drive A, then press any key to continue (7). Line 10 formats the disk, which is where the first tricky input redirection technique takes place.

The REM statement in line 9 reminds you that the data in ENTERN must contain a carriage return/linefeed plus the "N" character followed by another carriage return/linefeed. This is supplied to answer the two questions that FORMAT (10) asks: "Strike ENTER when ready" and after the formatting, "Format another (y/n) ?" If you forget to supply the "N", DOS will sit and wait for input. Because input is redirected from the file, if the N isn't there, you're keyboard is locked and you may have to reset to get control of your computer.

Also, the output of the FORMAT command is redirected to the NUL statement. This way, a user will not know that the diskette is being formatted (unless they have a good ear and can "hear" it being formatted.)

The final step is to copy the files from the special subdirectory (12) to drive A. Again, the ECHO command is used (11, 13) to tell the user exactly what's going on.

The batch file in FIG. 7-4 is time consuming because it always reformats the diskette before continuing. The example in FIG. 7-5 is faster. This program is a slight modification of the first batch file. The difference takes place in line 8, where DEL A:*.* is used instead of FORMAT to clean the disk of any files. The redirected input for the DEL command is provided by the YES file. YES contains a "Y" followed by a carriage return/linefeed. This input will answer the question "Are you sure?" and the redirected output will make the entire operation invisible to the user.

```
 1: @ECHO OFF
 2: REM Program files update
 3: REM can be run from any subdirectory on drive
 4: C:
 5: ECHO Updating program files subdirectory
 6: ECHO Insert diskette "ONE" in drive A and
 7: PAUSE
 8: DEL A:\*.* <C:\SYSTEM\UTIL\YES >NUL
 9: ECHO Copying files . . .
10: XCOPY \BATCH\DISK\*.* A: >NUL
11: ECHO Done!
```

Fig. 7-5. This batch file is a faster backup program.

If redirected input were not provided in line 8, the batch file would stop and wait for either "Y" or "N" to be pressed. Because output is redirected to the NUL device, the user wouldn't have a clue what was going on. Also, unlike the FORMAT command example, the YES file need only contain a "Y" and a carriage return/linefeed. There are no further questions asked by DEL *.*, so the "Y" is sufficient to erase all the files.

Finally, to add some zip to this batch file, the XCOPY command is used to copy a whole slew of files at a time. Unlike COPY, which reads and copies one file at a time, XCOPY reads as many files as will fit into RAM at a time, then writes them out at once. Combined with >NUL, this makes the updating procedure run extremely fast.

CTTY

The CTTY command is one of those strange, last-minute things Microsoft probably threw into DOS. It's an interesting command, but a dangerous one. Still, with the right technique, you can translate that danger into something extremely useful.

As any UNIX fiend can attest, any command ending in *TTY is something a novice shouldn't mess with. The same is true for CTTY. What it does is to change the CONsole device. Primarily, it allows you to change the console device to the AUX, or serial port device. (Any serial port, from AUX or COM1, up to COM4).

To demonstrate this, I hooked up a null modem cable between my PC and a Macintosh. After running a communications program on both systems (and making sure the BPS, or Baud, was set properly and other things were working), I "shelled out" of the PC's communications program and typed:

```
CTTY AUX
```

This transferred the console device from the screen and keyboard to the serial port and, indirectly, to the Macintosh. The screen and keyboard on the PC were no longer used for input or output. In fact, the keyboard was frozen. Even pressing CTRL–BREAK had no effect. Yet, when I turned to the Macintosh—there was DOS! I typed all the commands: DIR, COPY—I even used EDLIN. They all worked. (Only DOS programs would work. Other programs that don't use the DOS functions will "hang" the computer.)

Incidentally, I called in a friend and told him I had an IBM Emulator program running on the Macintosh. I had him going for a while. (*See* FIG. 7-6.)

To surrender control of the PC away from the Macintosh (or whatever you have hooked up to your serial port), you must type:

```
CTTY CON
```

I typed this on the Macintosh and, voilà, control was returned (gladly) by the Macintosh to the PC. So what does this have to do with batch files?

Ever run a batch file and want the user absolutely not to break out of it? How about AUTOEXEC.BAT? Ever want that to run uninterrupted? The answer is to

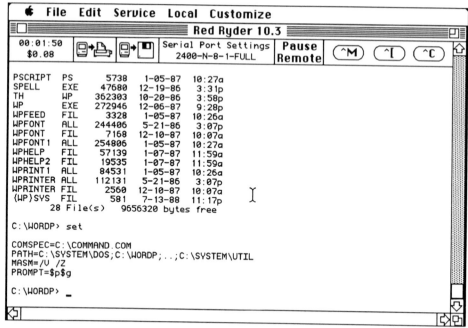

Fig. 7-6. This is a Macintosh communications program "running" an IBM PC after CTTY AUX.

turn off the keyboard using CTTY AUX. But always remember to return control back again with CTTY CON. In fact, using a batch file is the only way you can issue these two commands using only one computer.

There is a problem, however. The problem is with CTRL–BREAK. When you press CTRL–BREAK from the keyboard, that character is still generated (actually, an interrupt is generated and it's the interrupt that causes the problem).

For example, when I was typing DOS commands on my Macintosh's screen, I was also typing on the PC's keyboard to see what would happen. CTRL–C didn't do anything, but pressing CTRL–BREAK caused the ^C character to appear on the Mac's screen:

```
C:\WORDP>  ^C

C:\WORDP>
```

Also, after I typed CTTY CON on the Macintosh, all those characters I typed on the PC appeared on the screen. They had been buffered.

I tried a few more batch files to use CTTY AUX and CTTY CON to shut off the keyboard. While they do work, there is a drawback: If the user types a CTRL–BREAK, the system will hang.

REPLACEABLE PARAMETERS AND VARIABLES

The final concept of "tools" you can use with batch files are replaceable parameters and variables. Like other programming languages, batch files can take advantage of these variables to manipulate information in a variety of circumstances.

There are three types of variables used in batch files:

1) Replaceable parameters

2) Environment variables

3) FOR command variables

Each of these variable types are different, and you should distinguish between them. Unfortunately, all of them look the same (more or less) in that they are designated as variables by the %, percent sign.

All of these variables are expanded by the batch file interpreter into the character strings they represent. This works just as it does for environment variables (*see* Chapter 4). You can turn ECHO ON in your batch files to see the variables expanded as the program runs. The only exceptions to this are the FOR command's variables, which do not expand.

Replaceable Parameters

Replaceable parameter variables are used to represent "arguments," or the text typed after your batch file command. Other programming languages, for example the C language compilers that are available under DOS, also take advantage of these parameters. This way, you can pass instructions to your batch file commands. For example:

```
C> UPDATE \SYSTEM\UTIL \LOTUS\JUNE
```

The name of the program is UPDATE. The first argument is \SYSTEM\UTIL and the second argument is \LOTUS\JUNE. Batch files allow you to use up to nine arguments and represent them by the replaceable parameter variables %1 through %9. When your batch file runs, using the above as an example, %1 will be replaced by "\SYSTEM/UTIL" and %2 will be replaced by "\LOTUS\JUNE".

There are ten replaceable parameter variables that your batch files can take advantage of:

%0 is the command file name, the name of your batch file

%1 is the first word after the batch file name

%2 the second word

%3 the third word

%4 the fourth word

%5 the fifth word

%6 the sixth word

%7 the seventh word

%8 the eighth word

%9 the ninth word

"Words" in this instance are a series of characters surrounded by a space. The characters could be a group of command switches, a filename, a drive letter, a pathname, or a word of English text. Surrounding a string of text with quotes will not make it all one word. Also, anything beyond the ninth word cannot be referenced unless the SHIFT command is used (see below).

The examples in FIG. 7-7 show how replaceable parameters would represent various arguments on the command line.

```
     %0    %1      %2
C> MOVE A:\*.* C:\SYSTEM\UPDATE

%0=MOVE
%1=A:\*.*
%2=C:\SYSTEM\UPDATE

     %0    %1     %2      %3
C> LOGIN 10:12 LITTLE  HENRY

%0=LOGIN
%1=10:12
%2=LITTLE
%3=HENRY
```

Fig. 7-7. This is how replaceable parameters represent various arguments on the command line.

The batch file in FIG. 7-8 can be used to display all the replaceable parameters on the command line. You can use it when writing a batch file to see how the parameters will fall and in what order. When this program runs it displays the contents of each of the parameters. See FIG. 7-9 for an example. Notice that I didn't use "ECHO %1 = %1"; this is because the batch file interpreter would translate both %1's into the variable's value.

Name: BATARG.BAT

```
 1: @ECHO OFF
 2: REM Batch file to display replaceable parameters
 3: ECHO Parameter 0 = %0
 4: ECHO Parameter 1 = %1
 5: ECHO Parameter 2 = %2
 6: ECHO Parameter 3 = %3
 7: ECHO Parameter 4 = %4
 8: ECHO Parameter 5 = %5
 9: ECHO Parameter 6 = %6
10: ECHO Parameter 7 = %7
11: ECHO Parameter 8 = %8
12: ECHO Parameter 9 = %9
```

Fig. 7-8. This displays all replaceable parameters on the command line.

```
C> BATARG C: THIS IS A TEST "HELLO, TOM"
Parameter 0 = BATARG
Parameter 1 = C:
Parameter 2 = THIS
Parameter 3 = IS
Parameter 4 = A
Parameter 5 = TEST
Parameter 6 = "HELLO,
Parameter 7 = TOM"
Parameter 8 =
Parameter 9 =
```

Fig. 7-9. The result of running Fig. 7-8 is shown here.

You can use any information on the command line simply by specifying the replaceable parameter variable in your batch file, as shown in FIG. 7-10. This batch file moves a group of files from one place to another. A move is actually a copy, then delete. So this batch file first copies the files (4) and then deletes the originals (5). Notice how the I/O direction tricks from the previous section are used to suppress the warning messages and whatnot. Also, ECHO is used often (3, 6) to let the user know what's going on.

```
Name: MOVE.BAT

1:  @ECHO OFF
2:  REM MOVE FILES FROM %1 TO %2
3:  ECHO Moving Files...
4:  COPY %1 %2 >NUL
5:  DEL %1 <C:\SYSTEM\UTIL\YES >NUL
6:  ECHO Files moved
```

Fig. 7-10. Specify the replaceable parameter in your batch file.

A typical run of the batch file in FIG. 7-10 might look like this:

```
C> MOVE A:\*.* C:\TEMP\UPDATE
Moving Files...
Files moved

C>
```

All the files from the root directory on drive A (A:*.*) are first copied to subdirectory \TEMP\UPDATE on drive C, and then deleted from drive A. The replaceable parameter %1 is given the value "A:*.*", and %2 is given the value "C:\TEMP\UPDATE". If you change @ECHO OFF to @ECHO ON and run the batch file again, you'll see FIG. 7-11.

```
C> MOVE A:\*.* C:\TEMP\UPDATE

C> REM MOVE FILES FROM %1 TO %2

C> ECHO Moving Files...
Moving Files...

C> COPY A:\*.* C:\TEMP\UPDATE >NUL

C> DEL A:\*.* <C:\SYSTEM\UTIL\YES >NUL
Y
C> ECHO Files moved
Files moved
```

Fig. 7-11. This is the run of Fig. 7-10 after a few changes.

See how %1 and %2 were replaced as the file ran? That "Y" between the last two commands was supplied by the \SYSTEM/UTIL\YES file. (Because ECHO is on, it was echoed to the console.)

There is a problem with this batch file.

If you don't supply any arguments, you'll get the following:

```
C> MOVE
Moving Files...
Invalid number of parameters
Invalid number of parameters
Files moved

C>
```

Doesn't look right, does it?

Testing for Nothing

Because not everyone is going to know if a command needs parameters or not, you'll need to test for their existence. To do this, you'll use the IF command and the equals assignment operator, = = .

Testing for nothing sounds difficult, yet it's an easy technique to remember. Just keep in mind that the batch file interpreter expands variables out to their string values when the batch file is run. If a variable isn't assigned to anything, then it will be expanded into nothing.

The common format for testing for nothing is:

IF *parameter string constant* = = *string constant*

If the above statement is true, then **parameter** doesn't exist. Remember, if there is no variable for **parameter**, it's not expanded. So, when the batch file is run, you'll have:

IF *string constant* = = *string constant*

This evaluates as true. For example:

IF %1TEST==TEST

If %1 is equal to "A:*.*" then the above statement will be expanded to:

IF A:*.*TEST==TEST

That statement is false. Otherwise, if there is no replaceable parameter %1, you'll get:

IF TEST==TEST

You can use any value for a string constant. Most popular is:

IF %1!==!

This is nice because it's brief. It tends to be confusing, however. A novice batch file programmer may wonder if ! doesn't mean something. Instead, I prefer to use "nothing" as my string constant:

IF %1NOTHING==NOTHING

If that statement is true, there is no replaceable parameter %1. You can also check for the reverse:

IF NOT %1NOTHING==NOTHING

This statement will come out true if there is a replaceable parameter %1 (the opposite of the previous example).

To incorporate these examples in the MOVE.BAT file, you only need to add two lines. Just to be nice about things, the batch file now displays an informative message if the first parameter is left out (the second parameter is optional, as it is with the COPY command).

```
 1: @ECHO OFF
 2: REM MOVE FILES FROM %1 TO %2
 3: IF %1NOTHING==NOTHING GOTO WARNING
 4: ECHO Moving Files...
 5: COPY %1 %2 >nul
 6: DEL %1 < C:\SYSTEM\UTIL\YES >NUL
 7: ECHO Files moved
 8: GOTO END
 9: :WARNING
10: ECHO Please specify a source filename
11: :END
```

Fig. 7-12. A few more changes are made to MOV.BAT.

See FIG. 7-12. Line 3 tests for the existence of the first parameter. If it doesn't exist, and NOTHING = = NOTHING, execution branches to the WARNING label (9). Line 10 echoes an error message and then the program ends:

```
C> MOVE
Please specify a source filename

C>
```

If a source filename (%1) is supplied, the test in line 3 fails and execution continues with the rest of the program. Line 8 skips over the warning message (9, 10) and ends the program with the :END label.

You don't need to specify NOTHING = = NOTHING each time you want to test for nothing. In this book, that's the example used because it's also easy to remember. Most of the time, you can get by using a single letter, character or number. The following are all acceptable methods of testing for nothing:

IF %1X = = X . . .

IF %1! = = ! . . .

IF "%1" = = " " . . .

IF NUL%1 = = NUL ...

IF X%1 = = X ...

SHIFT

SHIFT is used primarily with replaceable parameters. It shifts the variable assignments of parameters %0 through %9—and beyond. SHIFT moves the value of the next highest replaceable parameter into the new lowest. Parameter %0 is SHIFTed away (goes bye-bye) and any parameters after %9 are shifted into %9, one for each use of the SHIFT command.

For example, after SHIFT is issued, the value of %2 becomes the new value of %1, %3 becomes %2, %4 becomes %3 and on and on until %9. For the value of %9, the batch file interpreter assigns any "words" to the left of %9 to %9. This way, you can read in arguments well beyond %9—but at the cost of loosing the original values of %1, %2 and so on.

The program in FIG. 7-13 shows how SHIFT alters the contents of the replaceable parameters %0 through %9. This program looks complex, but there's a lot of repeat. First, a GOTO statement (3) causes execution to jump to the :START label (7). The next line tests to see if argument %0 is equal to nothing. The first time through, it will be equal to SHIFTARG, the name of the program. But each time after that, its value will change until it's equal to the final word typed on the command line. When this happens, %1 will equal nothing and the statement, evaluated to *true*, will branch to the :END label (29). A similar test is performed on the first replaceable parameter, %1 (10). This ensures a short program run in case no arguments were typed after SHIFTARG.

Name: SHIFTARG.BAT

```
 1: @ECHO OFF
 2: REM Shift and display parameters
 3: GOTO START
 4: :LOOP
 5: ECHO ==== Shifting ====
 6: SHIFT
 7: :START
 8: IF %0NOTHING==NOTHING GOTO END
 9: ECHO Parameter 0 = %0
10: IF %1NOTHING==NOTHING GOTO END
11: ECHO Parameter 1 = %1
12: IF %2NOTHING==NOTHING GOTO LOOP
13: ECHO Parameter 2 = %2
14: IF %3NOTHING==NOTHING GOTO LOOP
15: ECHO Parameter 3 = %3
16: IF %4NOTHING==NOTHING GOTO LOOP
17: ECHO Parameter 4 = %4
18: IF %5NOTHING==NOTHING GOTO LOOP
19: ECHO Parameter 5 = %5
20: IF %6NOTHING==NOTHING GOTO LOOP
21: ECHO Parameter 6 = %6
22: IF %7NOTHING==NOTHING GOTO LOOP
23: ECHO Parameter 7 = %7
24: IF %8NOTHING==NOTHING GOTO LOOP
25: ECHO Parameter 8 = %8
26: IF %9NOTHING==NOTHING GOTO LOOP
27: ECHO Parameter 9 = %9
28: GOTO LOOP
29: :END
```

Fig. 7-13. This is how SHIFT alters parameters %0 through %9.

After line 12, each IF statement tests for existence of each replaceable parameter. If it exists, it's displayed. Otherwise, execution branches back to the :LOOP statement (4). The ECHO statement in line 5 breaks up the output of the program and lets the user know when a SHIFT statement has taken place. Line 6 contains the SHIFT command that shifts the variable's values.

The best way to see how the file works is to run it (see FIG. 7-14). Graphically, you see how SHIFT moves the values from each replaceable parameter. Because the program tests for the existence of a variable, and bases its "looping" on it, not a lot of space is wasted with the display.

An excellent example of how the SHIFT statement can be used appeared earlier in this book. The COPY2 program uses SHIFT to move several files (as many as can fit on the command line) from one place to another. It uses SHIFT to read in all the filenames—a feat that wouldn't be possible had only variables %1 through %9 been available (see FIG. 7-15).

```
C> SHIFTARG this is a test
Parameter 0 = SHIFTARG
Parameter 1 = this
Parameter 2 = is
Parameter 3 = a
Parameter 4 = test
==== Shifting ====
Parameter 0 = this
Parameter 1 = is
Parameter 2 = a
Parameter 3 = test
==== Shifting ====
Parameter 0 = is
Parameter 1 = a
Parameter 2 = test
==== Shifting ====
Parameter 0 = a
Parameter 1 = test
==== Shifting ====
Parameter 0 = test
C>
```

Fig. 7-14. This is the run of SHIFTARG.BAT.

Name: COPY2.BAT

```
 1: @ECHO OFF
 2: REM A 'Gang Copy' batch file example
 3: IF %1NOTHING==NOTHING GOTO HELP
 4: SET DISK=%1
 5: ECHO Copy a group of files to drive %DISK%
 6: :LOOP
 7: SHIFT
 8: IF %1NOTHING==NOTHING GOTO END
 9: COPY %1 %DISK% >NUL
10: ECHO %1 copied to %DISK%
11: GOTO LOOP
12: :HELP
13: ECHO COPY2 Command format:
14: ECHO copy2 [drive:[\path]] [file1] [file2] .... [fileN]
15: :END
16: SET DISK=
```

Fig. 7-15. This is the COPY2.BAT we have seen before.

The program in FIG. 7-15 also works along a loop structure (between lines 6 and 11). Also, you'll see a test for no parameters in line 3 and a warning message in lines 13 and 14.

The SET instruction in line 4 is used to "remember" the original starting disk location. This location will eventually be SHIFTed off into oblivion. So the variable %DISK% is used to remember the target destination in line 9, also in line 10 for display.

The NOTHING = = NOTHING test in line 8 determines the end of the loop. And finally, being good users of the DOS environment, the program releases its environment variable in line 16.

This program can easily be modified to delete a group of files, or to move files from one drive to another. See if you can do so on your own. Examples are listed at the end of this chapter.

Environment Variables

The environment and environment variables were discussed in Chapter 4. They are variables, however, that can be used in batch files and, as such, fit nicely into the format of this chapter.

Environment variables are different from replacement parameters in that their values are set, and remain, in the system's environment table. Also, the way they're used is different. Unlike replaceable parameters, environment variables are surrounded by percent signs:

%DRIVE%

%STATUS%

%USER NAME%

Environment variables are created by the SET command. They consist of any characters, letters, numbers—or even spaces—up to an = (equal sign). The variable is translated to upper case by DOS, though you can use upper or lower case when specifying the environment variable between percent signs.

The variable name will be replaced by the string assigned to it when a batch file runs. This is part of the batch file interpreter's variable expansion that also takes place with replaceable parameters. Using the SET command, you assign the environment variable to any string of characters (after the equal sign), though the string will not include the carriage return character at the end of the line.

SET DRIVE = A:

SET STATUS = ON

SET USER NAME = Orville the Robot

Though the variable name is translated to upper case, DOS uses whichever case you typed for the variable's data. So, for the above examples:

```
ECHO %STATUS%
```

displays: ON

ECHO %USER NAME%

displays: Orville the Robot

You should note that the expansion will not take place on the command line. It is assumed that the previous two examples would be used in a batch file.

The nice thing about environment variables is that you can create them on the fly. Only remember to reset them when you're through, otherwise you may run out of environment space. To reset the variable, simply re-assign its contents to nothing:

SET VARIABLE =

SET STATUS =

SET USER NAME =

Environment variables are good for storing data, and, as was previously shown, you can use them to temporarily save replaceable parameters as well:

SET TEMP=%1

This assigns the variable TEMP to whatever the parameter %1 is set to. However, you cannot "swap" the contents of two environment variables. For example, observe the following:

SET LOGIN=JULES
SET NAME=LOGIN

This creates two variables in the environment. The first is LOGIN, which has the value "JULES", and the second is "NAME" which has the value "LOGIN". To give NAME the same value as LOGIN, you'll need to use LOGIN as a variable (and remember, this only works in a batch file):

SET NAME=%LOGIN%

When the batch file containing that line runs, %LOGIN% is replaced (expanded) by the batch file interpreter with "JULES". So the end result is that both NAME and LOGIN will equal "JULES".

This can make for a nifty application that saves the system's path:

Name: SAVEPATH.BAT

```
1: @ECHO OFF
2: SET TEMP=%PATH%
3: PATH=C:\SYSTEM\DOS;C:\LOTUS;U:
4: CD \LOTUS
5: 123
6: SET PATH=%TEMP%
```

This batch file runs the program *123* in the \LOTUS subdirectory. But, before that, it saves the PATH in a temporary variable, TEMP. The PATH is reset in line 3, presumably to something that the *123* program likes better than the standard path. Then, after *123* is run (5), the old path is restored.

Before going off and creating batch files like this, be forewarned: You will run out of environment space quicker than you can believe. If that happens, you can always add the SHELL command to your CONFIG.SYS file and specify a larger environment. (Refer to Chapter 4.)

FOR Variables

The third type of variable you'll encounter in a batch file is used by the FOR command. FOR uses two types of variables, depending on if you use FOR in a batch file or in DOS:

% (one percent sign)   DOS

%% (two percent signs)   Batch files

In either case, the character %, is followed by a single character to represent the variable.

The FOR variable is used twice in the FOR command. The first time is to assign the variable to a group of files; the second time is as a wildcard in a DOS command:

```
C> FOR %V IN (*.*) DO COPY %V *.BAK
```

The first use of the variable %V (in DOS) assigns it to the set of files in parenthesis. In this case, %V is equal to every file in the current directory.

The second use of the variable %V is in the DO command. In this case, %V will represent each file on disk, one at a time. FOR repeats the command COPY %V *.BAK for each file found that matches (*.*). Keep in mind that this is not the same thing as "COPY *.* *.BAK." Though that command would work, FOR reads in the files represented by (*.*) one at a time and assigns them to the variable %V.

```
C> FOR %F IN (*.BAT *.COM *.EXE) DO XCOPY %F A:
```

The variable %F will be assigned to three values, *.BAT, *.COM and *.EXE. The second part of the FOR command will then be executed three times, each time %F will be replaced by those three file definitions. This is the same as issuing the three separate commands:

```
C> XCOPY *.BAT A:

C> XCOPY *.COM A:

C> XCOPY *.EXE A:
```

The important things to remember about FOR's variables are:

- In a batch file, two percent signs are used
- In DOS, only one percent sign is used
- The variable name is only one letter long and, with versions of DOS prior to 4.0, cannot be a number
- The FOR command's variable is only used with the FOR command

For Extra Credit

The two batch files in FIG. 7-16 and FIG. 7-17 are modifications to the COPY2.BAT program discussed earlier. The batch file in FIG. 7-16 deletes a group of files, and the batch file in FIG. 7-17 moves a group of files.

Notice how each file makes use of SHIFT, testing for nothing, as well as I/O redirection to suppress messages. The only thing that isn't tested for in these programs is the existence of the files. To test for that, you can use the IF EXIST %1 statement, and then skip over the COPY or DELETE statement if that particular file isn't found. (See, there's always a way to improve upon things.)

```
Name: DEL2.BAT

 1: @ECHO OFF
 2: REM A 'Gang Delete' batch file
 3: IF %1NOTHING==NOTHING GOTO HELP
 4: ECHO Delete a group of files
 5: :LOOP
 6: IF NOTHING%1==NOTHING GOTO END
 7: DEL %1 <C:\SYSTEM\UTIL\YES >NUL
 8: ECHO %1 is/are gone . . .
 9: SHIFT
10: GOTO LOOP
11: :HELP
12: ECHO DEL2 Command format:
13: ECHO del2 [file1] [file2] .... [fileN]
14: :END
```

Fig. 7-16. This batch file deletes a group of files.

Summary

There are quite a few "tools" used to create batch files. The first is the tool you use to write the batch file. This can be with a word processor, text editor, or with DOS and the COPY CON function. Overall, the best way to write a batch file is with a good text editor.

Other tools for creating batch files are the batch file commands themselves. These include special batch file directives, of which there are only a few, plus all the DOS commands and your program and application's names.

Name: MOVE2.BAT

```
 1: @ECHO OFF
 2: REM A 'Gang Move' batch file
 3: IF %1NOTHING==NOTHING GOTO HELP
 4: SET DISK=%1
 5: ECHO Moving a group of files to path %DISK%
 6: :LOOP
 7: SHIFT
 8: IF %1NOTHING==NOTHING GOTO END
 9: COPY %1 %DISK% >NUL
10: DEL %1 <C:\SYSTEM\UTIL\YES >NUL
11: ECHO %1 moved to %DISK%
12: GOTO LOOP
13: :HELP
14: ECHO MOVE2 Command format:
15: ECHO move2 [drive:[\path]] [file1] [file2] .... [fileN]
16: :END
17: SET DISK=
```

Fig. 7-17. This batch file moves a group of files.

The final set of tools are the % (percent) variables that you can use in batch files. These variables come in three flavors: replaceable parameters, or those items you type after the name of your batch file on the command line; environment variables; variables used with the FOR command.

8
Batch File Structure

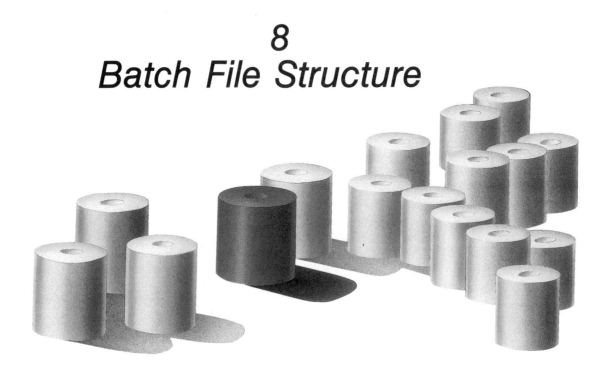

Most hard core programmer types will really get a laugh over the title of this chapter. The reason is that batch files inherit a lack of structure simply because of their nature (the way they began). There are, however, a few elements of structure—call it style, call it esthetics—that come in handy when writing batch files. Mostly, these are hints that allow you to better modify your batch files in the future. But for the purposes of conversation, and just to make Pascal programmers irate, I'll refer to it as batch file structure.

The purpose of this chapter is to acquaint you with those threadbare elements of structure that apply to batch file programming. This includes three areas: General structure, or how best to assemble a batch file (perhaps this can best be described as "consistency among batch files"); Labels and the GOTO statement, which are used to bring order and flow to a batch file; subroutines and batch file chaining which are also elements of structure that are covered here.

IS IT REALLY A PROGRAMMING LANGUAGE?

Yes, batch file programming is a real programming language. By definition, a programming language is a form of communication between a human and a computer. The human uses the programming language to tell the computer what to do. In this sense, batch file programming more than qualifies.

Batch file programming is similar to other programming in that you compose a source code file, consisting of instructions that the computer understands. Unlike compiled languages, batch file programs are interpreted. Some of the hard liners may claim that any interpreted language is not really a programming language at all. Wrong. It still qualifies.

Second, batch file programs can make use of variables, albeit only string variables, and it really can't do much with the variables other than display them or compare them. (No searches, no direct input from the user.)

Third, batch file programs can make decisions and take action. Through use of the GOTO statement and labels, different parts of the batch file program can be executed. Using IF and variables, loops can be performed in batch files—and those loops can be executed and exited by evaluating certain conditions.

How is batch file programming unlike other programming? For starters, no one will ever write a commercial application using batch files. Sure, you could try. But will people buy it? There are just better and faster ways to communicate with a computer than batch file programming.

Also, batch files have no inherent math functions. A lot of programming derives from simple math, addition, subtraction, division and multiplication. For batch files, this is impossible (and really out of the scope of things).

Batch files were never intended to be a substitute for real programming. But this doesn't mean that they don't come in handy. Even the most sophisticated applications will use a batch file to help you install the program. Later in this book, you'll see a complete DOS "shell" program implemented entirely by batch files.

The only way to summarize this is by saying that batch files are limited by their design, yet unlimited in application. There is only so much that batch files were designed to do—only certain things that they do best. Yet, they do those things well. On the other hand, because of the unlimited amount of software available to DOS (including batch file utilities), the things that batch files can do is virtually unlimited.

STRUCTURE

Believe it or not, you can do a lot to help your batch files along by writing structured programs. This isn't in the classic sense of structured programming. For example, some programming languages insist you follow a structure along these lines:

1) Using massive amounts of "remark" or "comment" statements, tell what the program is going to do, remembering to add your name, date, class section and teacher's name. (That was added as a joke because the only time anyone really cares about this is when you're in school.)

2) Define all the variables used in this program. (Does anyone really do this *before* they write the program?)

3) Write all the modules, or subroutines, used by this program.

4) Write the program itself.

5) Exit properly.

Fortunately, batch files can be programmed a little more loosely than that. Actually, most of that "structured" approach was from the old mainframe computer days. Because actual computer time was limited, programmers would write an entire program on paper before keying it in (or using punch cards). They would turn the program into the computer center, and the staff would place it on a stack with a bunch of other programs to run.

Then, during the midnight hour, the staff would run the program. They would place the output (if any) in a box, along with the list of errors. Then the programmer would have to rewrite the entire thing, or just the parts that didn't work.

In a nutshell, that's how structure evolved. The same lunatics who implemented that regimen, sought to apply it to microcomputers. Alas, the concept of "one person/one computer" never occurred to them. It took geniuses like Bill Gates of Microsoft to write a BASIC programming language that better understood the one person/one computer concept.

With one computer/one person, you can write your programs and run them at the same time. It's more of an on-the-fly operation. You could go in and modify your code as you were working on it. Add variables as you need them, modify routines, make adjustments. This is the way most microcomputer programming is done today. Most of the old timers, and those who were educated by them, will say this is "bad programming." Yet the most popular and fastest microcomputer applications written today are developed that way. The worst programs? The slow ones? The ones no one likes? They're done the old way.

Batch File Structure

An example of a type of batch file structure is shown in the following batch file program skeleton:

```
1: @ECHO OFF
2: REM this is a description of the program
3: ECHO tell them what's going on
4: ...
5: ...
6: :END
```

That's a simple structure. First comes the initial ECHO OFF statement (1), followed by a REM statement (2). For shorter batch files, you probably will leave out the REM statement. But they're a must for longer batch files, especially when a batch file is using replaceable parameters and variables.

The ECHO statement (3) is optional. I use them to tell the user that a batch file is running, and what the batch file does. Before DOS 3.3, you could always tell a batch file was running because you'd see:

ECHO OFF

on your screen. But with the implementation of the @ sign to suppress batch file listings, you no longer see the initial ECHO OFF. So I usually put an ECHO statement in a batch file to either give the name of the batch file, or tell what the program is about to do. Optionally, you could follow the ECHO statement with a PAUSE command, allowing the user to "break out" of the batch file if necessary:

```
ECHO This program erases your hard disk; Press Control-Break
to stop or
PAUSE
```

This gives them the option of pressing CTRL–BREAK to stop the batch file, or "Strike a key when ready . . ." to continue.

Finally, an :END label is added to the end of the batch file. END is not a reserved batch file word (though it should be; allowing you to exit from a batch file at any point). I've used it throughout this book and in my own batch files "just in case." If you were to modify this batch file, having an END label would help in case you wanted to "leave early."

As batch files grow more complex, and you start using IF to make decisions, you'll add labels and routines. In most cases, you will evaluate those decisions to either execute one part of your batch or another. For example, say you're writing a batch file to decide whether to print a group of files or simply save them in a temporary directory.

The program in FIG. 8-1 has two parts that will be executed depending on the results of the IF statement (4). If the environment variable DESTINATION equals "PRINTER," lines 8 through 10 are executed. If not, lines 5 through 7 are executed. After the first routine (5, 6, 7) is executed, it "jumps over" the second routine to the :END label (11).

```
 1:  @ECHO OFF
 2:  REM To Print or To Temp?
 3:  ECHO Print/Store files; One moment
 4:  IF %DESTINATION%==PRINTER GOTO PRINTIT
 5:  REM This code saves the files to disk
 6:  IF EXIST C:\WS\DATA\SPOOL\*.* COPY C:\WS\DATA\SPOOL\*.*
     C:\TEMP >NUL
 7:  GOTO END
 8:  :PRINTIT
 9:  IF NOT EXIST C:\WS\DATA\SPOOL\*.* GOTO END
10:  FOR %%F IN (C:\WS\DATA\SPOOL\*.*) DO COPY %%F PRN >NUL
11:  :END
```

Fig. 8-1. Here is a batch file that decides whether to print or save files.

Jumping over routines, as in the above example, is common in batch files—and a source of confusion. Some batch files will make a lot of decisions and have many routines. Jumping around in these batch files and following their flow can drive you mad. Of course, there is one possible solution: pretty printing.

Pretty Printing

Pretty printing is a term (I don't know where it came from) that applies to writing program source code. It's used by BASIC programmers for the most part because, like batch files, most BASIC interpreters lack any type of structure.

When you take a programming language like C and compare its source code to BASIC, you become amazed at how "neat" the code looks. C is interesting to read because it has an elegant structure (see FIG. 8-2). (Actually, the structure is not required by the C compiler. Yet, tradition dictates that the above type of format be used for C programs.)

```
/* C example */

#include <stdio.h>

#define MAXSIZE      20

main()
{
      int list[MAXSIZE];
      int size=0,num;

      do {
           printf("Type number: ");
           scanf("%d",&list[size]);
      } while ( list[size++] != 0 );
      size--;
      num = max(list,size);
      printf("Largest number is %d",num);
}

max(list,size)
int list[],size;
{
      int dex,max;
      max = list[0];
      for ( dex = 1; dex<size; dex++)
           if( max < list[dex] )
                max = list[dex];
      return(max);
}
```

Fig. 8-2. This is an example of C program source code.

BASIC, on the other hand, really has no structure. It's all one long list of commands (see FIG. 8-3). Seeing how hard BASIC is to read, certain BASIC programmers would take advantage of spaces and REM statements to make the listing a bit easier on the eyes. So the same program could read as in FIG. 8-4.

```
 10 REM BASIC EXAMPLE
 20 DIM MAXSIZE(20)
 30 LET SIZE=0: LET DEX=0: LET NUMBER=1
 40 WHILE NUMBER<>0
 50 INPUT "Type number:",NUMBER
 60 MAXSIZE(SIZE)=NUMBER
 70 SIZE=SIZE+1
 80 WEND
 90 DEX=MAXSIZE(0)
100 FOR X=1 TO SIZE
110 IF DEX<MAXSIZE(X) THEN DEX=MAXSIZE(X)
120 NEXT
130 PRINT "Highest number was";DEX
```

Fig. 8-3. This is an example of a BASIC program.

```
 10 REM BASIC EXAMPLE
 15 '
 20 DIM MAXSIZE(20)
 30 LET SIZE=0: LET DEX=0: LET NUMBER=1
 35 '
 40 WHILE NUMBER<>0
 50     INPUT "Type number:",NUMBER
 60     MAXSIZE(SIZE)=NUMBER
 70     SIZE=SIZE+1
 80 WEND
 85 '
 90 DEX=MAXSIZE(0)
100 FOR X=1 TO SIZE
110     IF DEX<MAXSIZE(X) THEN DEX=MAXSIZE(X)
120 NEXT
125 '
130 PRINT "Highest number was";DEX
```

Fig. 8-4. This is Fig. 8-3 spaced to be more readable.

Apostrophes are abbreviations for the REM statement. Here they are used in lines 15, 35, 85 and 125 to break up the various sections of the program. The two loops (the WHILE/WEND loop in lines 40 through 80 and the FOR/NEXT loop in lines 100 through 120) have their contents indented. This makes it easy to see where the loop starts and ends. If "nested" loops were used, their contents would be further indented.

The BASIC interpreter (or compiler) doesn't give a hoot about extra spaces or tab characters in the listing. It won't speed up or slow down the program any. It makes it easier to read and follow the program flow, however. The same can be done with batch files (see FIG. 8-5).

```
 1: @ECHO OFF
 2: REM To Print or To Temp?
 3: ECHO Print/Store files; One moment
 4:
 5: IF %DESTINATION%==PRINTER GOTO PRINTIT
 6:
 7:    REM This code saves the files to disk
 8:    IF EXIST C:\WS\DATA\SPOOL\*.* COPY C:\WS\DATA\SPOOL
       \*.* C:\TEMP >NUL
 9:    GOTO END
10:
11: :PRINTIT
12:    IF NOT EXIST C:\WS\DATA\SPOOL\*.* GOTO END
13:    FOR %%F IN (C:\WS\DATA\SPOOL\*.*) DO COPY %%F PRN >NUL
14:
15: :END
```

Fig. 8-5. Extra spaces can make batch files easier to read.

The batch file interpreter doesn't care about extra spaces on the line. Also, you can include blank lines in a batch file—no problem. COMMAND.COM interprets them as if you just pressed ENTER alone on the command line. The only thing that may happen is, if you have ECHO ON, you will see the command prompt displayed a few times. That's it. Otherwise, you can liberally use blank lines in your program to clean up their appearance.

LABELS AND *GOTO*

This book has shown you a lot of labels and quite a few GOTO statements, but still has yet to explain them. Sorry about that.

Basically, the GOTO statement works with labels to give your batch files a smidgen of structure. Using both GOTO and labels, you can execute specific portions of your batch file, avoid others, and "bail out" quickly if need be.

Labels

A label in a batch file is designated by the colon character. The label doesn't include the colon, but follows it. Labels can be up to 127 characters long but only the first 8 are important.

:*label*

label is eight or fewer characters, including letters and numbers, but not the period (.) character. (Other characters are allowed, but it's wise to only use letters and numbers.) Upper and lower case are treated as the same.

A space denotes the end of the label and the start of optional comments (see below):

:LOOP

"Loop" is the perfect name for a well-used label.

:10

Numbers are also okay for labels. Though it's best to make your labels descriptive where possible:

:PRINT

:GETINPUT

:ALARM

:ERROR

Remember that only the first eight characters are important, so:

:ZEDDIDIAYA

and

:ZEDDIDIAYO

are both considered the same label, though they may be in different parts of the batch file.

```
1: @ECHO OFF
2: GOTO LABEL
3: REM where will it go?
4: :Label One
5: ECHO after one
6: :LABEL
7: ECHO after two
```

Fig. 8-6. Lines 4 and 6 are labels.

In FIG. 8-6, lines 4 and 6 are labels. The GOTO in line 2 will branch to the matching *label*—in this case, line 4. (All characters after the space are ignored, so "Label One" equals "LABEL" according to the batch file interpreter.) The output of the program will be:

```
after one
after two
```

Essentially, what happened in the above example is that the second label was ignored. In all cases where a program has two identical labels, the second one will be ignored (more on this below).

When the batch file interpreter encounters a line starting with a colon, it assumes the line is a label and skips it. In fact, any line in a batch file starting with a colon is skipped; it's not even displayed when ECHO is turned ON:

```
1: :FIRST LABEL
2: :SECOND LABEL
3: :THIRD LABEL
```

Running the above batch file example would produce no output—even though ECHO is not used, and therefore is ON.

Labels are only used by the GOTO command. Otherwise, you can use labels as a form of comment within your batch file, or as a combination of both:

```
:LABEL This is a comment after the label "LABEL"
```

Anything after the colon is ignored by the batch file interpreter. The rest of the line can be used for comments.

GOTO

Normally, batch files execute one line at a time, one line after the other. There are times, however, when you may want to execute a specific part of the batch file or skip other parts. That's where GOTO comes in handy.

GOTO is a batch file statement Microsoft borrowed from its BASIC. In fact, it behaves a lot like the BASIC GOTO statement. What it does is to transfer batch file execution to the line containing a label specified by GOTO:

GOTO *label*

label is up to eight characters long and specifies a label somewhere else in the batch file. After the GOTO statement, the batch file interpreter will look for the *label* and then start executing commands after that line. If *label* isn't found, you'll see the following error message:

```
Label not found
```

and the batch file immediately stops executing.

```
GOTO END
```

After the above statement, the batch file interpreter will begin reading lines in the batch file, searching for those lines starting with a colon, signaling a label. As each label is found, the interpreter will compare that label with the one after GOTO. If found, execution transfers to that new line.

GOTO searches from the beginning of the batch file all the way to the end. Then, if the label isn't found, the "Label not found" error occurs, and the batch file will stop. This is important to remember if you use the identical label twice. The second label appearing in the program will never be used (*see* FIG. 8-7).

Before running this program, try to look at it and figure what it would do. The output is as follows:

```
PASSED LABEL1
Strike a key when ready . . .
PASSED LABEL 1
Strike a key when ready . . .
```

```
 1: @ECHO OFF
 2: REM GOTO TEST PROGRAM
 3: :LABEL1
 4: ECHO PASSED LABEL1
 5: PAUSE
 6: GOTO LABEL1
 7: ECHO THIS LINE IS AFTER THE GOTO STATEMENT
 8: :LABEL1
 9: ECHO PASSED THE SECOND LABEL1
10: PAUSE
11: GOTO LABEL1
```

Fig. 8-7. The second label in this program will never be used.

(and on and on.) GOTO will only find the first of two identical labels.

Using GOTO with IF

Because so much of batch file programming is borrowed from the BASIC programming language, it's important to note the differences. One that will doubtless pop up from time to time is using GOTO with the IF statement:

IF *condition* GOTO *label*

IF is basically a testing statement. It tests *condition* to see if it's either true or false. If true, then whatever follows *condition* is executed. In the above example, the GOTO *label* statement would be executed.

The important thing to remember here is that:

> The IF *command*
> *does not use* THEN

So don't catch yourself using the following syntax:

IF *condition* THEN *label*

It won't work.

Endless Loops

One of the hazards of using GOTO, or any looping statement in any program, is the possibility of entering an endless loop. That happens when the same set of instructions are executed repeatedly:

```
1: @ECHO OFF
2: :ETERNITY
3: REM A lot going on, but nothing happening
4: GOTO ETERNITY
```

In the above example, lines 2 through 4 are executed repeatedly—an endless loop. Most good programmers will introduce some code into the loop to determine an end point. Otherwise, you can stop a batch file the traditional way by pressing CTRL–BREAK:

```
Terminate batch job (Y/N)?
```

Pressing **Y** stops your computer from repeatedly executing the same commands over and over.

Sometimes an endless loop may be necessary. If so, you may want to add some lines to the program to let the user know how to get out of it:

```
ECHO The following may take a long time
ECHO If you want to stop, press Control-Break
ECHO and answer "Y" to the question.
```

or, you can use ECHO with the PAUSE command to give the user a chance to think in the middle of the loop:

```
ECHO This may take a few more times.
ECHO Press Control-Break to stop, or
PAUSE
```

That second ECHO command is used a lot before the PAUSE statement. The net effect on the screen reads:

```
This may take a few more times.
Press Control-Break to stop, or
Strike a key when ready . . .
```

Both the ECHOed message and the PAUSE command flow together nicely, giving the message a good consistency.

Is GOTO Bad?

Don't let the programming gurus kid you about GOTO, you can't write a program without it. Some of the Pascal programmers (yes, them again) claim that GOTO is the bane of programming. "Good programmers never use GOTO." Bah! Look at assembly language: it's full of GOTO statements (though they're called "jumps" instead). Because every other language eventually is translated to machine code (just like assembly), you can firmly attest to the programming prudes that you can't program without GOTO. So use it freely, but wisely.

SUBROUTINES AND CHAINING

Batch files can run other batch files. In fact, quite a few AUTOEXEC batch files will end with another batch file. After all, the name of a batch file is a command, so why not include other batch files in your batch files?

The answer lies in a flaw of logic that most beginning batch file programmers soon discover. Suppose you're writing a batch file called MENU.BAT. In the middle you want to use a second batch file, LOCATE.BAT, to position the cursor on the screen:

```
1: @ECHO OFF
2: REM Main Menu batch file
3: CLS
4: LOCATE 1 12
5: ECHO Main Menu
6: ...
```

Assuming that LOCATE is a batch file to move the cursor (and 1 and 12 are parameters), what will happen is that the screen will clear (3), and then the LOCATE.BAT file will be run. LOCATE will move the cursor to row 1, column 12, and then return to DOS.

Huh? Most users assume execution would return to line 5. It doesn't. When batch files quit, they return to DOS. They don't "remember" who called them, or how they were started. Real applications, .COM and .EXE programs, return execution to the batch file interpreter. But using one batch file inside another stops the first and starts the second. This is known as chaining.

Chaining

Chaining happens when one batch file "runs" another, the first one stops and the second takes over. This could be quite advantageous and avoid a lot of GOTO structures, as in the example of FIG. 8-8. This program could be called LOGIN.BAT. After LOGIN, the user types their name on the command line (in caps). Then, this program runs other batch files, depending on which user has logged in. Because all the files specified in lines 5 through 8 are batch files, execution will not return to this batch file. This avoids a whole multitude of GOTO statements.

```
 1: @ECHO OFF
 2: REM Program to run individual user's batch files
 3: IF %1NOTHING==NOTHING GOTO HELP
 4: ECHO Welcome to the machine, %1
 5: IF %1==STEVE LOTUS.BAT
 6: IF %1==DIANE DIANE.BAT
 7: IF %1==BILL WORD.BAT
 8: IF %1==PEGGY ACCOUNT.BAT
 9: :HELP
10: ECHO Sorry, I don't know you, %1
11: ECHO Contact the machine coordinator for help
12: :END
```

Fig. 8-8. This is an example of "chaining."

For the majority of batch file programmers, however, chaining batch files is not what life is all about. Fortunately, IBM came to the rescue with the addition of the CALL batch file directive, added in DOS 3.3.

CALL

CALL works like the BASIC programming language's GOSUB statement. It allows you to run a second batch file from your current batch file, then, when the second batch file is done, execution returns to the first batch file.

CALL *batchfile*

batchfile is the name of a batch file, including the optional drive letter and pathname. After CALL **batchfile** is executed, the batch file program **batchfile** is run. When **batchfile** stops, control returns to the first batch file.

Using the example from the previous section, the program can now "call" the LOCATE.BAT file by editing line 4 of his program to read:

```
4: CALL LOCATE 1 12
```

This will execute the LOCATE.BAT file, then return to the original batch file, line 5, and pick up where it left off.

See FIG. 8-9. The first batch file calls the second batch file in line 5. In the second batch file, control returns to the first after line 6. What you'll see on the screen is shown in FIG. 8-10.

```
Name: FIRST.BAT

1: @ECHO OFF
2: REM First batch program
3: ECHO This is the first batch file program
4: ECHO Transferring control to SECOND.BAT...
5: CALL SECOND.BAT
6: ECHO Back in the first program
7: :END
```

```
Name: SECOND.BAT

1: REM Second batch program
2: REPT = 20
3: ECHO Now we're in the second program
4: REPT = 20
5: PAUSE
6: :END
```

Fig. 8-9. The first program calls the second.

```
C> FIRST
This is the first batch file program
Transferring control to SECOND.BAT...
=====================
Now we're in the second program
=====================
Strike a key when ready . . .
Back in the first program
C>
```

Fig. 8-10. This is the run from the programs in Fig. 8-9.

Control passes from one batch file to another, as seen by the output. If ECHO is OFF in the first batch file, it will be off in the second as well. This is why the second file doesn't have (nor need) an initial ECHO OFF statement.

By the way, the REPT command (SECOND.BAT, lines 3 and 5) is a supplemental program included on the diskette available with this book. It REPeaTs a single character the specified number of times. In this case, it displays 20 equal signs. For some reason, and in some versions of DOS, ECHO will not display 20 equal signs and does one of these:

ECHO is off

That's why I wrote REPT and made it available on the Supplemental Programs Diskette.

Breaking Out

You should note that if you press CTRL–BREAK in a secondary batch file, control returns to DOS—not the first batch file. CALL doesn't act like the command processor shell's EXIT command. Any time a batch file is canceled with CTRL–BREAK, the following message is displayed:

Terminate batch job (Y/N)?

If Y is pressed, control returns to DOS.

COMMAND /C

For DOS versions prior to 3.3, the CALL command isn't available. This doesn't mean that you can't "call" one batch file from another, however. The secret is to use a second copy of the command processor, COMMAND.COM. (This method still works under later versions of DOS as well.)

COMMAND /C *batchfile*

batchfile is the name of a batch file, including the optional drive letter and pathname. After COMMAND /C *batchfile* is executed, the batch file program *batchfile* is run. When *batchfile* stops, control returns to the first batch file.

You can change line 5 in FIRST.BAT above to read:

```
5:  COMMAND /C SECOND.BAT
```

COMMAND /C uses COMMAND.COM to invoke a second copy of the command processor, like a shell. That's the only difference between COMMAND /C and CALL. Oh, and COMMAND /C is a lot slower than CALL. Otherwise, if you're still using an older version of DOS, replace all occurrences of CALL in this book with COMMAND /C.

Summary

Though batch files really lack any type of formal structure, there are things you can do that will bend them that way. The first is to use a consistent program "skeleton," use REM comments liberally, and always have an END label. The second method involves indenting lines and using blank lines to create a "pretty printing" effect. The third method is using the batch file directives GOTO and CALL to implement specific portions of code or to call external batch files. Though it isn't officially a structure, it is one step closer to writing better batch files.

9
Troubleshooting

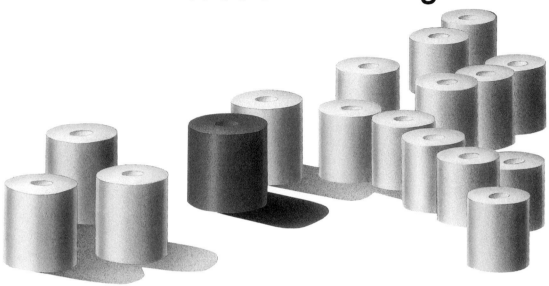

Isn't "troubleshooting" a wonderful word? Think about it. It's so violent. When you think about the word (more specifically the two words trouble and shooting), a vision comes to mind of sitting down in a harshly lit room, shirt sleeves rolled up, pencil in hand, ready to track down some annoying problem. Not a pleasant situation.

But, when I think about "trouble-shooting," I think of this beast: trouble. It's lurking out there somewhere, and I have a gun. A big one. That's what makes troubleshooting interesting. You don't even need a license.

Fortunately, troubleshooting batch files doesn't require a gun (and will probably never receive an "R" rating). Instead, this chapter contains everything having to do with batch file "trouble." This isn't limited to batch file errors and how to fix them. I've also included the ERRORLEVEL statement. Even though it has nothing to do with a batch file error, you can use ERRORLEVEL to aid in troubleshooting some common batch file problems—and to make your batch files smarter.

THINGS *DOS* WON'T LET YOU DO WITH BATCH FILES

No one ever accused batch files of being all powerful. Yet, there are some things that you'd think would work in a specific manner—but they don't. Some things DOS just won't let you do with batch files. Prominent among them are using I/O redirection on the same command line as the batch file name.

There are also certain reserved filenames that DOS won't let you use with batch files. Actually, you can't even name .COM and .EXE files these names. Though this isn't really a no-no, just don't scratch your head wondering why your COPY.BAT file won't run. (See below.)

Also, the ECHO command hasn't been known to be particularly predictable. Because ECHO sometimes doesn't behave the way you think it would, it's also been included in this section.

I/O Redirection

One thing that would be nice would be to pipe the output of a running batch file to the printer, or to automatically provide input to a batch file. This could be used effectively for self-running demonstration programs. Alas, I/O redirection is not allowed by the batch file interpreter. Any of the following characters are ignored after you type the name of a batch file program:

> < |

You may experience some peculiarities if you try to use these. First of all, don't expect them to work. In some cases, however, it may appear that they work. For example:

```
C> TEST > TEMP
```

TEST is a batch file and TEMP will (hopefully) be a file on disk that contains TEST's output. Of course, this will never happen. A brief attempt will be made, however, to create a TEMP file as you can see by listing the DIRectory:

```
Volume in drive C is MISSING
Volume Serial Number is ABCD-1234
Directory of  C:\BATCH\DISK

TEMP                    0   8-01-88   8:39p
          1 File(s)     9584640 bytes free
```

Unfortunately, TEMP contains nothing. This doesn't mean, however, that the batch file didn't run. Batch files will operate if you attempt to use I/O redirection: it's the I/O redirection that won't work.

A Possible Solution

Though I/O redirection isn't possible on the command line, DOS lets you use it freely inside a batch file. If you want the output of a batch file to be sent to a file, a possible solution would be to use I/O redirection inside the batch file to redirect the output. You could even write a special version of the batch file that would provide the output automatically.

Take one of the directory sorting programs discussed earlier in this book:

```
Name: DSN.BAT

1: @ECHO OFF
2: REM Sort directory by name
3: DIR | SORT > ZIGNORE.ME
4: MORE < ZIGNORE.ME
5: DEL ZIGNORE.ME
```

You could write a modified version, and call it DSNDISK.BAT. That version will use replaceable parameters to send its output to a disk file as well as the screen; or you could just delete line 5 above, but study FIG. 9-1 before you start editing.

```
Name: DSNDISK.BAT

1: @ECHO OFF
2: REM Sort directory by name--disk output version
3: IF %1N==N GOTO NORMAL
4: DIR | SORT > %1
5: ECHO Data saved in %1:
6: :NORMAL
7: DIR | SORT > ZIGNORE.ME
8: MORE < ZIGNORE.ME
9: DEL ZIGNORE.ME
```

Fig. 9-1. This program uses replaceable parameters.

This is the same program—from line 7 on. The difference is in a test for a replaceable parameter (3). If there is no parameter, the batch file performs the same as DSN.BAT, with no errors. Otherwise, the sorted output is sent to the file specified after DSNDISK on the command line (4), and then a message is displayed letting the user know that the file was saved (5).

```
C> DSNDISK TEMP
Data saved in TEMP:
```

(sorted directory listing would follow.)

Lines 3 through 6 could be added to any program where you wanted optional I/O redirection to disk. Just remember to type the filename after the command.

Some clever readers may think about testing for the character > on the command line using IF. For example:

```
IF "%1"==">"
```

This won't work. Remember, DOS ignores > and < and ¦ if they're typed on the command line after a batch file. ">" will never be read as a parameter. Also, using the character > with the IF statement is not allowed. Again, DOS assumes you want to redirect the output of the IF command. If you try this, you'll get a "File creation error" message.

Doing I/O redirection on the input side is next to impossible. It's best to use the replaceable parameters on the command line than attempt any tricky input redirection—unless, of course, you're using the YES, NO, ENTER, and ENTERN files covered in Chapter 7.

Reserved Names

The following are names of internal DOS commands. If you name a .COM, .EXE or .BAT file any of these names, those files will never run. Internal DOS commands always take priority over all other program names on disk:

BREAK	ECHO	REN
CALL	ERASE	RENAME
CD	FOR	RD
CHCP	GOTO	RMDIR
CHDIR	IF	SET
CLS	MD	SHIFT
COPY	MKDIR	TIME
CTTY	PATH	TYPE
DATE	PAUSE	VER
DEL	PROMPT	VERIFY
DIR	REM	VOL

% Signs

The percent sign, %, is a valid character in a filename, but you should be aware of using the character % in your batch files.

Have you ever wondered why the FOR command requires only one percent sign when used at the DOS prompt and two percent signs when used in a batch file? You can tell why if you turn ECHO ON and look at the FOR command as it's displayed. The batch file contains:

```
FOR %%F IN (*.*) DO DIR %%f
```

But you will see (with ECHO ON):

```
FOR %F IN (*.*) DO DIR %F
```

The batch file interpreter uses the percent sign to identify a variable. However, you can use the percent sign as the percent character by specifying it twice. When the batch file interpreter sees two percent signs, it translates them both into a single percent sign character.

```
ECHO %%
```

This command echoes one percent sign character to the display. ECHO will echo only one percent sign character for every two you have listed. So:

ECHO %%%

displays only one percent sign, whereas:

ECHO %%%%

displays two.

If a filename contains a percent sign, such as:

ANNUAL%

Specify the percent sign twice when you reference the file in your batch file program:

ANNUAL%%

ECHO Oddities

The ECHO command has three distinct functions:

1) Turn the echoing of batch file commands on or off
2) Echo character strings to the display
3) Display the status of the ECHO command.

In my humble opinion, the third function of the ECHO command is utterly useless. ECHO, without any arguments, displays the current status of the ECHO command. So:

ECHO

all by itself yields:

ECHO is on

or:

ECHO is off

Most users assume that ECHO by itself will "echo" a blank line. It doesn't. Instead, it displays one of the above status messages. This is perhaps the most annoying thing about ECHO.

Lost in Spaces

Some enterprising users figured that you could follow ECHO with some spaces. After all, spaces are characters, and ECHO followed by spaces should just ECHO those spaces to the screen. The result would be a blank line, right? Wrong:

`ECHO is off`

Depending on the version of DOS, ECHO followed by spaces is interpreted the same as the ECHO command alone on the line. (Earlier versions of DOS may display the spaces). In fact, all spaces up to the first non-space character are ignored by some versions of DOS:

`ECHO            test`

This command may just display "test" as the first four characters on the next line. Using the TAB key with some versions of DOS will not work either.

Generally, you should include some non-space character to start a blank line, or a line without any text on it:

`ECHO !`
`ECHO !      test`
`ECHO !`

This always displays:

`!`
`!      test`
`!`

Another character to use is character 255. This extended ASCII character is actually a blank, but it's also a non-space character. (Use the ALT–keypad trick to enter character 255.)

If you follow ECHO with a space, and then type character 255, a blank line is displayed.

Dot Commands

In earlier versions of DOS, you could use a period to "echo" a command:

`.You may now turn off your computer.`

DOS versions prior to 3.0 ignored the dot character and anything after it. So this served well as a substitute for ECHO. This trick should be avoided, however, if you want to be compatible with later versions of DOS.

Long Lines

Each line of a batch file can contain 128 characters. Actually, that's 127 characters, plus the ENTER key. ECHO and the space that follow it take up five characters, which leaves you 122 to get your message across. If you exceed the 122 character limit, DOS may do one of two things: truncate the string, or totally hang.

By the way, you can get more than 122 characters after the ECHO statement in one of three ways (or a mixture of all three):

1) By using an environment variable (or more than one) that expands out to a long string.

2) By using a replaceable parameter (more than once) that expands out to a long string.

3) By using a text editor and writing a long string after the ECHO command.

ON and OFF

Because ECHO ON and ECHO OFF are two ways of using ECHO, any string you try to display that starts with "on" or "off" will not be displayed. Instead, ECHO will be turned either on or off. (That makes sense.)

A way around this is to use character 255 as described above. If you precede the word ON or OFF with character 255, ECHO will not interpret it as the ON or OFF switch.

I/O Redirection (Again)

ECHO sends its output to a device, normally the console. You can, however, use I/O redirection with ECHO for some special effects. My favorite is:

ECHO ^L > PRN

This ejects a page from the printer, and it comes in quite handy.

Because ECHO allows I/O redirection, you cannot use any of the following characters in an ECHO string:

> < |

DOS will interpret those characters as I/O redirection symbols, and the results of your ECHO command will not be what you expect them to be. For example:

ECHO Insert backup disk ONE and press <Y> at the prompt.

This will send the string "Insert backup disk ON and press" to a file called "AT" and redirect input from a file called "Y". Not what you wanted.

With DOS 4.0, you can enclose the I/O redirection characters in double quotes and use them. For example:

ECHO The greater-than symbol is ">"

This displays:

The greater-than symbol is ">"

All three of the I/O redirection symbols can be used within double quotes in this manner.

Forbidden Characters

Besides the above quirks, ECHO also acts funky when used with the following characters in the manner noted:

=

ECHO followed by any number of equal signs is the same as type ECHO by itself; the equal signs will not be echoed to the screen. If you follow the equal signs with any other non-space character, however, they will be displayed. A possible solution is to, instead of using the equal sign, use character 205 which is similar looking.

%

The percent sign is not displayed by itself. Instead (in a batch file), you need to specify two percent signs for every one you want displayed.

;

The semicolon works along the same lines as the equal sign. When used by itself, or in any number, it's the same as typing ECHO by itself. The solution is to follow the semicolon with a non-space character.

,

Comma operates the same as the equal sign and semicolon. Follow it by a non-space character if you want it to be displayed.

USING *ERRORLEVEL*

ERRORLEVEL is used to test a program's return code. When certain programs quit, they optionally send a return code back to DOS. This code value can be used by other programs, or by the batch file command ERRORLEVEL.

ERRORLEVEL, or more specifically a program's return code, is a primitive form of communications between that program and DOS. The sad part is that most programs, including most DOS programs, fail to take advantage of the return code.

ERRORLEVEL *value*

value is a value compared with the previous program's return code. It can be any number from 0 through 255. The meaning of the value depends on the program, though a value of zero typically means a success (or that the program didn't offer a return code).

ERRORLEVEL is used with IF to test *value*. If the return code from a program is greater than or equal to *value*, then the IF statement is true. Note that in this instance an equal sign after ERRORLEVEL is optional:

```
IF ERRORLEVEL 6 GOTO OOPS
```

If the preceding program returned an ERRORLEVEL value of 6 or more, batch file execution will continue at the label :OOPS.

```
IF ERRORLEVEL 0 ECHO That was smooth
```

This statement causes "That was smooth" to be echoed to the console. Why? Because ERRORLEVEL will always be greater than 0.

ERRORLEVEL Testing

Only five programs that come with DOS return ERRORLEVEL values (*see* Appendix I):

BACKUP
FORMAT
GRAFTABL
KEYB
RESTORE

Several applications programs return ERRORLEVEL values. But for the most part, only third-party utility programs take advantage of ERRORLEVEL values.

For the above DOS utilities, BACKUP offers five return code values as follows:

0   Normal Exit

1   No files were backed up (all were already backed up or none existed).

2   File sharing conflicts. Not all files were backed up.

3   CTRL–BREAK was pressed, halting the backup.

4   Error, program stopped.

The batch file example in FIG. 9-2 shows how ERRORLEVEL can be used to communicate these messages to a user. (Remember, "BACKUP" is already used as the name of the BACKUP program. If you named your backup batch file BACKUP, the BACKUP.EXE (or .COM) program would be run instead.)

The batch file in FIG. 9-2 backs up a hard drive (drive C) to diskettes in drive A (5). The BACKUP switches are set to back up the entire drive, but only those files modified since the last backup. The ECHO statement in line 4 ends with "then" because the first line displayed by BACKUP is "Insert a disk . . ." (It makes for a smooth display.)

After the BACKUP command come the ERRORLEVEL tests, from highest to lowest (6 though 9). You'll also see how each label is also used as a REM statement to explain what the various return codes mean (12, 15, 18, 21). When ERRORLEVEL 0 is returned, execution falls through to line 10, then branches to the :END label. Otherwise, messages particular to each return code are displayed.

Even Better Uses

Perhaps the most useful purpose of the ERRORLEVEL variable comes with two utility programs on the supplemental programs diskette: ASK and READKEY. These are two variations on some popular public domain utilities. In fact, some similar batch file utility programs come with popular packages such as the Norton Utilities.

ASK is used to display a line of text and then wait for Y or N to be pressed. If Y is pressed, an ERRORLEVEL of 0 is generated. If N is pressed, an ERRORLEVEL

Name: BACK.BAT

```
 1: @ECHO OFF
 2: REM Backup the hard drive
 3: ECHO Backing up the hard drive ...
 4: ECHO Have a stack of disks handy, then
 5: BACKUP C:\*.* A: /S/M
 6: IF ERRORLEVEL 4 GOTO ERROR4
 7: IF ERRORLEVEL 3 GOTO ERROR3
 8: IF ERRORLEVEL 2 GOTO ERROR2
 9: IF ERRORLEVEL 1 GOTO ERROR1
10: ECHO Backup was successful
11: GOTO END
12: :ERROR4 -- error, program stopped
13: ECHO Some kinda error took place
14: GOTO END
15: :ERROR3 -- Control-Break pressed, stopping the backup
16: ECHO Backup halted!  (You pressed Control-Break)
17: GOTO END
18: :ERROR2 -- File sharing conflicts
19: ECHO There are file sharing conflicts.
20: ECHO Please contact the network administrator for
    assistance
21: GOTO END
22: :ERROR1 -- Nothing to backup
23: ECHO No files found to backup, no need to proceed
24: ECHO Bye!
25: :END
```

Fig. 9-2. This program shows how error levels can be communicated to the user.

of 1 is generated. This way, you can get feedback from the user in your batch file:

```
ASK Is it okay to go on?
IF ERRORLEVEL 1 GOTO END
```

ASK displays the string "Is it okay to go on?" and then waits for either Y or N to be pressed (upper or lower case). If the user presses N, ERRORLEVEL 1 is returned and the program ends. Otherwise, the program goes on.

READKEY comes in many variations. In Chapter 10 you will use DEBUG to create a READKEY program (called RKEY) that returns the ASCII code value of a key pressed on the keyboard. The READKEY program available on the Supplemental Programs Diskette does that, as well as return relative values for the function keys, number keys, and alpha keys.

See FIG. 9-3. After the string is displayed (4), READKEY will accept any single character input (5). That character's ASCII code value will then be available to your

```
Name: RANGE.BAT

 1: @ECHO OFF
 2: REM An example of READKEY
 3: :START
 4: ECHO Type a 1 or a 2
 5: READKEY
 6: IF ERRORLEVEL 51 GOTO RANGE
 7: IF ERRORLEVEL 50 GOTO TWO
 8: IF ERRORLEVEL 49 GOTO ONE
 9: :RANGE
10: ECHO --That number is out of range
11: GOTO START
12: :ONE
13: ECHO --You typed the number 1!
14: GOTO END
15: :TWO
16: ECHO --You typed the number 2!
17: :END
```

Fig. 9-3. This program accepts a 1 or 2 key press.

batch file via ERRORLEVEL (6, 7, 8). In this case, the values you want are 49 for "1" and 48 for "0". The first ERRORLEVEL statement eliminates any characters out of range (6) and goes to the :RANGE label (9) to display a warning (10). The program then repeats (11). This also happens for ASCII code values less than "1" or "2"; the ERRORLEVEL test fails in line 8 so the message is displayed.

Each of the messages displayed by ECHO (10, 13, 16) are preceded by two dashes. This offsets the message from the character entered. (A side effect of the READKEY utility is that it does not display the character just entered followed by a space or a linefeed.)

ERROR TRAPPING

There are two ways to "trap" potential errors in batch files. The first is to anticipate what an error might be. You will notice that the two preceding batch file examples (above) used ERRORLEVEL, and some fancy branching, to detect errors and display error messages. If you know what a potential error could be, it's easier to program around it.

The second type of error to trap for is a bit harder to catch. These are batch file errors that occur because of simple typos, or some errors DOS may throw at you. In batch files, these errors are hard to predict and next to impossible to remedy. A list with explanations is provided here, however, to assist you in tracking down causes.

IF EXIST

One of the most common errors encountered in a batch file is "File not found." It means you either mistyped something when you created the batch file, or something actually happened to the file in question. In either case, the prescription is to always use IF EXIST to see if the file is there.

```
IF EXIST DATAFILE.001 ECHO It's there!
```

If the file DATAFILE.001 exists, "It's there!" is displayed on the console.

```
IF NOT EXIST E:\SPOOL\*.* GOTO SKIP
COPY E:\SPOOL\*.* C:\TEMP
:SKIP
```

The above snippet of code might be part of a SHUTDOWN batch file. Assume E: is an electronic disk. This code is used to remove all files from the electronic disk and place them in the \TEMP directory on the hard drive. If only the middle line were used in a batch file and E:\SPOOL was empty, then an error message would be displayed. This way, IF NOT EXIST tests to see if the directory is empty. If no files exist, the line containing the COPY command is skipped.

You can test for any file on disk using IF EXIST. You cannot, however, check for subdirectories. If a subdirectory exists and it's full, then a statement such as:

```
IF EXIST C:\SUB\*.*
```

will work. If \SUB exists and it's empty, however, then the above statement will be false. Even if you try:

```
IF EXIST C:\SUB
```

the test will be negative. So to specify files within a subdirectory, rather than the subdirectory's name, use IF EXIST.

Batch File Errors

There are quite a few batch file specific errors you might come across. Additionally, you could come across any of the by-now-familiar DOS error messages from the classic "File not found" (which IF EXIST will catch) to "Abort, Retry, Fail, Ignore."

The following are error messages that you might see when running your batch files:

Batch file missing

Cannot start COMMAND, exiting

FOR cannot be nested

Label not found

No free file handles/Cannot start COMMAND, exiting

Out of environment space

Syntax Error

Terminate batch job (Y/N)

Fortunately, most of these errors have specific reasons for appearing. When you do see them, the following explanations will come in handy.

Batch file missing   The batch file you're running can no longer locate itself to load in the next line. This might happen if you accidentally deleted or renamed the batch file, if the batch file contains unusual characters (it was made by a word processor and saved improperly), or if you changed drives or diskettes. Sometimes, if you change your PATH statement, the batch file can get lost. Also, if you're accessing your batch file via a SUBSTituted drive and you un-assign the drive, then the batch file can get lost.

Cannot start COMMAND, exiting   This error occurs if you're using COMMAND /C to "call" other batch files but there are too many files already open. The solution is to increase the number of files that can be open at a time by increasing the number specified with the FILES statement in your CONFIG.SYS file.

FOR cannot be nested   You attempted to use a second FOR as the *command* portion of a FOR command. For example:

```
FOR %F IN (*.*) DO FOR %A IN (*.BAK) DO ...
```

The solution is to try to figure out another way to implement the FOR command.

Label not found   This is one of the few commands that will halt a batch file instantly. If the batch file interpreter cannot locate a label associated with a GOTO statement, the above message is displayed and the batch file immediately stops. The solution is to check your spelling, or add the label where it should go. (See Chapter 8 for more information on labels.)

No free file handles/Cannot start COMMAND, exiting   This is the same type of error that happens when you call another batch file with COMMAND /C. (This error happens with earlier versions of DOS.) See "Cannot start COMMAND, exiting" above.

Out of environment space   You attempted to alter the environment and there is no more room. This can happen with the PATH, PROMPT, or SET commands. The solution is either to reset certain environment variables to zero, or to give yourself more room in the environment by using the /E switch of the SHELL command in your CONFIG.SYS file. You can also run a second copy of COMMAND.COM with the /E switch specified, but remember to EXIT back to your original copy before the batch file is through.

Syntax Error   This is one of the most common batch file errors, but is not that serious. It won't halt your batch files like "Label not found" does, but if you have

ECHO OFF, it can be frustrating. Generally speaking, a "Syntax Error" only crops up when you forget to type something. In batch files this happens a lot when one equal sign is used instead of two with the IF statement:

IF %STRING%=TEST ECHO "Syntax Error"

Other DOS commands may use the "Syntax Error" message from time to time, though the majority of DOS commands have their own unique and confusing error messages. To hunt down Syntax Errors, first check for single equal signs. Then, turn ECHO ON and watch your batch file as it executes. You should be able to find the offending command and then edit it.

There is another, trickier error associated with the IF statement. Suppose you fix your IF statement with two equal signs:

IF %STATUS%==ON GOTO MAIN

If you still get "Syntax Error" with the above format, what DOS is telling you is that the environment variable (STATUS) isn't equal to anything (it's undefined). Essentially, the batch file interpreter expands it to:

IF ==ON GOTO MAIN

Because there is nothing on one side of the double equal sign, you have a syntax error. To fix this you can use the old quote trick:

IF "%STATUS"=="ON" GOTO MAIN

The statement will still evaluate true if %STATUS% is equal to ON. If %STATUS% isn't equal to anything, however, the batch file interpreter will see:

IF ""=="ON" GOTO MAIN

and you won't get your Syntax Error.

Terminate batch job (Y/N)   Although not really an error message, "Terminate batch job" isn't the friendliest way to stop a batch file from executing.

What this message means is that either CTRL–C or CTRL–BREAK was pressed. The batch file interpreter asks the user if they want to stop the batch file or continue. Pressing Y continues—pressing N stops.

But where does it stop?

As a rule of thumb, whichever line is being executed when CTRL–C or CTRL–BREAK is being pressed will not be executed. FIGURE 9-4 demonstrates how CTRL–BREAK stops a batch file.

Run the program in FIG. 9-4, and then press CTRL–C or CTRL–BREAK to stop it. Answer N to the question, then see where the batch file picks up. It usually ignores the line being executed when CTRL–BREAK was pressed (see FIG. 9-5). Line 7 in the FIG. 9-5 run was never executed. Keep this in mind when you halt long batch files; especially with ECHO OFF, because you don't really know what you're stopping.

```
Name: HALT.BAT

 1: @ECHO OFF
 2: ECHO Press Control-Break to stop me!
 3: ECHO This is line 1
 4: ECHO This is line 2
 5: ECHO This is line 3
 6: ECHO This is line 4
 7: ECHO This is line 5
 8: ECHO This is line 6
 9: ECHO This is line 7
10: ECHO This is line 8
11: ECHO This is line 9
12: ECHO Be faster next time ...
```

Fig. 9-4. This program demonstrates how *Ctrl—Break* stops a batch file.

```
C> HALT
Press Control-Break to stop me!
This is line 1
This is line 2
This is line 3
This is line 4
This is line 5
This is line 6
T^C

Terminate batch job (Y/N)? n
This is line 8
This is line 9
Be faster next time ...
C>
```

Fig. 9-5. This is the run from HALT.BAT.

If you're concerned about users messing up a batch file, give them a good place to break out by using the PAUSE command. The following is a common technique:

```
ECHO Press any key to go on, or press Control-Break to stop
ECHO and answer "Y" to "terminate batch job"
PAUSE
```

Here, PAUSE is used to allow the user to press CTRL–BREAK. This way, a serious operation won't be interrupted. Also, remember that pressing CTRL–BREAK in a called batch file returns control to DOS, not to the calling batch file.

One Last Thing
One Last Thing

No, I typed two of those titles on purpose. Occasionally you might get a double command at the end of your batch file. Say the final command in your batch file is:

```
ECHO All Done!
```

but you see on the screen:

```
All Done!
All Done!
```

The reason for the double display is an oddity with some versions of DOS. The problem is a missing carriage return/linefeed character combination. (You probably used a text editor to create the document and forgot to press ENTER after the final line.)

To fix things up, go in and add ENTER using your text editor.

Summary

Troubleshooting batch files is not as scary as it sounds. Instead, it involves minding your p's and q's and paying attention to several rules.

The restrictions DOS places on your batch files are: you cannot do I/O redirection on the same line as you start your batch file; you cannot name a batch file using the name of an internal command.

The ECHO command behaves rather oddly at times. It can be doubly frustrating because ECHO seems to vary with each release of DOS. There are alternative ECHO programs available (including SAY on the Supplemental Programs Diskette), however, that solve most of these problems.

Two batch file directives, ERRORLEVEL and EXIST, can be used to detect certain conditions in batch files. ERRORLEVEL contains a return code from a previously run DOS program or utility—and it can additionally be used to get a single character of input from the user. EXIST is used to test for the existence of files, and can be used to avoid "File not found" errors.

Finally, there are several errors, specific to batch files, that can occur. The most common is using a single equal sign with the IF statement (rather than the required double equal sign = =). Other errors can best be detected by turning ECHO ON and observing your batch file as it runs.

Part Three

Beyond
Batch Files

WHEN you go beyond batch files, you're breaking the limits of what batch files can do. After all, batch files were only designed with a limited purpose in mind. Yet, as most users discover how useful they can be, they want more.

Sadly, DOS doesn't provide that extra power that most advanced batch file programmers want. Instead, you'll have to turn to other sources: utility programs; third-party programs, and batch file enhancement languages. It's these sources that complete batch files, making them more useful and powerful than DOS does.

10
Beyond Batch Files

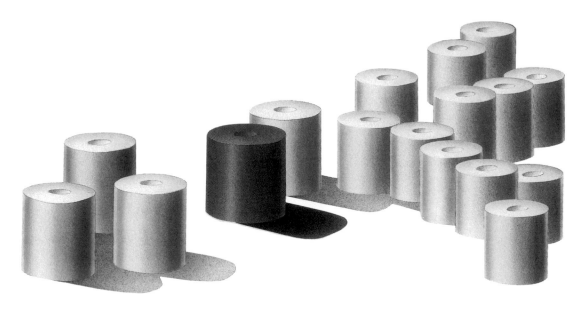

There are quite a few layers of "beyond batch file" techniques. Most of them covered in this chapter deal with supplemental batch file programs. First up to bat (what a horrid pun!) are utility programs—both public domain and third-party.

The second and third players are programs that come with DOS—programs that let you write other programs. These are the BASIC programming language and DEBUG. BASIC integrates quite nicely with batch file programs for picking up and taking care of a few simple, mundane tasks. DEBUG can be a powerful (and deadly) program. But in this instance, DEBUG is used to build some useful utilities.

ADDITIONS TO BATCH FILE COMMANDS

Besides the limited number of batch file commands DOS gives you, there are virtually thousands of supplemental programs and utilities, all of which can be added to your batch file command repertoire. You can use these programs to enhance your batch file performance, as well as to make your batch files more interesting and capable.

There are two sources for these batch file command additions. The first is the public domain. (Where is that anyway?) That's a place where programmers and philanthropists deposit programs and utilities free of charge for everyone to use. You can locate these programs on an electronic bulletin board system, or on national on-line systems such as GEnie or CompuServe. Or you can order disks full of these programs from places like PC–SIG.

The second source consists of third party software or utility programs. These are the programs you buy off the shelf, and for which you pay money. Though some public domain programs call themselves "shareware," meaning that they want a donation, they are not the same as these "real" programs. For one thing, third-party programs usually come with a money-back guarantee and phone support. They're thoroughly tested and, in most cases, well worth the money.

Public Domain Utilities

There are so many DOS public domain utilities, it would be futile to attempt to list them all. Some books try, but seeing that new and better utilities are constantly being written, it's not worth the effort. As a bit of advice, just keep your eyes open, attend user group meetings, and keep in touch with other PC enthusiasts and you'll catch wind of most of them.

Out of the many utility programs, only a handful apply to batch file programs. Below I've listed eight of the crème de la crème. This isn't by any means all of them, just some that I've found particularly useful.

DSIZE.COM   I've been looking for DSIZE for years. It scans a floppy disk in the indicated drive and returns an ERRORLEVEL code depending on the disk's format:

DSIZE *drive*

drive is the letter of a floppy drive.

The ERRORLEVEL codes returned are as follows:

0   Unrecognized format

1   160K diskette

2   180K diskette

3   320K diskette

4   360K diskette

This is handy for including in a FORMAT testing batch file. If DSIZE returns an ERRORLEVEL of zero, then the diskette is probably blank and can be formatted safely. Otherwise, the diskette contains some data, and you can display a warning message.

Note that a potential flaw in this thinking is that DSIZE assumes that the diskette is already formatted. If not, DOS displays the classic "Abort, Retry, Fail" error message.

ECOH.COM   ECOH works like DOS's ECHO function, with a twist: the string echoed is displayed in reverse:

ECOH I am in inverse type.

This displays "I am in inverse type" on the screen using black letters on a white background. Astute readers will recognize that you can do this using the ECHO command with ANSI escape characters as follows:

ECHO ESC[7m I am in inverse type.ESC[7m

(Remember to replace ESC with ^V[or ^[or whatever your text editor accepts as the ESCape character.) The advantage to ECOH, however, is that it doesn't rely upon ANSI to produce inverse type.

INPUT.COM   INPUT is a program that reads the keyboard and returns an ERRORLEVEL return code relative to the key pressed. Unlike other similar programs, if the user presses ESCape then ERRORLEVEL 255 is generated, which can come in handy.

INPUT, is followed by a string of characters to scan for:

INPUT "ABCDE"

Pressing **A** (upper or lower case) returns ERRORLEVEL 1; pressing **B** returns ERRORLEVEL 2; and so on.

REPLY.COM   REPLY is another in a series of "get input" programs that reads one character from the keyboard and translates that character, somehow, into an ERRORLEVEL code. The advantage of REPLY is that it waits ten seconds for input and, if there isn't any, returns an ERRORLEVEL of zero. Of course, you may not think of this as an advantage. If so, there are similar utilities you can use.

With REPLY you can narrow down the keys the user can press by listing valid key combinations after the REPLY command:

REPLY ynq

Here, REPLY waits ten seconds for either **Y**, **N** or **Q** to be pressed (upper and lower case are treated the same). If Y is pressed, an ERRORLEVEL of 1 is returned; if N is pressed, ERRORLEVEL 2 is returned; and if Q is pressed, ERRORLEVEL 3 is returned. REPLY assigns ERRORLEVEL values based on the position of the responses. So for:

REPLY abcdefghijklmnopqrstuvwxyz

A generates an ERRORLEVEL of 1, and **Z** generates an ERRORLEVEL of 26.

SWEEP.COM   Sweep is one of those "can't live without" utilities. SWEEP is followed by a command, such as:

SWEEP DEL *.BAK

What SWEEP does is to issue the command for the current directory, plus all subdirectories under the current directory. So, if the above command were typed in your root directory, SWEEP would scan all subdirectories on your hard drive and issue the command DEL *.BAK.

WAITN.COM   WAITN is used to pause for a number of seconds. It's ideal for briefly pausing the screen—especially when you don't want to rely upon the user to press ENTER.

WAITN 20

The command pauses for 20 seconds.

WAITUNTL.COM   WAITUNTL, also known as WAITTIME.COM, is another "must have" batch file addition. I don't know how many times I've heard people begging for some kind of "alarm clock" command that will start a certain function at a specific time of day. Well, this is it.

WAITUNTL is followed by a specific time in 24-hour (military) format. It waits until that time comes to pass, and then the batch file continues. This way you can include time-specific events in your batch files.

```
WAITUNTL 16:09:00
```

This command directs WAITUNTL to pause batch file execution until nine minutes after 4 o'clock in the afternoon.

Norton Utilities

Aside from the public domain goodies discussed above, there are programs you can buy that contain all sorts of batch file utilities. Perhaps the best all around is *Norton Utilities*, put out by Peter Norton Computing. There are two versions of the program: The *Norton Utilities 4.0* and the *Norton Utilities Advanced Edition*. You want the advanced edition.

The *Norton Utilities*, or "NU," are a series of small, individual programs that serve to enhance your computer. Several of the commands deal with disk management: unfragmenting the hard drive, scanning and repairing files and, most famous of all, the undelete program that has saved many a user's life.

Out of the 24 utilities that come with *NU Advanced Edition*, you'll find five to be extremely useful in batch files. (I like quite a few more of the utilities than that: Directory Sort, File Find, and so on, but only five of them will benefit batch files directly.)

ASK   ASK is yet another in a long series of programs that takes a single keystroke of input and translates it into an ERRORLEVEL value. The Norton ASK, however, has an option prompting string, as well as a list of valid keys:

```
ASK "Enter the function you desire: ", 123
```

ASK displays the string enclosed in quotes and then waits for either the 1, 2, or 3 key to be pressed. Each key is assigned an ERRORLEVEL value from 1 through 3 (based on their order), just like REPLY and INPUT above.

BEEP   BEEP is a handy program that beeps your computer's speaker. Of course, ECHOing a CTRL–G will do the same thing, but not in the many ways that the NU's BEEP command will.

BEEP is followed by a number of optional switches or, if you'll believe it, a filename containing pitches and durations that will play a small tune. BEEP's switches set the duration, frequency, repetition and wait factors of a tone, giving you quite some harmonic freedom. In fact, you could even alert the dog with some of the pitches possible.

FA   FA stands for File Attributes, and it's used to change certain aspects of a file. For example, using FA you can make a file visible or invisible. Also, you can use FA to change the read-only and archive values of a file; but seeing what most later versions of DOS can do with using the ATTRIB command, FA is best used for hiding and un-hiding things.

FA SECRET.BAT /HID+

This command HIDes the file SECRET.BAT, making it invisible (but it still exists on disk). The DIR command will not list SECRET.BAT, but if you type SECRET, the file will execute.

FA can also be used to find any hidden or otherwise altered files:

FA *.* /S/U

This command displays all "unusual" files in the current directory, as well as all unusual files in any subdirectories off the current directory.

One of my favorite batch files to have is HIDE.BAT. It uses FA to hide batch files:

Name: HIDE.BAT

```
1: @ECHO OFF
2: IF %1NOTHING=NOTHING GOTO END
3: FA %1 /HID+ > NUL
4: ECHO %1 hidden
5: :END
```

Using this batch file, I can type:

C> HIDE SECRET.DAT

and the HIDE batch file will run Norton's FA program, hiding whatever file I specify.

SA   SA stands for Screen Attributes and it's the famous Norton Utility command that will permanently change the color characteristics of your display.

The nice thing about SA is that it uses plain English commands:

SA BRIGHT WHITE ON BLUE

As you might have guessed, this command changes the screen colors to a bright white foreground (letters) on a blue background.

TM   Time Mark (TM) is one of the most interesting of all the NU batch file commands. It works like a stopwatch, keeping track of elapsed time.

TM START

This command starts the stopwatch. Now your batch file could execute, or a certain activity could take place.

TM STOP

This command stops the stopwatch and displays the elapsed time since the TM START command was issued.

TM operates up to four independent clocks and keeps track of each elapsed time. It can be quite useful for log entries or billing purposes when computer time is important.

Supplemental Programs Diskette

Windcrest Books, Inc., is offering a Supplement Programs Diskette—a companion disk—to go along with this book. On the diskette you'll find all the batch file examples listed here, except for Norton's, as well as public domain batch file utilities, and some programs that I've written myself.

One of the best parts of writing this book has been sitting down and thinking about which utilities would be the best to go with batch files. As I completed each chapter, a new utility would pop up in my head. I'd thir.k, "Yeah, that would come in handy." Then I'd sit down, fire up the assembler, and write the utility.

Granted, my first profession is a writer, not a programmer. But all the programs have been tested and they all work. They're not public domain programs, nor are they third-party. Instead, the only way to get them is to order the companion diskette that comes with this book. (There is a form near the back of this book.)

If you order the disk, and I encourage you to, you'll get the following programs I've written. I think all of them will help you to write better batch files. (Complete documentation for all of these files is included on the *Supplemental Programs Diskette.)*

ASK.COM   ASK is yet another one of those read key/return ERRORLEVEL utilities. But, unlike the Norton Utilities ASK, this one comes on the *Supplemental Diskette* for far less than you'd pay for the complete *Norton Utilities.*

ASK optionally displays a string that asks a yes or no question. The user can then type only a Y or N (either case). For Y, ERRORLEVEL 0 is returned; for N, ERRORLEVEL 1 is returned.

ASK Continue?

This displays the word "Continue?" and waits for either Y or N to be pressed.

BLANKS.COM   I wrote BLANKS because of the inadequacy of the ECHO statement to display a blank line. If you use BLANKS all by itself in a batch file, it will display a single blank line. Otherwise, you can follow blanks with any value (up to 255) and it displays that many blank lines.

BLANKS 6

This command causes six blank lines to be displayed.

BOX.COM   BOX is one of my pride and joys, though few people understand how to use it to its full extent. I wrote it for menu-generating batch file commands to make the screen look prettier.

What BOX does is to draw a box (using either block graphics, single lines, or double lines) at any position on the screen.

BOX ALL

This command draws a box around the edge of the screen. If anything is already drawn on the screen, it will not be erased by the box.

Also, box will draw a box around a specified string. In this instance, BOX only encloses the string; it does not draw a box elsewhere on the screen:

BOX "Hackers do it on computers"

If you add a /C, the box will be centered on the screen (see FIG. 10-1), adding another interesting effect.

```
┌─────────────────────────────────────┐
│  Hackers do it on computers          │
└─────────────────────────────────────┘
```

Fig. 10-1. BOX encloses a text string.

CLZ.COM   CLZ is a program a friend sent me—I don't know where he got it. What it does is to clear the screen in an interesting fashion. I took the original CLZ program, cleaned it up, and rewrote it, leaving the original flavor intact. (I added a proper exiting routine and made the cursor go to position "1,1" when the program was finished.)

CLZ is just an alternative to CLS, though it's more visually interesting.

GREET.COM   GREET is a program I include in all my batch files that others use around the office. GREET displays one of three messages, depending on the time of day:

Good morning,

Good afternoon,

Good evening,

If any text follows GREET on the command line, that text is echoed after the above greeting:

GREET Dan

displays, "Good morning, Dan" depending on the time of day. People really get a kick out of that one.

HOLD.COM   HOLD was written to counter the lameness of the batch file PAUSE command. What PAUSE does is to display "Strike a key when ready . . . " and then wait for a keypress. What it should do is allow you to include an optional message after PAUSE, a message that would be displayed a line above the "Strike a key'' message. The DOS manual says PAUSE does this—but only when ECHO is turned off.

HOLD can be used in two ways. The first is just like PAUSE. HOLD by itself displays the message ''Press any key to continue . . .''. But when HOLD is followed by an optional string, it first displays that string, then the ''Press any key'' message:

```
HOLD Insert the diskette "OLDFILES" in Drive A and
```

This displays the following:

```
Insert the diskette "OLDFILES" in Drive A and
Press any key to continue
```

That's what PAUSE should have done in the first place.

LOCATE.COM   I wrote LOCATE.COM after writing LOCATE.BAT (in Chapter 3). LOCATE.COM does the same thing: position the cursor anywhere on the display:

```
LOCATE 5,10
```

This positions the cursor at column 5, row 10 (the coordinates are in X-Y order). If no coordinates are given, LOCATE homes the cursor. (Also, if bad coordinates are given, LOCATE returns an ERRORLEVEL code of 1.)

You can follow LOCATE with an ECHO statement to position a string of characters at any spot on the screen:

```
LOCATE 20,5
ECHO Main Menu
```

READKEY.COM   Yes, here's yet another read key/return ERRORLEVEL program. But this one has some interesting advantages that none of the others offer. All by itself, READKEY simply returns the ASCII value of a key pressed as the ERRORLEVEL value. READKEY, however, has three optional switches that allow you to narrow down the choices:

The A switch limits READKEY's input to only the alphabet characters, A through Z (case doesn't matter). When /A is specified, READKEY returns an ERRORLEVEL value relative to the characters offset within the alphabet, so A is ERRORLEVEL one, B is ERRORLEVEL two, and so on.

The N switch limits READKEY's input to only the numbers, 0 through 1. Again, as with the /A switch, the ''1'' returns an ERRORLEVEL of one, ''2'' returns ERRORLEVEL two, and on up to ''9''. A special case is the ''0'' key, which returns ERRORLEVEL zero.

The F switch does something no other ''read key'' utility does: It reads the function keys, F1 through F10. For ''F1,'' an ERRORLEVEL of one is returned, for ''F2,'' an ERRORLEVEL of two is returned, and so on.

The E switch determines whether the key pressed will be displayed or not. Normally, the key is displayed, but when /E – is specified, the key will not be displayed.

Also, an optional prompting string can be specified after the switches:

READKEY /F "Enter function key:"

This displays "Enter function key:" then waits for F1 through F10 to be pressed. READKEY then returns a corresponding ERRORLEVEL value, depending on the key pressed.

REPT.COM   REPT was written to spiff up the display, and take care of one of the shortcomings of the ECHO command. What REPT does is to repeat a specific character a certain number of times, similar to the BASIC language STRING$ statement.

REPT * 20

This reads, "Repeat the * (asterisk) character twenty times." After the above command, you'll see twenty asterisks on your screen.

Some users like to use a string of equal signs to separate items in their batch files:

REPT = 80

This command displays 80 equal signs.

RESTPATH.COM   You'll like RESTPATH. It was written to solve a program that batch file programmers have puzzled over for years: How to restore your original drive and subdirectory after running a batch file.

Say, for example, that you're running a batch file that changes drives, then directories to run a specific program. Once the program is done, how do you change back to your original directory? There is no way to "remember" the current directory without doing some fancy batch file footwork.

Ta da! RESTPATH to the rescue!

RESTPATH uses the CD command and I/O redirection to remember from which drive and path you started your batch file. For example put the following command at the top of your batch file:

CD > C:\TEMP

This redirects the output of the CD command to the file TEMP in your root directory (on drive C). TEMP will contain something like:

C:\WP\WORD

When the batch file is over, the RESTPATH command can be used:

RESTPATH C:\TEMP

RESTPATH reads the TEMP file, then restores the drive to C and the path to \WP\WORD. (You can then add a second line to the end of your batch file to delete C:\TEMP.)

RESTPATH does its job quickly and silently. Because it has no output, it returns the following ERRORLEVEL values: 0, meaning everything went okay; 1 meaning that a file wasn't found; and 2 meaning that the path could not be restored (the file probably wasn't created with CD >).

SAY.COM   SAY was another program written to solve some of my frustrations with the ECHO command. In fact, SAY works just like ECHO, but with two exceptions.

You can SAY anything—even nothing—and SAY repeats exactly what you want. Just like ECHO, type SAY followed by any string and that string is displayed to the console—even a blank line, or the word ON or OFF or anything.

Secondly, if you end the string with a semicolon, the string displayed will not be followed by a carriage return/linefeed. (This works like the semicolon in the BASIC language PRINT statement.) Using the semicolon technique, you can follow the SAY command with a REPLY or INPUT statement and have the display look cleaner than when using ECHO to display the string.

TSTAMP.COM   TSTAMP is a quick utility I wrote that spits out the date and time in a short format. After typing TSTAMP, something like the following will be echoed to the display:

```
17:49:06 08/06/89
```

That's the current time and date in the "short" format. This program uses DOS (as all the others do) so that its output can be redirected to a file. This makes TSTAMP ideal for keeping log files, as well as just a quick way to find out what time it is.

VERNUM.COM   VERNUM might come in handy someday—if DOS ever changes radically. What it does is to return the current version number of DOS as an ERRORLEVEL value. Version numbers are returned as shown in TABLE 10-1.

Table 10-1.

Version	ERRORLEVEL
4.0	40
3.3	33
3.2	32
3.1	31
3.0	30
2.1	21
1.0	0

The batch file example in FIG. 10-2 shows how VERNUM.COM might be used.

```
Name: VERNUMT.BAT

 1: ECHO off
 2: ECHO This tests vernum
 3: VERNUM
 4: IF ERRORLEVEL 40 GOTO VER40
 5: IF ERRORLEVEL 33 GOTO VER33
 6: IF ERRORLEVEL 32 GOTO VER32
 7: IF ERRORLEVEL 31 GOTO VER31
 8: IF ERRORLEVEL 21 GOTO VER21
 9: ECHO You have a *very* early edition of DOS
10: GOTO END
11: :VER40
12: ECHO DOS Version 4.0 is in use
13: GOTO END
14: :VER33
15: ECHO DOS Version 3.3 is in use
16: GOTO END
17: :VER32
18: ECHO DOS Version 3.2 is in use
19: GOTO END
20: :VER31
21: ECHO DOS Version 3.1 is in use
22: GOTO END
23: :VER21
24: ECHO DOS Version 2.1 is in use
25: :END
```

Fig. 10-2. VERNUM.BAT is an example of how VERNUM.COM can be used.

BATCH FILES AND *BASIC*

The original IBM PC, and all versions since, have had the BASIC programming language built into their ROM. This was because, back in the good old days, every computer came with a built-in version of BASIC and IBM wanted to be just like everyone else. In most cases, the BASIC programming language also served as the computer's operating system! But today, with inexpensive software widely available, learning to program your computer in BASIC is an all-but-forgotten art.

BASIC integrates nicely with batch files. In the first place, BASIC comes with most versions of DOS. (It's a disk-based version of BASIC called GW BASIC. IBM computers have a special "supplemental" version of BASIC that comes on PC–DOS diskettes; that version won't run on any other computers.) As long as the BASIC interpreter is on your system's path, you can access and run BASIC programs from anywhere on your system.

There is a problem, though: Don't get carried away with writing supplemental BASIC programs for your batch files. In other words, if you start writing more and more of your batch file using a "supplemental" BASIC program, then you should question why you're writing the batch file in the first place. If a BASIC program would better suit your needs, write the program in BASIC.

Also, this book doesn't offer any programming tips on BASIC. If you'd like to learn BASIC programming, or need a reference, refer to the books mentioned in the introduction of this book. You don't need to know how to program BASIC to type in the routines in this section. But if you intend on further using BASIC, I'd recommend picking up those books.

Manipulating the Environment

BASIC is perfect for writing quick little routines—time savers and other functions that batch files are incapable of. Of primary interest to batch file programming is BASIC's ability to assign and manipulate the environment. Two BASIC functions do the work:

ENVIRON

ENVIRON$

ENVIRON is used like the SET command from DOS:

ENVIRON("*variable* = *string*")

variable becomes an environment variable and **string** becomes the variable's data. This works just like:

SET *variable* = *string*

ENVIRON$ is used to display the contents of environment variables, or to list them by their number (relative to the top entry in the environment table):

ENVIRON$(*value*)

value is a number from 1 to 127. It represents the variables in the environment in order, from 1st through 127th. Because this is a function, you'll need to assign ENVIRON$ to a variable, or use it with the PRINT statement (it won't work by itself):

```
PRINT ENVIRON$(1)
```

This command displays the first variable's data in the environment table. Alternatively, you can use the following format:

```
PRINT ENVIRON$("PATH")
```

This command displays the contents of the PATH variable—or any variable listed in the quotes.

There is one minor drawback to using ENVIRON and ENVIRON$. For some reason, assigning variables with ENVIRON is only a temporary thing. During the research for this book I tested both functions. ENVIRON continually produced "Out of Memory" errors no matter how long the variables were. Also, when I was able to assign a variable—once I quit BASIC and returned to DOS, that variable was gone. (The SET command did not display it.)

On other computers (besides an IBM PC/XT), and with other versions of DOS (besides PC–DOS 3.3) and BASIC, these functions may behave differently, but for the purposes of researching this book, I didn't get them to work properly.

If they did work, a BASIC program along the lines of the following could be in order:

Name: GETDATA.BAS

(All BASIC programs have the .BAS filename extension.)

```
10 REM Program to assign an environment variable
20 LINE INPUT "Variable data:",VD$
30 VD$="DATA="+VD$
40 ENVIRON(VD$)
50 SYSTEM
```

This BASIC program asks for a string of text (20). Then it creates the string "DATA =" plus whatever text you entered (30). So, for example, if you typed in "My Name", the string created in line 30 would be "DATA = My Name". Line 40 uses ENVIRON to pass the variable DATA and the string you entered to the environment table. Line 50 exits BASIC and returns to DOS.

To incorporate this BASIC program into your batch files, you add the line:

BASICA GETDATA

That's the name of the BASIC language interpreter, BASICA, followed by the name of the BASIC program you want to run. Because the BASIC program returns to DOS (line 50 above), this line would execute just like any other program in a batch file—with the added advantage of assigning an environment variable.

A Possible Solution

As I pointed out earlier, I never could get ENVIRON or ENVIRON$ to work with my IBM PC. But still, I have batch files where it would be nice to include some method of assigning environment variables. BASIC still provided a solution.

One of the most frustrating things when dealing with BATCH files is not being able to accept input from the keyboard. That is, anything beyond the one character you can read with programs like ASK and READKEY and then return to the batch file via ERRORLEVEL. But to get a whole string of characters is different. You can puzzle over this a long time, and eventually you'll figure out that there's no way to do it. Sure, a utility could be written to accept input and assign that input to an environment variable. But why do that when BASIC provides a solution?

The solution works like this: The problem is to get input from the user and assign that input to an environment variable, NAME. To do this we'll go through three steps:

1) Run a batch file that needs the data for NAME.

2) Run a BASIC program that gets the input, then creates a second batch file to SET the value of NAME.

3) Call the second batch file that sets the NAME variable, then return to the first batch file.

This is tricky, so pay close attention.

First, we write a batch file that needs the input. The input will be handled jointly by BASIC and the second batch file, SETVAR.BAT. For now, here's the first batch file:

Name: READNAME.BAT

```
1: @ECHO OFF
2: REM This batch file will read your name
3: ECHO Just like magic, this batch file knows who you are!
4: REM Clear old NAME variable...
5: SET NAME=
6: BASICA SETVAR
7: CALL SETVAR
8: ECHO Pleased to meet you, %NAME%
```

This batch file is straightforward, with a few ECHOes and REMs tossed in to let us and the user know what's going on. The secret, tricky part is in lines 6 and 7. Line 6 runs the BASIC program interpreter, BASICA, and runs the BASIC program SETVAR. After BASIC is done, control returns to DOS and, in line 7, the batch file SETVAR is called.

FIGURE 10-3 is a listing of the BASIC language program SETVAR.BAS. This program actually creates the batch file program SETVAR.BAT (it writes it out to disk).

Name: SETVAR.BAS

```
100 REM BASIC program to build a call-able batch file
110 REM disable CTRL-C and CTRL-BREAK for no interrupts
120 KEY 15,CHR$(4)+CHR$(46) 'CONTROL-C
130 KEY 16,CHR$(4)+CHR$(70) 'CONTROL-BREAK
140 ON KEY (15) GOSUB 240: KEY (15) ON
150 ON KEY (16) GOSUB 240: KEY (16) ON
160 REM ask for input
170 LINE INPUT "Enter your name: ";N$
180 OPEN "SETVAR.BAT" FOR OUTPUT AS 1
190       PRINT #1,"@ECHO OFF"
200       PRINT #1,"REM BASIC-created batch file"
210       PRINT #1,"SET NAME=";N$
220 CLOSE 1
230 SYSTEM
240 RETURN 230
```

Fig. 10-3. This program actually creates a batch file.

To type in the program, go into BASIC by typing BASICA at the DOS command prompt. Remember to type in the line numbers, and carefully watch your work. Do not run the program until you've saved it to disk! To save the file, type:

```
SAVE "SETVAR.BAS"
```

and press ENTER. To run the program, type RUN. SETVAR.BAS automatically returns to DOS. Otherwise, to manually return to DOS, type the BASIC command SYSTEM.

Lines 120 through 150 disable CTRL–C and CTRL–BREAK. This is necessary because, if the user pressed them while the BASIC program was running, control would return to BASIC, not DOS. Here, if either of these two keys are pressed, they execute the subroutine at line 240. Line 240 returns the user to line 230, which dumps them back into DOS. This way the program cannot ever exit to BASIC.

Line 170 asks for input from the user, and stores the input in the BASIC variable N$ (pronounced N-string). Next comes the tricky part.

Lines 180 through 220 create the batch file program SETVAR.BAT. (Only a twisted genius would think of creating a batch file for the sole purpose of assigning an environment variable. No—it wasn't me.)

Line 180 "opens" SETVAR.BAT for output. The "output" mode erases any file already called SETVAR.BAT, so we know we won't be appending or messing with any file already on disk. The next three lines create the contents of SETVAR.BAT.

Line 190 writes the first line of SETVAR.BAT using the PRINT statement. As usual, the first line is your typical "@ECHO OFF" statement.

Line 200 writes a REM statement. This is rather useless, but it does let you know where the batch file came from.

Line 210 is the key. It writes a line in the batch file that contains "SET NAME = " and then N$, which is whatever string you typed in line 170. The command line is then created just as it would be in any other batch file, but in this instance, it's customized!

Line 220 CLOSEs the batch file, writing it out to disk, and line 230 returns to DOS.

Now that BASIC is done, the next line in the batch file (READNAME.BAT) is executed, line 7:

```
7: CALL SETVAR
```

The newly created batch file SETVAR is called. SETVAR looks something like this:

```
1: @ECHO OFF
2: REM BASIC-created batch file
3: SET NAME=winston mcgillicutty
```

BASIC created this batch file. The user typed in **_winston mcgillicutty_** and BASIC created a batch file incorporating that string. After SETVAR runs, "NAME = winston mcgillicutty" is in the environment table. Control returns to

READNAME.BAT (the original batch file) and the following is ECHOed on the display:

`Pleased to meet you, winston mcgillicutty`

BASIC can be used in a variety of ways like this, creating and writing custom batch files that take advantage of the SET statement. There's only one warning (which was stated earlier): Just make sure you don't get carried away. Also, you should know that when you enter BASIC to run a BASIC program, such as:

`BASICA SETVAR`

the BASIC interpreter will first clear the screen. Keep this in mind if there's a message you want the user to read before the BASIC program runs. You may want to add a PAUSE statement before a line such as that above.

Writing .COM Programs with BASIC

Aside from supplementing batch file programs, BASIC can be used to create utility programs. These aren't BASIC programs, but .COM programs that are originally written in assembly language. BASIC is used in this case as a catalyst, a tool by which you can transform the raw data of the .COM program into a .COM file on disk.

This technique is really far removed from batch file programming. Yet, quite a few of the magazines use it to allow everyone to duplicate their utilities.

For an example, I'm using the GREET.COM utility mentioned above. GREET.COM simply displays a friendly message followed by any optional data on the command line. It was originally written in assembly language. Using BASIC, however, we can re-create the program. This works sort of like Dr. Frankenstein creating his monster from bits and pieces of dead people (sort of).

By the way, no .COM program or utility starts out this way. This technique simply makes those programs and utilities available to anyone who wants to type them in using BASIC.

The technique works like this: First, the .COM program is written and debugged. Then its contents, the individual bytes that make up the machine language instructions, are "dumped" in hexadecimal format. These bytes are then placed in BASIC language DATA statements.

The BASIC program then opens a .COM file on disk (similar to what was done with SETVAR above). The bytes are read from the DATA statement and then written to the .COM file on disk. When the last byte is ready, the .COM file is CLOSEd and the BASIC program ends.

This technique allows anyone with a BASIC interpreter to write the program, copying down all the DATA bytes, then run that program to create the .COM program.

The following is a BASIC program that creates the GREET.COM utility. It employs a checksum method to determine whether all the DATA values that the user enters are the same as printed in FIG. 10-4. Remember to type in the program

Name: GREET.BAS

```
100 REM A BASIC program to build GREET.COM
110 CLS
120 PRINT "Building GREET.COM"
130 PRINT"(C) Copyright 1988, TAB Books"
140 DEFINT V,C
150 C=0
160 OPEN "R",#1,"GREET.COM",1
170    FIELD #1,1 AS VALUE$
180    FOR X=1 TO 117
190       READ A$
200       V = VAL("&H"+A$)
210       C=C+V: LOCATE 3,1: PRINT "Checksum =";C
220       LSET VALUE$ = MKI$(V)
230       PUT #1
240    NEXT X
250    IF C=11382 THEN PRINT "Checksums match--file okay!":
       GOTO 270
260    PRINT "Bad checksum--check your DATA statements!"
270 CLOSE
280 DATA EB, 27, 90, 47, 6F, 6F, 64, 20, 24, 4D, 6F, 72, 6E
285 DATA 69, 6E, 67
290 DATA 2C, 24, 45, 76, 65, 6E, 69, 6E, 67, 2C, 24, 41, 66
295 DATA 74, 65, 72
300 DATA 6E, 6F, 6F, 6E, 2C, 24, 0D, 0A, 24, BA, 03, 01, B4
305 DATA 09, CD, 21
310 DATA B4, 2C, CD, 21, 80, FD, 0C, 73, 06, BA, 09, 01, EB
315 DATA 0F, 90, 80
320 DATA FD, 11, 73, 06, BA, 1B, 01, EB, 04, 90, BA, 12, 01
325 DATA B4, 09, CD
330 DATA 21, A0, 80, 00, 3C, 00, 74, 11, 98, 8B, C8, BB, 81
335 DATA 00, 8A, 07
340 DATA 8A, D0, B4, 02, CD, 21, 43, E2, F5, BA, 26, 01, B4
345 DATA 09, CD, 21
350 DATA B8, 00, 4C, CD, 21
```

Fig. 10-4. This BASIC program creates the GREET.COM utility.

exactly as listed, including line numbers. To save the program, type:

SAVE "GREET.BAS"

and press ENTER. To return to DOS, type SYSTEM.

Be extra careful typing in the DATA statements (280 through 350). The program will let you know if you've made a mistake by displaying the "Bad checksum" message. If that happens, double-check the values you typed in.

Most of the details of this program tend more toward a BASIC language tutorial, rather than anything to do with batch files. Briefly, lines 160 through 270 are responsible for creating the file. The FOR–NEXT loop, between lines 180 and 240, uses the READ statement to read in the values from the DATA statements. Line 210 calculates and displays the checksum value, and lines 220 and 230 write the value to disk.

To run the program, type RUN. You'll see a numeric display as the program builds its checksum. When the program is done, it writes GREET.COM out to disk. When you see the BASIC "Ok" prompt, type SYSTEM to return to DOS. Now you can test your GREET.COM utility.

BATCH FILES AND *DEBUG*

DEBUG can be a useful tool. But like all useful tools, it can also be a deadly weapon. Use it cautiously.

DEBUG has many faces. It can be a memory peeker, a disk peeker, a program peeker, a miniassembler, a debugger, a tracer, and a million other things. The problem with DEBUG is that it's cryptic in its command structure, and that scares a lot of people away from using it. And, of course, it has the ability to really muck up your hard drive. That, too, will scare some people away.

In this section, you're going to see how DEBUG can be used to write programs. The first example is another self-creating program, similar to the BASIC program SETVAR.BAT. The second example shows how to use DEBUG to write a simple version of the READKEY.COM program discussed in section 10.1.

In section 10.4 you'll see how DEBUG can be used to "patch" programs, and how batch files can be used to remove some of the deadliness of some DOS commands.

DEBUG as Assembler

Like BASIC, DEBUG can be used to write programs. In this instance, the programs can be written using a miniassembler built into DEBUG. This assembler is quite limited, yet for quick-and-dirty purposes—especially batch files—it can come in quite handy.

Some users' first encounter with DEBUG is with their hard drive. Some hard drives need to have a low-level format performed on them. To do this, you need to access the hard drive's ROM, which is located on its controller card. DEBUG allows you to access that ROM and run the low-level formatting code that's written in the controller card's BIOS.

The controller card's BIOS is located in memory segment C800 (hexadecimal). This is true for all PC/XT compatible hard drives. Most Western Digital hard drive controllers have their low-level formatting routine located at offset 5 within memory segment C800. Other hard drive controllers may use a different location, CCC (hex) also being popular.

You enter DEBUG by typing DEBUG at the DOS command prompt:

```
C> DEBUG
-
```

The hyphen is DEBUG's prompt. Here you can examine memory, load programs, examine raw data on disk, and disassemble or assemble programs. The command to perform a low-level disk format (the Western Digital version) is:

```
-GC800:5
```

This reads "Go memory segment C800 and start executing the machine code instructions at offset 5." You can optionally specify an equal sign after the G:

```
-G=C800:5
```

Be careful not to try this command on your computer's hard drive: it will perform a low-level format and erase your disk's data.

A Booting Example

A better demonstration is a small batch file I picked up off a national computer network. This batch file works similarly to the BASIC program, SETVAR, in that it creates a second program and then runs that program. In this instance, it's a batch file that creates an assembly program using DEBUG.

If you recall from the first part of Chapter 2, the Intel 8088 microprocessor starts its day by executing the instruction at memory segment FFFF (hex), offset 0. Using a technique similar to the low-level disk format, a batch file can be written, shown in FIG. 10-5, that will execute that instruction, which will reset your computer.

```
Name: REBOOT.BAT

 1: GOTO BEGIN
 2:
 3: RCS
 4: FFFF
 5: RIP
 6: 0000
 7: G
 8:
 9: :BEGIN
10: DEBUG < REBOOT.BAT
```

Fig. 10-5. This batch file will execute a reset.

Before running REBOOT.BAT, take a look at it. The first instruction (1) branches to the :BEGIN label (9). Here, the batch file performs a sort of cannibalization, using itself to create the assembly language program through I/O redirection. Line 10 uses that data from the batch file as input for DEBUG. (Be sure to include a complete pathname before REBOOT.BAT.)

With I/O redirection, DEBUG will attempt to interpret the batch file as DEBUG instructions. Line one will be meaningless to debug, so it will produce an error message. The second line is blank, and will provide the Enter character needed to continue DEBUG.

Lines 3 through 7 provide the code that will reset the computer.

Line 3 resets the code segment register, and line 4 supplies the memory segment address, FFFF (hex).

Line 5 sets the instruction pointer, and line 6 supplies the instruction pointer's address: the offset from memory segment FFFF (hex), where our "program" will execute.

Line 7 is the "G" that sets everything in motion . . . and the system reboots.

"Code segment register," "Memory segment address," "Instruction pointer," "Memory offset." These terms are not required to know batch file programming. If you'd like to learn more about them, you can try understanding DEBUG by using the DOS reference manual, or refer to the book list in the introduction.

If you haven't tried it already, run the REBOOT program to make sure it works. Because ECHO is never turned off, you'll see the batch file as it runs—briefly, because the system will reset before you know it.

Creating READKEY

Besides using a batch file to execute a program via DEBUG, you can use DEBUG to write useful utilities. The following is the assembly language source code for a RKEY.COM program. This utility is similar to READKEY.COM that comes on the supplemental programs diskette. The difference is that this RKEY.COM accepts any keypress, and then translates that keypress into an ERRORLEVEL value equal to the key's ASCII code value.

Name: RKEY.ASM

(You don't need to type this in)

```
mov ah,1         ;read/wait for key press
int 21h          ;DOS function call
mov ah,4Ch       ;Exit to DOS
int 21h          ;DOS function call
```

The first duty of this program is to read the keyboard. DOS function call number one waits for a character from the keyboard (actually, from the standard input device). That key's ASCII code value will be returned in register AL.

DOS function 4C (hex) is used to return to DOS with an ERRORLEVEL code value. The code value is in register AL. The previous function puts the code value of the keypress in the AL register for us, so we simply return to DOS with the ERRORLEVEL intact.

There are two ways to create this program. The first is to write it in DEBUG and then save it to disk. The second is to write a batch file program that does the same thing.

To compose the program using DEBUG, enter DEBUG and type the **A** command, directing DEBUG to go into the miniassembler mode:

```
C> DEBUG
-A
234D:0100
```

The number 234D may not appear on your screen, but some other four-digit hex number will. This is the memory segment in which you're writing your program. The other four numbers are an offset within the segment. All programs written in debug start at offset 100 (hex). Incidentally, all numbers in debug are in hex (base 16) notation.

Type the rest of the commands as follows:

```
234D:0100 MOV AH,1
234D:0102 INT 21
234D:0104 MOV AH,4C
234D:0106 INT 21
234D:0108 ^C
```

(Press CTRL–C on the last line to stop input.)

You've now entered four lines of assembly language code. To save this code to disk, you'll first need to tell the assembler how many bytes to write. The code above is eight bytes long. To tell the assembler this you need to modify the CX register. Type the following:

```
-RCX
```

DEBUG responds by displaying the current value of the CX register, and a colon prompt. Enter the new value for CX at the colon prompt:

```
CX 0000
:8
```

Type 8 and press ENTER.

Next you need to give the file a name. So as not to confuse it with the original READKEY (which may be on your disk), name it RKEY. Type:

```
-N RKEY.COM
```

Now you can use the W command to write the file to disk:

```
-W
Writing 0008 bytes
```

DEBUG responds by telling you it's written eight bytes to disk. Press Q to leave DEBUG:

```
-Q

C>
```

Now that you're back in DOS you can try out your new RKEY command. You can type RKEY on the command line, in which case DOS will wait for you to press a key, then redisplay the command prompt. (Who ever knew this could be so simple?)

Better still, type in the batch file program in FIG. 10-6 to test RKEY. This program uses RKEY (5) to read in a character from the keyboard. That character's ASCII code value is then compared with the ASCII code values of "1" and "2." The program uses IF–ERRORLEVEL tests to determine whether the key was in range and, if so, displays a message, and then quits. Otherwise, an "out of range" message is displayed (10) and the program loops through the same routines over again (3 through 9).

```
Name: RANGE.BAT

 1: @ECHO OFF
 2: REM An example of RKEY
 3: :START
 4: ECHO Type a 1 or a 2
 5: RKEY
 6: IF ERRORLEVEL 51 GOTO RANGE
 7: IF ERRORLEVEL 50 GOTO TWO
 8: IF ERRORLEVEL 49 GOTO ONE
 9: :RANGE
10: ECHO --That number is out of range
11: GOTO START
12: :ONE
13: ECHO --You typed the number 1!
14: GOTO END
15: :TWO
16: ECHO --You typed the number 2!
17: :END
```

Fig. 10-6. This program uses RKEY to read in a character from the keyboard.

FIGURE 10-7 shows a batch file program that also creates RKEY. If you were a little reluctant to create the batch file using DEBUG, then MAKERKEY.BAT does the same thing—but safely. This program borrows some technique from REBOOT.BAT. The difference is that this program will return you to DOS, rather than reset your computer. Also, once completed, you'll have the RKEY.COM program on disk.

```
                          Name: MAKERKEY.BAT

                           1: GOTO BEGIN
                           2:
                           3: A
                           4: MOV AH,1
                           5: INT 21
                           6: MOV AH,4C
                           7: INT 21
Fig. 10-7. This batch file creates RKEY.    8:
                           9: RCX
                          10: 8
                          11: N RKEY.COM
                          12: W
                          13: Q
                          14:
                          15: :BEGIN
                          16: DEBUG < MAKERKEY.BAT


                          C> MAKERKEY

                          C> GOTO :BEGIN

                          C> :BEGIN

                          C> DEBUG < MAKERKEY.BAT
                          -GOTO BEGIN
                             ^ Error
                          -
                          -A
                          234D:0100 MOV AH,1
Fig. 10-8. This is a run from MAKERKEY.BAT.    234D:0102 INT 21
                          234D:0104 MOV AH,4C
                          234D:0106 INT 21
                          234D:0108
                          -RCX
                          CX 0000
                          :8
                          -N RKEY.COM
                          -W
                          Writing 0008 bytes
                          -Q

                          C>
```

When you run MAKERKEY.BAT, your screen will show output that looks something like FIG. 10-8.

PATCHING BY RENAMING

Another thing you can do with DEBUG is to patch programs. That is, you load the programs into DEBUG, and then modify them. Needless to say, this is a very dangerous thing to do. Some users will go so far as to path their COMMAND.COM file, replacing the names of DOS commands with their own commands.

Usually what happens when you patch a program using DEBUG, is that it won't run. Worse, sometimes it will crash your system. (Now you can imagine why it would be folly to "patch" COMMAND.COM.) So why do it?

One reason is for security. For example, using DEBUG, you can load COMMAND.COM into memory and search for the DEL command (an internal command). You can then manually rename DEL to something odd, like T-Z. The T-Z command now replaces DEL, but the users of that computer don't know that offhand. Instead, they continue to type DEL to erase files. What is the difference? A batch file named DEL has taken over the internal DEL command's place. The DEL.BAT file may look like this:

```
1: @ECHO OFF
2: REM DEL batch file, replaces DEL command
3: IF %1NOTHING=NOTHING GOTO ERROR
4: COPY %1 C:\JUNK > NUL
5: ECHO %1 Files deleted
6: GOTO END
7: :ERROR
8: ECHO No filename(s) given
9: :END
```

This batch file command doesn't delete anything. Instead, it copies all the files that DEL would erase to a |JUNK directory on drive C. This way, the system manager could walk by at another time, examine the files, and then delete them using T-Z. This also saves a lot of heartache for those times when users delete files and then want them back. In this case, the system manager could simply copy the "deleted" files back from the |JUNK directory.

Internal commands need to be patched by using DEBUG with COMMAND.COM, but external commands can be fixed simply by renaming them.

As an example, consider FORMAT. You can rename FORMAT.COM to something no one would ever type: ZGBLQZFM.COM. Then, somewhere else on the disk, have a FORMAT.BAT file that actually does the formatting job, but checks to see if drive C, or some other important drive, is about to be formatted. If so, an error message could be displayed, or the program may just refuse to format. (Or it could beep very loudly, and let everyone else in the office know that someone just made a dumb mistake.)

But overall, patching programs is a task too risky to undertake. It's just too easy to botch things up. If you do take a stab at it, remember to experiment first with the file on the floppy drive system. Then, if everything checks out, copy the file to your hard drive. I'm not offering any guarantees—and the publisher of this book, myself, and your computer store cannot be held accountable for anything that may happen because of your patching.

Summary

Going beyond batch files means using more than what DOS gave you to write interesting and useful batch file programs. You can do this with public domain, shareware, or third-party utilities available through bulletin boards and shareware libraries.

Besides the utilities, you can also take advantage of BASIC and DEBUG, two programs that come with DOS, to supplement your batch files. BASIC can be used to write quick routines—even to write batch files themselves. DEBUG can be used for many purposes, one of which is to write small utility programs that supplement batch files.

11
Beyond•Bat

Beyond•Bat is an extension language, designed to supplement and enhance batch files. What the makers of Beyond•Bat have done is to take an original, good idea—batch files—and improve upon it immensely.

Beyond•Bat gives you the power of a complete programming language; with math functions, file I/O, complex decision making, advanced variable storage, and structure. It's almost like a BASIC program language interpreter built right on top of COMMAND.COM.

Beyond•Bat augments the existing batch file commands with dozens of supplemental commands. In a way, Beyond•Bat is really a programming language on its own. Yet, it's still related to the good ol' batch file language supplied with DOS.

By taking advantage of Beyond•Bat's features, you can program a complete and menu-driven command shell for DOS. This includes items such as order entry screens and file access. Personally, I'm amazed by it all. If you're a batch file guru, or want to be one, this is a program worth looking into.

HOW IT WORKS, AND WHAT YOU GET

Programs that augment the way batch files work can operate in two manners:

1) Memory Resident

2) Interpreted.

(This doesn't apply only to Beyond•Bat, but also to any batch file enhancing language.)

A memory-resident batch file enhancement program works like any other memory-resident program: it loads itself into memory and then waits until it's needed. In the case of a batch file modification program, the memory-resident portion monitors the command line, waiting for a batch file to be interpreted. When a batch file is run, the program takes over, adding its power to the batch file commands executed.

An *interpreted* batch file enhancement program must be called before the batch file is run. Typically, the name of the program is listed, followed by the name of the batch file to be run (sort of like running the BASIC interpreter from the previous chapter). The interpreter then reads in the batch file commands and executes them one by one.

Memory-resident batch file enhancers have the advantage of always being in memory. Because they're always there, any batch file you run at any time will automatically be executed without having to type an extra command. Interpreted batch file enhancers have the advantage of not taking up the memory required by the memory-resident programs. Fortunately, Beyond•Bat lets you have it both ways with two programs: BEYOND.COM and BB.COM:

BEYOND.COM is the memory-resident batch file enhancer. It loads itself into memory then stays there, waiting to interpret your enhanced batch files.

BB.COM is the interpreter version. You type the name of your enhanced batch file after BB on the command line. For example:

C> BB MENU

This causes BB to interpret the enhanced batch file MENU.BAT.

The memory-resident BEYOND.COM behaves a little bit faster than BB.COM, the interpreted version. The above example, BB MENU, will take a while to load. Once in memory though, it will run faster than any batch file you've ever seen.

Beyond•Bat comes with a lot of interesting programs and utilities. The programs and related files come on one 360K floppy, and over 100 demonstration and sample files come on another.

With Beyond•Bat, you get the following:

* A completely menu-driven DOS shell that you can customize
* A text editor that can also be used in a memory-resident "pop-up" mode
* The Beyond•Bat language

The Beyond•Bat language is used to create the enhanced batch files. As was mentioned above, it looks a lot like the BASIC programming language, though anyone familiar with batch file programming can adapt to it quickly. (In fact, you'll probably go ape over it.)

Also interesting are the data entry screens, referred to as "panels." These are input screens that you can design and customize. For example, you can create a custom order-entry screen and use it right in your batch file. (Does it suddenly dawn on you that, with all these features, Beyond•Bat has truly gone beyond the realm of a simple batch file? I guess that's how it got its name.)

About the nicest thing that Beyond•Bat comes with is a thick, informative 374-page manual. The manual is well organized, full of illustrations and sample programs. Plus, it has a complete reference in the last few chapters on all aspects of Beyond•Bat: the two programs, memory-resident and command line; the editor; the script language; and the commands for building input panels.

A BEYOND•BAT EXAMPLE

Beyond•Bat can run the plain, simple batch files that you probably now have dotting your disks. But it's real power lies in its enhanced batch language.

To tell the difference between an enhanced Beyond•Bat file and a plain old DOS batch file, Beyond•Bat looks at the first character on the first line of a batch file. If the character is an asterisk, then the file is an enhanced, Beyond•Bat batch file. Otherwise, Beyond•Bat passes the file off to DOS for "normal" execution.

To compare Beyond•Bat with DOS batch files, I modified an earlier batch file example to run under the BB interpreter. The file I chose was RANGE.BAT from Chapter 10 (see FIG. 11-1). RANGE was an interesting choice because it contains READKEY—a statement not found in the standard DOS batch file language.

```
Name: RANGE.BAT

 1: @ECHO OFF
 2: REM An example of RKEY
 3: :START
 4: ECHO Type a 1 or a 2
 5: RKEY
 6: IF ERRORLEVEL 51 GOTO RANGE
 7: IF ERRORLEVEL 50 GOTO TWO
 8: IF ERRORLEVEL 49 GOTO ONE
 9: :RANGE
10: ECHO --That number is out of range
11: GOTO START
12: :ONE
13: ECHO --You typed the number 1!
14: GOTO END
15: :TWO
16: ECHO --You typed the number 2!
17: :END
```

Fig. 11-1. This is RANGE.BAT from Chapter 10.

FIGURE 11-2 is the Beyond•Bat file I wrote that does essentially the same thing. The file was written with a text editor, just like RANGE.BAT (though I could have used Beyond•Bat's text editor).

Right away you can notice some differences: The asterisk is a comment character, including the required first asterisk to let the interpreter know that this

Name: RANGEBB.BAT

```
 1: *
 2: * Beyond*Bat program that works like RANGE.BAT
 3: *
 4: -start
 5: READ LINE &VALUE "IType a 1 or a 2: "
 6: IF (&VALUE=1) goto value1
 7: IF (&VALUE=2) goto value2
 8: TYPE "That number is out of range!"
 9: goto start
10: -value1
11: TYPE "You typed a one"
12: STOP
13: -value2
14: TYPE "You typed a two"
```

Fig. 11-2. This is RANGE.BAT modified to run under the BB interpreter.

is a Beyond•Bat batch file, and the dash signifying a label instead of a colon. Also, all of these commands are Beyond•Bat commands. There are not DOS utilities like READKEY.COM that are required because of any limitations.

READLINE in line 5 displays a prompting string and places the value input into the variable &VALUE. (Isn't it nice to use variables like this?) READLINE reads an entire line so, unlike READKEY, you'll need to press ENTER to end input.

Lines 6 and 7 contain two IF statements that compare the value entered (&VALUE) with the numbers one and two. If a match is found, execution branches to the indicated label. Otherwise, execution falls through to line 8 where a message is displayed, and in line 9 the program branches to the "start" loop to ask the question over again.

Lines 10 through 12 contain the procedure executed if a 1 was pressed. The interesting thing here is the STOP statement in line 12. STOP exits to DOS immediately, so there's no need for a "GOTO END" statement, as with DOS batch files.

Lines 13 and 14 display the message if a 2 was pressed. Like batch files, after the last line is read (14), control is returned to DOS.

BEYOND•BAT COMMANDS

The following is a list of some of the Beyond•Bat script commands, script functions, and variables (most of the file I/O commands aren't listed). A complete reference to all the commands, functions and variables is included in the Beyond•Bat manual. TABLES 11-1, 11-2 and 11-3 are provided to arouse your curiosity.

As you can see, the Beyond•Bat language is quite extensive. What you can't see from the above commands are things such as the panel control for data input and file manipulation.

Table 11-1.

Command	What it does
*	Identifies a line as a comment (like REM).
–	Identifies a label (like :).
ARGSTRING	Replaces the default &ARGSTRING variable with new data.
BEEP	Beeps the speaker in a variety of manners.
CANCEL	Cancels a function, such as printing.
CHAIN	Executes another script file (but does not return).
CHDIR	Changes directories, like DOS.
CLEAR	Clears the screen, like CLS.
CLOSE	Closes a file opened with the OPEN command.
CURSOR	Moves the cursor to a particular row and column.
DISPLAY	Used to display a panel and for providing input.
EXIT	Exits from the script processor with an optional return code.
GLOBAL	Defines variables as global, for use in all chained and called scripts.
GOSUB	Calls a subroutine within the current script.
GOTO	Branches execution to a specific label.
IF	Tests for a true condition by comparing variables and then executing an optional command.
LOCAL	Defines variables as local.
LOOP	Allows one section of code to be executed over and over (a loop) for a specific or infinite number of times.
ON	Causes the script to constantly monitor a condition and when that condition is true, branch to a specific routine.
OPEN	Opens a file for manipulation.
PRINT	Prints a file.
PRIVATE	Defines variables as private to certain routines.
PRTSCREEN	Prints the screen.
QUIET	Suppresses output of a command, similar to using "> NUL."
RETURN	Returns from a subroutine called via GOSUB.
RUN	Runs a program or DOS command.
SET	Sets certain script options—not like the DOS SET command at all.
SMSG	Displays a message on the status line.
SORTARRAY	Sorts an array variable.
STACK	Places a string of characters into the keyboard buffer.
STOP	Stops script execution and returns to DOS, like pressing CTRL–BREAK.
WAIT	Waits for a specific date or time and then executes a command.

Table 11-2.

Function	What it does
&ARGNUMBER	Returns the number (&n below) of an argument in a string.
&ASCII	Returns the hexadecimal value of a character at a certain offset within a string.
&CALCULATE	Evaluates an arithmetic expression enclosed in parentheses.
&CHARACTER	Returns an ASCII character for a hexadecimal value.
&DAYOFWEEK	Returns the day of the week (Monday, Tuesday, etc.) when given a date in the format MM/DD/YY.
&DAYOFYEAR	Returns the day of the year (from 1 to 365) when given a date in the format MM/DD/YY.
&DECIMAL	Returns the decimal value of a hexadecimal number.
&DISKSIZE	Returns the size of a specified disk.
&DISKSPACE	Returns the amount of free space left on a disk.
&DOSENVIRONMENT	Returns the data (string) of a DOS environment variable.
&GDATE	Returns a Georgian date for a specific Julian calendar date (if you can believe that!).
&HEXADECIMAL	Returns a hexadecimal number from a decimal value.
&HOURS	Converts time in seconds to HH:MM:SS format.
&INSTRING	Returns the position of a target string within a search string.
&JDATE	Converts from a Georgian date to a Julian calendar date.
&LEFT	Left-justifies or truncates a string.
&LENGTH	Returns the length of a string.
&LOWER	Converts a string to lowercase.
&MASK	Replaces characters in a string with X's.
&REPLACE	Replaces the occurrence of one string with another.
&REVERSED	Spits out a given string in reverse.
&RIGHT	Right-justifies or truncates a string.
&SECONDS	Converts time in a HH:MM:SS format to total number of seconds.
&TRIM	Removes leading and trailing blanks from a string.
&UPPER	Converts a string to uppercase.

Table 11-3.

Variable	What it stands for
&0	The name of the script file.
&n	A replaceable parameter, from 1 to "n" (like %1).
&ARGSTRING	The complete command line to start the script.
&BACKGROUND	A yes-or-no variable that tells whether Beyond • Bat is memory-resident or not.
&BLANK	A "blank" variable, set to the space character. Used to test for no input.
&CR	A variable set to the carriage return character.
&DATE	Contains the current date.
&DOSRETCODE	Set equal to the previous program's return code (ERRORLEVEL).
&DOSVERSION	Set equal to the version of DOS.
&ERROR	A yes-or-no variable depending on if the last command issued ends with an error.
&INKEY	Returns the next keystroke.
&LF	A variable set to the linefeed character.
&MONITOR	A variable equal to the type of monitor you have, "MONO," "COLOR," or "BW".
&NULL	A variable set to the null character, ASCII 0.
&NUMBER	The number of replaceable parameters entered on the command line.
&PACTIVE	A yes-or-no variable determining if the printer is on (active).
&SCOLUMN	Set to the screen column where the cursor is located.
&SLINE	Set to the screen row where the cursor is located.
&TIME	Contains the current time.
&TIMEOUT	A yes-or-no variable depending upon the WAIT command. If WAIT has timed out, &TIMEOUT will equal YES.
&TIMETH	Contains the current time plus thousandths of a second.
&YEAR	Contains the current year (four digits).

One thing that ran through my mind as I studied the various commands was "Gee, this certainly is a lot like BASIC." For more powerful batch files, Beyond•Bat is a wonderful thing. For data entry though, you might prefer a program designed to do it properly.

ORDERING INFORMATION

Beyond•Bat is marketed by Relay Communications, Inc. These are the same folk who market the Relay Gold communications programs. Because (sadly) batch file programming is not atop everyone's software shopping list, you'll probably have to order Beyond•Bat from them directly.

Beyond•Bat requires an IBM PC, XT, AT, PS/2 or compatible and DOS version 2.0 or later. In the memory-resident mode, Beyond•Bat requires at least 165K of RAM.

Relay Communications, Inc.
41 Kenosia Avenue
Danbury, CT 06810
(203) 798-3800
(800)-84-RELAY (orders and information)

Summary

Beyond•Bat is a powerful, all-purpose extension to the basic batch file programming directives. It offers incredible power and versatility. It might be a little too involved for most purposes, but if having it all—bells whistles and entry panels—is what you want, then Beyond•Bat is your ticket to happiness.

12
EBL

EBL is Frank Canova's Extended Batch Language—a batch file enhancer. It offers a complete extension to the DOS batch file language, plus it allows DOS batch file commands to be intermingled with EBL commands.

EBL offers an advanced programming language, user input, advanced string handling, arithmetic operations, comparisons, advanced control structures, tracing facilities, error trapping, and it's not that hard to get used to. In fact, it's quite similar to the BASIC programming language and, although I'm not familiar with it, the manual states that it's similar to the EXEC2 language that comes on a VM/370 computer.

BEHIND THE SCENES—WHAT YOU GET

The main program behind EBL is BAT.COM. BAT.COM acts as an interpreter. You specify EBL commands after typing BAT to start a line in a batch file. This way, you can mix EBL's extended batch file commands with regular DOS batch file commands in the same program.

There are two ways to run an EBL batch file. The first is to start each line of the batch file with BAT, as follows:

```
BAT * This is an EBL batch file
BAT * These lines are comments
BAT READ What is your name:> %0
BAT TYPE Howdy, %0
```

"BAT" essentially runs the BAT.COM program (so make sure BAT.COM is on your path). BAT then interprets the information that follows it. In this example, you will be prompted for your name, and that information will be saved in the variable %0. The next line uses the TYPE command (EBL's version—not the DOS TYPE command) to display "Howdy," followed by your name. For example:

```
What is your name: SANDIE
Howdy, SANDIE
```

The second method of running an EBL program is to make BAT.COM permanent by specifying the /P switch. This avoids the necessity of starting each line with the word "BAT.":

```
@BAT /P * This is an EBL batch file
* These lines are comments
READ What is your name:> %0
TYPE Howdy, %0
```

BAT /P tells EBL to make the BAT.COM interpreter resident. This way the rest of the batch file can contain EBL commands with the word BAT. You'll also note that the initial BAT is prefixed by an @ (at) sign. This suppresses the EBL commands from being displayed. (Normally, EBL is always in ECHO OFF mode—but the first line is still displayed—unless it starts with an @.)

To mix DOS batch file commands with EBL's commands, you have two choices. If you're using EBL by starting each line with "BAT" then simply specify a DOS command (don't start the line with BAT):

```
BAT * This is an EBL comment
BAT TYPE Here's your directory of drive C:
DIR C:
```

In this example, the first two lines are interpreted by EBL. The third is simply a DOS command.

If you're using the /P switch to make BAT permanent, you'll need to use the LEAVE command to exit EBL and return to the normal DOS batch file mode:

```
BAT /P * This is an EBL comment
TYPE Here's your directory of drive C:
LEAVE
DIR C:
```

The LEAVE command in the third line suspends EBL and allows the rest of the file to be interpreted using DOS's batch file interpreter. To continue with EBL, simply start it up again on a later line using BAT or BAT /P.

A second command, SHELL, can be used to issue only one DOS command. For example:

```
BAT /P * This is an EBL comment
TYPE Here's your directory of drive C:
SHELL DIR C:
* We're still in EBL
```

Only line 3 is a DOS command, issued via the EBL SHELL command. EBL picks up immediately after line 3 with another comment.

EBL comes on a diskette full of programs and examples. The main program is BAT.COM. Additional external functions are available in two library files, BATFUNC1.COM and BATFUNC2.COM. There is also a floating point (mathematical) function library called BATMATH3.COM, and if you have an 8087 math co-processor, you can even use BMATH87.COM.

The demos on the diskette are the most impressive. BATDEMO.BAT will be the first one you probably will run. It will amaze you that all the functions and fancy displays are available via a batch file language. To amaze yourself even further, TYPE the batch file on the screen to see how easy it looks.

The only drawback to picking up EBL (either from an electronic BBS or from a user group's software library) is that there is no on-line documentation. Typing BAT on the command line by itself lists the commands and functions, but doesn't explain what any of them do. So, in order to be fully proficient at EBL, you'll need to pick up the manual. For that, you must pay the shareware fee of $49. (See the end of this chapter for more information.)

AN *EBL* EXAMPLE

Again, for the example I'll use RANGE.BAT (as was done for Beyond•Bat in the previous chapter).

RANGE.BAT asks you to type either a 1 or 2, and then lets you know which key you typed. It's important to note (in this second go-round) that even a program as simple as this isn't possible using the native DOS batch file language. The RKEY program must be written to allow DOS to be interactive with a user (*see* FIG. 12-1).

```
Name: RANGE.BAT

 1: @ECHO OFF
 2: REM An example of RKEY
 3: :START
 4: ECHO Type a 1 or a 2
 5: RKEY
 6: IF ERRORLEVEL 51 GOTO RANGE
 7: IF ERRORLEVEL 50 GOTO TWO
 8: IF ERRORLEVEL 49 GOTO ONE
 9: :RANGE
10: ECHO --That number is out of range
11: GOTO START
12: :ONE
13: ECHO --You typed the number 1!
14: GOTO END
15: :TWO
16: ECHO --You typed the number 2!
17: :END
```

Fig. 12-1. Here's RANGE.BAT again!

FIGURE 12-2 is the EBL version of the batch file that does essentially the same thing. Line 1 loads EBL and makes it permanent. The @ (at) sign is used to suppress the command from being echoed to the screen. Line 2 is the START label. As with Beyond•Bat, labels in EBL begin with a hyphen.

```
Name: RANGEBL.BAT

 1: @BAT /P * EBL--make BAT permanent
 2: -START
 3: READ Type a 1 or a 2 %0
 4: IF %0 = 1 THEN GOTO -ONE
 5: IF %0 = 2 THEN GOTO -TWO
 6: TYPE That number is out of range
 7: GOTO -START
 8: -ONE TYPE You typed the number 1!
 9: EXIT
10: -TWO TYPE You typed the number 2!
```

Fig. 12-2. This is the EBL version of RANGE.BAT.

In line 3, the user is asked to input either a 1 or 2 and their input is saved in the variable %0. The two IF statements in lines 4 and 5 compare the input to the numbers 1 and 2. If there is a match, execution branches to the labels ONE or TWO, respectively. If not, line 6 displays the message "That number is out of range," and in line 7 execution branches back to the START label.

Line 8 contains the label ONE and an EBL command. EBL allows you to place commands after a label (a good idea that DOS should borrow). If the user presses the 1 key, execution will branch to line 8 and then they'll be returned to DOS via the EXIT command in line 9.

If the user presses the 2 key, execution branches to the label at line 10, and the message "You typed the number 2!" is displayed.

Superficially, this example is very similar to the Beyond•Bat example of the previous chapter. Both execute the commands flawlessly and with a little more logic than DOS batch files.

EBL COMMANDS AND FUNCTIONS

TABLE 12-1 is a brief list of EBL's commands and functions. In addition to these commands, the following math functions can be performed:

+   Addition
−   Subtraction
*   Multiplication
/   Division
$ Substring (return location of one string within another)
&   Concatenation (connect two strings together)

Table 12-1.

Command	What it does
*	Identifies a line as a comment (like REM).
—	Identifies a label (like :).
BEEP	Bleeps the speaker (like ECHO ^G would).
BEGSTACK	Stuffs text (characters) into a keyboard stack—sort of a forced method of redirected input. An "END" statement ends the series of characters that are stuffed into the keyboard stack.
BEGTYPE	Marks the beginning of a series of strings that will be displayed on the screen. An "END" statement ends the series.
CALL	Calls a subroutine within the batch file. CALL can optionally pass parameters to the subroutine.
COLOR	Changes the color of the text on computers equipped with a color monitor.
ELSE	Used with a single or nested IF statement to make decisions.
EXIT	Leaves the batch file and returns to DOS.
GOTO	Branches batch file execution to a specific label.
IF	Used to make decisions based on evaluations. EBL's **IF** command allows you to compare variables using < (less than), = (equal to—case insensitive), = = (equal to, case sensitive), > (greater than), and < > (not equal to).
INKEY	Reads a single character from the keyboard.
LEAVE	Suspends execution of EBL commands and returns batch file control to DOS. (It doesn't exit to DOS.)
READ	Reads input from the user into one or more variables. Both READ and INKEY can have optional prompting strings.
READSCRN	Reads input directly from the screen. Using this command, your program can read text strings displayed by other programs and then act on them accordingly.
RETURN	Returns control from a subroutine back to the line following the previous CALL command.
SHELL	Returns to DOS to execute one command. After a SHELL, batch file control returns to EBL.
SKIP	Jumps forward a number of lines in the batch file. SKIP is like GOTO, but it skips a number of lines rather than branching to a specific label.
STACK	Stuffs characters into a keyboard stack, almost like I/O redirection.
STATEOF	Searches disks and directories to see if a specific file exists.
TYPE	Displays a text string on the screen.

EBL makes quite extensive use of variables. Aside from the environment and replaceable parameter variables (%0 through %9), EBL gives you 21 others: six predefined and 15 global variables.

The six predefined variables are as follows:

% Q   "K" if characters are coming from the keyboard, or "S" if they are coming from EBL's keyboard stack.

% R   A return code in hexadecimal (base 16).

% S   The space character.

% V   The default disk drive.

%%   The percent character.

%(The left paren (otherwise, EBL would interpret a left paren as the beginning of an equation).

The 15 global variables are represented by the letters A through O. These variables can be assigned and used by your EBL batch files as you see fit.

EBL comes with several external function libraries:

BATFUNC1.COM   Common external functions

BATFUNC2.COM   Special external functions

BATMATH3.COM   Floating point functions

BATALLF.COM   All of the above functions

BMATH87.COM   8087 co-processor math functions

You add these functions to EBL's basic functions by specifying one, or a combination, of the above programs in your AUTOEXEC.BAT file. You can, instead, specify each of them individually before trying them out. (Unless the program has been run, its external functions will not be available to EBL.)

TABLES 12-2, 12-3, and 12-4 list the routines available in each of the external function libraries.

ORDERING INFORMATION

EBL is available through the Seaware Corporation in Florida. Because of the popularity of EBL, however, you can probably download it from a BBS, or order it from a shareware software warehouse (it's on PC–SIG's diskette number 124).

EBL is shareware. That means the software is distributed free of charge. If you use it, you're expected to pay for it. An enticement to this fact is that there is no "on-disk manual" that comes with EBL. So you really need to pay Seaware the $49 to get the manual and start using the product. (The manual is well worth it, by the way.)

Table 12-2.

BATFUNC1 Command	What it does
CENTER	Centers a string of characters.
CHDIR	Changes directories or drives.
DATE	Returns the current date.
GETDIR	Returns a string giving the name of the current subdirectory.
KEYPRESSED	Returns a "T" or "F" (true or false) depending on if a key has been pressed.
LEFT	Returns a specific number of characters from the left side of a string.
LOCATE	Positions the cursor on the display.
LOWER	Converts a string of characters to lowercase.
RIGHT	Returns a specific number of characters from the right side of a string.
STRIP	Removes characters from either side of a string.
TIME	Returns the current time.
UPPER	Converts a string of characters to uppercase.
WHATFUNC	Identifies which of EBL's external function packages have been loaded.

Table 12-3.

BATFUNC2 Command	What it does
C2H	Converts characters to hexadecimal values.
D2H	Converts decimal values to hexadecimal values.
H2C	Converts hexadecimal values into character strings.
H2D	Converts hexadecimal values into decimal values.
INT86	Executes an 8086 INT instruction.
PEEK	Reads a byte value from a memory location.
POKE	Puts a byte value at a specific memory location.
REBOOT	Resets the computer.
WHATFUNC	Identifies which of EBL's external function packages have been loaded.

Table 12-4.

BATMATH3 BATMATH87 Command	What it does
ABS	Returns the absolute value of a number.
FLOAT	Returns a floating point result of a mathematical operation.
FRAC	Returns the fraction value of a number.
INT	Returns the integer value of a number.
WHATFUNC	Identifies which of EBL's external function packages have been loaded.

EBL requires an IBM PC, XT, AT, PS/2 or compatible and DOS version 2.0 or later.

Seaware Corporation
P.O. Box 1656
Delray Beach, FL 33444
(407) 395-2816

Summary

Between the two batch file extender packages discussed here, I personally like to work with EBL. The reason is that EBL is more batch-file-like than Beyond•Bat. Beyond•Bat is very, very powerful and has quite a few features I wouldn't use personally. If I were in a business situation with many employees, however, I would probably choose Beyond•Bat for that reason. Both packages offer features way beyond what DOS offers. The power is worth the price.

Part Four

Hard Disk Strategies

HERE is where batch files get put to use. Sure, you can use the techniques described in this book to write some really efficient and useful batch files, but how can you put them to work? How can you use the knowledge provided here to give yourself the ideal system?

13
Managing Your Hard Disk

A hard disk is the best thing you can buy for your computer. It gives you fast and virtually unlimited storage. Floppy users: imagine having all your programs and data on one big, quick disk. No more need to juggle diskettes or examine gooey labels for the file you want.

One of the problems associated with a hard disk, however, is that its organization is up to you. You can put your files and programs anywhere on the hard disk. If you're smart, you'll organize your system into subdirectories. If you're even smarter, you'll develop a backup strategy that keeps safety copies of all your files and programs on "emergency" diskettes; but how can you learn that?

The DOS manual offers only weak, watered-down suggestions on hard disk organization and management. It assumes you'll learn about it on your own—or, better yet, have a service representative come out to your office and do it for you. Ha! You'd be better off putting all your files in the root directory and using the hard disk in the worst possible manner.

Because there's no official method of hard disk organization, many people turn to books on the subject. I co-authored one such book with Andy Townsend, and it's available through TAB Books (see the Introduction for more information). The way I learned about hard disk management was through trial and error.

I was one of the first users, at my previous job, to have a DOS hard disk system. I fiddled with it for hours, organizing subdirectories, writing batch files. I must have moved, deleted, renamed, and created dozens of subdirectories before I finally came upon my ideal setup, which you'll read about later.

Of course, not everyone is like me—or you for that matter. Different users require different things. If you're installing a hard disk and writing batch files for someone else, you'll need to know what they need and then work to meet that need. That's the subject of this chapter—learning how to organize a hard disk to meet a specific need.

Also, this part of this book doesn't assume to be an end-all to hard disk management. There is a lot to organizing a hard drive and using it effectively. If you still have questions or concerns after reading the next few chapters, I'd advise you to pick up a good book on the subject. (No further hints are needed on which book to get!)

WHAT IS HARD DISK MANAGEMENT?

No one reading this book should be without a hard disk. There are two reasons for this.

The first reason is that today's software requires the storage capacity and speed that a hard drive offers. If you're using floppy disk drives alone, then the amount of time a hard drive will save you is worth the cost.

The second reason is that hard drives are not expensive at all. The first hard drive available for my ancient TRS-80 Model III cost just under $2,000. It held a staggering five megabytes of data. Just last week I bought a 30 megabyte hard drive for under $300. That's ten dollars per megabyte compared with $400 per megabyte in 1983. Also, consider that floppy disk drives cost about $80 each, and only store a fraction of what a hard drive does. You just can't beat the price. Buy one.

Once you have a hard disk, you'll need to organize it. The organization is done via subdirectories and whatever other approaches you'd like to take. This is a flexible system. Because there are no mandatory subdirectories (unlike UNIX and Xenix, or even OS/2 to some extents), you can put files wherever you want, name the directories whatever you want—it's all up to you.

Just in case you need some assistance, though, the following are two key points to hard disk management:

1) Organization

2) Backing up

Organization is the easy part. Basically, it says to put programs and files in their own subdirectories.

Backing up is the hard part. Some would consider backing up to be the "minor" part, but it is important. Besides DOS, BACKUP should be the only other program that you absolutely use every day. Hard disks may be reliable, but they're not indestructible.

ORGANIZATION

Organization is easy. I'll start by describing the worst-case scenario of organization: putting all your files in your hard drive's root directory. This is done by one type of person: those who don't know better.

Users used to floppy drives just put everything on "the disk." But a hard drive is a very big disk. If you put everything on a hard drive, you're really going to confuse yourself. A hard drive can potentially have thousands of files on it, unlike the typical floppy which may average only 30 to 60 files.

I won't go into the problems of having 2,000 files all on one drive, all in the same directory. (Well, I will mention filename conflicts, fragmented and slow directory access, and a generally tacky appearance that will make even novice hard drive users shun you.) DOS offers three useful utilities to keep this from happening:

MKDIR or MD

CHDIR or CD

RMDIR or RD

Using these three internal commands, primarily MKDIR and CHDIR, you can organize your hard drive into subdirectories. That's all the DOS manual says. How you do it is up to you.

Of primary concern is to keep your root directory clean. Somewhere, in the marble pillared halls of hard disk management, there is the following phrase chiseled into an arch:

Keep the root
clean

This refers to that biggest goal of hard disk management: organization. The root, or top, directory of a hard disk should have only three files in it:

COMMAND.COM

AUTOEXEC.BAT

CONFIG.SYS

Even then, all three of these files are optional. COMMAND.COM can be placed in another directory (using the SHELL command in CONFIG.SYS, in which case CONFIG.SYS needs to be in the root). Also, AUTOEXEC.BAT and CONFIG.SYS can be removed, if need be.

Other than those three files, everything else should be a subdirectory entry. Your goal is to create those subdirectories carefully and logically, and then place your programs and files into them.

In this section, I'll show you three approaches. None of them are right and none of them are wrong. They're just three popular ways of tackling the same problem. Also included are various batch file examples to supplement each of the three directory structures.

Simple Approach

If you're just starting out, you can forget the "example" provided for you in the DOS manual. It's impractical. Instead, you should start with the basics: Create a subdirectory for DOS. (*see* FIG. 13.1) The DOS directory was created by typing:

```
C> MD DOS
```

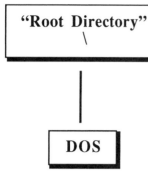

"Root Directory"
\

DOS

Fig. 13-1. Illustrated here is a DOS subdirectory.

To see what it looks like, change to your DOS directory:

```
C> CD DOS
```

Pull a directory and you will find /DOS void of files:

```
C> DIR
```

```
Volume in drive C is BRAND NEW
Volume Serial Number is 000A-0001
Directory of  C:\DOS

.               <DIR>       2-17-89    8:56p
..              <DIR>       2-17-89    8:56p
        2 File(s)   32491072 bytes free
```

Your next task is to copy all your DOS programs and files from your DOS distribution diskettes into the /DOS directory on your hard drive. Put the DOS diskette in drive A and type:

```
C> COPY A:*.* C:\DOS
```

or, because you're already "in" the DOS directory, you can type:

```
C> COPY A:*.*
```

Some of the files copied will be duplicates. For example, you don't need a second copy of COMMAND.COM in your /DOS directory, so delete it:

```
C> DEL COMMAND.COM
```

(Make sure you're in the /DOS directory before typing that command!)

You can also delete any other files you might think you'll never need. I'd advise against deleting anything now (other than COMMAND.COM). Later, though, you can delete some of the files you'll never use to free up some space. (You'll still have the originals on the distribution diskette in case you need them.)

If your version of DOS came with more than one diskette, insert each succeeding diskette into drive A, and copy files from them as well:

```
C> COPY A:*.*
```

DOS 4.0's INSTALL Program

Finally, after half a dozen or so versions of DOS, IBM decided to include a full-blown installation program with DOS 4.0. This program really saves time over installing DOS with the old method, and the INSTALL program is smart. It doesn't insist that you start everything over from scratch. The program installs DOS on a new system, creating a DOS subdirectory, or updates an older version of DOS to 4.0. A major improvement.

The INSTALL program is actually an upgrade of the old SELECT program (which just set the country and other system information). It's completely menu-driven, meaning you make your choices mostly by moving a highlight bar with the arrow keys and then pressing ENTER when you see what you like.

INSTALL is very informative and has help screens all over the place. Another nice thing is the consistency of the keys used in the program: Pressing F1 always gets you help; pressing ESCape cancels an operation. (I did have a problem accessing the non-existent F11 key on my old, original IBM keyboard, however.)

If you have a new hard drive system, INSTALL sets everything up for you. If your hard drive already has an older copy of DOS, INSTALL updates all your DOS files (no matter where you've hidden them). The program will even move some files out of the way to make room for its own files. (I was impressed by that one.)

Once everything is set, INSTALL tells you to reset your system and, voilà, you have a hard drive with DOS 4.0 on it.

There are a few drawbacks, however. The first is that IBM refuses to recognize third-party hardware. For example, when you choose which type of printer you're using (for the DOSSHELL program), only IBM's printers are listed. If you don't have an IBM printer, you should choose "other."

A second inconvenience is that only IBM's display adapters are listed for your system's graphics mode. Granted, if you're using a color display, chances are it's compatible with IBM's (because IBM is still calling the shots in the PC graphics arena). But the program doesn't recognize my Hercules Graphics Plus monochrome graphics adapter. (Hopefully someone else, probably Hercules, will come out with a driver.)

Finally, the DOSSHELL program is set up only to work with an IBM mouse. If you look far enough into the manual, you'll find the secret instructions for getting DOSSHELL to work with a Microsoft mouse (which is what I have). Because most other computer mouses can emulate the Microsoft mouse, this driver should work fine.

One thing INSTALL won't do for you is to organize your directory structure. That's still up to you.

Organizing Directories

After you've put DOS on your hard drive, neatly tucked away into its own subdirectory, you should create subdirectories for each of your applications programs. For the example, I'll assume you have a spreadsheet (SuperCalc), data base program (R:BASE), word processor (MultiMate), and a directory for playing games (see FIG. 13-2).

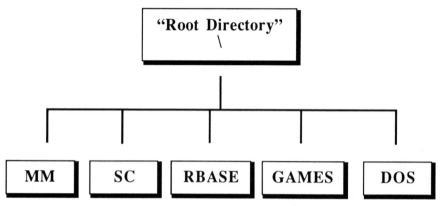

Fig. 13-2. Here are more subdirectories.

Into each of these subdirectories you'll install the respective programs. Then, as a second layer of organization, place under each subdirectory various data files. For example, the following subdirectories might go under the MM subdirectory:

\LETTERS

\MISC

\WORK

\POETRY

\NOVEL

You can have as many subdirectories as you like, one for each category of your writing. Rather than have only a second layer of subdirectories, you can go nuts with organization and create something like FIG. 13-3. You can get as detailed and as organized as you like. In fact, the more the better.

Setting the Path

All this organization means that you'll need to supply your system with a fairly useful PATH command—one that can anticipate just about any situation.

If you only had one subdirectory layer of data files under your programs' subdirectories, the following path would work nicely:

```
PATH = C:\DOS;..
```

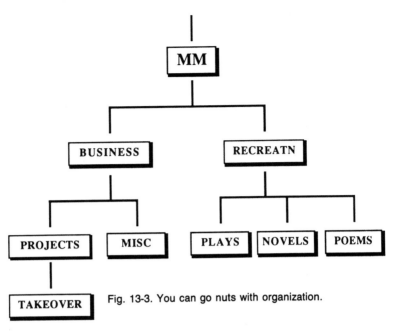

Fig. 13-3. You can go nuts with organization.

Remember how ".." equals the parent directory? This would allow one layer of data subdirectories below each of your primary program subdirectories to have access to the program files. Also, DOS should always be on the path, allowing you access to all the important external DOS commands.

If you choose to go with a highly specific and organized subdirectory structure, then the following path might come in handy:

```
PATH = C:\DOS;C:\MM;C:\SC;C:\RBASE;C:\GAMES
```

Okay. Let's get real nuts. Use the SUBST command to "alias" some popular directories:

```
SUBST D: C:\DOS
SUBST M: C:\MM
SUBST S: C:\SC
SUBST R: C:\RBASE
SUBST G: C:\GAMES
```

Now your path will look like this:

```
PATH = D:\;M:\;S:\;R:\;G:\
```

Remember to add the LASTDRIVE command to your CONFIG.SYS file if you use SUBST. Also, if your system already has a drive D, SUBST won't let you alias D: for /DOS; choose another letter.

Detailed Approach

The following is a more detailed approach to using subdirectories. It's a hybrid between the above, simple example, and a totally souped system that will be discussed next. This is the exact system I use on my computer at home—and have used successfully for five years. It proves to be quite flexible.

The first step to this approach is to group your files and programs. For most people, this isn't necessary. But if you use more than one word processor, or spreadsheet, or if you write programs, this type of organization will come in handy.

The primary "branch" of the directory tree structure I call SYSTEM. Under the SYSTEM directory are all files associated with my computer SYSTEM—each placed into its own subdirectory: DOS, for the DOS programs; UTIL, for miscellaneous utilities; MACE, for the MACE utilities; NORTON, for the Norton Utilities; HERCULES, for the Hercules graphics card utilities; MOUSE, for my mouse programs; TOOLS, for my backup program and other hard disk tools (caching programs and electronic disk drivers); and BORLAND, which contains the SideKick and SuperKey programs (see FIG. 13-4).

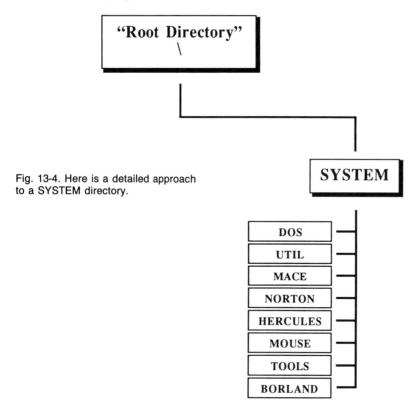

Fig. 13-4. Here is a detailed approach to a SYSTEM directory.

I also use a number of word processors. Each of them is kept in the WP directory (see FIG. 13-5).

In a third main subdirectory, I keep all the other files I use on my system. This includes a spreadsheet, plus a C and Assembly language development system (see FIG. 13-6).

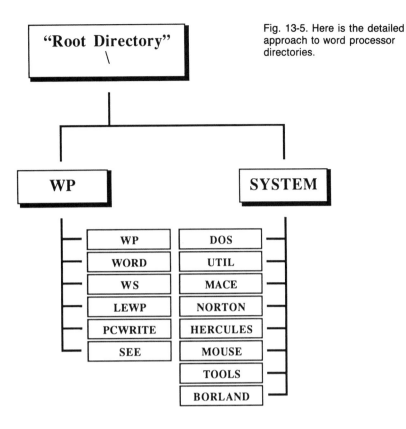

Fig. 13-5. Here is the detailed approach to word processor directories.

"Root Directory"
\

WP   SYSTEM

WP	DOS
WORD	UTIL
WS	MACE
LEWP	NORTON
PCWRITE	HERCULES
SEE	MOUSE
	TOOLS
	BORLAND

In addition to all those second-level subdirectories, there are third- and fourth-level directories. For example, under the /OTHER/MASM directory are about a half dozen directories for the programs that I've written in assembly language (including an /OTHER/MASM/BATCH directory for the files written for this book).

Two other main subdirectories exist off the root directory: /TEMP and /WORK. (Some users might have a /JUNK directory instead of /TEMP.)

/TEMP is my temporary files subdirectory. I put into that subdirectory just about anything and everything. For example, when I get a new program to try out, I install it in /TEMP. If I like the program, I figure out where else on the hard drive to put it, and then make a permanent subdirectory for it.

I also place into /TEMP files that I download from national networks or local electronic bulletin boards. I can then examine them to see if they're worth keeping or not—keeping them all in once place until I know what to do with them.

/WORK contains a varying number of subdirectories depending upon the projects with which I'm working. Normally, I keep data files in subdirectories under the appropriate program subdirectory. For example, /OTHER/SS/DATA contains all my spreadsheet data, and /WP/WP/LETTERS contains all my correspondence written in WordPerfect. But the contents of /WORK vary and might not necessarily relate to another program in another subdirectory.

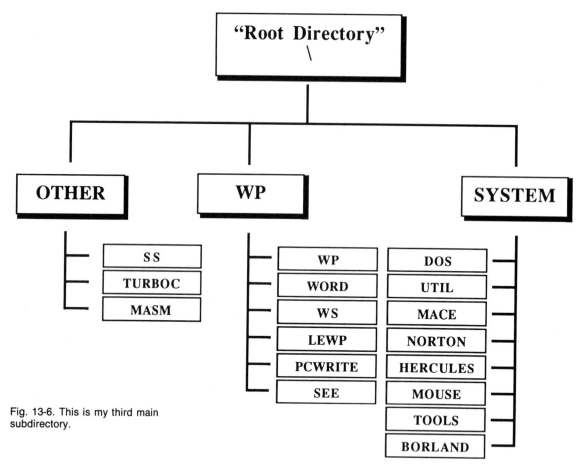

Fig. 13-6. This is my third main
subdirectory.

For example, if I'm working on a novel or play, I'll put it under /WORK. If I'm working on a large project for the office, using spreadsheet data and graphics, I'll put all those files in their own subdirectory under /WORK to keep them together.

Organization is the key, and this subdirectory structure keeps me organized. The problem is that things can get rather unruly after a while. My path is as follows:

PATH = C:\SYSTEM\DOS;C:\SYSTEM\UTIL;C:\WP\WP;..

This means I don't have ready access to quite a few programs. Of course, I could use drive "aliasing" with SUBST to get at some important files, and to place them on the path, but, as I said earlier, I've been using this system for five years and really don't want to change it. If you'll keep reading, however, you'll see one possible solution.

Complex (Best) Approach: Using Batch Files

The complex approach is my solution to the problems I've encountered with my system at home. Basically, this organizational strategy is wide open. You can have as few or as many subdirectories as you like.

Consider a directory structure as in the previous example, but just to make things interesting, mentally add in database, communications, integrated software, desktop publishing, and games subdirectories. Under each of these subdirectories add more subdirectories for different programs, and then more subdirectories for data. Soon, your subdirectory tree is approaching the great oak in stature.

Assuming that you use all those programs, you're in for one heck of a joy ride. There is no way you should list all those directories on your path. Consider that each time you type in a command, DOS looks for the program (first .COM, then .EXE, then .BAT) in the current directory, then in every subdirectory on the path. That's three times the number of path entries you have. That's a lot.

The solution is in batch files. For each program you might ever need on disk, you write a batch file. The batch file takes care of all the details. To make it work, however, you still need to set the path, but you add the name of a special batch file subdirectory:

```
PATH = C:\SYSTEM\DOS;U:\;C:\SYSTEM\BATCH;..
```

/SYSTEM/DOS is left on the path because the DOS programs are very important and you should have a direct path to them at all times. "U:" is an alias for a utility program subdirectory. Because you probably use a lot of utilities on your system, you should also have access to it. (Incidentally, making liberal use of the SUBST command to alias drive letters is another way to whittle down a complex subdirectory structure.)

The ".." entry is kept in the path because it will still come in handy when you "manually" change directories to run programs. But for the most part, all the programs you run will be executed via batch files in the /SYSTEM/BATCH subdirectory.

For example, the following batch file runs your spreadsheet:

```
Name: SS.BAT

1: @ECHO OFF
2: REM Run Spreadsheet
3: C:
4: CD \OTHER\SS
5: PATH = C:\SYSTEM\DOS;C:\SYSTEM\UTIL;C:\OTHER\SS
6: SS
7: REM Restore old path
8: PATH = C:\SYSTEM\DOS;U:\;C:\SYSTEM\BATCH;..
```

For every program on your disk, there will exist a batch file. In fact, you only need change a few things to make the SS.BAT file run a word processor:

```
Name: WORD.BAT

1: @ECHO OFF
2: REM Run Microsoft Word
```

```
3:  C:
4:  CD \WP\WORD
5:  PATH = C:\SYSTEM\DOS;C:\SYSTEM\UTIL;C:\WP\WORD
6:  SS
7:  REM Restore old path
8:  PATH = C:\SYSTEM\DOS;U:\;C:\SYSTEM\BATCH;..
```

Because all these batch files are in the batch file subdirectory, you will always have access to any of your programs. If you add software to your system, simply write a new batch file to run that program and put the batch file in /SYSTEM/BATCH (or whatever your batch file subdirectory is called).

Some programs may use batch files to start themselves. For example, the following batch file is used to start the PAINT program that comes with the *Microsoft Mouse*:

```
Name:  PAINT.BAT

1:  FRIEZE P1
2:  PBrush E 1HER 720 348 0
```

You could put this ready-made batch file into your batch file directory, but change it as follows:

```
1:  @ECHO OFF
2:  REM Paint Program
3:  C:
4:  CD \OTHER\PAINT
5:  PATH = C:\SYSTEM\DOS;C:\OTHER\PAINT
6:  FRIEZE P1
7:  PBRUSH E 1HER 720 348 0
8:  PATH = C:\SYSTEM\DOS;U:\;C:\SYSTEM\BATCH;..
```

Now the PAINT program is available all over your hard drive.

This method can further be simplified by taking full advantage of SUBST to shorten some popular directories.

BACKING UP

No one likes to back up, but it really isn't a bother if you do it right. The object is to develop a backup strategy. Now, I'm not going to sit here and wag my finger at you, explaining how important backups are. You should know that.

There are quite a few "fast" backup programs on the market, offering themselves as better alternatives to the DOS BACKUP program. Because this isn't a complete book on the subject, I'm just going to say to use the BACKUP program that came with DOS. It may not be blindingly fast, but it's free, and it works. But first a rule:

Always RESTORE *files to a hard drive*
with the same DOS version that was used for the BACKUP

Backup has changed over the years. The latest version of BACKUP is actually quite smart—and quite incompatible with past releases. If you're going to backup your hard drive because you're reformatting it for a new version of DOS (which isn't necessary, by the way), you will want to BACKUP using the new DOS's BACKUP program. (First, boot the new version of DOS, then run the BACKUP program.)

Normally, however, an entire hard disk backup isn't always necessary. Instead, using the strategy mentioned below—you will be able to get by safely with a minimum of time wasted on backups.

1) Back up your entire hard drive at least once a month.

2) Back up the files you use every day, every day.

Daily backup is the most important. At the end of each day you should back up the files you work on. For example, when I'm done using my computer tonight, I will have backed up all the files and subdirectories that have to do with this book.

Step one is only necessary once in a while. For most users, you'll typically work on one project over a period of time. During that time, the majority of files on your hard drive will just sit there, not being used or modified. There's no point in backing up the entire drive in those instances. Backing up your current work is much more important.

The only times you'll want to back up your entire hard drive are:

- before taking the computer in to be repaired—even if the problem isn't related to the hard drive.
- before moving the computer.
- before installing a new piece of hardware.
- before upgrading to a new version of DOS. (You may want to optionally re-format the drive with the new version of DOS, then RESTORE your files to it.)
- once a month.

If you follow these simple rules, you should be able to use your system without much worry of the effects of a hard disk crash or accidental erasure of important files.

To ensure that you're doing your proper amount of backing up, use the CALL command to include the FIG. 13-7 batch file in your SHUTDOWN batch file. If you don't have a SHUTDOWN.BAT file, then just type the name of this batch file every day before you shut down the computer.

You will notice that the name of the DOS BACKUP program has been changed to B__U. This is so you can call this batch file BACKUP.BAT without any conflicts.

Name: BACKUP.BAT

```
 1: @ECHO OFF
 2: REM BACKUP.BAT program: provides various types of
    backup
 3: REM This program should be on the path so that it's
    available
 4: REM at all times.  Also, note that the DOS BACKUP.COM
    program
 5: REM has been renamed to B_U.COM.
 6: REM This program incorporates programs on the
    supplemental
 7: REM programs diskette.  Like:
 8: :MAIN MENU
 9: CLZ
10: BOX C=20,1;63,18
11: LOCATE 30,3
12: ECHO Hard Disk Backup Options
13: LOCATE 25,6
14: ECHO F1 - Backup the entire hard drive
15: LOCATE 25,8
16: ECHO F2 - Backup only modified files
17: LOCATE 25,10
18: ECHO F3 - Backup only C:\WP\BOOK
19: LOCATE 25,12
20: ECHO F10 - Cancel
21: :GETINPUT
22: LOCATE 30,15
23: READKEY /F Your choice:
24: IF ERRORLEVEL 10 GOTO END
25: IF ERRORLEVEL 3 GOTO ONLY
26: IF ERRORLEVEL 2 GOTO MODIFY
27: IF ERRORLEVEL 1 GOTO ALL
28: GOTO GETINPUT
29: :ONLY
30: CLZ
31: BOX "Backing up C:\WP\BOOK to drive A:"/C
32: B_U C:\NOVELS\BATCH A:
33: GOTO END
34: :MODIFY
35: CLZ
36: BOX "Backing up modified files only"/C
37: B_U C:\*.* A: /S/M
38: GOTO END
39: :ALL
```

Fig. 13-7. This program helps you back up your hard disk.

```
40: CLZ
41: BOX "Backing up entire hard drive"/C
42: B_U C:\*.* A: /S/H
43: :END
44: LOCATE 1,24
```
Fig. 13-7. Continued.

BACKUP makes liberal use of some of the programs on the supplemental programs diskette—among them: CLZ, LOCATE, READKEY and BOX. If you have these programs, be sure that they're on your system's path. (Put them in a UTILITY subdirectory, if you have one.) These programs serve primarily to give this backup program a pretty interface (*see* FIG. 13-8).

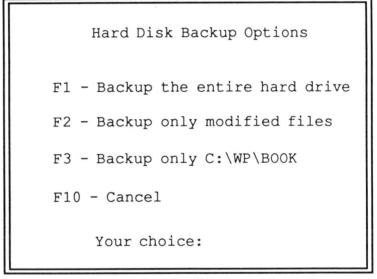

```
              Hard Disk Backup Options


      F1 - Backup the entire hard drive

      F2 - Backup only modified files

      F3 - Backup only C:\WP\BOOK

      F10 - Cancel


              Your choice:
```

Fig. 13-8. Here is BACKUP.BAT's user interface.

The "main menu" is generated between lines 8 and 21. First, the screen is cleared in a fancy way (9) and a box is drawn (10). The menu text will be located inside the box using a combination of LOCATE and ECHO statements.

Input for the batch file is provided by the READKEY statement in line 23. The /F switch tells READKEY to read the function keys as ERRORLEVELs 1 through 10. Lines 24 through 27 evaluate the input and branch to the appropriate subroutine.

Lines 29 through 33 back up files from a specified directory, specifically a directory in which you do most of your recent work. Again, CLZ is used to clear the display (30), and BOX is used to display a message (31). In line 32 the BACKUP command (renamed B_U) is run to do the backup. (If BACKUP.COM weren't renamed, and "BACKUP" were used instead of "B_U," the BACKUP batch program would continually run itself.) Once the backup is completed, batch file execution branches to line 43. Incidentally, the example uses C:/WP/BOOK. For your own backups, you will probably change this.

Lines 34 through 38 back up only those files modified since the last backup. The /S switch of the BACKUP command backs up all subdirectories under the current directory (in this case, that's the entire drive), and /M is used to backup only modified files.

Lines 39 through 43 back up all files on the hard drive—a complete backup. The /F option is new with DOS 3.3. It allows BACKUP to run the FORMAT program in case it encounters an unreadable disk. If you have DOS 3.3, you should always specify the /H command. (Be sure FORMAT is on your system's path when you do so.)

The very last line of this batch file moves the cursor to the bottom left position on the screen (44). This is in case you press F10 to cancel the batch file. If the cursor isn't moved, your system prompt will appear in the middle of the screen (because of READKEY and the LOCATE statement) and look awkward.

OTHER HELPFUL HINTS

Hard disk organization and backing up are the major components of managing your hard disk, but there are many more less important, but still significant, aspects of hard disk management. Again, this isn't a complete book on the subject, but you may look into some of the following techniques to complete your "ultimate system."

Menuing/Shell Software

I extremely dislike menuing or "shell" software, so I'm going to be very brief. Basically, this software is supposed to help you use your computer by avoiding DOS. I think that's like someone helping you learn to drive your car by not teaching you the rules of the road. Unfortunately, DOS shells proliferate, and quite a few users (gulp) like them.

Menuing or shell software allows you to use your system with that one-keystroke effect. Basically, some genius (you, usually) builds the shell program, telling it where all your files are located, and which keys will activate those files. Then the shell program takes over and, using a graphics display, will allow you to "easily" manipulate your computer system using that keystroke.

For beginners, and the computer reluctant, these programs are fine. In fact, the next chapter shows you how to write one using batch files and what you've learned about DOS from this book.

DOSSHELL

Version 4.0 of DOS comes with its own shell program. It's not a bad program, either. (Though I still feel the same way about shell programs in general.)

DOSSHELL features an easy-to-use menu interface. If you have a mouse, it's even more easy to use. Without the mouse, DOSSHELL is awkward to use but still manageable (but you can forget getting at that F11 key if you don't have one).

You can run programs from the shell, or simply use the shell's utilities to manage your system. Advanced capabilities of the shell allow you to customize its operating, allowing new users to take advantage of the shell in as painless a manner as possible.

One drawback to DOSSHELL is that it still insists upon using some dreadful computer terms. "Open" is used to run a program. Although "(start)" appears right next to Open, I think it would be better if that menu option were simply "Run." Also, the DOS neophyte still has to pick the program they want to run from a scrolling list of files. Why can't these shells simply list all the .COM, .EXE, and .BAT files in a directory instead? (This gets into a whole area of complexity about programming shells—one which I don't have the space here to rant about.)

Other than those minor gripes, the DOSSHELL is something to sit down and take a good look at—especially because it comes with DOS. Future releases of DOSSHELL, plus some innovative user-patches, may make it something to keep an eye on for future reference.

Other DOS Shells

There are dozens of shell programs on the market. Some are ridiculously low in price, for example *DOS-A-MATIC*. The most popular is *Direct Access*, available from Delta Technology.

DOS-A-MATIC is available from Marin Pacific Software, 1001 Bridgeway, Suite 514, Sausalito, CA 94965.

Direct Access is available from Delta Technology, 1621 Westgate Road, Eu Claire, Wisconsin 54703. Because of the popularity of *Direct Access*, you can pick it up at any software store.

Keyboard Enhancers

Way back when DOS was young, some enterprising software hackers figured out that you could "hook into" the keyboard interrupt vector inside the machine. While this sounds dangerous and stupid to everyone reading this, some amazing products developed. Of primary concern are keyboard enhancers.

Keyboard enhancers are programs that allow you to record and play back a series of keystrokes—like a tape recorder. Most of them are activated by pressing a certain key combination, say ALT-+. After typing ALT-+, the keyboard enhancer program (memory-resident, of course) memorizes all the keys you press, up until the time you press ALT-+ again. Then it asks you to assign those keystrokes to another key. Say you choose F1. Now, every time to press F1, the keyboard enhancer will repeat, or play back, all the keystrokes you recorded. Neat-o.

Using these enhancers, you could make typing long pathnames and answering repetitive questions easy. Alternatively, if you were paying attention in Chapter 3, you could use ANSI.SYS to do the same thing (*see* FIG. 13-9).

This is the same NIFTY.BAT program introduced in Chapter 3. The difference is that I've changed the string commands to make them a bit more useful (and apply them to the theme of this chapter).

One of the keyboard enhancers, *SuperKey* from Borland, also allows you to have "pop up" screens. For example, you can program the ALT-H (for Help) key to have a little help window appear each time it's pressed. You can change the menu

```
Name: NIFTY.BAT

 1: @ECHO off
 2: ECHO ^[[0;104;"C:";13p;"CD \";13p
 3: ECHO ^[[0;105;"CD \WP\WP";13p
 4: ECHO ^[[0;106;"DIR A:"13p
 5: ECHO ^[[0;107;"DIR *.BAT";13p
 6: ECHO ^[[0;108;"DEL *.BAK";13p
 7: ECHO ^[[0;109;"DEL TEMP*.*";13p
 8: ECHO ^[[0;110;"FORMAT A:";13p
 9: ECHO ^[[0;111;"CD \WORK\BOOK";13p
10: ECHO ^[[0;112;"CD \SYSTEM\TOOLS";13p
11: ECHO ^[[0;113;"SHUTDOWN";13p
```

Fig. 13-9. You can use ANSI.SYS to enhance your keyboard.

being displayed. For example, during the run of one batch file you can echo the message:

```
ECHO Press Alt-H for help
```

Then, using *SuperKey*, you can define the pop-up menu for ALT–H. When the user presses that key, zip!, up comes the menu. People are impressed by this.

Eek! A Mouse

Whether you like them or not, mouses are here to stay. In fact, trying to use the OS/2 Presentation Manager without a mouse is a waste of time and an exercise in frustration. If you don't have a mouse now, you will be buying one within three years. Promise.

To make owning a mouse attractive, the mouse makers (aside from Disney) supply their input devices with a bunch of interesting programs "for free." You usually get a painting program, a few games, a sample something-or-other that you're supposed to practice using your mouse with—and they also toss in a menuing program.

The menuing program can come in really handy. Sadly, the documentation for writing your own menus suffers, but you can still use the menus provided. One of them is bound to be used with DOS.

Using a DOS menu with a mouse is fun. Depending on the rodent, the menu may pop up on the screen when you press a mouse button. You'll then be able to choose from a list of popular DOS commands using the mouse. Unfortunately, the mouse interface really doesn't work well with DOS—not at this time at least.

Helpful Batch Files

One last thing you can do to help manage your hard disk is write some useful batch files, like the one in FIG. 13-10. This program first checks for any files in your

```
Name: CLEAN.BAT

1: @ECHO OFF
2: REM This batch file removes all offending files from the
   drive
3: REM Even if you don't have a \JUNK directory
4: IF EXIST \JUNK\*.* DEL \JUNK\*.* <YES
5: CD \
6: REM Use the SWEEP utility to remove unwanted files
7: SWEEP DEL *.BAK
8: SWEEP DEL KILL*.*
9: SWEEP DEL TEMP*.*
```

Fig. 13-10. CLEAN.BAT checks and deletes JUNK directory files.

/JUNK directory. If any files are found, they are deleted. Next, the SWEEP utility
is used to march down your subdirectories, deleting all *.BAK, then KILL*·*, then
TEMP*·* files.

Log Batch Files

A second type of batch file that comes in handy is a log batch file. This batch
file maintains a list of activities: who was using the computer and when they started
and stopped. Because IBM computers keep track of the time, all that's needed is
a program to "spit out" the current time.

I wrote two programs that assist in creating a computer log for the hard disk
management book I co-authored with Andy Townsend. They are STIME and ETIME.
STIME displays the following:

```
Start Time = Thursday, February 18, 1988 @ 11:14 am
```

ETIME displays:

```
End Time = Thursday, February 18, 1988 @ 11:15 am
```

Using these two files and I/O redirection, you can create a logfile letting you
know what you've used your computer for, and for how long. For example, FIG.
13-11 is a modification of the SS.BAT program discussed earlier in this chapter.
Line 6 of FIG. 13-11 ECHOes "Work on Spreadsheet", appending it to whatever information is already in the file LOGFILE.DAT in the WORK subdirectory on
drive C. Then STIME is used to append the start time to the file (7). After you're
done spreadsheeting, ETIME appends your finish time to the file (8). At the end
of the day, LOGFILE may look like FIG. 13-12.
The last two lines were probably added by a SHUTDOWN.BAT file. Another
ECHO statement was simply used to add "System Shutdown." And a final ETIME
>> C:/WORK/LOGFILE.DAT was used to add the final shutdown time.

```
 1: @ECHO OFF
 2: REM Run Spreadsheet
 3: C:
 4: CD \OTHER\SS
 5: PATH = C:\SYSTEM\DOS;C:\SYSTEM\UTIL;C:\OTHER\SS
 6: ECHO Work on Spreadsheet >> C:\WORK\LOGFILE.DAT
 7: STIME >> C:\WORK\LOGFILE.DAT
 8: SS
 9: ETIME >> C:\WORK\LOGFILE.DAT
10: REM Restore old path
11: PATH = C:\SYSTEM\DOS;U:\;C:\SYSTEM\BATCH;..
```

Fig. 13-11. This is a modification of the SS.BAT program.

```
Work on Spreadsheet
Start Time = Wednesday, August 3rd, 1988 @ 11:57 pm
End Time = Thursday, August 4th, 1988 @ 7:32 am
Work on Word Processor
Start Time = Thursday, August 4th, 1988 @ 7:34 am
End Time = Thursday, August 4th, 1988 @ 7:49 am
System Shutdown
End Time = Thursday, August 4th, 1988 @ 7:55 am
```

Fig. 13-12. This is a sample run of the batch file in Fig. 13-11.

Using a simple logfile system such as this, you can print a written record of your computer time and, if you have them, bill your clients accordingly; or, with just a few extra lines in some batch files, you could have individual user's names ECHOed to a logfile. It makes tracking computer usage easier.

Summary

Hard disk management is a complex area to go into, but still one that's perfect for batch files. Fundamentally, hard disk management boils down to hard disk organization and backing up.

As far as organization goes, a good way to use files and programs on your hard drive is via batch files kept in a special batch file subdirectory. Each batch file runs your programs, customizing the path and environment.

For backing up, various BACKUP batch files can be written and, using the RKEY function from a previous chapter, or any of the key reading utilities provided on the Supplemental Programs Diskette, you can customize the backup to be as specific or general as you need.

Finally, there are numerous other programs available that will assist in hard disk management, organization and use. There are menu generating and user "shell" programs that can make using your system easy; keyboard enhancers that provide complex macro functions; the computer mouse for users who are afraid of the keyboard; and other helpful batch files you can write to make your system more manageable.

14
Batch File Menus

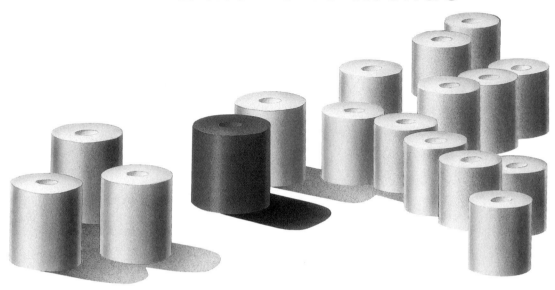

I know, I know. Anyone who's read the previous chapter will be thinking to themselves, "Golly, he just spent part of the last chapter ripping menu programs to shreds. Now what?"

The truth is that menuing and shell programs can make a computer system a lot easier to use. Face it, not everyone is going to enjoy using a computer as much as you do. In fact, there is a faction out there that claims computers have no place being used by people who don't like them. Yet, it will happen. When it does, it's nice to give those people a break by making the system a little more tolerable.

This chapter shows you how you can using batch files to create a comfortable, insulating shell program; a menuing system that will make the computer easier to use.

CREATING A BATCH FILE SHELL PROGRAM

A lot of people complain that DOS is too technical. While this is true, it's also true that the more technical and complex something is, the easier it is to manipulate it into something that isn't. Using your knowledge of DOS, plus the hints provided in this book, you can create a program that will make using DOS a lot easier for the compu-phobes and DOS-terrified among the general populace.

I think you'll find that writing these shell programs is a lot easier using batch files—plus a few slight-of-hands with PROMPT and PATH. If you like, however, you can always buy those commercial shell programs. The problem is that you already know batch files. With the commercial programs, you'll need to learn the way they do things before you can get off and running. So why take the extra trip?

Three Steps to Writing a Shell Program

There are three points to writing a good shell program. Keep these in mind, and your efforts will be successful:

Point one is never to assume that your user is dumb. This is one thing that immediately turns people off to computers. Never talk down to a user or make them feel inferior. The "this is the on/off switch" approach may work for some simple-minded people, but most of the people who use computers are motivated and productive individuals. They simply may not have the time to learn something as cumbersome as DOS. Give them a break, and have your shell program treat them as they deserve.

The second point to writing a good menuing system is to know what the user wants. No, they don't want to "use the computer." If they do, they should learn DOS. Instead, there may be only one or two operations that someone needs to do on the computer. Find out what your user's tasks are, and then write your menu program to accommodate them.

The third point is never to get too cute. Actually, points one and two are the most important. I added this point because (well, three makes a good number and) some programmers get carried away with shell programs. Fancy displays, moving icons, cutsie little bleeps and zippy noises may make the computer "seem fun to use," but they annoy most people after a while. Think productivity and efficiency, and you'll realize that being cute is only used to sell software—not get the job done.

Now that you know these steps, you'll need to apply them. For your own practice, it's good to work with a subject you know: Yourself. In the real world, however, you'll probably end up writing a shell program for someone else. (Remember step two: what do they want?) For this book, I'll use the example of Peggy, a former publisher of mine who does basically four things with her computer:

- Writes letters and memos
- Sends TELEX messages
- Works a spreadsheet
- Reviews a data base and generates reports

Peggy knows how to use the software responsible for those four jobs very well. (Remember, she's not dumb!) Her problem is with using DOS, which she really doesn't have time to mess with. To make her job a little easier, I'll show you how I would build a batch file menu system customized to her needs.

Designing the System

To implement the shell, you should first structure the user's system to meet their needs and, indirectly, to satisfy your own sense of organization. This involves creating all the required subdirectories, and setting up an appropriate file structure. For simplicity's sake, make only one subdirectory for each different program on the computer, plus a subdirectory for DOS. Then place, under those subdirectories, data directories where your users will put their files.

(Remember, the user still needs to know about filenames, saving and loading. You should never confuse someone by making them remember subdirectories and backslash combinations. Let the shell's batch files take care of that for you.)

FIGURE 14-1 shows the directory structure I would set up for Peggy. Each one of the programs she uses is placed into its own subdirectory. Then, under the SYSTEM subdirectory are three additional subdirectories: DOS, BATCH, and UTILITY. Into each of the program subdirectories (DBASE, WP, SS, PCCOM) the respective programs would be installed: the database program, the word processor, the spreadsheet, and a communications program for sending the TELEX messages. Under each of the program subdirectories would be placed a data subdirectory (not shown in FIG. 14-1).

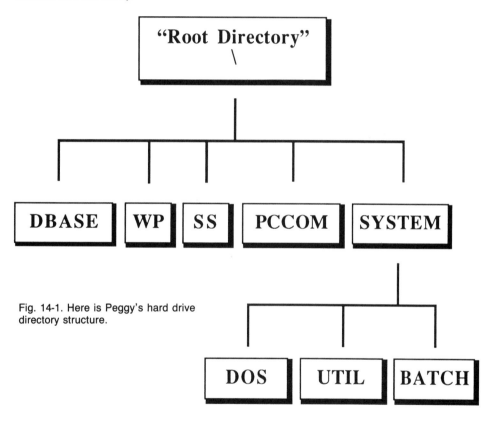

Fig. 14-1. Here is Peggy's hard drive directory structure.

At this point, you might wonder why Peggy would need such a complex /SYSTEM directory. After all, a single subdirectory could contain all DOS files, batch files and utilities and still keep her system simple. There are two reason.

The first is for organization. Her system will be run by batch files. To make managing them easier, I'm putting them all in one place. Sure, I could have put them in a /BATCH subdirectory off the root, but putting it in /SYSTEM (along with /UTIL) keeps the root directory "clean."

The second reason is for myself—or whoever the office computer manager is. Not only will Peggy be using her computer, but the local office computer guru will as well. If that guru is me, I'll want to set up a system that I am familiar with, and that I can get around quickly. So I went with a familiar structure.

CONFIG.SYS and AUTOEXEC.BAT

The following is an example of Peggy's CONFIG.SYS file. If I knew that she was running a particular program that required a specific configuration, I'd make sure that the proper statements were placed in CONFIG.SYS. For demonstration purposes, I'll use the following:

```
1: FILES=20
2: BUFFERS=33
3: DEVICE = C:\SYSTEM\DOS\ANSI.SYS
4: LASTDRIVE=Z
```

I'm giving Peggy ample room for files and buffers (1 and 2), just in case her database program requires it. Also, the ANSI.SYS driver is installed (3), and LASTDRIVE is set to Z so that I could take advantage of the SUBST command if needed.

The following is an example of the system's AUTOEXEC.BAT file:

```
1: @ECHO OFF
2: REM Peggy's AUTOEXEC.BAT
3: PATH=C:\SYSTEM\DOS;C:\SYSTEM\BATCH;C:\SYSTEM\UTIL;..
4: \DOS\UTIL\ASTCLOCK
5: CD \SYSTEM\BATCH
6: MENU
```

There's really nothing fancy here. Line 3 sets the path to the three most popular directories, plus the special ".." entry which specifies the parent directory. (This comes in handy because of the way Peggy's data directories are set up.)

Line 4 sets the system clock. You will note that the complete path is used for this command. While just "ASTCLOCK" would have worked (because line 3 already set the path to /DOS/UTIL), it's much faster to specify a direct path.

Line 5 changes directories to the /SYSTEM/BATCH subdirectory, and finally the program MENU is run.

MENU.BAT

MENU, the final command in AUTOEXEC, is a batch file. It's the "main menu" batch file where Peggy makes her decisions. For example, she could type "1" here to start word processing. Remember, the point to all this is to make the system easier for Peggy to use.

FIGURE 14-2 is the key program that makes Peggy's computer painless to use. It does three things.

First, MENU.BAT makes sure that the system is currently logged to drive C, and the current directory is /SYSTEM/BATCH (5, 6).

Name: MENU.BAT

```
1: @ECHO OFF
2: REM Peggy's shell program, main menu
3: REM Make sure we're in the right directory
4: REM for displaying messages
5: C:
6: CD \SYSTEM\BATCH
7: CLS
8: TYPE MENU.MSG
9: PROMPT $e[17;30HChoice:
```

Fig. 14-2. This is the key program that makes Peggy's computer painless to use.

Second, the screen clears (7) and a text file is displayed (8). The text file displays Peggy's menu choices. It could have easily been done with ECHO statements, but that method proves slow and awkward looking. It's much better to display the text file. (This batch file assumes the text file to be in the /SYSTEM/BATCH directory; otherwise a full pathname would be used in line 8).

Finally, the tricky part is to incorporate the system prompt as an input device. Line 9 sets the prompt first with an ANSI command, and then with the word "Choice: " (followed by a space character).

The ANSI command is ^[[17;30H. This moves the cursor on to row 17, column 30 on the screen. At that point, the word "Choice" is displayed. The net effect is of an integrated menu display (see FIG. 14-3).

To the unsuspecting user, "Choice:" simply looks like a place to input a number. However, it's really the vicious and cryptic DOS prompt in disguise.

At this point, Peggy can press 1, 2, 3 or 4 to get her work done, or press A, B or C to do the special functions. Each number or letter must be followed by an ENTER (as is true of all DOS commands). Again, the secret here is that all those one-letter responses are batch files (see FIG. 14-4). The file 1.BAT file runs Peggy's word processor. It first changes directories (3) and then the PATH to be more accommodating to the word processor (4).

In line 6, the word processing program is run. Then, after Peggy is done word processing, the old PATH is reset (8), the system changes directories to the batch file subdirectory (9), and finally the MENU program is run again (10), making the circle complete.

The other batch files, 2 through 4, are only simple modifications to 1.BAT (see FIG. 14-5).

Name: A.BAT

```
1: @ECHO OFF
2: CLS
3: ECHO You're now in DOS...
4: VER
5: ECHO Type "MENU" to return to the menu program
6: PROMPT $p$g
```

```
┌─────────────────────────────────────────────────┐
│ ┌─────────────────────────────────────────────┐ │
│ │               Main Menu                       │ │
│ │                                               │ │
│ │   Type the number of the item you want:       │ │
│ │                                               │ │
│ │       1. Word Processing                      │ │
│ │                                               │ │
│ │       2. Spreadsheet                          │ │
│ │                                               │ │
│ │       3. Data base                            │ │
│ │                                               │ │
│ │       4. Send Telex                           │ │
│ │                                               │ │
│ │   Special Functions:                          │ │
│ │                                               │ │
│ │       A. Return to DOS                        │ │
│ │                                               │ │
│ │       B. Backup Files                         │ │
│ │                                               │ │
│ │       C. Turn computer off                    │ │
│ │                                               │ │
│ │           Choice:                             │ │
│ │                                               │ │
│ └─────────────────────────────────────────────┘ │
└─────────────────────────────────────────────────┘
```

Fig. 14-3. Here is Peggy's main MENU.

Name: 1.BAT

```
 1: @ECHO OFF
 2: REM Run the word processor
 3: CD \WP
 4: PATH=C:\SYSTEM\DOS;C:\SYSTEM\BATCH;..;C:\WP
 5: REM Enter the word processor's name:
 6: WP
 7: REM All done, go back to the menu
 8: PATH=C:\SYSTEM\DOS;C:\SYSTEM\BATCH;C:\SYSTEM\UTIL;..
 9: CD \SYSTEM\BATCH
10: MENU
```

Fig. 14-4. This is the batch file for word processing.

Name: 2.BAT

```
 1: @ECHO OFF
 2: REM Run the spreadsheet
 3: CD \SS
 4: PATH=C:\SYSTEM\DOS;C:\SYSTEM\BATCH;..;C:\SS
 5: REM Enter the spreadsheet's name:
 6: PLAN
 7: REM All done, go back to the menu
 8: PATH=C:\SYSTEM\DOS;C:\SYSTEM\BATCH;C:\SYSTEM\UTIL;..
 9: CD \SYSTEM\BATCH
10: MENU
```

Name: 3.BAT

```
 1: @ECHO OFF
 2: REM Run the data base
 3: CD \DBASE
 4: PATH=C:\SYSTEM\DOS;C:\SYSTEM\BATCH;..;C:\DBASE
 5: REM Enter the data base's name:
 6: DBASE
 7: REM All done, go back to the menu
 8: PATH=C:\SYSTEM\DOS;C:\SYSTEM\BATCH;C:\SYSTEM\UTIL;..
 9: CD \SYSTEM\BATCH
10: MENU
```

Name: 4.BAT

```
 1: @ECHO OFF
 2: REM Send a TELEX
 3: CD \PCCOM
 4: PATH=C:\SYSTEM\DOS;C:\SYSTEM\BATCH;..;C:\PCCOM
 5: REM Enter the communication program's name:
 6: AEMS
 7: REM All done, go back to the menu
 8: PATH=C:\SYSTEM\DOS;C:\SYSTEM\BATCH;C:\SYSTEM\UTIL;..
 9: CD \SYSTEM\BATCH
10: MENU
```

Fig. 14-5. These batch files are for spreadsheet, database and communication applications.

This is the batch file that "returns" Peggy to DOS (or, more likely, returns the office computer manager to DOS). The most important change is the PROMPT statement in line 6, which restores the system to a typical drive/pathname type of prompt. MENU can still be typed at this point to return Peggy to her menuing system. (If the PROMPT is not changed back, it will continue to be the word "Choice" displayed near the center of the screen.)

Name: B.BAT

```
1: @ECHO OFF
2: REM Backup the disk
3: CLS
4: ECHO Make sure you have a pile of diskettes handy.
5: PAUSE
6: BACKUP C:\*.* A: /S/F
7: ECHO ^G
8: MENU
```

This is just a quick and dirty example of a backup routine. A much better routine was covered in the previous chapter, and could easily be incorporated here by changing it's name to B.BAT. The only thing odd here is the ECHO ^G statement in line 7. This causes the computer's speaker to beep, alerting Peggy that the backup is complete. Then, as is true with all these batch files, control returns to the menu.

Name: C.BAT

```
1: @ECHO OFF
2: REM this is Peggy's shutdown.bat file
3: CLS
4: ECHO Stand by to turn your computer system off
5: REM Put the computer's PARK program here:
6: PARK
```

Again, this is another quick and dirty example of a shutdown batch file. The only thing this one does is to park the hard drive (6) once it's done. Other items could be added to C.BAT if they were required before Peggy turns her system off.

If you do design this type of menuing system, about the most important thing to remember is to turn it off when you're done. This implies the simple steps performed in the example A.BAT above. Changing the system prompt using the ANSI commands is really nice for inputting information in a "menu," but for regularly running a system, it's a pain.

ADDING COMPLEXITY

While the above example of a batch file shell does the job, it's really not as smooth as it could have been. I avoided adding too much complexity to it so you could see the basic idea. Still, there are many nice little touches you can add to enhance the performance and appearance of a batch file shell.

You can add different layers to this type of shell as deep as you want. For example, different menu options could display different menus (and change the prompt again). Everything still works the same way—you're just running another MENU.BAT file rather than running a program.

You can also get fancy with the CALL statement, using certain batch files as subroutines; or you can opt to use the READKEY utility instead of using the PROMPT command for input. READKEY has the advantage of controlling input. However, it has the disadvantage of not giving you immediate access to the system if you need it.

You should try to avoid using groups of ECHO statements wherever possible. Create text files with your information listed in them. If you feel like getting creative, use the color ANSI commands for fancy menu displays.

Finally, as the coup de grace of the batch file shell, you can use enhanced batch file languages such as Beyond•Bat or EBL to write your shell. This is taking one foot out of DOS and planting one foot in a customized shell program. In other words, it might be a better choice to buy a program that already does the job for you if you need that complexity. Yet, it's still another way you can enhance a shell or menuing program.

Using PATH

One weak point of the above shell example was how the PATH kept changing. This could be avoided by adding variables in the environment for each possible path, then using SET to change the Path. If you try this, remember to specify enough space in the environment. (See Chapter 4.)

The following are environment variables that could be defined by AUTOEXEC:

```
WPPATH=PATH=C:\SYSTEM\DOS;C:\SYSTEM\BATCH;..;C:\WP
SSPATH=PATH=C:\SYSTEM\DOS;C:\SYSTEM\BATCH;..;C:\SS
DBPATH=PATH=C:\SYSTEM\DOS;C:\SYSTEM\BATCH;..;C:\DBASE
COMPATH=PATH=C:\SYSTEM\DOS;C:\SYSTEM\BATCH;..;C:\PCCOM
SYSPATH=PATH=C:\SYSTEM\DOS;C:\SYSTEM\BATCH;C:\SYSTEM\UTIL;..
```

To change the path, the new path can be specified in a batch file as follows:

```
PATH=%WPPATH%
```

That's it! To restore the path, use the following:

```
PATH=%SYSPATH%
```

The batch file interpreter expands the variable names (between the percent signs) when the batch file is run. The net effect will be the same, but with a lot less typing.

Here's an even better trick. If you'll notice, the first part of the path is always the same. Therefore, it would be easier and take up less space if the following variable were established:

```
SAME=C:\SYSTEM\DOS;C:\SYSTEM\BATCH;..;
```

This way, setting or changing the path is as easy as:

```
PATH=%SAME%C:\WP
```

and:

```
PATH=%SAME%C:\SS
```

and so on.

As you work with your own shells, and see how they run, you'll probably think of more tricks. Just keep in mind the third point from earlier in this chapter: Don't get carried away with being too cute!

RESTPATH

As your menu files get more complex, you'll want them to perform more and more tricks. Some of them, the PATH command in the previous section as an example, are possible using the tools DOS gives you. Others aren't as easy, which is why I wrote the RESTPATH command.

RESTPATH isn't necessarily for batch file menus. It's for any system that's run via batch files in a /BATCH subdirectory. The problem with running your system this way is that you never know from where your batch file started. For example, assume for some reason that you're on drive I in the "root" directory. (Drive I is a SUBSTituted drive.) You want to run an UPDATE batch file.

What UPDATE does is to copy key files from your hard drive to a diskette in drive A. To do this, UPDATE changes drives and directories to find all the files you want copied. When UPDATE is done, it's in the drive and directory of the last file copied. Yet, you started out on drive I. How could the batch file return you to where you started?

(Think about this one for a time. How could it be done? I stewed over this for about two hours before it finally came to me—okay, okay, I had a jelly donut as well!)

Here's a hint. The CD command is used alone to display the current drive and directory. You can redirect the output of CD to a file:

```
CD >> C:\CDIR
```

This puts the name of the current drive and directory into the file CDIR in the root directory on drive C. CDIR may contain something like the following:

```
I:\WORK\MAKEUP
```

That's the current directory. But how can we get that information back into DOS, allowing us to get back to that drive and directory?

The answer is RESTPATH. RESTPATH is used with the CD command's redirected output to restore you to the same directory from which you started. To move you back to drive I and the /WORK/MAKEUP subdirectory, you'd enter:

```
RESTPATH C:\CDIR
```

The file CDIR contains "I:/WORK/MAKEUP". RESTPATH reads this information, then logs to drive I and the /WORK/MAKEUP directory.

So, to bring an end to this question, here is how to restore your drive and directory for all your batch files. At the top of your batch files, put the following command:

```
CD > C:\CDIR
```

    (Or you can use "TEMP" or put the file in a JUNK directory.)
Then, near the bottom of your batch file, add the following two commands:

```
RESTPATH C:\CDIR
DEL C:\CDIR
```

This restores the path, bringing you back to where you were when you started—and then the CDIR file is neatly removed. Convenience at its best.

You should note, however, that RESTPATH has no output. Instead, it uses ERRORLEVEL values to communicate to your batch file what happened. The ERRORLEVEL values returned by RESTPATH are as follows:

0) Drive/directory properly restored

1) File not found, the file specified after RESTPATH was not found or no file was specified

2) Syntax error, the information in the specified file was probably not a drive/directory listing or not created by CD >

It might be added that: testing for these errors is rather fruitless. Because RESTPATH will probably be used at the end of a batch file, there's really nothing more you can do, as far as restoring the drive and directory is concerned.

A friend pointed out, however, that you could conceivably use RESTPATH as a quick replacement for a combination change drive/directory command. So, for example, instead of having the following two lines in a batch file:

```
I:
CD \WORK\MAKEUP
```

you could simply use:

```
RESTPATH C:\BATCH\MPATH
```

MPATH would contain "I:/WORK/MAKEUP". This way, RESTPATH would be quicker than using the two separate commands.

The HelpFile System

A good example of adding complexity to a batch file menu system is provided on the supplemental programs diskette. It's a batch file that offers useful information on the diskette, and it's what I call the HelpFile system. Though this one is specific to the programs and file that come on the supplemental programs diskette, it could really be used in a variety of circumstances and for a number of purposes.

HelpFile takes into account almost every trick in the book (this book) as far as manipulating batch files is concerned. In fact, many of the sample programs and custom utilities written for this book were created with HelpFile in mind.

FIGURE 14-6 is a listing of HelpFile's main program, called HELP.BAT. This batch file can be divided into five parts:

1) Lines 1 through 8 are the introduction, mainly comments.

2) Lines 9 through 21 set up the program—establishing a path and displaying introductory information on the screen.

3) Lines 22 through 34 compose the main menu, displaying selections and then waiting for input

4) Lines 35 through 37 act upon the input the user provides.

5) Lines 38 through 48 provide the end of the batch file—resetting variables, the path, and the directory to what they were before the batch file started.

Part one is simply a setup. After the initial ECHO OFF, several REM statements provide comments and other information about the batch file. This section could be much longer, explaining who wrote the batch file and when they wrote it, what it does, explaining what the variables are, and how they are modified—all that stuff they taught you in programming class that you can safely ignore for now. I avoided entering all that information just to make the batch file shorter on disk (and, besides, it's all written down here anyway!).

Part one ends on line 8. This is where the variable IN is tested. IN is set to "YES" by the other batch file's HELP.BAT runs. Because HELP.BAT doesn't CALL these batch files (it simply branches to them, which is more convenient and in some cases necessary), it uses the IN variable to determine if another batch file has just been run, or if the user typed HELP.BAT from the command line. If another batch file called HELP.BAT, then IN will equal "YES," and part two is skipped.

Part two sets the system path and displays the initial HelpFile screen. Line 9 saves the current path in the OLD variable, and line 10 uses CD with I/O redirection to place the current drive and directory in the file KILLME on drive A (it's assumed that this program will be run from the Supplemental Programs Diskette in drive A).

Line 15 sets the path to the two directories on drive A that contain HelpFile's program and the utilities that are used by this batch file. Lines 16 through 20 display the initial HelpFile information screen. Then line 21 waits for any key to be pressed before going on to part three.

Part three of this batch file displays the main menu. If the environment variable IN (line 8) was set to "YES", then batch file execution would have automatically

Name: HELP.BAT

```
1: ECHO OFF
2: REM Add an @ sign in front of ECHO OFF if this is DOS
   3.3 or later
3: REM ****************************
4: REM *                          *
```

Fig. 14-6. This is HELP.BAT.

```
 5: REM *     The HelpFile System     *
 6: REM *                             *
 7: REM ****************************
 8: IF "%IN%"=="YES" GOTO MAIN
 9: SET OLD=%PATH%
10: CD > A:\KILLME
11: REM --- Change the path to reflect your own set up,
    depending on where
12: REM --- you install HELPFILE.
13: REM --- You'll need access to your utilities as well
14: REM --- as the HELPFILE directory
15: PATH=A:\HELPFILE;A:\BOOKUTIL
16: CLS
17: BOX s=b "The HelpFile System"/c
18: CD HELPFILE
19: TYPE INTRO.MSG
20: BOX s=s "Press any key"/c
21: READKEY
22: :MAIN MENU LOOP
23: SET IN=NO
24: CLZ
25: BOX s=d "Main Menu"/c
26: TYPE MAIN.MSG
27: BOX c=15,4;65,16
28: LOCATE 30,14
29: READKEY /F "Enter your choice:"
30: IF ERRORLEVEL 10 GOTO EXIT
31: IF ERRORLEVEL 3 A:\HELPFILE\F3.BAT
32: IF ERRORLEVEL 2 GOTO BRANCH2
33: IF ERRORLEVEL 1 CALL A:\HELPFILE\F1.BAT
34: GOTO MAIN
35: :BRANCH2
36: CALL A:\HELPFILE\F2.BAT
37: GOTO MAIN
38: :EXIT ROUTINES
39: REM Restore directory and remove temporary files:
40: RESTPATH A:\KILLME
41: DEL A:\KILLME
42: REM Restore path:
43: PATH=%OLD%
44: REM Clear our variables:
45: SET OLD=
46: SET IN=
47: CLS
48: :END
```

come here. You'll notice how the MAIN label also incorporates a comment that fully describes what it is (line 22).

The first thing done in the main menu loop is to reset the IN variable to "NO" (23). Next, the screen is cleared with the special CLZ utility (24). A box is drawn around "Main Menu" and it's centered at the top of the display (25). The MAIN.MSG file is typed to the screen (avoiding a long sequence of ECHO statements) and then a box is drawn around it (26, 25). Finally, the LOCATE utility is used to position the cursor in the box (28) and the string "Enter your choice" is displayed by READKEY (29). Here, READKEY waits for input from the user, and because the /F switch is specified, only the function keys will be read.

Once the user presses a key, part four of the batch file is executed. Here, ERRORLEVEL is used to test the keys pressed. Because ERRORLEVEL matches all values greater than or equal to what is listed, the first value tested for is 10, for F10 (30). If that's the case, the exit routines (part five) are executed at line 38.

If the user presses F3 (or any other F-key between F4 and F9), the batch file F3.BAT is executed (31). If the user presses F2, batch file execution branches to the BRANCH2 label at line 35. In line 36, the CALL command is used to execute the batch file F2.BAT. CALL was chosen over executing F2.BAT, simply to add variety to this batch file.

If the user presses F1, CALL is used to execute F1.BAT. When control returns to HELP.BAT in line 34, the main menu section of this batch file will be executed again.

Part five is the shutdown part of this batch file, starting at line 38. The purpose here is to restore the state of the computer back to what it was before the program started. First, RESTPATH is used to restore the drive and directory to what they were before the batch file started (40). Next, the file used by RESTPATH is removed from the root directory of drive A (41). The old path is restored in line 43 and, in lines 45 and 46, the environment variables used by this batch file are cleared from the environment table. Finally, the screen is cleared (47) and the batch file ends.

You will notice the END label in line 48. It's not used by this batch file, yet it could be used by some addition at a future date.

Summary

Even though I personally detest menu-driven computer systems, it's possible to use the knowledge you've gained from this book to successfully write a batch file menu system. This system can be used by those people who detest DOS but need to get work done anyway.

The way you implement a batch file menu system is by examining the needs of the person who will use it. Once that's done, simply keep the system clean, avoiding junking up the batch file menus with a lot of bells and whistles, and you should have a happy—and productive—computer user on your hands.

Part Five

Batch File Cookbook

THIS part of the book is a reference work—like a cookbook, but more like an encyclopedia. It provides information on each of the DOS and OS/2 batch file directives, plus a few extra DOS and OS/2 commands that are primarily used by batch files.

15
Cookbook Introduction

The following is a list of each of the batch file directives in this reference:

% (percent)	COMMAND	IF
: (colon)	ECHO	NOT
= = (double equal signs)	ENDLOCAL	PAUSE
@ (at)	ERRORLEVEL	REM
ANSI	EXIST	SET
CALL	EXTPROC	SETLOCAL
CLS	FOR	SHIFT
CMD	GOTO	

Each directive is listed alphabetically, with the single character commands and operators listed in their ASCII order (%, :, = , @). Provided with each directive is a description of what it does, how it relates to DOS, plus an example program and a test run.

You can use this section as a reference when writing your own batch files. Every effort has been made to make sure that this information is up to date and works with each version of DOS. Where exceptions occur, they are noted.

Reference

At the top of the page is the name of the batch file directive. Single character commands are followed by their name in parentheses, such as % (percent) or = = (double equal signs).

Below the name of the batch file directive is its type. There are no official types, only the four that I use to describe the various directives:

1) Command—ANSI, CALL, CLS (just about everything else)

2) Statement—REM, IF

3) Variable—ERRORLEVEL, EXIST

4) Operator—= = (double equal signs), NOT

A command batch file directive is a direct order, it does something immediately. For example, GOTO branches to the indicated label; CALL executes a second batch file; SET assigns an environment variable. Most batch file directives are commands.

There are only two statements: REM and IF. IF is a statement because it involves a decision based on a comparison. It doesn't really give a direct order. REM isn't a command because it simply identifies a comment; it does nothing by itself.

The only variables, aside from the % (percent) variables, are ERRORLEVEL and EXIST. These two variables are used with the IF statement to hold a program's return code or determine if a file exists.

The operators are = = (double equal signs) and NOT. Both of these are used with the IF statement to compare variables or to negate the result of a test, respectively.

After identifying whether the batch file directive is a command, statement, variable or operator, four items are determined:

- Whether the directive can also be issued directly on the command line
- The DOS versions in which the directive can be used
- The OS/2 modes in which the directive can be used (real or protected)
- The type of command: internal or external

If a batch file directive can be used on the command line, the cookbook will list the following:

Command line: Yes

otherwise, "No" is listed. There is an explanation of why this is so at the end of the entry.

The "DOS versions" entry indicates when the batch file directive was introduced. Only a few of the directives have been around since DOS version 1.0. More were introduced with version 2.0, and more with version 3.3:

DOS versions: 2.0 and up

If the batch file directive is an OS/2-protected-mode-only command, then "N/A" is listed for the DOS version.

DOS versions: N/A

The "OS/2" entry determines whether the batch file directive can be used with OS/2. Nearly all batch file directives can be used in the OS/2 real mode. However, some directives are specific to the protected mode only:

OS/2: Protected mode

The "type" entry indicates whether it's internal or external. Internal commands are part of COMMAND.COM and always remain in memory. External commands are located on disk:

Type: Internal

Following these items is a description of the command and what it does. For example:

@ hides command lines in a batch file, preventing them from being displayed. It's normally used with the initial ECHO OFF command.

This is followed by the format of the command. Optional parameters are listed after (or before) the command:

@ *commands*

Below this is a description of the optional parameters, along with a few examples of how the batch file directive is used.

A program example is provided to show the batch file directive in a simple batch file. If there are any variations of usage, additional program examples are provided, along with "test runs" that describe or illustrate the batch file's output.

A final section titled "IN DOS . . ." is used to describe how the batch file directive behaves differently at the DOS command prompt—or if it behaves at all.

At the end of the entry is a list of similar or related commands, plus a reference to a specific chapter in this book (where applicable).

% (percent sign) COMMAND

Command line—	No
DOS versions—	2.0 and up
OS/2—	Real and Protected modes
Type—	Internal

% (percent sign) is used to identify a variable in a batch file. It has three separate applications: replaceable parameters, environment variables, and for use with the FOR statement.

Replaceable Parameters

Format: *%value*

value is a number from zero through nine. It specifies the items typed on the command line in the order that they were typed. %0 is the name of the batch file; %1 is the first item typed after the batch file name; %2 is the second; %3 is the third; and so on. Items are separated by the space character.

Examples

C> TEST THIS IS A TEST

"TEST" is the name of the batch file. "THIS IS A TEST" are the compose the individual items used by the replaceable parameter variables. In order, they are:

%0 TEST

%1 THIS

%2 IS

%3 A

%4 TEST

As the replaceable parameter variables are encountered in the batch file, the batch file interpreter will expand them to their appropriate values. For example:

ECHO %1

will be replaced by:

ECHO THIS

when the batch file runs. Replaceable parameters allow your batch files to work with variables, but only variables entered on the command line.

Program Example 1

```
1: @ECHO OFF
2: ECHO Replaceable parameters are:
3: ECHO One   = %1
4: ECHO Two   = %2
5: ECHO Three = %3
6: ECHO Four  = %4
```

Test Run 1   The following is typed to start the batch file:

C> TEST FIRST SECOND THIRD FOURTH

Replaceable parameters are:

    One   =   FIRST
    Two   =   SECOND
  Three   =   THIRD
   Four   =   FOURTH

If a replaceable parameter variable doesn't exist (one wasn't entered on the command line), then that variable will be equal to the null string ("").

Environment Variables

Format: **%name%**

name is the name of an environment variable assigned with the SET command. It can be any length and include spaces and reserved characters. **name** is expanded by the batch file interpreter to equal the string assigned to it by SET.

Examples

```
SET test=Hello, Sandie
```

This places the string "TEST = Hello, Sandie" into the environment table. TEST, the variable name, is capitalized by the SET command. To use the variable TEST, it must be surrounded by single percent signs:

```
ECHO %TEST%
```

The batch file interpreter searches the environment table for TEST. If found, it expands TEST into the appropriate string. In the above example, this would be:

```
ECHO Hello, Sandie
```

Had the variable TEST not been found, the batch file interpreter would "expand" it to a null string:

```
ECHO
```

In other words, no error would occur.

Program Example 2

```
1:  @ECHO OFF
2:  SET STATUS=IN
3:  IF "%STATUS%"=="IN" GOTO FOUND
4:  ECHO Not in
5:  GOTO END
6:  :FOUND
7:  ECHO Status is %STATUS%
8:  :END
```

Test Run 2

```
Status is IN
```

FOR Variables

Format: **%*char***
Format: **%%*char***

char can be any single character except for the greater-than sign, less-than sign, pipe symbol and comma. With DOS versions prior to 4.0, ***char*** cannot be a number. It is used by the FOR command to specify a group of files. If the FOR command is used at the DOS prompt, then only one percent-sign should be specified. When FOR is used in a batch file, two percent-signs should be specified.

The batch file interpreter does not expand the FOR variable. (It does, however, "eat" one of the percent signs—which is why two of them need to be specified inside a batch file.) Instead, FOR uses its variable as a placeholder for the commands used with the FOR statement. The variables represent a group of files the commands act upon.

Example

```
FOR %A in (*.BAK TEMP*.* JUNK*.* KILL*.*) DO DEL %A
```

The command "DEL %A" will be repeated for each of the files represented between the parentheses. The %A is the placeholder for those filenames. In this example, FOR is used to DELete four separate groups of files.

Program Example 3

```
1: @ECHO OFF
2: FOR %%F IN (*.DOC README %1) DO TYPE %%F
3: :END
```

Test Run 3   (The batch file will TYPE to the screen any file in the current directory with a .DOC extension, any file named README, and any file matching the replaceable parameter variable %1.)

In DOS . . .

The character % is only used with the FOR command on the DOS command line. In this instance, only percent-sign needs to be specified with the FOR variable.

DOS does not use the replaceable parameter variables %0 through %1, nor will it expand them or environment variables.

It's also important to note that DOS considers the % character a valid character for a filename. However, the batch file interpreter will not see a single % in a filename (because of how it deals with variables). If you specify a filename in a batch file, and that filename has a % in it, you must specify % twice. Therefore:

```
ANNUAL%.DAT
```

should be listed in a batch file as:

```
ANNUAL%%.DAT
```

ALSO SEE . . .FOR, ECHO, SET, SHIFT, = = (double equal signs)

: (colon) COMMAND

Command line— Yes
DOS versions— 2.0 and up
OS/2— Real and Protected modes
Type— Internal

The character : (colon) is used to identify a label. The label is used by the GOTO statement, however, the : character is not specified by GOTO.

Format: *:label comments*

label is the label identifying the line. It can be from one to eight characters long, and can contain any characters except for a period, semicolon, equal sign, or characters not allowed in a filename (see Appendix E). If the label is followed by *comments*, then the space character identifies the end of the label and the start of the *comments*.

    comments are any optional characters appearing after the label. The batch file interpreter ignores any characters after the eighth character of a label, or after the space character, whichever comes first. You can use this "feature" to include comments with your label. For example:

```
:HERE <- This is where I want you to branch
```

"HERE" is the label. The rest of the line is ignored by the batch file interpreter and is used as a comment.

Example

```
:LABEL1
```

    The : is used to identify the label named "LABEL1". If the following command were issued:

```
GOTO LABEL1
```

the batch file interpreter would scan the entire batch file (from start to finish) for the : character followed by "LABEL1". If found, batch file execution will pick up at the following line. If not found, a "Label not found" error will result, and the batch file will immediately stop.

The colon can also be used alone on a line. In this instance, the colon serves only to "pretty up" the listing:

```
@ECHO OFF
:
ECHO Don't I look nice?
:
```

Of course, blank lines are allowed in batch files, as well as using the colon alone.

```
1: @ECHO OFF
2: GOTO LABEL1
3: REM This line is skipped
4: :LABEL1
5: ECHO I found it!
6: :END
```

```
I found it!
```

When the batch file interpreter encounters a line starting with a : character, it assumes that line to be a label and ignores it (does not execute the line as a command). Therefore, you can also use the colon character simply as a device for adding comments to a file. But be careful not to confuse those comments with a label elsewhere in the program.

```
1: @ECHO OFF
2: :THIS IS A COMMENT
3: ECHO batch file starting...
4: GOTO THIS
5: REM this line will probably be skipped
6: :THIS
7: ECHO I'm Done!
8: END
```

```
batch file starting...
batch file starting...
batch file starting...
```

(etc.)

GOTO looks for the first matching label from the top of the file through the bottom. Because the colon in line 2 is carelessly used as a comment, execution never branches to the intended label at line 6.

In DOS . . .

The colon is a reserved character in DOS, used to separate a drive letter from a pathname. If you type a colon on a command line in DOS, you'll get a "Bad command or filename" error.

ALSO SEE . . .GOTO, REM

= = (double equal signs) OPERATOR

Command line— N/A
DOS versions— 2.0 and up
OS/2— Real and Protected modes
Type— Internal

The characters = = (double equal signs) form a comparison operator used with the IF command. It's similar to the single equal sign used with IF-THEN statements in BASIC.

Format: **variable** = = **string**

variable and **string** are two string values that are compared by the = = operator. Both can be variables or both can be strings, though typically the first value is either a replaceable parameter variable, or an environment variable. If both strings are equal, the IF statement is true (see IF).

Both sides of the double equal signs must have some value. If you forget either one of the values, or if one value is a variable that turns out to be empty, then you'll get a Syntax Error. (See the second example below.)

Examples

```
IF %STATUS%==IN
```

This command compares the value of the environment variable STATUS with the string IN. If both sides of the equal sign are equal (both strings are the same), then the IF test will be true.

```
IF "%1"==""
```

This command uses the double equals sign to check to see if the variable %1 is equal to anything at all. If so, the IF test will pass (because '""' = ='"", %1 is not expanded by the batch file interpreter). However, if %1 is equal to something, the batch file interpreter will expand it, and the IF test will fail.

```
IF "%NAME%"=="Shelly Ann"
```

In this instance the IF test may fail. Unlike BASIC and other programming languages, "Shelly Ann" is considered two separate items by the IF command. Even if NAME does equal "Shelly Ann", the batch file will error because it assumes "Ann" to be a command and not part of the comparison test.

```
1:  @ECHO OFF
2:  SET TEST=in
3:  IF "%TEST%"=="in" ECHO It's %TEST% there!
4:  SET TEST=
5:  :END
```

Test Run

```
It's in there!
```

Format: **variable**CONST = = CONST

When used in the above format, = = tests for the existence of a variable.

variable is either an environment variable or a replaceable parameter. CONST is a string constant, either a single letter or a complete word. If **variable** exists, the IF statement will be false. Otherwise, because the batch file interpreter expands **variable** into nothing (a null string), the statement will be true.

```
IF !%1==!
```

If the replaceable parameter isn't set to anything, then the IF statement is true. Otherwise, %1 is equal to something. Note that this strategy will always avoid a possible Syntax Error in case a replaceable parameter has no value.

Other variations on this format are:

"**variable**" = = " "

NUL**variable** = = NUL

In DOS . . .

The IF statement works on the command line. However, environment variables are not expanded by the command line interpreter—therefore, an IF test would be rather silly.

ALSO SEE . . . IF, % (percent)

@ (at) COMMAND

Command line—   No
DOS versions—   3.3 and up

314   PART FIVE: BATCH FILE COOKBOOK

OS/2— Real and Protected modes
Type— Internal

The character @ hides command lines in a batch file, preventing them from being displayed. It's normally used with the initial ECHO OFF command.

Format: **@commands**

commands are batch file or DOS commands. @ is placed before batch file commands so that the commands will not be displayed. @ suppresses the displaying of commands, regardless of whether ECHO is ON or OFF.

Example

`@ECHO OFF`

This command is usually used as the first line in a batch file. ECHO OFF suppresses the batch file from being listed to the screen as it's run. The @ sign suppresses ECHO OFF from being displayed. The net result is a "silent" batch file.

Normally @ is only used once with the initial ECHO OFF statement. However, you could use @ for every line in the batch file to stop it from being displayed. See Program Example #2 below.

You can write an entire batch file and precede each line with an @ sign to suppress the display. However, you should not put an @ sign in front of a label. In fact, the batch file interpreter will not display any line beginning with a colon character, whether ECHO is on or off.

Program Example 1

```
1: @ECHO OFF
2. ECHO The initial @ECHO command did not display on the
screen.
3: :END
```

Test Run 1   The initial @ECHO command did not display on the screen.

Program Example 2

```
1: @ECHO These strings are echoed to the screen,
2: @ECHO but because of the @ sign, you do not see
3: @ECHO the ECHO command displayed.
```

Test Run 2

```
These strings are echoed to the screen,
but because of the @ sign, you do not see
the ECHO command displayed.
```

In DOS . . .

@ does not work on the DOS command line. (Think about it—it would be redundant: The @ command would turn off the display!)

@ is a valid character in a filename. If you want to specify a program or file in your batch program that starts with the @ character, you must use two @ signs. Therefore, to run the program @NOON in your batch file, you'll need to specify:

```
@@NOON
```

ALSO SEE . . . ECHO

ANSI COMMAND

Command line—	Yes
DOS versions—	N/A
OS/2—	Protected mode only
Type—	External

ANSI is used to turn the ANSI screen driver on or off.

Format: ANSI *switch*

switch is either ON or OFF. ANSI ON turns the ANSI driver on; ANSI OFF turns it off.

After issuing the ANSI ON command, OS/2 displays the following:

```
ANSI extended screen and
keyboard control is on.
```

After issuing ANSI OFF, the following is displayed

```
ANSI extended screen and
keyboard control is off.
```

ANSI ON is usually used in the OS2INIT.CMD batch file. This way, each new protected mode session you start will be able to use ANSI.

Example

```
ANSI ON
```

This command turns the ANSI screen driver on. ANSI commands issued in batch files will now control the screen, change screen color, or reassign keys on the keyboard.

```
ANSI OFF
```

This command disables the ANSI screen driver. Normally, ANSI is off.

```
1: @ECHO OFF
2: ANSI ON
3: ECHO ^[[2J
4: ANSI OFF
```

```
ANSI extended screen and
keyboard control is on.
```

(The screen will be clear.)

```
ANSI extended screen and
keyboard control is off.
```

In DOS . . .

DOS and OS/2 Real mode batch files have no control over the ANSI driver. It must be loaded when the computer is first started by installing the ANSI.SYS device driver in the CONFIG.SYS file.

ALSO SEE . . . Chapter 5

CALL COMMAND

Command line—	Yes
DOS versions—	3.3 and up
OS/2—	Real and Protected modes
Type—	Internal

CALL allows you to call another batch file, then return to the original batch file. It works like the GOSUB command in BASIC.

Format: CALL *filename*

filename is the name of a batch file. CALL will execute all the commands in the batch file and then execution returns to the calling batch file.

Normally, when you use the name of another batch file as a batch file command, the first batch file stops and control passes to the second batch file. However, by using CALL, you can have one batch file run several other batch files. Control always returns to the original batch file program.

Example

```
CALL NEXT.BAT
```

The above command causes the batch file NEXT.BAT to be run. After NEXT.BAT is finished, execution returns to the statement immediately after CALL in the first batch file.

Program Examples

Name: CALL1.BAT

```
1: @ECHO OFF
2: ECHO Running second batch file now
3: CALL CALL2.BAT
4: ECHO Back in first batch file again.
5: :END
```

Name: CALL2.BAT

```
1: ECHO Now executing second batch file...
2: PAUSE
3: :END
```

Test Run

```
Running second batch file now
Now Executing second batch file...
Strike any key when ready . . .
Back in first batch file again
```

You should note that the second batch will continue with the same ECHO state as the first batch file; therefore, if ECHO is OFF in the first batch file, it will continue to be off for each batch file CALLed.

In DOS . . .

CALL does work on the command line, but it's unnecessary; simply type in the name of a batch file you want to run and save yourself five keystrokes.

ALSO SEE . . . COMMAND, GOTO

CLS COMMAND

Command line—	Yes
DOS versions—	1.0 and up
OS/2—	Real and Protected modes
Type—	Internal

CLS clears the screen and moves the cursor to the "home" position, location 1, 1.

Format: CLS

CLS has no options, though its output (the ANSI escape sequence to clear the screen) can be redirected to a file.

After the CLS command is issued, either directly from the command prompt or in a batch file, the screen will be cleared and the cursor moved to the home position.

Example

CLS

After the above command, the screen will be cleared.

CLS is used when you want your batch file to start off on a clear screen. It really comes in handy with older versions of DOS that left the tell-tale batch file marker "ECHO OFF" lingering on the screen.

Program Example

```
1: @ECHO OFF
2: CLS
3: ECHO Off to a fresh start
4: :END
```

Test Run   (The screen will clear.)

Off to a fresh start

You can use the ANSI escape sequences to clear the screen with the ECHO command. The ANSI clear screen sequence is ESC[2J:

ECHO ^[[2J

This ECHO command will also clear the screen.

In DOS . . .

CLS is more of a DOS command than a batch file-specific command, but it's best put to use in batch files.

ALSO SEE . . . Chapter 3

CMD COMMAND

Command line— Yes
DOS versions— None
OS/2— Protected mode only
Type— External

CMD is used to run a second copy of CMD.EXE, the OS/2 command processor.

Format: CMD *switches commands*

switches can be one of two switches specified after CMD: /C and /K.

/C is used to specify certain *commands* that will be passed to the copy of the command processor. The *commands* can be any OS/2 command or command line, including the name of a batch file. After the *commands* have been executed by the new command processor, control returns to the original command processor.

/K is also used to specify *commands* for the new copy of the command processor. The difference between this switch and /C is that /K keeps the command processor in memory after *commands* have been executed. Control does not return to the original command processor (you must type EXIT to return).

If both *switches* and *commands* are omitted, then a second copy of the command processor is started. The old environment, including any environment variables such as PATH and COMSPEC strings, are copied to the new command processor's environment. Typing EXIT returns you to the previous command processor.

Examples

```
CMD /K DIR
```

This command causes a second copy of the command processor to be run. The first command given to the processor will be DIR. After the directory is listed, control stays with the second copy of CMD.EXE. To return to the original CMD.EXE, type EXIT.

```
CMD /C NEXT.CMD
```

CMD is used to run a second copy of the command processor. The second copy of CMD.EXE runs the protected mode batch file, NEXT.CMD. Once NEXT.CMD has finished, control returns to the original copy of the command processor.

Program Example

```
1: @ECHO OFF
2: ECHO Now running second command processor
3: ECHO Type EXIT to return here.
4: CMD /K
5: ECHO Welcome back!
```

Test Run

```
Now running second command processor
Type EXIT to return here.
[C:\OS2]EXIT
Welcome back!
```

Control returns to the middle of the batch file, to the line right after the CMD /K command was issued.

In DOS . . .

The COMMAND.COM program can be run a second time to start up a second copy of the DOS command processor. COMMAND only has the /C switch that works exactly as it does for CMD.EXE above.

ALSO SEE . . . COMMAND, CALL

COMMAND COMMAND

Command line—	Yes
DOS versions—	2.0 and up
OS/2—	Real mode only
Type—	External

COMMAND starts a secondary command processor. In batch files, COMMAND is used with the /C switch to "call" another batch file.

Format: COMMAND /C *filename*

filename is the name of a batch file. After COMMAND /C is typed, the batch file *filename* is executed. When *filename* is done, control returns to the first batch file, not DOS.

Normally, when a second batch file is included as a command in a batch file, the first batch file stops and the second one starts. Control is never returned to the first batch file.

Using COMMAND /C, you can "call" batch files, similar to the GOSUB statement in BASIC. After the second batch file is done, control returns to the first.

Example

```
COMMAND /C SECOND
```

The batch file interpreter will look for and load the file SECOND.BAT. After SECOND.BAT has run, control returns to the current batch file.

Program Examples

```
Name: COMM1.BAT

1: @ECHO OFF
2: ECHO Running second batch file now
3: COMMAND /C COMM2.BAT
4: ECHO Back in first batch file again.
5: END
```

```
Name: COMM2.BAT

1: @ECHO OFF
2: ECHO Now executing second batch file...
3: PAUSE
4: :END
```

Test Run

```
Running second batch file now
Now Executing second batch file...
Strike any key when ready . . .
Back in first batch file again
```

If you get a "Bad command or filename" error when running the first program above, it's probably because COMMAND.COM isn't on your system's path. You can solve this by changing line 3 in COMM1.BAT to:

```
3: C:\COMMAND /C COMM2.BAT
```

or, to be really nifty about things, you can use the environment variable COMSPEC, which naturally contains the location of your COMMAND.COM file:

```
3: %COMSPEC% /C COMM2.BAT
```

COMMAND also has a second switch, /P, similar to the /K switch for CMD.EXE (see CMD). The /P switch will keep COMMAND.COM in memory, but it also causes COMMAND.COM to run any AUTOEXEC.BAT file found in the root directory. You could run a second batch file simply by naming it AUTOEXEC.BAT and putting it in the root directory. But this isn't the purpose Microsoft had in mind for the /P switch. (See the SHELL command in Chapters 2 and 5.)

In DOS . . .

COMMAND can be used to "call" a batch file as described above, though it's redundant. Instead, COMMAND is used at the DOS prompt to start another command processor. The complete environment table, including PATH, PROMPT, and COMSPEC, is copied and a new copy of COMMAND.COM is loaded into memory. To leave the new copy of COMMAND.COM, type EXIT.

ALSO SEE . . . CMD, CALL, GOTO, Chapter 2

ECHO COMMAND

Command line— Yes
DOS versions— 2.0 and up

OS/2— Real and Protected modes
Type— Internal

ECHO turns command echoing on or off. Also, ECHO sends an optional string of characters to the display.

Format: ECHO

When used without any parameters, ECHO merely repeats the current "state" of the ECHO command. For example:

ECHO is off

or

ECHO is on

Format: ECHO *switch*

switch is either ON or OFF. The default is ECHO ON, meaning that all commands in a batch file are displayed as they are executed. Normally, ECHO OFF is used at the start of every batch file to suppress the echoing of commands.

ECHO OFF

This command suppresses the echoing of batch file commands to the screen. The batch file will run silently unless an ECHO ON statement is encountered.

Format: ECHO *string*

string is a string of up to 124 characters that will be echoed to the display, or console device.

Examples

ECHO

This displays either "ECHO is on" or "ECHO is off" depending on the current state of the ECHO command.

ECHO ON

This command turns echo on. Because ECHO is always ON each time a batch file starts, you don't normally need to use this command unless you have previously turned ECHO off. Also, you don't need to end a batch file with ECHO ON to "reset."

ECHO OFF

This command turns off the echoing of commands during batch file execution.

ECHO Sandie makes the best cookies

sends "Sandie makes the best cookies" to the console. Because ECHO uses DOS's devices, you can also use I/O redirection with ECHO to send the output elsewhere. For example:

```
ECHO Jim is here >> LOGFILE
```

appends the string "Jim is here" followed by a carriage return and linefeed to the file LOGFILE.

```
ECHO ^L > PRN
```

This command comes in very handy. It sends a Control L character to the printer device, PRN. The effect of this command is to eject a page from the printer.

```
ECHO .
```

This command is used to ECHO a "blank line" to the display. Normally, when ECHO is used by itself, it repeats the status of the ECHO command. However, when followed by a period, ECHO displays only the period. (In older versions of DOS, ECHO followed by some spaces would display only the space; but, with the new and improved versions of DOS, ECHO followed by spaces is the same as ECHO followed by nothing.)

When ECHO is used in a batch file with either an environment variable or a replaceable parameter variable, it ECHOes the contents of that variable. (Actually, what happens is that the batch file interpreter first expands the variable and then ECHO displays that expanded string.)

```
ECHO %STATUS%
```

If the environment variable STATUS is set equal to "IN," then the batch file interpreter expands it as follows:

```
ECHO IN
```

The word "IN" will be displayed.

```
ECHO %1 is the first argument
```

The batch file interpreter will expand %1 to the value of the first replaceable parameter, the first item typed after the name of the batch file on the command line.

Program Example 1

```
1: @ECHO
```

Test Run 1

```
ECHO is on
```

```
1: @ECHO ON
2: REM THAT LINE REALLY ISN'T NECESSARY
3: ECHO YOU CAN SEE EVERYTHING AS IT RUNS
4: :END
```

Test Run 2

```
C> @ECHO ON

C> REM THAT LINE REALLY ISN'T NECESSARY

C> ECHO YOU CAN SEE EVERYTHING AS IT RUNS

C> :END
```

In DOS . . .

Because ECHO generates redirectable output, the main reason for using it on the command line is with I/O redirection. For example, ejecting a page from the printer with ECHO ^L > PRN, appending data to the end of a text file with > >, or creating new, one-line text files.

ALSO SEE . . . COMMAND, GOTO % (percent), @ (at)

ENDLOCAL COMMAND

Command line— Yes
DOS versions— N/A
OS/2— Protected mode only
Type— Internal

ENDLOCAL restores the environment settings and changes to the drive and directory that were active when the SETLOCAL command was issued.

Format: ENDLOCAL

ENDLOCAL restores the drive, directory and environment that were saved by a SETLOCAL command. You can use ENDLOCAL as often as you like in your batch files. Each time it's used your original drive, directory and environment will be restored.

ENDLOCAL need only be specified if you wish to restore your drive, directory and environment before the batch file stops. Otherwise, the OS/2 batch file interpreter restores your drive, directory and environment when the batch file is finished (provided a SETLOCAL command was previously issued).

ENDLOCAL

After the above command is encountered in a batch file, then the drive, path and environment will be restored to exactly what they were when the SETLOCAL command was issued.

Program Example

```
 1: @ECHO OFF
 2: ECHO Here's how we start:
 3: CD
 4: SET
 5: REM Save stuff
 6: SETLOCAL
 7: ECHO Now let me change some things...
 8: A:
 9: CD \OLD
10: PATH=\
11: PROMPT=Help!
12: CD
13: SET
14: ECHO And now, back to normal:
15: ENDLOCAL
16: CD
17: SET
18: :END
```

Test Run

```
Here's how we start:
C:\OS2
COMSPEC=C:\OS2\PBIN\CMD.EXE
PATH=C:\;C:\OS2\BIN;C:\OS2\PBIN
PROMPT=$i[$p]
Now let me change some things...
C:\OLD
COMSPEC=C:\OS2\PBIN\CMD.EXE
PATH=\
PROMPT=Help!
And now, back to normal:
C:\OS2
COMSPEC=C:\OS2\PBIN\CMD.EXE
PATH=C:\;C:\OS2\BIN;C:\OS2\PBIN
PROMPT=$i[$p]
```

In Dos . . .

The only way to retain the contents of the environment table in DOS would be to start a new copy of the command processor. The batch file could then end with an EXIT statement, by which the contents of the environment would be restored.

The RESTPATH program on the Supplemental Programs Diskette can be used to restore an original drive/directory. (See Chapter 10 and Appendix K.)

ALSO SEE . . . SETLOCAL, SET

ERRORLEVEL VARIABLE

Command line—	N/A
DOS versions—	2.0 and up
OS/2—	Real and Protected modes
Type—	Internal

ERRORLEVEL is a variable that contains the return code for a previously run program. ERRORLEVEL is used only with the IF statement.

Format: IF ERRORLEVEL *value commands*

value is a comparison value for ERRORLEVEL. It ranges from 0 through 255, and is compared with the return code of a previously run program. If the return code (the value of ERRORLEVEL) is greater than or equal to *value*, then the IF test is true, and the specified *commands* are executed.

The tricky thing about ERRORLEVEL is remembering that it compares values greater than or equal to the return code of the previous program. Also, keep in mind that not every program has a return code. Only a few DOS programs and some utilities take advantage of this feature.

Examples

```
IF ERRORLEVEL 13 GOTO LABEL
```

If the return code of the most recently run program is 13 or greater, batch file execution branches to the label LABEL.

ERRORLEVEL is often used with several IF statements to determine the exact return code of the most recently run program:

```
IF ERRORLEVEL 5 GOTO FIVE
IF ERRORLEVEL 4 GOTO FOUR
IF ERRORLEVEL 3 GOTO THREE
IF ERRORLEVEL 2 GOTO TWO
IF ERRORLEVEL 1 GOTO END
REM Must be ERRORLEVEL zero here...
```

```
 1: @ECHO OFF
 2: REM It's assumed the program BLECH returns an
 3: REM ERRORLEVEL value of either 1 or 0
 4: BLECH
 5: IF ERRORLEVEL 0 GOTO ZERO
 6: ECHO Errorlevel one returned
 7: GOTO END
 8: :ZERO
 9: ECHO Errorlevel zero returned
10: :END
```

Test Run

```
BLECH!
Errorlevel one returned
```

In DOS . . .

The ERRORLEVEL variable always has a value of zero when an IF statement is used on the command line.

ALSO SEE . . . IF, EXIST, NOT

EXIST VARIABLE

Command line—	N/A
DOS versions—	2.0 and up
OS/2—	Real and Protected modes
Type—	Internal

EXIST is a variable set to either true or false depending on if a specified file exists. EXIST is used only with the IF statement.

Format: IF EXIST *filename commands*

filename can be an individual file's name, or a group of files specified via wildcards. It cannot be the name of a subdirectory. If *filename* exists, then the IF test is true, and the specified *commands* are executed.

Examples

```
IF EXIST README TYPE README
```

If the file named README exists, the command TYPE README will be executed. Otherwise, the IF test fails and the next line in the batch file will be executed.

```
IF EXIST C:\JUNK\*.* GOTO KILLALL
```

If any files exist in the /JUNK subdirectory on drive C, batch file execution will branch to the label KILLALL.

EXIST can also be used with the NOT conditional. In that case, the IF statement is true only if the specified file or files do not exist.

```
IF NOT EXIST *.* ECHO Directory Empty!
```

```
1: @ECHO OFF
2: IF EXIST *.BAT GOTO FOUND
3: ECHO There are not batch files here!
4: GOTO END
5: :FOUND
6: ECHO There are batch files here!
7: :END
```

```
There are batch files here!
```

In DOS . . .

EXIST can be used with IF on the command line to test for the existence of a file or group of files.

ALSO SEE . . . IF, ERRORLEVEL, NOT

EXTPROC COMMAND

Command line—	N/A
DOS versions—	N/A
OS/2—	Protected mode only
Type—	Internal

EXTPROC is used to start a batch file interpreter besides CMD.EXE. Using EXTPROC, you can have a third-party batch file processor execute your batch file commands.

Format: EXTPROC *filename*

filename is the name of a batch file processor.

EXTPROC must be the first command given in a batch file. Normally, CMD.EXE executes OS/2 batch files. However, by using EXTPROC, you can have a third-party batch file interpreter do the job. This avoids the memory-resident mess that most DOS batch file enhancing programs must go through.

`@EXTPROC FASTBAT.EXE`

This line, the first line in the batch file, specifies the program FASTBAT.EXE as this batch file program's batch file processor. From this line on, FASTBAT will be executing the batch file commands.

Program Example   Because no secondary batch file processors exist for OS/2 yet, a Program Example and Test Run are not possible. Just remember that EXTPROC must be the first command in the batch file. (Other commands in the batch file may be specific to the external batch file processor.)

In DOS . . .

Third-party batch file extension languages are readily available for speeding up batch file execution, or just providinga richer batch file programming environment. (See Part III of this book for more information.)

ALSO SEE . . . Chapters 10, 11, and 12

FOR COMMAND

Command line—	Yes
DOS versions—	2.0 and up
OS/2—	Real and Protected modes
Type—	Internal

FOR is used to repeat a command for a given set of filenames.

Format: FOR %*variables* IN (*set*) DO *command*

variable is the name of the FOR variable. It's a single letter or character, but is neither a number nor the symbols <or> or ¦ . *variable* is used to represent each of the filenames specified by *set*. In DOS, *variable* is preceded by a single percent-sign. In batch files, *variable* is preceded by double percent-signs.

set specifies a group of filenames—either individual filenames or groups of filenames with wildcards.

command is a DOS command. The DOS command will be performed on the filenames mentioned in *set* via the *variable*. In other words, *variable* is used as a placeholder for each of the filenames in *set*. Don't forget the DO before *command*.

Using FOR, you can repeat a specific DOS command for several groups of files. This avoids having to type the same command a number of times for a number of files.

Examples

`FOR %A IN (*.COM *.EXE *.BAT) DO DIR %A`

%A is the **variable**. It will be used to represent the three groups of files specified in the **set**: *.COM, *.EXE, and *.BAT. For each of those files, the command "DIR %A" will be performed. The final result will be a directory of all .COM, .EXE and .BAT files in the current directory.

The above command does the same thing as the following:

```
DIR *.COM
DIR *.EXE
DIR *.BAT
```

%A takes on each of the filenames in the **set** for the DIR command.

```
FOR %F IN (JUNK TEMP KILLME OLD) TO DEL %F
```

This command will delete all the following files in one fell swoop: JUNK, TEMP, KILLME and OLD.

Program Example

```
1: @ECHO OFF
2: FOR %%D IN (*.DOC MANUAL PRINTME.*) DO COPY %%D PRN
3: END
```

Test Run   (All files with the .DOC extension, the file named MANUAL, and all files starting with PRINTME will be copied to the printer.)

In DOS . . .

The FOR command can be used at the DOS prompt to cut down on your typing time. Remember to specify a single percent-sign at the DOS prompt, and only use double percent-signs in batch files.

ALSO SEE . . .% (percent)

GOTO COMMAND

Command line—   N/A
DOS versions—   2.0 and up
OS/2—   Real and Protected modes
Type—   Internal

GOTO is used to branch batch file execution to a specified label.

Format: GOTO *label*

label is a name used to identify the line to which execution branches. It can be from one to eight characters long and can contain any characters except for a period, semicolon, equal sign, or characters not allowed in a filename (see Appendix E). If the label is longer than eight characters or contains a space, only the first eight characters, or any characters up to the space, will be considered as the label.

By using GOTO, you can have your batch file skip over sections of code, branch to a specific routine, or execute one part of the code over and over. GOTO works well with the IF statement to act upon a certain condition.

The batch file GOTO works exactly the same as the BASIC language GOTO command. The difference is that a label is used in batch files, rather than a line number.

After the batch file interpreter encounters a GOTO statement, it searches the entire batch file from start through finish for the *label*. If the *label* is not found, the batch file stops immediately with a "Label not found" error. Lines containing labels are identified by a leading colon (:) character.

Example

```
GOTO STEP5
```

This causes the batch file interpreter to GOTO the line starting with :STEP5.

The batch file interpreter always searches for a label starting from the top of the batch file down to the bottom. Only the first matching label is used, so duplicate labels will be ignored by GOTO.

Program Example 1

```
 1: @ECHO OFF
 2: REM Test the GOTO statement
 3: GOTO LABEL1
 4: :LABEL2
 5: ECHO At label two
 6: GOTO END
 7: :LABEL1
 8: ECHO At label one
 9: GOTO LABEL2
10: :END
11: ECHO Done!
```

Test Run 1

```
At label one
At label two
Done!
```

Program Example 2

```
 1: @ECHO OFF
 2: REM A Shifting example
 3: :LOOP
```

```
4:  IF "%1"=="" GOTO END
5:  COPY %1 A:
6:  SHIFT
7:  GOTO LOOP
8:  :END
```

Test Run 2   (The program copies a group of files to drive A.)

Test program #2 uses GOTO to form a loop. The GOTO in line 7 continuously executes lines 3 through 6. Line 4 tests for the end of the loop, in which case GOTO is again used to end the batch file.

In DOS . . .

The GOTO statement does not cause an error on the command line, nor does it do much of anything else either.

ALSO SEE . . . : (colon), CALL

IF STATEMENT

Command line— Yes
DOS versions— 2.0 and up
OS/2— Real and Protected modes
Type— Internal

IF is used to test for a condition. If the condition is true, then a DOS command will be executed.

Format: IF **condition command**

condition is an evaluation made by the IF command. There are three sets of **condition**s that IF can evaluate using the following:

= = (double equal signs)

ERRORLEVEL

EXIST

= = (double equal signs) are used to compare two string values. Either string value may be a replaceable parameter or environment variable. If the two strings are equal, then the IF statement is true and the indicated **command** is executed.

ERRORLEVEL is a variable that contains the return code from a previously run program. ERRORLEVEL is followed by a comparison value. If the return code is equal to or greater than that value, the IF statement is true and the indicated **command** is executed.

EXIST is used to test for the existence of a file or group of files (using wildcards). If the indicated files exist, then the IF statement is true and the indicated **command** is executed.

The NOT prefix can be used with any of the above **conditions** to reverse their results. For example, IF NOT EXIST tests to ee if a file does not exist, IF NOT **string** = = **string** tests to see if two strings are not equal. In these cases, if the results of the IF comparison are NOT true, then the indicated **command** is executed.

command is any DOS or batch file command. It can even be another IF statement. Keep in mind, however, that unlike other versions of the IF command in other programming languages, the batch file IF does not have a corresponding THEN statement. If you use THEN, you'll get an error.

Examples

```
IF %STATUS%==IN GOTO MAIN
```

If the string value of the environment variable STATUS is equal to "IN", then the command GOTO MAIN will be executed. Otherwise, the next statement in the batch file is executed.

```
IF ERRORLEVEL 1 ECHO Ouch!
```

If the return code from the most recently run DOS program is equal to one or more, then "Ouch!" will be echoed to the screen.

```
IF EXIST READ.ME TYPE READ.ME
```

If the file named READ.ME is found in the current directory, then it will be TYPEd to the screen.

```
IF NOT "%1"=="" GOTO CONTINUE
```

When a NOT appears in an IF statement, it helps to read it from the inside out. Therefore, this IF statement checks to see if the first replaceable parameter exists:

```
"%1"==""
```

If %1 is equal to anything, the IF test will be false. However, because NOT is specified, the reverse will hold true and the command GOTO CONTINUE will be executed. IF %1 is not equal to anything, the IF test will be false (because NOT is used).

IF statements can also be "nested." That is, one IF statement can follow another:

```
IF %FIRST%==CHERRY IF %SECOND%==CHERRY IF %THIRD%==CHERRY
ECHO You just won seven bucks!
```

Program Example

```
1: @ECHO OFF
2: REM If test program
3: IF EXIST *.* ECHO There are files here!
```

```
 4:  IF %PROMPT%==$p$g GOTO YAWN
 5:  IF %PROMPT%==$P$G GOTO YAWN
 6:  ECHO My, what an interesting prompt you have
 7:  GOTO END
 8:  :YAWN
 9:  ECHO You have a boring prompt
10:  :END
```

```
There are files here!
You have a boring prompt
```

In DOS . . .

The IF statement can be used on the command line without any modifications. However, an ERRORLEVEL test in an IF statement will always return a value of zero.

ALSO SEE . . . = = (double equal signs), ERRORLEVEL, EXIST, NOT

NOT OPERATOR

Command line—	N/A
DOS versions—	2.0 and up
OS/2—	Real and Protected modes
Type—	Internal

NOT is used with the IF statement to reverse the results of the IF statement's test.

Format: IF NOT **condition command**

condition is an evaluation made by the IF statement. It is either a string comparison using = = (double equal signs); a test for a file's existence using EXIST; or a return code test using ERRORLEVEL. NOT precedes the **condition**. If the **condition** evaluates to true, NOT reverses it to false. If **condition** evaluates to false, NOT reverses it to true.

command is a DOS or batch file command. Normally, if **condition** is true, **command** is executed. However, when NOT is specified, **command** will only be executed when **condition** is false.

```
IF NOT EXIST READ.ME ECHO No READ.ME file was found
```

This IF statement tests for the existence of a file named READ.ME. If the file does not exist, the IF statement is true and "No READ.ME file was found" will be displayed.

```
1:  @ECHO OFF
2:  IF NOT EXIST *.BAT GOTO NONEFOUND
3:  ECHO There are batch files here!
4:  GOTO END
5:  :NONEFOUND
6:  ECHO There are no batch files here!
7:  :END
```

Test Run

```
There are batch files here!
```

In DOS . . .

NOT can be used with the IF statement on the command line just as it's used in batch files.

ALSO SEE . . . IF

PAUSE COMMAND

Command line— Yes
DOS versions— 1.0 and up
OS/2— Real and Protected modes
Type— Internal

PAUSE is used to display a message, and then wait for the user to press a key on the keyboard.

Format: PAUSE **message**

message is an optional message displayed before the PAUSE command's message. You should be careful when specifying a **message** because it's not displayed to the screen like the ECHO command. Instead, the only way to see the **message** is to keep ECHO ON.

Besides the optional message, PAUSE displays the following:

```
Strike a key when ready . . .
```

It then waits for the user to press a key on the keyboard. Once a key is pressed, the batch file continues.

It's important to note that not every key will cause the PAUSE command to continue. The "a key" description is rather vague to many users. In fact, the following keys will have no effect with the PAUSE command:

Shift keys: Left, Right, ALT, CTRL (control)
Option keys: CAPS LOCK, NUM LOCK, SCROLL LOCK
Dead keys: 5 on the cursor pad, Foreign language dead keys

PAUSE

After the above command, the following is displayed:

```
Strike a key when ready . . .
```

After the user presses a key, usually the spacebar, the batch program continues.

PAUSE is useful in batch files to give the user a chance to read a message, or to make a decision. For example:

```
ECHO Press Control-Break to stop or
PAUSE
```

The above two commands are often used one after the other to give the user a chance to "Break out" of a batch file. The display will show:

```
Press Control-Break to stop or
Strike a key when ready . . .
```

If the user strikes any key, the batch file continues; otherwise, by pressing CTRL–BREAK, the batch file will ask if the user wants to stop, and they can press Y to get out.

```
1: @ECHO OFF
2: PAUSE
3: ECHO And now, with ECHO ON...
4: ECHO ON
5: PAUSE Doesn't this work great?
```

```
Strike a key when ready . . .
(a key is pressed)
And now, with ECHO ON...

C> PAUSE Doesn't this work great?
Strike a key when ready . . .
```

In DOS . . .

PAUSE can be issued at the command prompt to display the same message as it does in batch files. After pressing a key, control returns to the command prompt.

ALSO SEE . . . ECHO

REM STATEMENT

Command line— Yes
DOS versions— 1.0 and up
OS/2— Real and Protected modes
Type— Internal

REM allows comments, or REMarks, to be used in batch files.

Format: REM *comments*

comments can be an optional string of characters, usually offering useful information about the batch file, or explaining a batch file procedure.

The REM statement is primarily used for placing comments into batch files. REM is not executed as a command, and anything following it is ignored by the batch file interpreter.

Examples

```
REM This is the tricky part
```

"This is the tricky part" is a comment specified after the REM statement.

```
REM Reset old path
```

This remark may appear before the SET command is used to change an environment variable.

```
REM IF EXIST *.BAK DEL *.BAK
```

In this example, REM is used to "comment out" a regular command in the batch file. To re-activate the command, the REM statement can be deleted.

Program Example

```
1: @ECHO OFF
2: REM ECHO This command will not work
3: REM ECHO because REM has made it into a comma.
4: ECHO Ah, so!
```

`Ah, so!`

In DOS . . .

REM can be used on the command line, in which case anything you type after it will be ignored by the command interpreter.

ALSO SEE . . . : (colon)

SET COMMAND

Command line—	Yes
DOS versions—	2.0 and up
OS/2—	Real and Protected modes
Type—	Internal

SET allows you to assign system, or environment, variables.

Format: SET *variable = string*

variable is the name of an environment variable. It can be any length, though shorter is better, and may contain letters and numbers and spaces (any characters before the equal sign). Upper case and lower case letters are converted to upper case when *variable* is stored in the environment.

string is a string of characters. When *variable* is used in a batch file, it will be replaced by *string*. If *string* is omitted, *variable* is removed from the environment. If *variable* already exists, any specified *string* replaces its previous value.

SET is used to create environment variables. These variables can be used for storing information or temporary string values. PATH and PROMPT are two environment variables, though they are set by the PATH and PROMPT commands. (They could be created with the SET command as well.)

If SET is used without both the *variable* or *string* values, it displays a list of the current variables in the environment table and their string values.

Examples

`SET STATUS=ON`

places the string STATUS = ON into your system's environment. When %STATUS% is used in a batch file, the batch file interpreter will expand it to "ON."

`SET GIRLFRIEND=Lola Palooza`

Sets "Lola Palooza" to the variable GIRLFRIEND. Lola Palooza need not be in quotes.

SET ANSWER="Goodbye, Matthew"

sets the entire string, "Goodbye, Matthew" into the environment table—even the quotes. When %ANSWER% is used in a batch file, it will be expanded by the batch file interpreter to "Goodbye, Matthew".

SET STATUS=

removes the variable STATUS from the environment. The equal sign must be specified.

Program Example

```
 1: @ECHO OFF
 2: SET TESTING=It works
 3: ECHO A demonstration of SET:
 4: ECHO Here is what the SET command displays by itself:
 5: SET
 6: PAUSE
 7: ECHO And here's a demonstration of SET assigning a
variable:
 8: ECHO TESTING=%TESTING%
 9: SET TESTING=
10: :END
```

Test Run

```
A demonstration of SET:
Here is what the SET command displays by itself:
PATH=
COMSPEC=C:\AUTOEXEC.BAT
Strike any key when ready . . .
And here's a demonstration of SET assigning a variable:
TESTING=It works
```

(You will note how the TESTING variable is removed from the environment in line 10 above; this frees the space used by the variable and is good practice when using temporary environment variables.)

In DOS . . .

Typing the SET command on DOS displays a list of assigned variables, as well as the system variables COMSPEC, PATH, PROMPT. Additionally, SET can be used at the command prompt to assign environment variables that can be used in batch files.

Environment variables cannot be echoed on the DOS command line. For example:

```
C> ECHO %STATUS%
```

This command simply displays %STATUS% on the following line. Only the batch file interpreter expands percent-sign variables.

ALSO SEE . . . ECHO, = =, %

SETLOCAL COMMAND

Command line—	Yes
DOS versions—	None
OS/2—	Protected mode only
Type—	Internal?

SETLOCAL saves the current drive, directory and environment settings.

Format: SETLOCAL

SETLOCAL remembers the drive, directory and environment at the time the SETLOCAL command was issued. After SETLOCAL, you can change your drive, directory, and environment. The original settings can be restored at any time using the ENDLOCAL command.

SETLOCAL can only be used once in a batch file. Any further use of SETLOCAL will be ignored by the OS/2 batch file interpreter.

(For a program example see ENDLOCAL.)

ALSO SEE . . . ENDLOCAL, SET

SHIFT COMMAND

Command line—	No
DOS versions—	2.0 and up
OS/2—	Real and Protected modes
Type—	Internal

SHIFT shifts the replaceable parameter values, %0 through %9.

Format: SHIFT

SHIFT has no arguments. Instead, after the SHIFT command is issued, the values of each of the replaceable parameters is shifted "down." For example: the value of %1 becomes %0, the value of %2 becomes %1, and so on.

After the SHIFT command, %0 is SHIFTed away. Any parameters after %9 are shifted into %9, one for each use of the SHIFT statement. This way, additional arguments (beyond %9) on the command line can be used as replaceable parameters.

`C> LOGIN 10:12 LITTLE HENRY`

The replaceable parameters for this command line are:

%0—LOGIN (the name of the batch file)
%1—10:12
%2—LITTLE
%3—HENRY

After the SHIFT command is used once, the replaceable parameters will be:

%0—10:12
%1—LITTLE
%2—HENRY

If SHIFT is used a second time, the replaceable parameters will be:

%0—LITTLE
%1—HENRY

```
1: @ECHO OFF
2: ECHO First parameter is now %1
3: SHIFT
4: ECHO But after the SHIFT command, it's %1
```

Test Run   (Assuming the following was typed after the name of the batch file: FIRST, SECOND.)

```
First parameter is now FIRST
But after the SHIFT command, it's SECOND
```

(For an excellent program example, refer to SHIFTARG in Chapter 7.)

In DOS . . .

The SHIFT command has no effect at the DOS command prompt. However, it is interesting in that you enter the word SHIFT and press RETURN, and nothing happens. Try doing this on an officemate's computer and it will leave them baffled (because they won't be able to find a SHIFT.COM file in any directory)!

ALSO SEE . . . %, = =

Appendices

A

ASCII

The Old ALT–Keypad Trick

Characters not on the keyboard—specifically, the Extended ASCII codes 128 through 255—can be entered using what's come to be known as the ALT-keypad trick. To enter these characters (any ASCII character, actually), press and hold the ALT key, type the character's decimal ASCII code on the keypad, then release the ALT key. Once the ALT key is released, the character appears.

For example, to enter the a character, ASCII 160, do the following:

1) Press and hold the ALT key.

2) Type **1** then **6** then **0** on the keypad.

3) Release the ALT key.

Voilá, you have the a character!

IBM ASCII Character Set

Display Character	Value Decimal	Hexadecimal	Binary

Control Characters:

Display Character	Value Decimal	Hexadecimal	Binary
^@ NUL	0	00h	00000000
^A SOH	1	01h	00000001
^B STX	2	02h	00000010
^C ETX	3	03h	00000011
^D EOT	4	04h	00000100
^E ENQ	5	05h	00000101
^F ACK	6	06h	00000110
^G BEL	7	07h	00000111
^H BS	8	08h	00001000
^I HT	9	09h	00001001
^J LF	10	0Ah	00001010
^K VT	11	0Bh	00001011
^L FF	12	0Ch	00001100
^M CR	13	0Dh	00001101
^N SO	14	0Eh	00001110
^O SI	15	0Fh	00001111
^P DLE	16	10h	00010000
^Q DC1	17	11h	00010001
^R DC2	18	12h	00010010
^S DC3	19	13h	00010011
^T CD4	20	14h	00010100
^U NAK	21	15h	00010101
^V SYN	22	16h	00010110
^W ETB	23	17h	00010111
^X CAN	24	18h	00011000
^Y EM	25	19h	00011001
^Z SUB	26	1Ah	00011010
^[ESC	27	1Bh	00011011
^\ FS	28	1Ch	00011100
^] GS	29	1Dh	00011101
^^ RS	30	1Eh	00011110
^_ US	31	1Fh	00011111

Standard Characters:

	32	20h	00100000
!	33	21h	00100001
"	34	22h	00100010
#	35	23h	00100011
$	36	24h	00100100
%	37	25h	00100101
&	38	26h	00100110
'	39	27h	00100111
(	40	28h	00101000
)	41	29h	00101001
*	42	2Ah	00101010
+	43	2Bh	00101011
,	44	2Ch	00101100
-	45	2Dh	00101101
.	46	2Eh	00101110
/	47	2Fh	00101111
0	48	30h	00110000
1	49	31h	00110001
2	50	32h	00110010
3	51	33h	00110011
4	52	34h	00110100
5	53	35h	00110101
6	54	36h	00110110
7	55	37h	00110111
8	56	38h	00111000
9	57	39h	00111001
:	58	3Ah	00111010
;	59	3Bh	00111011
<	60	3Ch	00111100
=	61	3Dh	00111101
>	62	3Eh	00111110
?	63	3Fh	00111111
@	64	40h	01000000
A	65	41h	01000001
B	66	42h	01000010
C	67	43h	01000011
D	68	44h	01000100
E	69	45h	01000101
F	70	46h	01000110
G	71	47h	01000111
H	72	48h	01001000
I	73	49h	01001001
J	74	4Ah	01001010
K	75	4Bh	01001011
L	76	4Ch	01001100
M	77	4Dh	01001101
N	78	4Eh	01001110
O	79	4Fh	01001111
P	80	50h	01010000
Q	81	51h	01010001
R	82	52h	01010010
S	83	53h	01010011
T	84	54h	01010100
U	85	55h	01010101
V	86	56h	01010110
W	87	57h	01010111
X	88	58h	01011000
Y	89	59h	01011001
Z	90	5Ah	01011010
[	91	5Bh	01011011
\	92	5Ch	01011100
]	93	5Dh	01011101
^	94	5Eh	01011110
_	95	5Fh	01011111
`	96	60h	01100000
a	97	61h	01100001
b	98	62h	01100010
c	99	63h	01100011
d	100	64h	01100100
e	101	65h	01100101
f	102	66h	01100110
g	103	67h	01100111
h	104	68h	01101000
i	105	69h	01101001
j	106	6Ah	01101010
k	107	6Bh	01101011
l	108	6Ch	01101100
m	109	6Dh	01101101
n	110	6Eh	01101110
o	111	6Fh	01101111
p	112	70h	01110000
q	113	71h	01110001
r	114	72h	01110010
s	115	73h	01110011
t	116	74h	01110100
u	117	75h	01110101
v	118	76h	01110110
w	119	77h	01110111
x	120	78h	01111000
y	121	79h	01111001
z	122	7Ah	01111010
{	123	7Bh	01111011
		124	7Ch	01111100
}	125	7Dh	01111101
~	126	7Eh	01111110
Δ	127	7Fh	01111111

IBM's Extended ASCII Character Set:

Ç	128	80h	10000000		▌	178	B2h	10110010
ü	129	81h	10000001			179	B3h	10110011
é	130	82h	10000010		┤	180	B4h	10110100
â	131	83h	10000011		╡	181	B5h	10110101
ä	132	84h	10000100		╢	182	B6h	10110110
à	133	85h	10000101		╖	183	B7h	10110111
å	134	86h	10000110		╕	184	B8h	10111000
ç	135	87h	10000111		╣	185	B9h	10111001
ê	136	88h	10001000		║	186	BAh	10111010
ë	137	89h	10001001		╗	187	BBh	10111011
è	138	8Ah	10001010		╝	188	BCh	10111100
ï	139	8Bh	10001011		╜	189	BDh	10111101
î	140	8Ch	10001100		╛	190	BEh	10111110
ì	141	8Dh	10001101		┐	191	BFh	10111111
Ä	142	8Eh	10001110		└	192	C0h	11000000
Å	143	8Fh	10001111		┴	193	C1h	11000001
É	144	90h	10010000		┬	194	C2h	11000010
æ	145	91h	10010001		├	195	C3h	11000011
Æ	146	92h	10010010		─	196	C4h	11000100
ô	147	93h	10010011		┼	197	C5h	11000101
ö	148	94h	10010100		╞	198	C6h	11000110
ò	149	95h	10010101		╟	199	C7h	11000111
û	150	96h	10010110		╚	200	C8h	11001000
ù	151	97h	10010111		╔	201	C9h	11001001
ÿ	152	98h	10011000		╩	202	CAh	11001010
Ö	153	99h	10011001		╦	203	CBh	11001011
Ü	154	9Ah	10011010		╠	204	CCh	11001100
¢	155	9Bh	10011011		═	205	CDh	11001101
£	156	9Ch	10011100		╬	206	CEh	11001110
¥	157	9Dh	10011101		╧	207	CFh	11001111
₧	158	9Eh	10011110		╨	208	D0h	11010000
ƒ	159	9Fh	10011111		╤	209	D1h	11010001
á	160	A0h	10100000		╥	210	D2h	11010010
í	161	A1h	10100001		╙	211	D3h	11010011
ó	162	A2h	10100010		╘	212	D4h	11010100
ú	163	A3h	10100011		╒	213	D5h	11010101
ñ	164	A4h	10100100		╓	214	D6h	11010110
Ñ	165	A5h	10100101		╫	215	D7h	11010111
ª	166	A6h	10100110		╪	216	D8h	11011000
º	167	A7h	10100111		┘	217	D9h	11011001
¿	168	A8h	10101000		┌	218	DAh	11011010
⌐	169	A9h	10101001		█	219	DBh	11011011
¬	170	AAh	10101010		▄	220	DCh	11011100
½	171	ABh	10101011		▌	221	DDh	11011101
¼	172	ACh	10101100		▐	222	DEh	11011110
¡	173	ADh	10101101		▀	223	DFh	11011111
«	174	AEh	10101110		∝	224	E0h	11100000
»	175	AFh	10101111		β	225	E1h	11100001
▒	176	B0h	10110000		Γ	226	E2h	11100010
▓	177	B1h	10110001		π	227	E3h	11100011

Σ	228	E4h	11100100	≥	242	F2h	11110010
σ	229	E5h	11100101	≤	243	F3h	11110011
↙	230	E6h	11100110	⌠	244	F4h	11110100
τ	231	E7h	11100111	⌡	245	F5h	11110101
◊	232	E8h	11101000	÷	246	F6h	11110110
θ	233	E9h	11101001	≈	247	F7h	11110111
Ω	234	EAh	11101010	·	248	F8h	11111000
δ	235	EBh	11101011	˙	249	F9h	11111001
∞	236	ECh	11101100	·	250	FAh	11111010
φ	237	EDh	11101101	√	251	FBh	11111011
∈	238	EEh	11101110	ⁿ	252	FCh	11111100
∩	239	EFh	11101111	²	253	FDh	11111101
≡	240	F0h	11110000	∎	254	FEh	11111110
±	241	F1h	11110001		255	FFh	11111111

B

ANSI.SYS Commands

In the following, the **n** represents an integer ASCII value. For example, if you want **n** to represent the value 42, then replace it with the ASCII characters "42", not the byte value 42. If more than one replaceable integer value appears in a command string, they are numbered **n1**, **n2** and so on.

"ESC" represents the escape character, ASCII 27 (1B hexadecimal, or "^[").

Locate Cursor

ESC[**n1**;**n2**H

n1 is a row number and **n2** is a column number. After the above command, the cursor will be positioned at row **n1** and column **n2**. If both parameters are omitted, as in ESC[;H, the cursor is sent to position 1,1—the upper left corner of the screen.

Position Cursor

ESC[**n1**;**n2**f

This command operates the same as the previous command, though it's not as common, and is rarely used.

Move Cursor Up

ESC[**n**A

moves the cursor up *n* number of rows. If *n* is omitted, the cursor moves up one row. If the cursor is at the top row, this command is ignored.

Move Cursor Down

ESC[*n*B

moves the cursor down *n* number of lines. If *n* is omitted, the cursor moves down one row. If the cursor is at the bottom row, this command is ignored.

Move Cursor Right

ESC[*n*C

moves the cursor right *n* number of columns. If *n* is omitted, the cursor moves right one column. If the cursor is at the far right column, this command is ignored.

Move Cursor Left

ESC[*n*D

moves the cursor left *n* number of columns. If *n* is omitted, the cursor moves left one column. If the cursor is at the far left column, this command is ignored.

Save Cursor Position

ESC[s

The current cursor position is saved. To restore it, use the following command.

Restore Cursor Position

ESC[u

restores the cursor to its position as saved by the ESC[s command sequence.

Erase Display

ESC[2J

This sequence clears the screen and puts the cursor into the upper-left corner.

Erase Line

ESC[K

The line that the cursor is on will be erased from the cursor's position to the end of the line.

Set Graphics Rendition

ESC[*n*m

n takes on a number of values, each changing the foreground and background color attributes of the screen:

0	Normal text
1	High-intensity
2	Low-intensity
4	Underline on (monochrome displays only)
5	Blinking on
7	Inverse video on
8	Invisible text
30	Black foreground
31	Red foreground
32	Green foreground
33	Yellow foreground
34	Blue foreground
35	Magenta foreground
36	Cyan foreground
37	White foreground
40	Black background
41	Red background
42	Green background
43	Yellow background
44	Blue background
45	Magenta background
46	Cyan background
47	White background

EXAMPLE: ESC[34m turns on a blue foreground color.

Two or more of the attributes can be selected at once using the following format:

ESC[*n1;n2*; . . . nnm

Different color attributes can be specified by separating each with a semicolon (;). The final attribute is followed by the lower case m. For example:

ESC[37;44m

This sets white characters on a blue background.

Set/Reset Mode

ESC[= *n*h

The "mode" in this case is the screen mode—the resolution of characters or graphics pixels. *n* carries 13 values, from 0 through 6 and from 14 to 19.

0   Monochrome text, 40x25
1   Color text, 40x25
2   Monochrome text, 80x25
3   Color text, 80x25
4   Medium resolution graphics (four color), 320x200
5   Same as 4, but with color burst disabled
6   High resolution graphics (two color), 640x200
14 Color graphics, 640x200
15 Monochrome graphics, 640x350
16 Color graphics, 640x350
17 Color graphics, 640x480
18 Color graphics, 640x480
19 Color graphics, 320x200

These commands are useful when creating special large character screens. For example, for children or the handicapped who have trouble reading the regular display.

Character Wrap ON

ESC[= 7h

Part of ANSI's VT100 legacy is the ability to "wrap" characters on the screen. That is, if a character is displayed in column 80 (the far right-hand column), the next character will be displayed on the next row in the first column. This is character wrap.

If character wrap is disabled, then all characters displayed after the 80th character on a line, and before a carriage return character, will be displayed in column 80. (*See* chapter 3 for a demonstration.) Character wrap ON is the default of the ANSI.SYS driver.

Character Wrap OFF

ESC[= 7l

This command disables character wrap. Note that the final character in the command string is a lowercase L, not the number one.

Keyboard Key Reassignment

ESC[*n1*;*n2*p

n1 is the ASCII code for a key to redefine. *n2* is the ASCII code that will be produced when *n1* is pressed. For example:

```
ESC[71,84p
```

This assigns capital "G" (ASCII 71) as capital 'T' (ASCII 84). Whenever a capital G key is typed, DOS will display a T. To reassign the lowercase characters, use the following:

`ESC[103;116p`

Keyboard String Reassignment

ESC[0;*n*;"**string**"p

n is an extended keyboard code. **string** is a string of characters that will be produced every time the specified key is pressed. For example:

ESC[0;113;"DIR"p

This assigns the string "DIR" to the key combination ALT–F10 (see below). To add a carriage return after the DIR command, use:

ESC[0;113;"DIR";13p

(*See* Chapter 3 for a complete example of keyboard reassignment.)

The extended codes for the function keys are as shown in TABLE B-1.

Table B-1.

	Normal	SHIFT	CTRL	ALT
F1	0;59	0;84	0;94	0;104
F2	0;60	0;85	0;95	0;105
F3	0;61	0;86	0;96	0;106
F4	0;62	0;87	0;97	0;107
F5	0;63	0;88	0;98	0;108
F6	0;64	0;89	0;99	0;109
F7	0;65	0;90	0;100	0;110
F8	0;66	0;91	0;101	0;111
F9	0;67	0;92	0;102	0;112
F10	0;68	0;93	0;103	0;113

NOTE ON KEY REASSIGNMENT: You can only "un-assign" the keys by rebooting your computer—or by running an un-assign program. Also, note that because most applications do not use DOS routines to read the keyboard, these reassignments will probably not take effect in any of your programs.

C

Keyboard Scan Codes

The PC's keyboard is controlled by a special microprocessor that's right inside the keyboard. When you press on a key, the microprocessor interprets the keypress and sends a code called a "scan code" for that key to the computer. Put simply, this is a funky way to read the keyboard.

This appendix contains a list of the scan codes generated by your keyboard. All these codes are the same for all IBM-compatible PCs. As can be seen by the charts at the end of this Appendix, the scan codes are laid out with really no rhyme or reason (when compared with other keyboards).

Scan Codes

1	Escape	30	A			
2	1 !	31	S	59	F1	
3	2 @	32	D	60	F2	
4	3 #	33	F	61	F3	
5	4 $	34	G	62	F4	
6	5 %	35	H	63	F5	
7	6 ^	36	J	64	F6	
8	7 &	37	K	65	F7	
9	8 *	38	L	66	F8	
10	9 (	39	; :	67	F9	
11	0)	40	' "	68	F10	
12	- _	41	` ~	69	NumLock	
13	= +	42	Left shift key	70	Scroll Lock	
14	Backspace	43	/	71	Home 7 (keypad numbers only)	
15	Tab	44	Z	72	Up arrow 8	
16	Q	45	X	73	PgUp 9	
17	W	46	C	74	– (keypad minus key)	
18	E	47	V	75	Left arrow 4	
19	R	48	B	76	5 (keypad only)	
20	T	49	N	77	Right arrow 6	
21	Y	50	M	78	+ (keypad plus key)	
22	U	51	, <	79	End 1	
23	I	52	. >	80	Down arrow 2	
24	O	53	/ ?	81	PgDn 3	
25	P	54	Right shift key	82	Insert key	
26	[{	55	* PrtSc (print screen)	83	Delete key	
27	] }	56	Alt key	84	Sys Req (AT keyboards only)	
28	RETURN	57	Spacebar	87	F11	
29	Control key	58	Caps lock	86	F12	

Keyboard Layouts

Fig. C-1. PC/XT

Fig. C-2. Convertible PC

Fig. C-3. PC/AT

Fig. C-4. Enhanced PC

D

PROMPT Commands

The following are command characters that can be included with the PROMPT command (to change your system prompt). All commands are preceded by a dollar sign.

Table D-1.

Command	Displays
$$	$, dollar sign character
$b	¦ pipe character
$d	the date (according to the system clock)
$e	the ESCape character
$g	> character
$h	backspace (erase previous character)
$l	< character
$n	the logged disk drive letter
$p	the logged disk drive and subdirectory
$q	= character
$t	the current time (according to the system clock)
$v	DOS version
$_	Carriage return/linefeed (new line)

ANSI.SYS commands are included by using $e, the ESCape character. (For examples of various prompts, refer to Chapter 3.) Any other characters, (including spaces) listed after the PROMPT command will become part of the system prompt.

The standard system prompt is ng, or the drive letter followed by the > character.

The date and time displayed by $d and $t are according to the country and other system parameters that can be set in the CONFIG.SYS file. *See* Chapter 4.

OS/2 adds the following commands to PROMPT:

Table D-2

Command	Displays
$a	The ampersand character, &
$c	Left parenthesis, (
$f	Right parenthesis,)
$i	Undocumented, possibly a hook into an internal routine

E

DOS Device Names

Shown here are the DOS device names:

AUX	First serial port
CLOCK$	System clock
COM1	First serial port
COM2	Second serial port
COM3	Third serial port
COM4	Fourth serial port
CON	"Console," keyboard or screen
LPT1	First printer
LPT2	Second printer
LPT3	Third printer
NUL	"Nul," or dummy, device
PRN	First printer

Filenames

The format of a filename is as follows:

filename.ext

filename is a string of from 1 to 8 characters (excluding those listed below).
ext is an optional string of from 1 to 3 characters, separated from **filename** by

360

a period.

Characters not allowed as part of a filename:

. " / \ [ ] : | < > + = ; ,

Also not allowed are spaces and any ASCII control code (decimal 31 or less). However, often not mentioned is that high-order, or "extended," ASCII characters are allowed as part of a filename.

Filenames can be preceded by a drive letter, followed by a colon. After the colon can come the file's full pathname.

Pathnames

A pathname is the full name of a file, including all subdirectories. Subdirectories are named just like files, and each is separated by a backslash. The only limitation on a pathname is that the entire name (including drive letter, colon, and filename/extension) can be no more than 63 characters long.

F

DOS Function Keys

When you enter text on the DOS command line, or in EDLIN, you're manipulating a "template." This template contains the same characters as were previously entered (either in DOS or EDLIN). Using special function keys, the template of text can be edited, saving typing time. The editing also takes place in any program that uses DOS Interrupt 21h, Service Ah (10 decimal) to read a line of text from the keyboard.

The following keys (delimited by dashes, and ended with a colon) can be used to edit a DOS command line, or a line of text in EDLIN:

F1 or Right arrow   Move right one character in the template.

F2 char   Display characters up to character **char.**

F3   Display remaining characters in the template.

F4 char   Deletes remaining characters up to the character **char**.

F5   Reset the template, replacing it with the characters entered so far.

F6 or CTRL-Z   Display a ^Z (end of file) character. This character is entered to signal the end of a file—especially when you're creating files from the keyboard using the COPY CON function.

F7   Display a ^@, the null character.

Left arrow or Backspace   Move left one character in the template. Note that backspace does not delete any characters in the template.

INSert   Begin inserting characters in the template. Press INSert a second time to re-enter the overwrite mode (new characters you type will replace the old characters in the template).

DELete   Remove characters from the template.

ESCape   Cancel editing on the template, replace with original template, move cursor to first character position.

CTRLDASHV (EDLIN only)   Typing a CTRL–V is a special prefix character used only in EDLIN. It causes the next character typed to be accepted as an ASCII control code. For example, the ESCape character is normally written as ^[. To enter this character in EDLIN using CTRL–V, type CTRL–V followed by [. To enter a CTRL–C, type CTRL–V followed by a C. (Refer to Appendix A for more information on control characters.)

Special Function Keys

The special function keys perform some miscellaneous duties while you're in DOS. There are ways to make other keys perform the same duties. Refer to Appendix B on ANSI.SYS under Keyboard String Reassignment for the gory details.

NUM LOCK   Activates the numeric keypad on some keyboards.

CAPS LOCK   Causes all alphabet characters to be displayed in upper case (the default is lower case).

SHIFT–PRTSC   Prints the contents of the screen to the printer. If the printer is turned off, some computers may ignore this command. Other computers will "lock up" and wait for the printer. If you have a printer, turn it on and let the screen dump continue. Otherwise, reset.

CTRL–P or CTRL–PRTSC   Turn on "echo" to Printer mode. All characters DOS sends to the screen (or any other program that uses the DOS print character functions) will also be sent to the printer. To turn this mode off, press CTRL–P, or CTRL–PRTSC, a second time. Again, as with SHIFT–PRTSC, if the printer is turned off, DOS may wait for it or display an error message.

CTRL–S or CTRL–NUM/LOCK   Pauses the display. To re-start the display, type a second CTRL–S. Unfortunately, typing a second CTRL–**NUM**/LOCK does not re-start the display. Just type any other key.

CTRL–C and CTRL–BREAK   Halts DOS from displaying or performing some other activity (copying, backing up, etc.) For some operations, CTRL–C will stop the going's on. Other times, DOS must receive a CTRL–BREAK (the "Break" key is actually *Scroll Lock*); it depends on how the program was written to intercept the DOS interrupt service 23h. Generally speaking, CTRL–BREAK will stop 'em cold 100% of the time.

ALT   The ALT key can be used in conjunction with the numeric keypad to produce any ASCII, or Extended ASCII, character. These characters are numbered from 0 through 255. To display any character, hold down the ALT key and type the character's number on the numeric keypad. For example, to produce ASCII 89 (the letter "Y"), do the following:

1) Press and hold down the ALT key.
2) Type an 8 on the keypad.
3) Type a 9 on the keypad.
4) Release the ALT key.

ASCII 89 will be displayed.

This works for all ASCII and Extended ASCII codes—even within applications programs. The only time this special ALT key character generation doesn't work is when certain memory-resident programs are loaded, for example, *SuperKey*.

G

EDLIN

EDLIN isn't the best text editor on the planet Earth. However, it does have some advantages over all other test editors: It comes free with DOS (so everyone has it), and it's one of the few editors that allows you to easily enter control characters in your text.

Summary of EDLIN's Commands

I—Inserts a new line at the current line. When creating a new file, pressing I inserts line 1.

*n*I—Inserts a new line number *n*.

.I—Inserts a new line at the current line.

#I—Inserts a new line at the bottom of the file

+*n*I—Inserts a new line *n* lines down from the current line number

–*n*I—Inserts a new line *n* lines up from the current line number.

L—Lists the 11 lines before the current line, the current line, and 11 lines after the current line.

*x*L—Lists 23 lines starting with line *x*.

,*y*L—Lists the 11 lines before line *y*, line *y*, and the 11 lines after line *y*.

x,yL—Lists the lines from **x** through **y**.

P—"Page" or print from the current line down 23 lines.

,yP—Print from the current line through line **y**.

x,yP—Print from line **x** through line **y**.

Delete:

D—Deletes the current line.

xD—Deletes line **x**.

x,yD—Deletes lines **x** through **y**.

,yD—Deletes all lines from the current line through line **y**.

x,.D—Deletes all lines from **x** through the current line.

Copy:

x,y,zC—Copies the block of lines from **x** through **y** and places them at line number **z**.

x,x,zC—Copies the single line **x** to line number **z**.

Move:

x,y,zM—Moves the block of lines from **x** through **y** and places them at line number **z**.

x,x,zM—Moves line **x** to line number **z**.

Search and Replace:

S **string**—Searches for the characters in **string**.

x,yS**string**—Searches for the characters in **string** between lines **x** and **y**.

x,y?S**string**—Searches for the characters in **string** between lines **x** and **y**, stops and asks "OK?" for each occurrence. Pressing Y continues the search, N cancels.

R**str1**^Z**str2**—Replaces all occurrences of **str1** with **str2**. ^Z is CTRL–Z.

x,yR**str1**^Z**str2**—Replaces all occurrences of **str1** with **str2** in the range of lines from **x** through **y**.

x,y?R**str1**^Z**str2**—Replaces all occurrences of **str1** with **str2** in the range of lines from **x** through **y**. When **str1** is found, replace stops and asks "OK?" Pressing Y replaces, pressing N cancels.

Edit:

n—Selects line **n** for editing.

–n—Selects line **n** lines up for editing.

+n—Selects line **n** lines down for editing.

.—Selects current line for editing.

Disk:

*n*A—Appends lines from the disk file into memory. (This command only works if the file being edited is too big to fit into memory.)

*n*T—Transfers text to disk starting with line *n*. If *n* is omitted, the current line is used

*n*W—Writes a specific number of lines to disk. (Used only for files too large to fit into memory at once.)

End:

E—Ends edit, saves file, renames original file to *.BAK.

Q—Cancels edit, does not save changes.

H

DEBUG Commands

All commands can be issued as either upper or lower case. All numeric values are in hexadecimal, or base 16, format.

A*address*—Enter the mini-assembler and start entering assembly language commands. *address* is optional; if omitted, 100h is used.

C *blk1 r blk2*—Compare the block of memory *blk1* with *blk2* for the range *r*.

D *address r*—Dump, or Display, memory contents at *address* for range *r*. *address* is optional and, if omitted, the current address is used.

E *address list*—Enter, or Edit, the bytes at *address*. *list* is an optional list of information to place at *address*. *list* can be ASCII data, in which case it should be enclosed in quotes.

F *address r list*—Fill the bytes starting at *address* for the range *r* with the values in *list*.

G *=address*—Go, or start executing instructions, at *address*.

H *n1 n2*—Add two values, *n1* and *n2*, then subtract them. The two results are displayed on the following line.

I *port*—Input one byte from the specified *port*.

L *address d s1 s2*—Load into memory at *address* from disk *d* (where 0 is drive A, 1 is B, etc.) the data from sectors *s1* through *s2*. If a program name has been specified with the N command, L alone loads that program into memory.

M *r address*—Moves the bytes in the range *r* to *address*.

N *pathname*—Names the program specified by **pathname**. Using the L or W command will cause that file to be loaded or saved, respectively.

O **port** *n*—Outputs the byte *n* to the port **port**.

P **address** *n*—Proceed, or execute the following instruction, such as an INT, CALL or LOOP instruction. **address** specifies the optional location of the instruction and *n* is a repeat count.

Q—Quit.

R **register**—Change the contents of the 8088 register **register**.

S *r list*—Searches for list in the range *r*. (*r* specifies two addresses.)

T **address** *n*—Trace, or execute the single instruction at **address**. *n* is a repeat count.

U **address**—Un-assemble the machine code at **address**. **address** may optionally be a range of memory locations, or a specific address followed by a range value.

W **address** *d* *s1* *s2*—Write the data at **address** to disk *d* (where 0 is drive A, 1 is B, etc.) sectors *s1* through *s2*. If a program name has been specified with the N command, W alone writes that program to disk.

XA *h*—Creates (allocates) a handle *h* to a specific number of pages of expanded memory.

XD *h*—De-allocates the handle created with XA.

XM *l*,*p*,*h*—Maps the logical expanded memory page *l* to the physical page *p*, using handle *h*.

XS—Displays the expanded memory status.

NOTE: DEBUG does not perform properly on files with an .EXE or .HEX filename extension. To DEBUG these programs, rename them first to a .BIN or .COM file extension, then use DEBUG.

I

ERRORLEVEL Return Codes

DOS programs that use ERRORLEVEL:

BACKUP

0   Normal Exit.
1   No files were backed up (all were already backed up or none existed).
2   File sharing conflicts. Not all files were backed up.
3   CTRL–BREAK was pressed, halting the backup.
4   Error, program stopped.

FORMAT

0   Normal Exit.
3   CTRL–BREAK was pressed, halting the format.
4   Error, program stopped.
5   N was pressed when the user was asked whether to format their hard
    drive.

GRAFTABL

0   Normal Exit.
1   A previously loaded character table has been replaced by the most
    recently specified table.
2   No previously loaded character table existed and no new table has been
    loaded.

3   An improper parameter was specified, nothing done.
4   Incorrect DOS version.

KEYB

0   Normal Exit.
1   Bad parameter (usually a syntax error).
2   Keyboard definition file not found or bad.
3   Unable to create table (memory problem).
4   CON device error.
5   Unprepared code page request.
6   Translation table not found.
7   Incorrect DOS version.

REPLACE

2   Source file(s) not found.
3   Source or target path was not found.
5   Read/write access denied. (Change the files with ATTRIB.)
8   Not enough memory to run REPLACE.
11 Bad parameter found or invalid format used.
15 Non-existent drive specified.
22 Incorrect DOS version.

RESTORE

0   Normal Exit.
1   No files found.
2   File sharing conflicts, not all files restored.
3   Control-Break was pressed, halting the restore.
4   Error termination, program stopped.

Batch File Example

The following batch file can be used to determine if a program has an ERRORLEVEL return code:

Name: ERRCHK.BAT

```
1: @ECHO OFF
2: REM Errorlevel checking program
3: ECHO Errorlevel checker version 1.0
4: IF nothing%1==nothing GOTO error
5: ECHO Running program %1...
6: %1 %2 %3 %4 %5 %6 %7 %8 %9
7: IF ERRORLEVEL 2 GOTO TWO
8: IF ERRORLEVEL 1 GOTO ONE
```

```
 9: IF ERRORLEVEL 0 GOTO ZERO
10: :TWO
11: ECHO Errorlevels higher than "1" detected
12: GOTO END
13: :ONE
14: ECHO Errorlevel of "1" detected
15: GOTO END
16: :ZERO
17: ECHO Errorlevel of zero returned
18: GOTO END
19: :ERROR
20: ECHO Program not specified.
21: :END
```

J

Batch File Error Codes

Aside from DOS errors ("File not found," "Bad command or filename") the following batch-file specific errors may pop up from time to time:

Batch file missing—The batch file you're running can no longer locate itself to load in the next line.

Cannot start COMMAND, exiting—You've used COMMAND /C to "call" other batch files and there are too many files already open.

FOR cannot be nested—You attempted to use a second FOR as the command portion of a FOR command.

Label not found—The batch file interpreter could not locate a label associated with a GOTO statement.

No free file handles
Cannot start COMMAND, exiting—See "Cannot start COMMAND, exiting" above.

Out of environment space—You attempted to alter the environment and there is no more room.

Syntax Error—A command was mistyped, or a double equal-sign not used with an IF statement.

Terminate batch job (Y/N)—Either CTRL–C or CTRL–BREAK was pressed to halt the batch file.

K

Floppy Disk Contents

This book has a companion floppy disk that you can order. On the disk you will find all of the batch files listed in this book, including the HELPFILE.BAT program discussed in Chapter 14, as well as public domain software and utilities.

In this appendix you'll find a listing of the disk's contents and filenames, as well as which files are public domain and which are shareware. Public domain programs are free—there's no charge. These programs were written by philanthropic programmers (some of them really, really bored) who donate all their labors to mankind.

Disk Contents

The floppy disk contains four subdirectories:

/BATPROGS
/BOOKUTIL
/HELPFILE
/OTHERS

/BATPROGS contains all the major batch files mentioned in this book, plus a few extras just to spice things up.

/BOOKUTIL contains all the special utility programs written specifically for this book. You will find these batch file utilities no where else.

/HELPFILE contains a special batch file menu system, discussed briefly in Chapter 14, that describes the contents of the entire disk. You run this shell system by running the HELP.BAT program in the root directory.

/OTHERS is a directory of public domain utilities, each of which will help enhance your own batch files. Some of the utilities were mentioned in this book. Others are special utilities that you may find interesting. Also, a few useful programs have been added, some of which make using your computer a lot easier.

Utilities

The following are brief descriptions of the utilities provided on the supplemental programs diskette.

Programs written specifically for this book:

ASK.COM   A "read key-return ERRORLEVEL" program that waits for a Y/N response.

BLANKS.COM   A program to display a number of blank lines on the screen.

BOX.COM   BOX draws graphic boxes around strings of text, or at any position on the display. It's ideal for creating menus or jazzing up a dull batch file.

CLZ.COM   A fancy CLS program.

GREET.COM   A program to display a timely greeting on your display. Use it to end your batch files, or to start off your AUTOEXEC.BAT file in a friendly way.

HOLD.COM   An improved version of the PAUSE command. HOLD allows you to optionally specify a prompting string before the "Press any key" message.

LOCATE.COM   A program to locate the cursor at a specific row and column on the screen.

MORE.COM   A filter program, similar to the DOS MORE filter, but conservative on screen space.

READKEY.COM   Another "read key-return ERRORLEVEL" program. Aside from returning ERRORLEVEL values relative to number or alphabet keys, READKEY can also be used to assign ERRORLEVEL values to the function keys.

REPT.COM   A program that will REPeaT a character a certain number of times. REPT saves typing time over using ECHO with a long string of dashes (or what have you).

RESTPATH.COM   RESTPATH is used with CD and I/O redirection to "remember" your starting drive and directory. If RESTPATH is issued at the end of a batch file, you will be returned to the drive and directory from which the batch file started.

SAY.COM   An intelligent version of the ECHO command.

TSTAMP.COM   A program to display a short version of the date and time. Ideal for use with computer log files.

VERNUM.COM   A program that returns the current version of DOS as an ERRORLEVEL value.

L

Product Information

The following products are mentioned in this book. The manufacturer or distributor's name is included here for those desiring additional information:

Beyond • Bat
Relay Communications, Inc.
41 Kenosia Ave.
Danbury, CT 06810
203-798-3800

EBL
Seaware Corp.
P.O. Box 1656
Delray Beach, FL 33444
305-392-2046

Norton Utilities, Advanced Edition
Peter Norton Computing, Inc.
2210 Wilshire Boulevard, #186
Santa Monica, CA 90403

PC–SIG
Public Domain/Shareware Stuff
1030D East Duane Ave.
Sunnyvale, CA 94086
408-730-9291

PC Write
Quicksoft
219 First North
Box 224-PMA1
Seattle, WA 98109
800-888-8088

See Editor
C Ware Corporation
P.O. Box 428
Passo Robles, CA 93447
805-239-4620

SideKick, SideKick Plus, SuperKey
Borland International
4585 Scotts Valley Drive
Scotts Valley, CA 95066

WordStar
MicroPro International
P.O. Box 7079
San Rafael, CA 94901
800-227-5609

Additionally, PC–SIG is an excellent source for hard-to-find utilities and useful public domain programs. Besides the programs that come on the supplemental programs disk, you should check out the following PC–SIG diskettes:

#82—BATCH FILE UTILITIES, various batch file utilities

#124—EXTENDED BATCH LANG., Version 3.05 of EBL

#205—DOS UTILITIES No. 13, some older, yet still useful utilities

#373—DOS UTILITIES No. 17, interesting and useful DOS utilities

#1000—NETHACK, a game, but it includes the NANSI.SYS driver

If you'd like to locate a specific program, give PC–SIG a call. Their tech support people are perhaps the most friendly and helpful you'll ever encounter.

Index

Index

Other Best Sellers From TAB

Other Best Sellers From TAB

☐ **TESTING COMPUTER SOFTWARE—Cem Kaner**

Now you can develop bug-free software! This book describes testing and test planning *in practice*. It covers the fundamentals, including test case design . . . the goals behind many types of testing tools . . . the various types of software tests . . . and their role in the software life cycle. New features covered include: analyzing bugs as you find them, a complete functional specification of a bug tracking system, an in-depth description of the different types of software errors, an explanation of how to test user manuals, discussions of design errors in the user interface, consideration of priorities, and testing group management. 312 pp., 32 illus.

Paper $21.95   Hard $27.50
Book No. 2763

☐ **IBM PC® GRAPHICS—John Clark Craig and Jeff Bretz**

Now, this practical and exceptionally complete guide provides the answers to questions and the programs you need to utilize your IBM PC's maximum potential. This is a collection of immediately useful programs covering a wide variety of subjects that are sure to captivate your interest . . . and expand your programming horizons. 272 pp., 138 illus., 8-page color section.

Paper $14.95   Hard $16.95
Book No. 1860

Send $1 for the new TAB Catalog describing over 1300 titles currently in print and receive a coupon worth $1 off on your next purchase from TAB.

(In PA, NY, and ME add applicable sales tax. Orders subject to credit approval. Orders outside U.S. must be prepaid with international money orders in U.S. dollars.)

*Prices subject to change without notice.

To purchase these or any other books from TAB, visit your local bookstore, return this coupon, or call toll-free 1-800-233-1128 (In PA and AK call 1-717-794-2191).

Product No.	Hard or Paper	Title	Quantity	Price

☐ Check or money order enclosed made payable to TAB BOOKS Inc.

Charge my   ☐ VISA   ☐ MasterCard   ☐ American Express

Acct. No. _____ Exp. _____

Signature _____

Please Print
Name _____

Company _____

Address _____

City _____

State _____ Zip _____

Subtotal	
Postage/Handling ($5.00 outside U.S.A. and Canada)	$2.50
In PA, NY, and ME add applicable sales tax	
TOTAL	

Mail coupon to:

TAB BOOKS Inc.
Blue Ridge Summit
PA 17294-0840   BC

ADVANCED
MS–DOS
BATCH FILE PROGRAMMING

If you are intrigued with the possibilities of the programs included in *Advanced MS-DOS Batch File Programming* (TAB Book No. 3197), you should definitely consider having the ready-to-run disk containing the software applications. This software is guaranteed free of manufacturer's defects. (If you have any problems, return the disk within 30 days, and we'll send you a new one.) Not only will you save the time and effort of typing the programs, the disk eliminates the possibility of errors that can prevent the programs from functioning. Interested?

Available on disk for the IBM PC at $24.95 for each disk plus $1.50 shipping and handling.